nce between the saint and the sinner is that
int has a past, and every sinner has a future.

ar Wilde, *A Woman of No Importance* (1893)

It was a very nice wedding—no one threw anything, and there was a dog fight.

—E.B. White, *The Letters of E.B. White* (Revised ed., 2006)

"Don't let's ask for the moon, we have the stars."

—*Now, Voyager* (1942)

Be not just a follower, not just a receiver of the command. . . .

Do not hope to go into an already prepared heaven.

There is no such heaven.

You must create, construct, and reconstruct a heaven of your own.

Then heaven is automatically yours.

—Rev. Sun Myung Moon, Leader's Address (1965)

We Have the Stars

We Have the Stars

a memoir

Pamela A. Moffatt

We Have the Stars
Published: November 2023
First Edition
Printed in the United States of America
ISBN: 979-8-9851619-0-8

Published by Joie de Cyrano, LLC

TABLE OF CONTENTS

— CHAPTER ONE —
MEETING THE UNIFICATION MOVEMENT

A starched white linen tablecloth pressed against my knee as I sat at a round table crowned with half a dozen gleaming water glasses. The atmosphere was crisp, electric. At my table, other writers came prepared with business cards and elevator speeches. I came with a pen and notebook to learn from this experience. Dozens of tables like ours dotted the room. One long rectangular table, where the emcee and session speakers sat, anchored the scene center stage beneath a large screen that flashed computer-projected graphics and PowerPoint slides for the writers' conference.

"I'm probably the only person here who's not publishing a book," I thought to myself. My peculiar past resided in this very room. If the people I was sitting with knew my story, I would no longer fit in even though I wore a nametag just like theirs. Surely, if they knew, they would see me as odd. Yet my memories, both fantastic and familiar, made me feel at home in the space now populated with strangers.

As expert presentations rolled along about marketing strategies, writing chops, and the latest software, I relived the last time I sat in this room of the New Yorker Hotel. Back then, I wasn't wearing shoes. No one was. Natty conference attire with shoes on felt alien. Funny how the nametags pinned to our spiffy lapels didn't describe who we really were.

While the writers at my table didn't know me, the walls and I were old friends though I'd been absent for decades. Like hands holding mine, we held a shared past; together we had heard whispered prayers, laughter, and songs. The walls remembered the hush of awe, the hopes, sobs, and songs of thousands who had been there with me years ago. In a rush, I remembered how possible it seemed back then to create a better world—one where people of all nations would live in peace, with love, and free to delight in the holy joyousness of life itself.

I no longer felt as naïve as the last time I sat in the New Yorker's Grand Ballroom. It was 1982 and none of us wore shoes, let alone nametags like folks at the conference. Back then, we sat knee-to-knee on the floor, hundreds upon hundreds of us from around the world. Many of those attending spoke little English. Even without nametags, we knew one another: if male, it was a brother; if female, a sister. And in the center of the room stood Father Moon. We called him Father. Those who knew him less well called him Reverend Sun Myung Moon. People who didn't know him at all called him the Antichrist.

It was in this room and by this man that I was to be matched for marriage to someone he selected. And while I had never been interested in having a traditional American marriage, which I envisioned as something resembling a 1950s sitcom with June Cleaver's boring life answering the phone or doing housework, or Lucille Ball's hijinks with Ethel, I was still allowing someone else to choose my spouse. Why, as a proto-feminist more interested in saving the world from destruction than domesticated bliss, would I allow this to happen?

To answer that question, I'd have go back to the year 1980. I don't recall if I voted that year, the year Ronald Reagan won; I doubt it. None of the candidates captured my attention with a vision for the kind of world I wanted to live in. Besides, I thought I'd found that world in Chapel Hill, North Carolina. I had fallen in love—not with a person, but with a town that encouraged self-starting creativity, individuality, and that valued the arts. PhDs with long hair drove city buses. Musicians played on street corners. My friends played in bands; I read poetry in bars. I was working, going to college, searching for God. Yes, God with the big G. Little did I know what awaited me the day I slung my backpack over my shoulders after class in UNC's Dey Hall, my footsteps heavy with books and literary ruminations.

Russian language studies had brought me to Chapel Hill from Boulder, Colorado—where I'd already completed two years of general undergraduate work. My aunt and uncle, both of whom had served in the military, offered me a chance to live in Moscow with them as a nanny for their son, my young cousin. I prepared for the trip with intensive language studies. But when the army cancelled their deployment, rather than return to Boulder, I opted to stay in Chapel Hill and took a gap year to work and qualify for in-state tuition. After a year of waiting tables, I relished being a full-time student again studying Russian, French, and economics.

Exiting the foreign language building, my eyes rested upon the manicured expanse of green grass and white oaks before me. I took a deep breath to get my bearings. Across the quad stood Old East, whose mortar walls seemed held aloft by ivy. My eyes homed in on a hound dog standing there. I missed my dogs: I'd left them with my parents in Colorado before classes started. I made my way to the beagle mix and knelt by him to scritch his ears. He snuffled into my armpit before unceremoniously flopping on his back for a belly rub.

I was in my element—mind full of matter, an amiable pooch, and sunshine under a Carolina blue sky before the mosquitoes started to bite. A sunbeam burst through the oak leaves, warming my face as I watched two backlit silhouettes approach. Squinting into the light, I could make out that one was a tall, curly-haired man with a large Roman nose, and the other a short, slightly rotund woman in a skirt.

The man, pale and thin with a few freckles, folded his legs effortlessly beneath him and started petting the dog too. He looked up shyly through his rather thick glasses and with a Midwestern accent said, "Pretty friendly, isn't he?"

"Yeah," I said, "looks like he's happy to stay here all day as long as someone keeps rubbing his stomach."

In an English accent the woman asked, "Are you a student here?" She had soft eyes and a smile that lifted the corners of her mouth into pronounced dimples.

"Yes, are you?"

"Not yet," the man answered. "We work with a student group called CARP—it stands for the Collegiate Association for the Research of Principles."

"What kind of principles?"

"The meaning of life, the relationship between human beings and God," he said.

"So, you're a church?"

Recently, seeking to quench my longstanding spiritual thirst, I'd visited a variety of churches, but I felt only a familiar sense of dissatisfaction with their theologies. None of them seemed equipped to explain the rapport between their spiritual stories and real life on earth. Among the more vexing topics for me was the enduring mystery of the trinity and worship of the incorporeal Jesus. I was open to different conceptions of God, but subscribing to unquestioning, blind faith put me off.

The man met my gaze evenly as he kept scratching the dog's belly. "No, we are a student movement. And we research the relationship between religion and science, mind and body—principles that unify different world religions."

This sounded promising. Turning his eyes back to the dog, and the dappled light coming through the leaves, my new friend seemed more interested in nature than in proselytizing. Prompted by my questions, he added: "We have dinner, give a lecture, and then talk about it. CARP was founded by Reverend Moon."

I was intrigued and tired of eating alone. My pastimes included mountain climbing, poetry readings, bicycling to bars to dance alone or clog with others. I had energy to burn and my trusty Huffy ten-speed got me wherever I needed to go. "What time does it start?" I asked.

"At 6 p.m. Would you like to come and have dinner?"

"Sure! What can I bring—a loaf of bread or something?" Not much of a cook, I hoped it was not a gourmet affair.

"You don't have to bring anything. But you understand it was founded by Rev. Moon?"

"Yes. Is that like the Hare Krishna?"

George Harrison's "My Sweet Lord" played in my head. In high school, I'd visited a convent as part of a spring break alternative workshop. I discovered that nuns did not always don sandals, scowls, or cowls, much less ride about on donkeys. Rather, the Benedictine sisters that hosted me wore street clothes, enjoyed beer and pizza, and drove a Mustang. So, I figured that Hare Krishna followers didn't always have to shave their heads or wear orange.

"No," the man continued. "We're a student group that researches principles. The Hare Krishna are Hindu. We are interreligious."

I liked the sound of that too; I was already learning something. I looked over the newspaper they had handed me. "So where do I go?" I asked, hoping I wouldn't have too far to pedal.

"We can pick you up and bring you to the center. By the way, my name is Briana and this is Paul," said the woman.

We exchanged pleasantries about places of origin. Paul had practiced and taught yoga in Arizona and New Mexico; Briana had been a teacher back in England. They were not much older than me, graduate-student age. I enjoyed their easygoing conversation and international awareness. And I was relieved that they offered me a ride as it had been a long day. The sunbeam that seemed to keep shining on us felt warm and auspicious.

"Okay, I live right over there," I said, pointing to the apartments across the street from Silent Sam. "I can meet you in the parking lot."

"Alright then, see you at six," said Paul.

And off they went. At the time, in an era before cell phones, it did not seem strange to make verbal agreements and expect them to be kept. I gave the dog a farewell belly rub, dropped my books at home, and rode my bike to buy a fresh loaf of sunflower bread. I didn't want to go empty handed. Within a couple of hours, right on schedule, I found their white van in the parking lot. We greeted each other through a rolled-down window and Paul hopped out to open the passenger door. I sat in the bucket seat by Briana, who drove. Along the way, we chatted about the weather, philosophy, and some of the other places we'd each lived.

Right about now, some readers might hear the relentless grinding of the two-note theme from *Jaws* and imagine an innocent girl on her way to be brainwashed by the nefarious Moonies. But that's not this story. I had traveled, lived abroad, and was more of a rebel than a follower.

Briana and Paul, for their part, while devout in their convictions, held the view that free will was essential to God's plan for humanity. Though I did not yet know how deeply they felt this, I sensed their gentleness all the same. They did not uphold Calvinist predestination or justification to eliminate another person's responsibility for his or her own life; nor did they believe that the ends justified any means necessary. Primarily, they espoused a desire to love and serve others as a unified, global family. John Lennon would not be assassinated for another month, and the song playing would have been "Imagine."

We pulled into to the driveway by a little ranch house in the suburbs. This was the CARP center. After taking my shoes off at the front door, I entered a tidy living room with the typical rental-style sofa, chairs, and coffee tables. A woman's voice with an Australian accent called from around the corner, "Oh you're here! I'm just finishing cooking; come on in the kitchen!"

Bridget, a tall, womanly brunette with laughing eyes greeted us in the kitchen with a cheery smile. "Oh, thank you for the lovely bread! But you didn't have to bring anything!" She offered me juice or water. I chose water and sat down at the Formica table on one of the chrome chairs with flower-power, tan-and-wheat-colored padding.

Bridget called out, "Chris! Tadashi-san! Pam's here!" and the other residents gathered from about the house. We shook hands as they arrived. Tadashi-san, a thin, natty gentleman from Japan; and Chris, a Polish-American from outside "Chi-cah-go," square-built with a thick tousle of blond hair. Altogether, there were five housemates from assorted countries—like many student-housing arrangements.

After supper, the dishes cleared, Bridget opened a large photo album at the kitchen table. I looked over her shoulder at page after page of smiling people of diverse races and nationalities in various landscapes posed in groups. As Bridget pointed to different people she knew, she looked peaceful and happy. The album gave an overview of what the workshops were like that she'd attended.

"This is nice," I said, wanting to be polite, "but I would really like to hear about the principles."

Tadashi-san, a little older and more serious, seemed to understand that I wanted to cut to the chase. We left the kitchen table and went to the living room. He pulled up a chair for me and set up a chalkboard on an easel. Paul grabbed a chair from the kitchen and sat beside me. The living room thus transformed into a classroom.

Tadashi-san stood in front of the chalkboard, then bowed his head, and closed his eyes as he greeted "Heavenly Father" and invited Him to join us. While this seemed similar to other church services I'd attended, his prayer felt more intimate somehow. The way Tadashi-san prayed was not a formal address to some distant Almighty, but an affectionate invitation to a divine being that seemed to be right there and interested in what he had to say.

After his "Amen," Tadashi opened his eyes, raised his head and then launched his explanation of the Divine Principle through his thick Japanese accent. As he spoke, he sketched diagrams on the board to illustrate historical periods, patterns of yin and yang, and other relationships in the natural and man-made world.[1]

As he spoke, Tadashi-san would regularly indicate a verse supporting some aspect of the Principle from the Bible—which he treated with reverence—and would have me read the passage. His presentation coincided with my own ruminations over the years. What really hit home was the idea that Jesus was not meant to go the way of the cross merely to satisfy a bloodthirsty God.

From childhood, I had recoiled at the idea of a loving God needing to kill his son. With all my heart, I felt that the crucifixion was a really bad idea. Conversations with my lawyer dad over the years had secured a strong desire within me to protect the innocent. Regarding the crucifixion, it seemed that humans had imposed their own bloodthirsty ways upon Jesus and projected some weird justification for their actions upon an innocent deity.

Dad used to say things like, "If Jesus had been born in our day, there would be electric chairs on church steeples instead of crosses." "You know, if you took the days of creation and just stretched them out over a few thousand years, it pretty much coincides with evolution." "Once upon a time, God and human beings were together. Then they were apart. God didn't move. Guess who did?" And my personal favorite, "God and I often disagree on things like the weather. But in the grand scheme of things, we see eye-to-eye."

When I was a little kid, questioning my Sunday school teachers about the nature of the trinity, I was never satisfied with the idea of a "Father, Son, and Holy Spirit." I felt there should be a woman among the big three. And it made no sense to me that Jesus was God and therefore prayed to Himself. Deep in my soul, I felt that if Jesus was beloved and good, and that if God was good, it could not possibly have been God's idea to crucify Jesus.

The Principle, as it was first described to me in that living room in Chapel Hill, brought to life people and situations from biblical history, but its analytical approach opened up a different sort of discourse. It combined a Western, Judeo-

---

[1] For those readers interested in a more in-depth explanation of the Divine Principle, I've provided a brief bibliography at the end of this book.

Christian theological perspective with Buddhist and Confucian thought. In this way, it opened up a multicultural dialogue on religious principles that could facilitate cooperation rather than a theological pissing contest. Dear to me was the idea that a God of love did not send Jesus to die, but to live. This thought, and more, found a home in the Principle, which I decided I would study over the next few weeks.

That evening, when Sarah and Paul dropped me off at home, we arranged to meet the following week. In the interim, between class work, clogging, and poetry readings, I read a collection of Rev. Moon's sermons entitled *Christianity in Crisis*. These sermons articulated and proposed resolutions for quibbles I'd had with churches I'd visited. I appreciated Rev. Moon's insight and practical understanding of how to unite disparate ideologies. His down-to-earth language and philosophy made sense and I wanted to learn more about it.

Over the course of several months, I would meet Paul and Briana after class; hear another chapter of the Divine Principle, followed by dinner and jocular conversation with "sisters" and "brothers," as they called one another at the center. When Paul prayed, like Tadashi-san, he spoke intimately with God; the way he said, "Heavenly Father," sounded as warm and familiar as "Pop" or "Dad." I was unaccustomed to the tender emotions he and others at the CARP center expressed to this invisible being. In the churches I'd visited, most prayers were written down and read, not spoken from the heart. This spurred me to investigate my own relationship with God. I prayed outside when I was jogging or walking, and whenever I talked with this invisible being I too began to call Heavenly Father, I felt a substantial spiritual presence.

After about six months, the CARP members offered me shared space with them in a "sisters' room" while I attended school. This appealed to me as my roommate was moving in with her boyfriend, and I needed a new place to live. Why move into a religious community rather than in with a friend? "Why not?" would have been my answer. As something new to try it seemed less dangerous than LSD, which I did not dare do, or mountain climbing, which I did. And it gave me an opportunity to enjoy the camaraderie of people from around the world. In many ways, living at the center resembled hosteling.

Yet I struggled with the CARP center's offer because it entailed a big change in my lifestyle. The rules included no dating or drinking. I was ready to take a break from the latter. As an athlete, I knew there could be advantages to teetotalism—especially given my own dad's alcoholism. I figured that developing a relationship with God was worth some modifications in my life. But the directive against dating felt more restrictive; I had a healthy libido and enjoyed the opposite sex. No dating seemed a little odd. I questioned my ability to commit myself to celibacy within a faith-based community. Part of me rebelled against the idea of not heading out with whomever I pleased and enjoying physical intimacy.

Late one afternoon, pondering whether I wanted to forfeit my casual lifestyle to participate in such a pious movement dedicated to world peace, I went on my typical jog about campus. Stopping before Wilson Library, I paused to stretch my arms straight above my head. Looking up, I noticed the clouds had formed an unmistakable image: Jesus on the cross, a crown of thorns upon his head, his jugular vein protruding from his arched neck. I could see him silently screaming in agony.

Taken aback, I felt this was God's direct reply to my question. It felt imperative, like He was telling me that my move into the center was important; that Jesus' heart was at stake. Moreover, I felt like I would be able to get to know God in a deeper way than I would on my own; that it would be experiential, not just theoretical. This vision also resonated with my frustration with the versions of Christianity I'd already encountered. It was as if Jesus himself was telling me that Christian dogma didn't have all the answers, as if he was confirming that a gap in understanding existed, a gap that had nagged me my whole life. This extraordinary information was relayed in an intuitive rush to my heart and mind. This was no result of wearing a hair shirt, fasting, or flagellating myself in some arcane ritual. This vision simply appeared. To me. While I was wearing sweatpants, a T-shirt, and sneakers on a balmy spring evening.

Even still, I remained skeptical. Internally, I said to God, "Okay, if this is really a vision, it will still be here after I touch my toes." It was. But instead of being impressed, I doubled down. "If this is *really* for real," I reasoned, "it will still be here after I touch my toes twice more." By this point it began to dissipate. I felt that God was saying, "I gave you the vision. Don't push it."

Moving day arrived. I packed as many clothes as would fit into a suitcase and filled a couple of milk crates with vinyl records. I gave away my few other possessions, a camera to a hiking buddy, and left the rest—my dishes, wok, and artwork—to my roommate. I wanted nothing from the past to interfere with my new spiritual commitment. I can't recall what I told my friends, although I doubt that I told them about having a vision of Jesus. I imagine I said something about going on a spiritual quest and how I didn't need my stuff. That much was true. Like Abraham, I was now ready to let go of my "Isaac"—whatever was most precious to me—in order to live for something bigger than myself. Having met the spirit of God, nothing else seemed to matter. I had been seeking my Heavenly Parent my whole life.

Decades later, after two divorces, three marriages, raising two children, having seen several loved ones through hospice—changed as I was from when I first decided to move into the CARP center—I still felt that divine spirit in the

New Yorker Hotel. My story came rushing back, and I knew I had to write it down.

— CHAPTER TWO —

My Unsaintly Preparation
for a Life of Faith

Even as a toddler, I never felt connected to the people who told me they were my parents. I felt as if I lived in a different reality—one where my invisible friends were real. Mom and Dad were kind, idealistic, flawed (who isn't?), and loving. They raised my siblings and me the best they knew how in a changing world. Far from any deficiency of theirs, the feeling that I did not belong to them originated with my own visceral sense of lineage and the spiritual world I perceived. I could not have articulated this as a two-year-old sitting in a highchair in our kitchen in Durham, North Carolina, mind you, but early on it felt as if I was awake and aware in ways they were not. From this vantage point, I felt connected to another, unseen origin, one that bound me to history and the wider world yet alienated me even from those physically close who loved me.

No one seemed to understand this better than my elder cousin, Craig. He was the big brother I always longed for, wisecracking, kind, and witty, though I'm not sure his little sister always felt that way. We'd meet only at summer family reunions in Pinehurst, North Carolina, an annual pilgrimage. But in those brief encounters, we shared a certain camaraderie. Horsing around, we'd create wild dramas involving armed rogues and trains made of empty boxes on the lawn, or we'd stage performances for the adults using a sheet on a clothesline for a curtain. Like me, he'd been to the hospital and had multiple surgeries. He had osteosarcoma, bone cancer. I had osteomyelitis, bone infection. I underwent surgery and treatment every other year from the second grade on. He was in the hospital even more often, and he died when I was thirteen. I never understood why I was spared, and he wasn't.

Luke 2:49 tells the story of Jesus' parents taking off with their other children and leaving him behind in Jerusalem by accident; three days later they return to find him with the rabbis, whereupon Jesus says, "Why were you searching for me? Didn't you know I had to be in my Father's house?"

This made complete sense to me when I first heard it. I understood how at home Jesus could feel with people who loved God. I understood how his own family, though trying to do all the right things, could misunderstand him. He embarrassed them because he was different. He spaced out. They had practical matters to attend and he didn't share their priorities. He'd stumbled onto something fascinating and wandered off. Preoccupied, his parents hadn't even noticed he was missing at first.

I'm not Jesus, of course, yet I felt the presence of love at my core, within the nucleus of every atom. My childhood experience with illness gave me life lessons; it was a not always a welcome gift given the discomfort. Like Buddha, I had the chance to live outside of my family's suburban "palace" during my long stays in the hospital. I witnessed the agony of others and learned that however great my pain, someone else was suffering far worse. I also learned to live in a fishbowl of public life, poked with needles, prodded with thermometers, subjected to cold bedpans, and observed by probing eyes at all hours of the day or night.

Back at home, I spent long hours alone—whole days, even—recuperating from osteomyelitis and, one year, rheumatic fever. My father worked. My mother's volunteer activities filled her schedule. When I was in the fourth grade, like many parents that year, they thought a Ouija board would make a good Christmas gift. I was intrigued. When friends came to visit, resting our fingertips on the indicator we'd ask the board questions. It would "answer" by moving the indicator to the words "Yes" or "No," or to individual letters.

I didn't cheat but always wondered if my friends were moving the indicator to spell out words, so one day I tried it on my own. To my surprise, the indicator scooted around spelling amazing things. Henceforth, bedridden and with oodles of time on my own, I'd regularly consult the board as a medium to communicate with, for the most part, friendly spirits. These beings would advise me of things the medical establishment tended to ignore back then. The treatment for rheumatic fever, for example, was Tetracycline antibiotics and bed rest. The spirits' advice? "T-A-K-E V-I-T-A-M-I-N-S."

So, I did. I didn't tell my parents about these things. I sensed invisible beings that others didn't seem to see. Yet visiting a school chum up the street, I discovered I wasn't alone with this awareness. My friend's mother insisted on a very tidy house—the kind where you had to take off your shoes at the door. She kept clear plastic covers on the living room furniture. It was a no-pet zone, and felt like a no-kid zone, too. My friend's family employed a maid who was thin, with high ebony cheekbones. She cleaned briskly and kept her long, dark hair pinned in a tight bun. One day, she looked both ways to be sure my friend's mother wasn't around, then wiped her hands on her apron, and invited us into the kitchen for some cookies. Sitting around the kitchen table, she told us ghost stories—supernatural events that had happened to regular folks. I don't remember the stories, but as she spoke, her hands seemed to have minds of their own and would weave images in the air while her voice rose and fell. Watching us, her eyes would grow wide with wonder as if seeing beings herself, then small with discernment as she checked to be sure we were paying attention. Her stories of the dead returning to engage with the living confirmed my spiritual experiences. She always added a moral to drive home how we had to be good and tell the truth because God knew everything. I was certain this woman had had experiences with spiritual beings like I had—not make-believe but for real. Though I couldn't tell my friend, her family's maid had made me feel less alone.

Emboldened that my spirit friends could be connected to God, I asked them how a baby came to be. Not yet knowledgeable of the mechanics of human sexuality, I was confused about this. I waited for the Ouija board's answer with my hands on the indicator. It started zipping around, letter by letter, that formed words and whole sentences. The somewhat confusing tale of two souls combining was G-rated, yet it made clear that a male and female spirit combined to form a new spirit and a physical body. To me that meant that human sex had another dimension; it was more than a visible materialistic proposition between organisms: it also had spiritual or eternal consequences. Heady stuff for a fourth grader who was not yet entirely sure what menstruation was! However, it increased my conviction that true love would be a spiritual event, not just a physical one.

That I would experience love on this other plane seemed to elude my parents. They focused on the physical realm with their myriad routines and responsibilities, yet I was convinced that all that mattered was unseen and potentially extraordinary. Intuitively, I could sense oceans of emotion and energy patterns surrounding living things and animating inanimate objects.

Physical pain from the osteomyelitis and its treatment that I experienced as a child wracked my captive body, but it could not control my mind and spirit. Eventually, unrelenting pain seemed to rip open my flesh and eject my soul, freeing me from my body's encasement. My spirit emerged through my crown chakra, at the top of my head. Then, my body felt like an observable object to me. My soul and I would notice how my body experienced pain. It still hurt, but I could reconceptualize the discomfort by placing it in a broader context. My spiritual self thus observed my bodily self. While I still inhabited the latter, my new-found awareness also helped me detach from or transcend it.

This new awareness also broadened my intuitive sense of those around me. I felt more sharply the pain of others—both patients and visitors—at the hospital.

The pain I experienced, though plenty enough to register for me, in reality oftentimes couldn't compare to what others suffered—that included the pain of fear, of sorrow, of lack of love, of bewilderment. I felt an easy camaraderie with the pure-hearted and mentally challenged. They, too, it seemed, sensed the unseen world beyond words and physical touch. So did poets, writers, artists, musicians, and the maid at my friend's house. There was an energy, a vibration of love; it felt tangible and real, and more enduring than physical pain or mundane words.

One gray day back in the hospital, I sat in my wheelchair beneath an IV tree. I had a needle up my arm, a sutured incision with a rubber drain tube beneath the bandage and brace around my leg that jutted out in front of me. A nurse parked an old woman in a wheelchair alongside me. Her thin gray hair barely covered her scalp. She was slumped over, her eyes half-shut. The nurse set the wheelchair brake and left. Suddenly, I felt a love vibration and the old woman jolted awake. She turned her head toward me and rasped, "Jesus is knocking on the door of your heart. You must let him in."

She babbled on about love, how even Jesus couldn't trespass. How we had to invite him to visit. Almost out of breath, she had to fight to get the words out. Her effort and earnest message tugged at my heart. I looked at her without knowing what to say when a nurse in terse whites clipped over. "Don't listen to that old woman," she said. "She's not in her right mind. She doesn't know what she's saying."

Abruptly, the nurse wheeled my new old friend away as though she posed a danger to me. The nurse's reaction made me contemplate the old woman's odd words all the more. I felt from my higher self that she had spoken to me with a message of God's love and that the nurse, in her authoritarian censorship, represented evil. I understood instantly that good would always be attacked by evil. That love would be attacked by hate. That wisdom could be hidden in the mouths of fools. That Jesus knocking at the door of my heart was not a mere evangelical doctrine. It was a message from beyond that God incarnate longed to dwell within my seven-year-old soul in a personal way. And that we are all meant to know this love.

My father was my spiritual compass as a child. He seemed to know everything. Despite the advice of the wheelchair messenger, I remained skeptical about relating to Jesus. Christology—though I would not have called it that until years later—continued to perplex me. In Sunday school at the Methodist church we attended, teachers insisted on the unity of the tripartite Father, Son, and Holy

Ghost. Their explanations did not satisfy me as much as the sugar cubes we kids raided from a glass bowl by the coffee dispenser in the fellowship room. Rather than navigate my Sunday school teachers' confusing conglomeration of Jesus, I liked the idea of going directly to God, avoiding the middleman, like Dad.

However much I adored my father, my love was not enough to keep him from becoming an alcoholic. The more his work frustrated him, the more martinis he would knock back over lunch at work and after dinner at home. My mom avoided his late-night rants by going to bed early. So, Dad would visit me in my little white canopy bed where I nestled tucked under the covers surrounded by my stuffed animals.

As a young girl, I longed for my father's love but couldn't fix his adult problems. I could only listen and agree with him adoringly, which seemed to satisfy him. He would sit on top of the covers and at the end of his diatribes, having confided in me his adult woes, he would lean over and kiss me goodnight on the forehead then go to bed to snore next to my mom.

One day just before dinner when I was in sixth grade, Mom paused my brother, sister, and me as we stampeded toward the kitchen table. "I have something to tell you," she said. "We are going to move to France."

She put it so matter-of-factly, it sounded as normal as a trip to visit the grandparents. Dad was changing jobs; we would move to France. My brother and sister were too young to remember our prior move, but for me, it felt like moving to New Jersey from Long Island, only people would speak a different language. We would take one dog with us and Dad, who was staying behind, would keep the other dog and the rest of the menagerie. Being hungry and more concerned about food than logistics, we kids were glad the meeting was short.

Mom often instigated adventures, so we were used to following her into the unknown. From outings to the Turtle Back Zoo, to museums, or opera in New York, she was always out to educate us. My parents were not divorcing. They wanted us kids to learn a second language and adapt to another culture. Mom, a great reader, wanted us to taste a little something of what Hemingway, Wolfe, and Fitzgerald had lived. By living in France, we were to be immersed not only in the French language, but in the literary and artistic heritage that had inspired some of her favorite American writers.

We set sail from New York Harbor on the *S.S. France*. For the first time in my life, I saw my mother cry after she said goodbye to my dad. It took about a week to get to Southampton. The next day, we arrived at Le Havre, where we took a train to Paris and then south to Aix-en-Provence, which would be our hometown for the next two years. My mother led the three of us kids through customs and train stations, while I handled Gael, our Irish Water Spaniel.

After a long day of train travel from the boat at Le Havre to the train station in Aix, we emerged from a taxi at our hotel late at night. We were new to town, new to France, and there had been some mix-up at the Trianon regarding reservations. There was a lot of hand gesturing and words I didn't understand. Then Ingrid, the receptionist offered a solution. My brother and I could stay with her. My mom and little sister went upstairs to bed taking the dog with them. My brother and I waited in the foyer for Ingrid to finish her shift at the receptionist desk. The prospect of adventure and standing so close to our bustling new town of Aix roaring with motorbikes and cars beyond the open front door made us both more alert. Ingrid, who was in her twenties, led us through mysterious back alleys to her tiny studio apartment. She pulled out some bedding so we could sleep on the floor in an area that was usually her living room. This was a crash course in kindness and trusting the universe.

The next day we trotted behind Ingrid, who must have been glad to be rid of us, to rejoin my sister and mom. Perhaps my mother's trust in strangers taught us to be trusting too. She spoke little French but could read it well. The hotel sorted out our sleeping arrangements and from then on, we all stayed together in one hotel room with enough beds until Mom found a place for us to live in the town center.

L'Hôtel Trianon felt like home by the time we moved to our rental apartment at 24 Place de l'Archevêché, facing the Cathédrale Saint-Sauveur. There, my brother and sister shared a room with soaring ceilings and windows that opened onto a small balcony. Adjacent to their room was a bathroom with a tub and a bidet. On the same floor, my mother's room had a balcony overlooking a quieter side street. Seventeenth-century portraits of ladies, gentlemen and cherubs smiled down from above the doors of the living, dining room and bedrooms and their fireplaces had black marble mantles. The furnishings were an eclectic mix of antique and utilitarian.

I discovered a hidden room up a narrow stairwell beyond the kitchen and WC. I claimed this little loft for my own. Back in the day, it must have been the servant's quarters. I loved its low plaster ceiling and the small square window that opened onto the courtyard. Early in the morning, I would hear the concierge's mops and buckets clinking along with the cathedral bells. Best of all, my dear sweet dad did not make nocturnal visits there to confide in me. With an ocean safely between us, we could carry on with an affectionate epistolary relationship. By letter, he appropriately resumed confiding in Mom, instead of me.

Letters would take two weeks, even *par avion*. Packages could take over a month to arrive. For urgent or timely communications, we'd walk to the post office, where we could send a telegram relayed by Morse code. On birthdays we'd receive pale-blue, parchment-thin telegrams with messages in blue-gray type: "Happy Birthday. Stop. Thinking of you. Stop. Love and hugs. Stop. Dad."

On the rarest of occasions, as a treat, Mom would take us all to spend an afternoon at the post office to make a phone call. We'd have to wait for what felt like hours until "Madame Claxton" was called and then we'd have to run to the phone booth with the flashing red light. Crammed inside the small wooden box, we'd huddle four sets of ears around the receiver Mom held to hear Dad's voice crackling between hisses and scratches of the international phone wires.

While stateside, I had served as a wife-like confidant—minus the sexual relations—to my father, and I became a linguistic liaison and confidant for my mother in France. Having assimilated French at the Lycée Rocher du Dragon, like many immigrant children, I translated for my mother in a variety of adult transactions, from banking, to apartment dealings, and later, with hospital jargon (hospitalized for osteo, I underwent surgery and antibiotic treatment) and legal issues (my little sister was hit by a car on her way to visit me at hospital—she became my roommate with a broken leg and arm). Plucky was my mother, yet despite her love of opera and the French language, she was tone deaf. It was difficult for her to learn French simply by parroting it the way her children were able to do.

My fluency in French took time to accrue. The disparity between my linguistic ability in my new language and my appetite for knowledge drove me to satiate my eagerness for expression by devouring books in English. I relished our trips to the *librairie* (bookstore), where Mom would treat us to armloads of lovely books. When Dad would visit a couple of times a year, he would delight us with jars of Skippy peanut butter tucked into his suitcase of clothes. But that was nothing compared to opening his trunk full of books in English—which was like opening a treasure chest.

In Aix, I gradually jettisoned my ugly duckling phase for somewhat less awkward puberty. My eyes seemed to improve, so I stopped wearing the thick trifocals I'd worn when I arrived. Nobody seemed to notice the braces on my teeth. I enjoyed feeling accepted at school for a change. Unlike in the US, my academic engagement was cultivated as an asset, rather than mocked as a liability. It felt liberating to be myself. We all wore a school uniform: a simple smock worn over our clothes with our name and class embroidered on it. This assured that we were judged not for our clothes, but for our scholastic effort, if not, as Dr. King would have desired, our character.

A typical school day would begin in the courtyard. Once through the gate, I would greet each person in my class with a kiss on either cheek—boys and girls. This entailed producing some sixty kisses in a row—an effort more athletic than romantic. It also created a familial atmosphere, as the boys could be rascals and the girls rather shrill. The teachers were sometimes formidable and classes quite strict on protocol. We had to stand at attention when called upon to answer a question or if an adult walked into the room. It was public school, yet a centuries-old code of decorum remained in place. All this I found comforting in its civility and charming in its archaic form.

My favorite class of all was math, as that was where I learned the most French. I delighted in the Cartesian plane and adored my math teacher, Madame Sap. She was slight of build, with a quick, deliberate walk. I knew she was an avid gardener—not only because I passed by her yard of roses on my way to school, but because of her sunbaked skin. A starburst of wrinkles set off the outer edge of each of her eyes, while others crisscrossed her forehead like racing serpents. I thought that there would be nothing better than to grow old with such beautiful wrinkles. They accentuated her deep brown eyes that twinkled and snapped.

Madame Sap did not tolerate nonsense. Unlike my sewing teacher, however, she never took a ruler to my knuckles. She corrected students with Socratic precision. When we were all stumped by a problem, her questions led us to unveil the answer, such that we would feel a sense of marvel, as though we had discovered the solution ourselves.

Exploring characterized our lives living in downtown Aix too. We could easily walk to museums, parks, restaurants, the grocery, or the open-air market. Mother would send us on shopping errands, and we would pick up all the items on her list, including the wine. We kids felt very grown-up living in town. Our Sunday morning ritual included a visit to the back-alley *crémerie* (dairy store). The shop was the size of a walk-in closet. Its stone walls smelled of ancient mossy dew. The *crémier* had bushy white eyebrows and white hair about his ears, a baldpate, and thick fingers with which he would deftly wrap fresh eggs in newspaper for us. He would put a dollop of whipped cream on wax paper and then wrap it in newspaper, too, for us to take home for our hot chocolate.

But the place I loved most of all was CHAM, the Club Hippique d'Aix Marseille, a riding stable on the edge of town. I could go there on foot if need be—it was only about three kilometers from home. Midweek and weekends, barring a family excursion, I went riding. I loved the Club Hippique because there I was not *l'Américaine* but *une cavalière*, another equestrian like everyone else. Before and after riding, I would do anything to be around the horses and the Noël family, who ran the place—groom and feed horses, hunt for and collect eggs the free-ranging chickens had laid, paint fences, clean tack, or help collect hay from the field. My brother loved to shovel manure with the guys. There, we learned all manner of "stable French"—the kinds of words you weren't supposed to use in school. Although they taught jumping as well as dressage, the Noël family knew how to communicate with earthbound language appropriate to handling people and the combined personalities of their ninety plus horses.

After a couple of years in France, it was home and I hated to leave. Had there been a war between France and the US, like Joan of Arc, I thought, I'd have fought for France. But being a minor, I returned with my family nevertheless, by ship, to New York Harbor in 1973. The harsh twang of American English that surrounded us seemed ugly and odd to my ears. Unlike in France, the American public transportation authorities insisted that our gentle dog wear a muzzle. We boarded a train at Grand Central Station heading west for Denver, Colorado, where Dad had moved during our stay in France. Our train chugged south, then west. My brother and I tagged along after a congenial black conductor. He let us stay outside with him on the platform between two railcars as we crossed the expanse of the Mississippi for the first time in our young lives.

My dad worked at the then futuristic Denver Tech Center. He found a house that sat on a couple of acres of prairie in Arapahoe County. Today the area, now called Aurora, has transformed into a teeming city. But when we arrived in the early seventies, our neighborhood was off dirt roads in what used to be unincorporated Southeast Denver, where the deer and the prong-horned antelope played. Neighbors raised horses. Beyond, vast cattle ranches were carpeted with miles of tough prairie grass, yucca plants, and prickly pear cactus. Sandy creek beds bordered by cottonwood trees traversed these prickly plains. You always knew where you were by the purple silhouette of the Rockies to the west. This was cowboy country.

I was fourteen and had leapfrogged from seventh grade into ninth. My high school's mascot was a buffalo that pastured near some Quarter Horses at a neighbor's house. Instead of walking to school through town to greet my classmates with endless kisses, I stood on a dusty dirt road to await a yellow school bus at 6:15 in the morning. No one said hello, not even the driver. Cowboys sat in the back. Besides their eponymous hats, they wore "shit-kicker" boots with pointy toes. When the bus stopped on a slope, the tobacco juice they spat onto the floor would ooze up the aisle.

I clung to my French identity and found respite in books and my studies. The osteo had followed me, so I had a couple of rounds of hospital stays, surgery, and crutches. Our neighbor, Reg, had a part-Arab, part-Standardbred gelding named Joe whose trot devoured miles in steady, long strides. After one hospital stay, just off crutches, I rode Joe in a twenty-five-mile endurance competition. I had been chatting with a fellow on a bay Quarter Horse mare. Approaching the finish line,

I let him pass me to place tenth to my eleventh. He seemed to need the win. I could see the glint of competitive eagerness in his eye beneath his cowboy hat. I felt proud of Joe, whose four legs I trusted more than I did my own two. I was fresh out of hospital and grateful to have completed the ride.

Joe was my first spiritual guide. Wherever we went together, I had the sense that heaven and hell were side by side. When we were united, galloping across the prairie was sublime. I was one with his rippling muscles, pounding hooves, his breath snorting in rhythm with mine. If we were disunited—usually by my own arrogance—I might find myself unceremoniously dumped into a patch of prickly pear cactus or headed full steam for a branch that could knock me right out of the saddle. Once, rearing and bucking his way to freedom, Joe lunged us both free of quicksand in an isolated part of Piney Creek. Another time, we'd roamed miles deep into a cattle ranch. The light passed quickly from dusk to night. In the dark, I could no longer find the Rockies on the western horizon to navigate home. I gave Joe his head. He got us home. In times like these it felt as though he'd indulged me, let me fantasize that I was the one in charge, when really he had known better all along.

I found American high school bewildering. Walking the prairie alone at night, I used to pray. The wind brought no answer for me, save for Joe and my studies. After school, riding Joe, sometimes with friends on horseback, I would try to make sense of my place in American culture, and indeed the universe. Shooting a rifle at a target in a neighbor's basement, I keenly felt how far from French culture I'd come. I hung out with high school kids a year or so ahead of me. They had access to cars—a ticket, of sorts, to insular freedom where we could smoke homegrown dope and travel beyond the cow pastures to buy 3.2 percent beer, a vestige of Prohibition in Colorado at the time for those over eighteen years of age but under twenty-one. None of my friends were even eighteen, but they managed the beer situation. Thus fueled, we would go to someone's basement, play ping-pong and listen to Lynyrd Skynyrd.

A drive-in theater lay just beyond the turf farms and stockyards that bordered the cattle ranches surrounding our rural neighborhood. The entry fee was based on the number of people in the car. Muffling laughter, a couple of us would hide in the trunk. This was less about the few dollars saved than the thrill of having flouted authority.

Overall, my friends and I were "good" kids. We did our homework, our household chores, and held the odd job babysitting or selling burgers at the Tastee Freeze near school. We did not identify with the local cowboy culture. We were more likely to go hiking, camping, or to a rock concert at the Red Rocks Amphitheater, than to a square dance at the local Farmer's Grange. None of us who attended public school went to church.

As a novelty, to experience bona fide American culture, I accepted an invitation to attend a football game—my first—at my high school. My friend Cindy had invited me, and her dad drove us to the game. As we watched the event, I noticed that people seemed very excited, what with the cheering and all. After the game, my friend went to use the ladies' room. Dawdling behind the bleachers, waiting for her to return, I was cold and bored. A group of drunken cowboys charged at me, "Rip her pants off! Let's go for it!" one of them yelled.

I took off running past the bleachers into the night. The ground—uneven, sculpted frozen mud—held as I bolted. But there were more of them than of me. They paced themselves like wolves, some holding back as they took turns sprinting at my heels. The hefty one caught up to me and pulled me to the ground. He'd lost his cowboy hat and leered into my face as he sat on my legs and held my arms splayed out. Another arrived out of breath. He sat on my feet. I struggled but couldn't get them off of me. I felt their heavy hands fumble clumsily through my clothes and unfasten my pants when past my face flew a cowboy boot on the end of a foot. It landed on the face of the hefty one. "Get the fuck off her, you assholes!" shouted a woman's voice. As soon as their grips loosened, I wriggled free and dashed, fastening my jeans, heart pounding, as I ran toward the light of the parking lot. I didn't look back but thanked the divine for my rescue.

I found my friend and her dad talking at the other end of the lot near the car. They were so busy chatting that they hadn't noticed I'd been delayed. I told them nothing about the attack or rescue. I was used to dealing with my pain alone; this was just another skirmish in some great battle between good and evil that reflected my own battles in hospital with pain. On a human level, I felt ashamed and confused. On the drive home, I prayed in silence and mapped my internal progress with God to discern how to relate to the world. In the end, I chalked up the attack to my failure to understand American culture. I longed for France.

My rescuer and I shared a school bus. Her complexion was pale thanks to the cowboy hat that constantly sat atop her long dark hair. She had small, keen eyes yet didn't excel in school. She commanded local respect as a champion barrel racer. I feared her rebuke for being weak and appreciated her fine, roan Appy mare I'd see as the bus chugged past the pasture behind her house.

"Thank you for what you did," I summoned the courage to mumble to her one day.

She looked away, "T'weren't nothin'."

We never became friends; still, I think of her cowboy boot flying past my face into that of my attacker's as the hand of God reaching out to save me.

I discerned grace, too, when Isabelle, a French riding buddy and exchange student, invited me to live with her family in France the following year. By then, my dad's drinking had increased in both quantity and frequency. Sober, he would dispense his version of the birds and the bees with biblical enthusiasm and down-home imagery: "If you ever get pregnant, there better be a star in the East!" His version of sex ed was, "You know what the best birth control is? A large pillow between your knees."

In spite of his practical guidelines, by age sixteen I found my breasts growing tender and my head poised over the nearest commode as I grew acquainted with morning sickness. My first ever boyfriend and I had been intimate. Or, as my little sister had shrieked running upstairs when she had found us naked together in my basement bedroom, "Mom! Pam and Kip are like Adam and Eve!"

But my symptoms did not occur until I was back in France, safely out of reach of Dad's paddle and US laws prohibiting abortion. The father of the child growing within me—my first and only boyfriend from Colorado—was stateside, now living with his parents in Florida, and I alone knew of the pregnancy. I wrote to him from France. The letter took two weeks to arrive. "Abortion would make sense," went his casual, unemotional response, which arrived weeks later—too late to be helpful. The combined time lag of our letters was nearly a month.

Before moving in with Isabelle and her family to attend school later that summer, I lived and worked at the Club Hippique on the outskirts of Aix-en-Provence. Relishing the return to my old haunts, I fed and groomed horses, cleaned tack, collected baled hay, and painted fences in exchange for room, board, dressage lessons, and the Noël family's no-nonsense bonhomie. However, my purpose in being abroad was to study. From my parents' point of view, living with Isabelle's family in Cap d'Ail, a French village less than three miles from Monaco, was supposed to improve my French and prepare me for college and, one day, the international job market. But I felt it was extremely generous of Isabelle's folks to put me up just for being Isabelle's friend.

I was grateful to be back home in France. My school required new students to take placement tests on-site so I had to travel some 125 miles by train from Aix to the Collège Franciscain, a Catholic *lycée* run by monks. Isabelle's family said I could stay at their place to take the exams even though they would be away that day.

It was daylight when I arrived at Isabelle's house in Cap d'Ail. A white villa off the Moyenne Corniche, it overlooked a steep granite slope abutting the sea. I hadn't any preconceived idea of what it looked like—only instructions on how to enter since no one was home. I unlocked the outer gate to the property using the code. The gate creaked as I pushed through beneath mimosa and pines. Unlocking the front door with the key I'd found as directed, I entered a house flooded with sun from the floor-to-ceiling windows. I left my suitcase upstairs in the bedroom, where I opened the double French windows. Looking down, I could see the first-floor balcony overhanging a cliff above the turquoise blue Mediterranean.

A walk beckoned. I scrambled down the steep path from the villa to the sea. At the foot of scrub pines and rugged alpine groundcover, I found a little vine with heart-shaped leaves. I took a cutting and rooted it in an abandoned paper cup that I found on the ground, adding soil. Back at the house, I set my new friend on the bedroom window ledge so I would have someone to come home to after my placement exams. I was confident about my math skills but a little nervous about the journey as I didn't know my way around and relied on instructions from Isabelle's folks.

I caught the city bus to Monte Carlo and got off at the legendary Casino near a jetting fountain and bright gardens. In the regal shadows of its Beaux-Arts façade, Lamborghinis, Ferraris, Mercedes, and Porsches awaited their drivers. I followed the main road up the hill (unavoidable as Monaco is perched on a cliff), then turned left to enter a narrow maze of sober, medieval alleys. Finding the school, I pushed open a towering wrought-iron gate that parted the high masonry walls—the sole entry into a cobblestone courtyard. As the gate closed behind me, I felt as if I'd stepped back into the sixteenth century. It wasn't just the architecture. I saw Franciscan friars in brown habits cinched with rope belts. They moved briskly as they kept order at the Collège. I couldn't believe this much pious austerity existed within walking distance of the decadent glitz and glamour of the Casino.

Franciscan frugality prevented the goodly monks from using much in the way of heat, light, or other luxuries like electricity. After I checked in and found my exam room, the hallways darkened as storm clouds settled. Rain pounded outside, and the cold clamminess of the building closed in around me. Morning sickness compounded the pressure of taking exams before a bevy of stern-looking monks. Though I wasn't Catholic, my status as a sullied girl did not escape me. I hoped the monks did not divine my condition. To them, I was *l'Américaine*. Like the only other two girls in the entire school, I would be a paying day student. I passed successfully into *Seconde C*, the junior year in the math and science track.

Rain streamed down the bus windows on the way back to Cap d'Ail. The sun had set. As I got off the bus, rain pelted my face and soon soaked my clothes. In the glimmer of a streetlight, I punched in the code to enter the villa's gate while my teeth chattered. At the door, I fumbled the key into the lock with numb fingers. Grateful when it finally released, I entered the pitch-black entryway. Inside, I felt up the walls in the dark for the switch and pushed the button. No light.

Panic rose in waves from my chest to my throat, then receded into calm as I thought of my host family's situation, and their generosity in letting me into their home in their absence. My French parents and siblings, including my friend Isabelle, were away in Malaysia. The eldest son, Jean-Luc, had died there. The boom of his sailboat had knocked him off the deck into the South China Sea, where he drowned, leaving his lover and her children to fend for themselves. The entire family had left France on a memorial pilgrimage. I felt their loss dwarfed my problems.

Rainfall pounded into a crescendo as gale-force winds howled outside. What had appeared a cheery place in the light of day had become an eerie, cold house that moaned and rattled like Marley's ghost. It was Monday. I had only been able to procure a can of tuna to eat, as the local bakeries and shops were closed. I had no idea where the fuse box was or what to do should I find it. French-style, everything was turned off, including the pilot light for hot water and gas for the stove. I fumbled through kitchen drawers in the dark but couldn't find a can opener. Taking a deep breath, I left the kitchen to feel my way up the winding stairwell to where I was supposed to sleep.

Lightning flashed, revealing the bedroom for an instant. The large windows I'd left open crashed together and apart again, the white curtains whipped free like specters. Gusts of wind drove the rain like daggers plummeting in through the windows. Thunder bellowed. As lightning flashed again, I could see past the window to a choppy gray sea. The rain-slicked boulders on the shore clung to what looked like a bottomless ravine, the railroad tracks submerged in darkness. As I fought against the wind to shut the windows, the small, heart-shaped vine in its little cup of dirt crashed to the floor. I fell on my knees and wept over it; it was a living, breathing friend to me, the only creature, it seemed, that knew I existed, knew all my secrets and accepted me with all my flaws. I collected the little plant off the floor and tenderly gathered the dirt that had fallen from the cup. As I tucked the salvaged soil about its fragile root, I prayed that my little vine might live. Then, I felt my way through the dark to the loo to vomit.

Scared to be pregnant, cold from the rain, hungry and without means to open my can of tuna, I crawled into bed, wearing socks for warmth. Sobbing, I started to scream along with each peal of thunder. Desperation forced me to call out to God. I'd felt the new life within me. I longed for love but felt none in this world. How could I bring a baby into a place of such pain and sorrow? And what about my education—how would I survive without it? Exhausted, I eventually fell asleep to the gradual waning of the storm.

As the sun rose, and so too did my resolve. My duties awaited at the stable and so the next day I returned by train to Aix. Having a baby would arrest my progress—I had to finish high school. After the train pulled into the station, without an appointment, I went directly to see my childhood pediatrician. My feet seemed to remember the way from years past.

Arriving at the office, I informed the plump, square-jawed Monsieur *le docteur* from my innocent youth that I'd been "knocked up." During my time at the stable, I'd acquired my share of vernacular French, and lacking the filters of educated codification, I didn't realize that the term *pleine* referred to pregnant horses, not women. He caught the gist of my dilemma, however, and avoided eye contact with me while he engaged his nurse as the go-between. She processed the necessary urine sample, confirming my assessment. Forthwith came the decision to return my body to its unpregnant state. The doctor procured an appointment for me at a clinic.

God, it seemed, had answered my prayers. I clutched the piece of paper on which the nurse had written the clinic's address in her tidy French script. All I had to do was show up. Daunted and nauseated, my head spun as my feet carried me past the two-headed cigar fountain on a stone wall and the graceful, cast-iron fountain in the Place d'Albertas. The Natural History Museum looked different. The ancient, gray and black grime that had listened to our childhood chatter years before had since been cleaned to an unfamiliar sandy brown. I felt disoriented in this strange newness. "Where are you now, God?" I asked inwardly, without tears or thunder. I ambled along, expecting no response beyond the address I already held in my hand.

Down the street rose a mirage of two old classmates from *lycée* in Aix, Emma and Christine. Approaching, they seemed scarcely to have changed from years past. I thought I was delirious from lack of food. The three of us had been buddies long ago. Emma and Christine's families lived far from the city center, in opposite directions. The probability of them being together and me meeting them on that particular sidewalk at that precise moment on that specific day after so many years apart was negligible. And in fact, Christine and Emma were normally not very close.

But it was them. To this day, I feel sure that the hand of God brought the three of us face-to-face. I had long since lost their addresses. And here I was in big trouble, needing big help, as God alone knew. After brief greetings, I told them straightaway of my ordeal. Without hesitation, Christine offered me a place to stay for the night, in addition to moral support.

Together, Christine and I took a bus to the edge of town. The women at the clinic explained what they were going to do. Christine held my hand and repeated what they had said in a less clinically euphemistic French that I could understand. They gave me some medications and I fell asleep. Afterwards, I felt woozy.

Helping me on and off the bus, Christine took me to her home, made some excuse to her parents about me being ill, and tucked me into bed. She brought me a cup of hot Chocolat Poulain and some toast. In the morning, I'd be traveling back to the Club Hippique to resume work before returning to Cap d'Ail and Monaco for the start of classes at the Collège Franciscain.

Through my own bumbling mistakes, I had found God. And God had rescued me with absolute love. I learned to trust God more than people—that is,

God showed me how people of good heart could be unconditionally loving, which to me, was the spirit incarnate.

My experiences as a child, adolescent, and young adult had forged within me a trust in an unseen being. My experiences of cause and effect with this ostensibly invisible being were such that I experienced divine love and creative energy through actual events and people. As such, the existence of the divine was real to me before I ever met the Unification movement.

So, what about all the rules that I chafed against in moving into the CARP center? I made a deliberate choice to humble myself to learn something new and unfamiliar through means I hadn't tried before. I chose to experiment with following a spiritual path. I wanted to challenge myself to see how my own relationship with God might evolve.

Still, the act of humility was an offering not easily given. In a capitalist society, the concept of "submission" could find an easy alliance with tyranny. Yet I did not see humility or submission as an excuse to avoid taking responsibility for my actions. By opting to participate in a spiritual community, I chose to suspend disbelief in order to empathize with and understand a different perspective, but I maintained my discrete autonomy before God.

So, when as an undergraduate I moved into the CARP center, I still wasn't as sure about my new brothers and sisters as I was about God. My new, sometimes quirky, friends seemed good-hearted. However, my interest lay mainly in studying and testing the Divine Principle for myself. I disliked the movie star attraction that Rev. and Mrs. Moon seemed to hold for many of the members. The photographs of this Korean couple placed strategically around the place seemed excessively venerated. Having never been much of a groupie, I found that odd.

Yet I felt confident that moving into the center was an experiment worth my time and effort. After returning the cheerful greetings of my new housemates, I entered the sisters' room, plopped my sleeping bag into a corner, and piled my clothes into a dresser drawer that had been emptied for me. Then I went to the prayer room for my own pow-wow with God before supper.

— CHAPTER THREE —

ON FOOD AND RELATIONSHIPS

At the CARP center, I opened my eyes in the morning not to an alarm but a song that penetrated the closed door of the sister's room. Paul would strum the guitar and sing, "It only takes a spark to get a fire going . . ." from Kurt Kaiser's "Pass It On" or some other folksy song. Not one to jump out of bed, I'd listen to the lyrics, stretch in my sleeping bag, sit up, and often just keel over onto my forehead in a snoozy morning prayer before leaving my cozy sleeping bag and rolling it up for the day.

Navigating around the other sisters in our shared washroom was a dance of sorts from toothbrushing and spitting in the sink to timing individual access in the loo. No time to dawdle with ablutions. We had to dress and make a beeline for the prayer room—an unfurnished bedroom down the hall. It provided a wide expanse of floor to sit upon and a lone, low altar table at one end with a few holy books, a photo of Rev. Moon and usually a vase with some fresh flowers.

Entering, I'd find a patch of floor to sit Japanese-style and pray silently until morning service began. We took turns leading this service and preparing the mini-sermons we gave each other. (Father's sermons were renowned for their length, easily lasting several hours and some even six hours or more.) Our talks were comparatively short and touched on insight we'd gained from experience, reflection and prayer. Our daily challenges, solutions and insight put flesh on the holy literature we read and tried to apply.

A final unison-prayer (each person saying their own prayer aloud simultaneously), followed by a representative prayer (where one person prayed and we all silently honored their words), closed morning service. Next came announcements, and we shared our goals for the day. Casual chatter ensued as we migrated to the kitchen to pray and sing again before eating breakfast. Anyone fasting nevertheless sat at the dining table and joined in the conversation. We all helped with cleanup before heading out for the day.

I spent the day on campus, in class, and offered my own silent prayer over lunch. When I returned to the center in the evening, we reconvened family-style, again praying aloud and singing before eating. Those fasting behaved like everyone else, helping with food preparation, serving others, participating in table conversation, and cleanup.

Over the years, I lived in various centers throughout the US and visited others in France and Korea. Each was as unique as the people who lived there. In my early days in the US, I observed some devotees who seemed so fervent in their desire for a spiritual experience to confirm their devotion it bordered on insecurity. It seemed odd to me to consider having a dream of Father Moon or some other spiritual experience an achievement. I'll never forget one brother rubbing holy salt in his eyes to force himself to cry in prayer. Father did not teach us to do such things. Feeling connected to the bigger whole, to the suffering of humanity, to the injustices of history, could cause me to weep sometimes, not always. But I didn't understand why anyone would force themselves to produce an external result without having the genuine feeling within. Mortifying the flesh by fasting or taking cold showers was the usual way people made an offering. To me, an offering was supposed to be unconditional like love, with no strings attached, no quid pro quo.

Like many others in the movement, I did not seek spiritual experiences to confirm my value before God. But I did try to understand what God wanted of me. I reflected and prayed to better understand the Divine Principle (DP) that Father Moon taught us. I often felt a spiritual whoosh when I prayed about it. DP seemed a useful tool like any worthwhile spiritual teaching or practice. Over time, with prayer and testing it for myself, I felt more patient and open to an ever-evolving understanding of the rapport between the spiritual and physical worlds.

About a year after I first joined CARP, I was transferred to Auburn, Alabama. Rev. Moon taught us that by learning to love many different types of people, we could grow our hearts. To that end, CARP centers regularly reorganized; all the reshuffling meant we got to know a broad range of people. These rotations made it easier to focus on one's internal growth instead of circumstances. A fresh setting made testing out new ways of relating easier and could revitalize attitudes because the new group of people wouldn't have preconceived notions. We were inwardly dynamic and growth oriented besides seeking to expand membership.

Each center had a spiritual leader—a.k.a. the "central figure" (CF). In Auburn, my new CF was a gentle and jovial Japanese brother named Akira. He was betrothed to a German sister. Akira suggested that I try a one-week fast. I decided to go for it. It would be my longest fast yet, and on it I'd take only plain water. I saw it as an opportunity for spiritual growth, to explore my own potential from within. And I wanted to use it as an unconditional offering for America or whatever God needed. I had no idea who kept the spiritual account books. I felt happy to make an offering, as if somehow I could help God.

Religious fasting was not for the sake of looking good for bikini season or dietary purification. Its historical practice was connecting to the theological concepts of sacrifice and offering. Denying the body to focus on the spirit has ancient roots. It's still a common path to attain higher states of consciousness and sensitivity toward the divine. However, during my seven-day fast, I had neither dreams of my guru nor apocalyptic revelations from God.

On the evening of day six, I did have a dream in which half a dozen bearded Lilliputians carrying giant forks over their shoulders ran toward me, a giant female Gulliver. Upon each fork, a single, perfectly caramelized sausage link was skewered. These little fellows charged me en masse. They beat me with the skewered sausages as they yelled, "Unite with central figure! Unite with central figure!" This dream pretty well summed up how I saw blind faith: something very important to small minds.

When I broke fast at midnight on the seventh day, all the brothers and sisters at the center gathered around the table to keep me company for my first repast. A sister served me miso soup and plain yogurt to gently rouse my stomach. Truth be told, I was disappointed at how lean this meal was. Yet I strove to be grateful and did not complain. When I reported my dream to the others, no one laughed. I was still hungry after my little meal. Based on my relationship to the divine, a seven-day hiatus from food called for a celebration more along the lines of a full spread of scrambled eggs with gooey cheese, sausage, grits, and coffee with real cream. Especially the coffee. Keeping to my spiritual discipline, however, I waited for an answer from God about this dilemma.

The following afternoon, I met a brother from Southeast Asia, who was studying at the University of Georgia. Knowing nothing about my fast, he gave me a full-sized chocolate bar. As a chocolate fanatic all my life, I was amazed. Chocolate was not on the center's menu so soon after a seven-day fast. I accepted this gift as though it had come from God personally. I felt that God not only knew me but loved me just the way I was. I relished every smooth, creamy, succulent ounce of that chocolate bar with no ill effects. Making the decision to accept and eat the chocolate made me my own central figure—not unlike Napoleon seizing the crown from the pope to render himself emperor. I took charge of my own spiritual life. I claimed ownership and responsibility for my own actions. No one else could be blamed for what I chose to do. I felt beloved and free to stand on my own two feet before God.

Food preparation itself was a form of prayer, from the loving gathering of ingredients—however humble they may have been—to sanctifying the groceries with "holy salt" back at home, to preparing the meal with gentle, loving thoughts. At each step, the cook was conscientious to transmit God's love into each morsel before it reached the lips of sisters and brothers. Center life was a constant exercise in mindfulness. Even the smallest act was an opportunity to invite God into the experience.

Holy salt was in fact regular table salt blessed by Father Moon. We each had a small portion from that original batch, or "seed," and we could multiply this through prayer. Like holy water in a Catholic church, sage smudging in Native tradition, or *aarti* smoke in a Hindu temple, holy salt provided a tangible element from creation to symbolize sanctification, and for this reason it was thought to embody the blessing of the invisible divine. By sprinkling holy salt on the groceries and praying over them—a ritual pause after the madcap commercialism of the grocery store—we expressed gratitude to the divine for the provisions and dedicated their use to good purpose.

Our mindfulness included not only recognizing the spiritual energy needed to gather, prepare, and receive food, but also to cultivate and transmit that energy or blessing into every activity at the center, whether cleaning, playing, working, or sleeping. When we entered the house, we shucked our shoes at the door, Japanese-style. This resonated with multiple religions and histories of sanctification (for instance, God telling Moses to remove his sandals before approaching holy ground).

Each month, one person would sanctify every corner of the center with holy salt, to cleanse and claim it for divine use. Our life was not otherworldly; rather, our inner intent and focus changed the quality of everyday activities. Reflecting back on this, I sometimes think of the Zen Buddhist expression I came to appreciate at the time: "Before Enlightenment, chop wood, carry water. After Enlightenment, chop wood, carry water." Same life, different reason for living.

Key to understanding CARP center mores was that most famous of food stories, the one about the forbidden fruit in the Garden of Eden. "Of all the fruits you may eat," the story goes, "but one." And of course, it's that one that causes all the problems of human history. The serpent tempts Eve to eat of it, and when she does, she is filled with fear and remorse. She then convinces Adam to partake of this wicked fruit, after which they realize they are no longer innocent. They experience shame in their nakedness and God boots them from the Garden of Eden[2].

Although Unificationists did not consider apples, pears, or any other literal fruit diabolical, one allegorical fruit was. That particular fruit, the one we were not to fondle never mind eat, was the one that could produce the fruit of one's loins. Sex was out of the question. We were to live in absolute chastity. And to that end, we had to go beyond even Jimmy Carter's level of devotion when he confessed, in his infamous *Playboy* interview, that he'd "committed adultery in my heart many times." Simply put, we had to change our thinking about sex. In a sense, our treatment of food and our surroundings was consistent with the way we established purity in our relationships. As a conscious act, we practiced agape rather than romantic love.

This was, for me, a novel concept. Emerging from a 1960s ethos of free love ("Make love, not war"), and my youth growing up in France reading D.H. Lawrence and other modernists, I'd been well versed in the concept of sexual intercourse as a natural and pleasurable shared experience between consenting adults. It was an era before AIDS, and I had all the usual post-pubescent vigor and appetite for engaging my body as much as my mind. While I expended energy in my studies, work, tutoring, teaching, and sports, none of these activities was so exhausting that the allure of sex eluded me.

To top it off, I was an incurable romantic and, once smitten, helpless prey should a poet, artist, or musician try to woo me. Since dad's pillow-between-the-knees idea hadn't really worked, it was not altogether bad that DP and center life motivated me to cultivate some mind/body unity and my own tools of restraint. Pausing sexual escapades in order to develop my soul required not only theology, but practice to unite my mind and body. Prayers that focused my mind on bigger issues—combined with more than a few voluntary cold showers—assisted me in this process.

To assure thorough saturation of this frigid blessing while showering, it was common practice to sing, as much to clock time as to focus the mind. One three-verse hymn, "Song of the Garden," when sung three times, ensured a good five minutes elapsed from start to finish. A brother once confided to me that when he and the other brothers heard a sister belting out this song, it was pretty much

---

[2] I use Judeo-Christian terms, primarily, to explain Unificationism. However, the concept of a "good world" into which "evil" entered due to human activity has deep, cross-cultural, and interreligious roots in ancient Buddhist, Hindu, Shinto, and Tao scriptures, the Greek myth of Pandora's box, and multiple African religious traditions. For more on these traditions and how they overlap, see Dr. Andrew Wilson's *World Scripture: A Comparative Anthology of Sacred Texts.* (IRF, 1991), available at http://www.unification.net/ws/theme053.htm.

impossible not to know that she was stark naked in the shower. Thereafter, I tried to curb the boldness with which my lungs so readily protested the freezing water.

Like taking a cold shower, gathering for meals also served as a way to meet God, whose presence existed within in all people. The spiritual discipline of prayer, combined with fasting and serving others food when I was not eating, taught me about sacrifice. Such practice may sound draconian, yet any parent experiences this. You see that your kids are fed before you eat. Ultimately, that was what CARP's "leadership training" was for—to help us learn how to be parents, to think of others before ourselves. Eating was not evil. Overcoming the failure to love with a true heart was our common challenge.

Our attitude toward food was not unlike our attitude about sex in that food was an offering to God. To sanctify what we took into our bodies, we prayed before meals so that our nourishment might serve God's purpose within us. Through our mindfulness of God's love, we sought to become vessels of love such that the food itself, as part of God's creation, would yearn to be consumed by us. This, we believed, was because all things respond to the original true love of God. Divine love is in DNA; it's in subatomic particles. It was not out of austerity, but for the sake of enduring joy of sharing our experience with God.

Thus, sex, according to Unificationism, insofar as it was an expression of divine love, was the greatest thing going on the planet—with the caveat, of course, that one engaged in this activity uniquely with one's eternal spouse. All you had to do was look around and see how everything wanted to connect and exchange elements from anions (negatively charged molecules) and cations (positively charged molecules) to human beings. The union of two people in true love was not only to produce children, but to experience God's love, spiritually and physically. This resonated with my lessons from the Ouija board days. Physical union bereft of spiritual compassion was unfulfilling. The way I saw it, we were all abstaining from sex for a while, so we could ultimately have the best sex ever—true love sex.

Theologically, Father Moon taught us that in a loving marriage, the physical union between a man and woman reflected the original unity of yin and yang, or the masculine and feminine energy within God. Thus, hot sex with one's spouse was thoroughly encouraged as the natural expression of God's own masculinity and femininity uniting in eternal love. But absolute chastity prior to marriage, and total fidelity within it, was the only way to reach that blissful state of total abandon and freedom in love everlasting.

And just as we fasted to make an offering to God, or delayed our meals by praying first, we sought to put our own lusty sexuality on ice to serve God. Like fasting, celibacy was meant to be for a limited time period—enough to grow and discipline ourselves spiritually. Living together in chaste community as brothers and sisters provided opportunities to learn how to love unconditionally, like family. We learned to serve people who had a wide range of personalities and backgrounds. Father Moon thought this was good training for marriage. Jesus said, "Love thy enemy." Rev. Moon said, "Marry the enemy." Ultimately, we were to put unconditional love into practice on a daily and most intimate level.

Center life, then, was akin to monks and nuns living in coed cooperation. At the center, no one told me not to wear cutoff shorts, miniskirts, or low-cut blouses, but over time, those items made their way to the back of the closet and less-revealing clothing became my go-to wear. I didn't feel comfortable flashing cleavage and thighs when I was aware that my brothers wanted to stay pure in their minds. They were frank and unafraid to tell me when too much skin on my part made matters difficult for them. And for their part, the brothers did not lounge around the center in Speedos.

Inwardly, I fully gave myself over to God. I let go, as one willfully suspends disbelief while reading a good book. I did a lot of bowing. Rather than reaching out in horizontal hugs or handshakes, we would acknowledge the divine in each other by bowing in greeting, in parting, or to acknowledge understanding. It was not obsequious, but Asian.

Life at the various centers I lived in had a vertical, almost Confucian sense of hierarchy modeled on family relationships where the younger honors the elder. At the Chapel Hill CARP center, Tadashi-san was the CF or central figure. As such, he served as a pastor, or rabbi, or imam. He took spiritual responsibility for our little group. He listened to people's issues, their personal struggles, and then prayed for them on his own time, often late into the night or extra early in the morning. He prayed aloud in his native Japanese, with tearful fervor. I overheard many leaders over the years pray with selfless humility and tears for the suffering of others. A small amalgam of such a leader's prayer might go something like this:

"Most beloved Heavenly Father, I am so sorry that I have not been able to show your heart better to your children, my sisters and brothers. They are trying so hard, Heavenly Father, but we come up short. We fail to love from your point of view. Please help me to inherit True Parents'[3] heart of attendance. How can I

---

[3] In its plural form, the term "True Parents" was a pastoral title used to designate a couple joined in love, humble before God, willing to take spiritual responsibility to unconditionally love not only those in their direct pastoral care, but all humankind. According to the Divine

bring your love to my sisters and brothers? Please help [so and so] to heal their heart and feel your love."

The hearts of many leaders I heard pray in the US in the early 1980s seemed sincerely humble before God. In those days, the typical CF was male, but could be a sister. Each CF had an assistant or someone in the "Mother" position who supported the center by praying, providing honest feedback in decision-making, and assuring everyone was fed. A third person was responsible for tending finances and accounting. In Chapel Hill, Briana fulfilled the Mother role, while Bridget did the accounting. All three positions were appointed, not elected. As I moved around living in different centers, this repeated pattern felt familiar; each center had a CF, a center mother, and an accountant among the members.

Distinct from the Unification Church, CARP—which stood for the Collegiate Association for the Research of Principles—seemed both more youthful and secular as a student movement. CARP centers exuded energy, empathy and camaraderie of a sort that seemed lacking in the more stringent or fundamentalist church centers, where the holiness hung in the air like fog resting in a cornfield. Many church members, it seemed to me, esteemed reverent silence and appreciated God's suffering more than God's joy.

College-age CARP members were noisier and bouncier; they engaged with boisterous enthusiasm in the wider world of study, work, and participation in non-CARP activities on campus, whereas the church members did more fasting and prayer vigils. When I joined, CARP-center life supported individual initiative, while the church, more saturated with Japanese members, reflected their cultural inclination to favor group conformity. They held an enthusiasm for following directions that confounded Americans deeply rooted in a laissez-faire, every man-for-himself-and-women-and-children-last Western upbringing.

Asian culture, in general, provided helpful insight into the core ethos of our discipleship. Traveling, eating, and living together gave us countless daily opportunities to work through cultural differences up close and personal. In CARP, we took pride in our focus on "leadership" training to develop each individual's skills. Given CARP members' unique and often outspoken characters, we lived "unity in diversity."

No CF had an easy job. He or she would rise earlier, pray more, and had the commission to love more than anyone else. Like a Resident Advisor in a college dorm, the CF juggled listening to people's problems and personality conflicts, yet in addition handled the logistics of mobilizing crews for various projects. The

---

Principle, all people were meant to become True Parents, parents capable of transmitting divine love. Rev. and Mrs. Moon were considered to hold that pastoral position of spiritual responsibility.

mother figure shared the pastoral roles of nurturing, serving, and spiritually counseling center members. Together, the CF and mother figure coordinated the practicalities of center life like fundraising (procuring product, finding venues to sell it, managing the proceeds), housing, and all that went into household management (assuring groceries were bought, meals provided, that the van was gassed up and ready to go), not to mention caring for the physical needs of all those living in the center (providing toothbrushes, tampons, winter coats, booking doctor appointments). Anyone could be called to the parental roles of CF or center mother, yet members regarded these positions with respect, as a divine calling—a mission, not a job. I was grateful that blessing was not bestowed upon me.

Father and Mother Moon (Hak Ja Han) were the model CF and mother figure in those days. By reading speeches they had given over the years, talking with elder sisters and brothers, and reading books that members, scholars, and journalists outside the movement had written, I pieced together some of the depth and scope of Father and Mother Moon's lives. In this way, I began to appreciate how they'd practiced aspects of the Divine Principle not only when it was inconvenient to do so, but when so doing put their lives in danger. And yet I still wasn't a groupie. Groupies possess a degree of fervor that escaped me—their enthusiasm, based on pure emotion, carries them without restraint. (Think of girls fainting at a Beatles concert or stampeding soccer fans.) In faith practice, there are those for whom devotion itself has a fervent attraction, one that completely bypasses intellectual reserve. This can engender a religious impulse to be deferential, to honor, to obey, to remain humble, chaste. When you're completely "in it" you don't think about it. However, I continued to think even as I let myself go in terms of my own relationship with God.

Father Moon's teaching inspired or directly guided people to varying degrees according to their personal inclination. The extent of unquestioning devotion anticipated also varied among branches of the movement. The church, for example, was rigorously ascetic. Church businesses, however, competed with their worldly counterparts. Business members enjoyed more freedom, such as the moderate consumption of alcohol. CARP was somewhere in the middle—like clean-cut Boy and Girl Scouts minus the uniform. Regardless of one's organizational affiliation, however, the more intimate one was with Father and Mother Moon, the more the practice of Confucian and Korean cultural traditions became evident. The casual disorder of Western, back-slapping, "horizontal" democracy seemed out of place around them.

When Father prayed, he shed many tears. Even without understanding Korean, I felt his emotional relationship to God. Father's voice would croon to comfort his Heavenly Parent, as if talking to a small child. Then, as the prayer took different trajectories, his intonation would lilt up and down in singsong or veer off into explosive declarations of determination. While the guttural quality of Korean suited Father's bold personality, before God, he became humble as a little child who adores his parent. His voice would change, even crack as he expressed his tenderness toward God. His compassionate embrace of this invisible being, the divine, the being we called Heavenly Father, or *Aboji*, created an atmosphere of vulnerability before history, an awareness of how the moment we were all sharing with him united us in a precious connection of love so strong it bonded heaven and earth. It was awe-inspiring, though not from any human charisma. Father's prayers invited divine presence that was made accessible to us all.

When Father was angry, he roared in Korean. Single handedly, he would protect God's heart. Father was always telling God not to worry about him, but others. He taught us how God had a broken heart. That the heinous, cruel things people—or nations—do to each other caused God to grieve as the loving parent of both the victims and the perpetrators. It was as if Father sought to shield God from those bullies who caused pain on a cosmic level. I bring this up because some folks who, like me, don't speak Korean fluently, only heard the volume but not the heart of Father's prayers. His anger was never a self-centered tantrum about his own situation. Rather, he blasted indignation toward that which prevented others from experiencing God's love.

His was a passionate expression of loving the sinner but hating the sin. In the Soviet Union, for instance, the state's rigid enforcement of atheistic communist materialism denied God's existence. The government militarily enforced this philosophy, and in so doing would block a child from finding his or her own True Parent. For indeed, as Father taught us, God was the original True Parent of humankind.

In Father's eyes, denying divine human value by reducing people to their materialistic parts and productivity was a crime against God. It went beyond slander; it was the equivalent of tearing a hungry infant from his mother's breast and throwing him into a cage.

Yet Father did not hate those behind the so-called Bamboo Curtain. Although Kim Il Sung had imprisoned Father for preaching, condemning him to a labor camp, decades later, having defied the odds and survived this hardship, Father met Kim Il Sung, had supper with him, and even forgave him. Returning to North Korea under these extraordinary conditions, at a time when it was still a crime against the state to speak of religion, Father nevertheless spoke about God to Kim Il Sung. Father wanted him to understand that he, too, was God's son.

Had Kim Il Sung understood this point and experienced that love relationship, he would not want to do anything to hurt God's heart. If the supreme leader understood his own original value and purpose, he would have understood the supreme value of each precious citizen in his nation. To open such a heart and mind to a new way of thinking would have required delicacy as well as strength, intuition as well as logic, forgiveness of human frailty as well as extended frank discussion of alternatives. One meal alone was not going to do that. Yet the audacity of Father's effort endures.

When Yoda says, "Do or do not. There is no try," (*Empire Strikes Back*, 1980), he's using tough-love pedagogy. I understood how challenging people could have its place to encourage growth. But tough love requires a masterful teacher, one who practices unconditional love. My horseback riding days at the Club Hippique in Aix had taught me this. Marie Christine and her brothers assigned horses to riders based not only on the rider's prowess or the horse's training, but also on the rider's character and the horse's personality.

In France at the time, all young men were required to serve in the military. In a tradition that dated back to the Middle Ages, these *militaires* (soldiers-in-training) had to be schooled in equitation. The *militaires* could be feisty ruffians, competitive with one another and eager to prove themselves in front of some pretty girl at the stable. Marie Christine might assign to such a pupil a stubborn horse that made it impossible for him to show off unless he treated his mount with respect. If cold-hearted, perhaps she'd match the rider with a mean and tricky horse that in making him hang on for dear life, would be humbling or require him to be slow and gentle. To a shy rider, she might assign a goofy mount, one that would force him to be bold to keep up with his comrades. Each student was matched with a horse according to what he or she needed to grow as an equestrian and as a person. And each horse was safeguarded both by the instructor and by having a rider with appropriate skills.

Father's talks varied in a similar manner to help us grow spiritually. His addresses were not mere flattery, full of fairies and unicorns, or descriptions of how great everything would be in heaven. He could be blunt about what was wrong with the world and what we could do to fix it, starting with our own relationship with God.

Over the years, I listened to thousands of hours of sermons, many at dawn: live. I attended intimate gatherings at Barrytown, the Manhattan Center, the New Yorker, Belvedere, East Garden, North Garden, and more at large public venues. On top of reading Father's words in translation, I listened to his speeches—recorded or simultaneously broadcasted—at home or in small private gatherings. Intrinsic to center life was listening to Father's words and discussing them. Years later, I would carry on this tradition with my husband and children even when we weren't involved with the church. We'd gather the family and read and pray together, not necessarily at dawn, but when our schedules meshed. As a family we also attended numerous events where Father and sometimes Mother spoke.

When Father verbally chastised one person or all of us during his lectures, he did so not to belittle us, but to dismantle the barrier of arrogance that blocked us from feeling God's voice within our own hearts. When he joked, or waxed poetic, the warmth of loving encouragement felt tangible, so we could open our hearts to God's love. A broad variety of people attended his sermons, so Father's demeanor fluctuated as he walked around the room and directly addressed one person or another over the course of a single talk. The context of the stories was ever changing and elucidated deeper aspects of the Divine Principle. But constant in every discourse was his urgency to share God's vulnerable situation, how God was a loving parent longing to rejoin His children, and how precious we kids are to God.

Taken out of context, portions of Father's sermons were often misinterpreted. People frequently did so to discredit him. Besides the full, deeper context of the Divine Principle, another interpretive variable was Father's personal rapport with those attending live. In intimate gatherings, he knew many in the audience personally. For their benefit, he joked about theology or human behavior in earthy ways. For example, emphasizing fidelity to one's spouse, he'd tease brothers about having a wiener roast of their own male appendages in heaven.

In addition to the personalities of those in the audience whom he knew and addressed with inside knowledge, the translator's personality further shaped the delivery of Father's discourse. On top of that, the art of translation itself could further produce misunderstanding. While any translation might be approximate, there were several levels of technical complexity in translating Father's sermons from Korean. First, Father spoke, as veteran translators in the movement confided, in an archaic form of Korean. His accent came from the agrarian area in which he was born, in what is now North Korea. Having grown up in the countryside, he could sling earthy, coarse language as well as any farmer. Second, as a scholar, he wrote and read ancient Chinese-Korean script, logo-syllabic characters called Hanja that predated the more direct, contemporary Korean Hangul. Third, written translations of his speeches often passed through a Japanese filter before settling into English. This was because translators were not always easy to find. Furthermore, the devoted and efficient native Japanese speakers sometimes eschewed Judeo-Christian or Buddhist imagery for more swarthy terminology from the days of emperor worship. So a message that might sound loving in Korean, once transformed into Japanese and retranslated into English, could stray far afield from the emotional warmth of the original discourse.

However, translation skills alone did not account for interpretive discrepancies. First, the historical context of the moment in which Father spoke (and the man didn't stop speaking for over 90 years—time for plenty of circumstantial twists and turns). Second, as mentioned, his personal—often longstanding—rapport with specific audience members. Third, with Father, there was still one more dimension to those in the room with him. In addition to our personal life stories and issues, we also brought with us some seven generations of our own peculiar ancestors into any given meeting. And he could see and hear them all.

I imagined each person with an invisible, inverted pyramid of family spirits above his or her head. All of us walk around not just as our individual selves, but as the fruit of our history and lineage. Each individual had an invisible, spiritual entourage of heroes, hooligans, saints, and just plain folks. Father, like a medium, sensed this and spoke to all of the ancestors as well as to all of us who were physically present in embodied form.

So, if Father directly lectured someone, I was in no position to judge either the person chastised or Father. He might have been addressing a spiritual ancestor of that person, perhaps directing the ancestor to straighten out their lineage. Spiritually, sometimes I could sense that. I did not see myself as above reprimand, so if others were scolded, I'd check my own heart. Father's tough-love outbursts were irregular. And even after what might sound like a vehement diatribe, with a twinkle in his eye, making funny faces, he'd turn around and compliment or tease the very people scolded.

Through the 1970s and 80s, "Rev. Moon," "brainwashing" and "cult" were splashed across the front pages of newspapers and *Time* magazine. It seemed strange to me to read such blarney. Father was just a great talker. He could teach for hours on end without a bathroom break. Lesser mortals in the audience would have to sneak out to tend their more earthbound needs. Still, it was difficult to leave, sort of like watching the World Cup. You know that the moment you turn away from the action, something important will happen. Father's talks had that quality, as he was spirit filled.

Over the years, I was acquainted with a number of leaders in the movement who spent extended quality time with Father. One was Rev. Hong, who joined CARP as a young man in Korea. His wife was Japanese, and they had a passel of children, one of whom, a boy, was autistic and a regular challenge for the family. Outside the church after a long meeting, I saw this gangly child grab hold of both his parents' hands on either side of him. Swinging between them wildly, both feet airborne as he laughed, his voice ricocheted through the parking lot as they walked to the parsonage. He was not a toddler but a strapping proto-teen, a lad in constant motion. His mom held on tight with weary yet loving determination, her eyes soft and patient, while his athletic dad seemed to handle the jerky flying motion with energy to spare. Rev. Hong had a thick shock of jet-black hair that tumbled, Elvis-like, across his forehead as he looked down at his son and pulled him up through the air with one hand.

One day, Rev. Hong told the congregation he had to attend a week-long leaders' meeting with Father. As he spoke, his face glowed, taut with the exuberance of youth and happy expectation. But when he returned from his week with Father, we didn't see him for days. There were rumors that he was bedridden, perhaps with a mortal illness. When he at last resurfaced, I asked him how his trip went. He cast down his eyes, shook his head, and said in a Korean-inflected English, "Father, he get up so early, every day 2:30 a.m. to pray, then *Hoon Dok Hae!*[4] Then he lecture. Sometimes until midnight. So difficult to keep up with Father. I need two weeks to recover!" When Rev. Hong told me this, he was a young man of robust health in early midlife. Father was in his eighties.

Father maintained rigorous daily prayer vigils. The large homes in which he and Mother ostensibly "lived" served as public meeting places at all hours of the day and night. When traveling, he met with leaders for hours on end in his hotel room, in addition to giving public addresses. I knew this to be so from regular first-hand reports from leaders I knew personally. After the advent of the internet, I read countless testimonies from brothers and sisters worldwide that corroborated Father's lifestyle.

Thus, it seemed that technology arose with Darwinian efficiency to make our communication far easier than that enjoyed by the first disciples of Confucius, Socrates, Moses, Jesus, or Mohammed. Yet, in my early days of the Unification movement in America, we practiced our faith in a way similar to that of the early Christians or the Jewish people, as one extended family of believers. People followed Father's tradition and the precepts of the Divine Principle with a genuine concern and care for each other's spiritual lives. I met people who were ready to sacrifice their own lives for the sake of their brother or sister. In the depth of prayers I heard, as well as in little gestures of kindness, I felt the spirit of love surrounded and protected us.

Summer came and went along with fundraising and various gatherings with others in the movement throughout the Southeast. I decided not to return to

---

[4] *Hoon Dok Hae* is a Korean term that means "gathering for reading and learning," a practice that usually involved reading aloud from some holy texts.

university in Chapel Hill but continue working with the movement. When I transferred to the CARP center in Atlanta, Georgia, I already knew many of the people there from our regional meetings. Beyond that, I knew that we shared the same values and lifestyle, whether or not we knew each other's personalities. We had an easy camaraderie from the intimacy of prayer and the simple kindness with which we sought to treat one another. For the most part, we maintained a similar schedule too, as did the whole movement: prayer and study at 5 a.m. followed by various activities throughout the day. We gathered in the evening to eat dinner together and share about our day. We slept in sleeping bags on the floor, sisters in one room, brothers in another.

In Atlanta, I attended classes on the Georgia State University campus, worked on the student paper, and served as a campus leader for CARP, primarily doing outreach. The campus sponsored a leadership retreat, which gave me an opportunity to mix with the leaders of other student movements at GSU. Politically, CARP supported Lech Wałęsa's Solidarity, the independent labor movement in Poland opposing the Communist government. We held lectures and staged demonstrations against the Russian invasion of Afghanistan.

While opposed to the annihilation of human rights anywhere, I myself was not what you would call right-wing, at least not in the way some of the other members were. I remained open minded to researching ethical, spiritual principles that could bring healthy, humanitarian outcomes as per the mission of CARP. Pursuant to that mission, I felt that putting the Divine Principle into practice included bridging political divisions to help realize common ideals that both the Left and the Right shared for our nation: freedom, peace, and healthy prosperity for all.

One night in Atlanta, I went with one of my center brothers, Jerry, to hear Stokely Carmichael, the pioneering civil rights activist and black intellectual, speak at GSU. The place was packed. We sat in the balcony.

Stokely said, "The black man is like a flea on the dog's back, suckin' blood, suckin' food stamps, suckin' welfare, suckin', suckin' suckin'! How do you get the flea off the dog? You kill the dog!"

Looking at the sea of listening people, I became acutely aware that Jerry, sitting on my left, the editor from the student paper, sitting two rows down, and I were the only white people in the packed auditorium.

Reaction against a history of racial prejudice was apparent outside the auditorium too. On the GSU campus, black fraternities and activist groups had meetings where they openly fundraised to send arms to support militant groups in Africa. Since I worked for the school paper as a reporter, I could attend these private meetings. In my capacity as a student leader pioneering CARP on campus, I knew and admired many of the black student leaders for their dedication, eloquence, and organizational ability. Together, we'd attended a leadership retreat to learn about best practices, share ideas, and break bread with each other. While I disagreed with any policy that resulted in violence, I understood their rancor and shared their passion for change.

When Stokely's speech ended, it was time for questions from the audience. I stood up from my chair and challenged some of his Marxist-influenced theories. At the conclusion, a flock of black Christians surrounded me. Jerry stood next to me, silent yet supportive. As I answered their questions, I realized that the Principle offered a philosophical challenge to Marxism in a way Christianity could not. Without the Divine Principle, Christianity was impotent. And indeed, in many ways, Marxism arose due to the failures of Christianity. The people who gathered around us gushed in gratitude for my challenge to Stokely's message of violence. But as soon as they heard we were with CARP, followers of Rev. Moon, they laid their hands upon our heads eager to cast out the devil from us.

In Atlanta, my passion to create a new history of true love in the nation of my birth infused ardor into my conversations with God. An hour could pass quickly as I paced back and forth alone in the prayer room, gesturing or holding my hands behind my back, declaring before heaven and earth what needed to change. I was not supplicating, but rather delineating—as though a secretary were taking notes on policies. I felt a personal responsibility before God to rescue America from its history of unrighteous bigotry and inept international awareness. I did not write down these prayers. They were inspired in the moment. Speaking, I felt the presence of powerful, enlightened beings in the spiritual realm. I called upon Martin Luther King, Jr., and Abraham Lincoln for help with the cause of unifying America beyond race, religion, and nationality. I felt bold and strong.

One day, praying as I walked around the neighborhood, a chill ran through me, although it was a typical hot summer afternoon. Suddenly, thunderhead clouds rolled across the sky, turning midday into dusk. Shadows overtook each house, tree and flower petal, encasing the landscape in gray. The wind picked up and sent a tin can rattling across the silent intersection. A solitary tumbleweed—redolent of my Colorado days—bobbed and bounced down the deserted street. Strange to see a tumbleweed in the heart of Dixie, I thought, yet there it was. The greater message, I felt, was that God intended to send a spiritual message to me. I shivered as wind whipped the chill of death around me. A clear message entered my heart: "This is what would happen if God left America." After that, my prayer modality switched, from dictating to God what I wanted, to supplicating myself before Him for mercy and repenting for the historic crimes of our nation. Within a week of Carmichael's speech, the former Black Panther Eldridge Cleaver came to speak at GSU at our behest.

Jerry and I needed an American flag of a size suitable for the auditorium. The university did not have one and neither did we. Who would have a flag big enough on such short notice? We brainstormed until a slow smile crept across Jerry's face. "The mayor!" he blurted out.

So, we walked to the mayor's office. Upon arrival, we explained to the receptionist that we needed to borrow a flag. She said, "Wait a moment, let me see if the mayor can see you." His door was ajar, and on the other side of it we heard a friendly voice call out, "Sure, send them on in."

We entered and shook Mayor Andrew Young's hand, and with his blessing, borrowed an American flag for our presentation. Walking back to the center, we took Martin Luther King Jr. Boulevard, and then cut through the projects to go home. Both sides of the quiet streets were lined by brick duplexes with cement front porches where people sat on rockers, talking over sweet tea. We took turns carrying the flag upright. It towered over us, turning Jerry and me into a two-person parade as we walked through this Atlanta neighborhood of the poorest of the poor.

Most of the elderly inhabitants were on welfare and had experienced the scourge of racism under Jim Crow laws. As we passed each house, people silently rose from their rockers; men took off their baseball caps and put their hands over their hearts. This was our America, broken yet united. We had to change this country for them. I felt so beholden to them, and also conflicted: merely debating political theory, I reasoned, would not be enough to make a lasting change.

Eldridge Cleaver's talk was not terribly well attended, though it was well delivered. Like Dr. King, he spoke with a preacher's lilt and cadence. Our regional CF, Dennis, center mother, Jacinta, Jerry, and I took Eldridge out to eat after his lecture. He had been an insider in the Black Panthers, but in spite of his militant reputation, his demeanor was affable and engaging. The five of us sat together at one table. I was sitting to his right. He had ordered only a sandwich, so I shared my salad with him.

Hearing that I'd lived in France, he described the mystical experience in Saint Tropez that led him to renounce Marxism. He'd described his embrace of that doctrine in his first memoir, *Soul on Ice* (1968). In the book he published ten years later, *Soul on Fire*, he detailed his more recent spiritual quest. As we ate, he told us in poignant detail about his conversion. He was at a party, standing on a balcony that overlooked the Mediterranean on a night I could easily picture from my time living near Monaco. He lifted his hands and painted in the air the huge harvest moon he saw that night. He said, "It was a bloody moon, a blood red moon, and I could see the trail of blood Lenin, Stalin and Mao left as I watched each one pass in front of the moon." Afterwards, he'd seen a vision of Jesus, so like the one I saw when I joined the movement. Hearing this, I felt that he and I were kindred spirits. He spoke of how he embraced all religions and wanted not merely to critique communism, but to offer a spiritual counter-proposal. I felt gratified that our efforts in CARP aligned so naturally with his own.

On the heels of Stokely's and Eldridge's visits to GSU, a thin, middle-aged woman pulled me aside in the hallway one day. She wore her gray hair in a loose bun, had on sensible shoes and a dress splashed in bright flowers. She told me she was a secretary while sneaking furtive looks up and down the hall. Then, she whispered, "Shhh, come to my desk at noon, I have something to tell you," before disappearing into her office.

Intrigued, if somewhat perplexed, I did as she asked. At lunchtime, her boss was gone so she could talk freely. "I found this memo in the trash," she said, shaking the small wastepaper basket below her desk excitedly. She showed me a torn piece of paper with an event reservation for an anti-cult conference at GSU. "My boss is a dean. He doesn't know that I keep a photo of Reverend and Mrs. Moon right here," she said, pointing to a small photo on her bookshelf, nestled amidst figurines and pictures of grandchildren. "No one can know about my beliefs, you understand? But you must do something! The purpose of this conference is to drive you off campus! Now go before anyone sees you here. And don't contact me again."

Though I was baffled that this woman was trying to hide her beliefs while keeping a portrait of Rev. Moon on her shelf, I of course honored her wish for anonymity. At the time, there was little academic research, never mind objective discussion, of "New Religious Movements." Rather, the word "cult" was often ascribed to the Unification movement, and anyone associated with it was assumed to be "brainwashed." I understood why my informant would not want to be tainted even by mere association with the movement. The ignorance and prejudice at that time was tremendous and held sway in the news.

I told Dennis about the event. He found a speaker and arranged for us to have an anti-deprogramming awareness program. We secured a couple of classrooms right across the hall from the anti-cult conference. In the end, both conferences were poorly attended, leaving large classrooms on either side of the hall full of empty seats. The main speaker was low key, and afterwards, we CARP members gave several lectures to one another. The organizers across the hall mostly looked sheepish. Meeting our opposition in the hallway, we offered them juice and cookies from our spread, but they rejected our overtures of friendship. It seemed, nevertheless, a spiritual victory to me. Meeting us, and witnessing our obvious lack of diabolical torture devices, perhaps helped to neutralize some of their conjectures about us so they could turn their attention elsewhere.

The born-again contingent on campus harbored a certain fear of unfamiliar faiths. Baptist parents might seek to deprogram their offspring if they became

Catholic, for instance. Speakers "saved by the blood" would describe Unificationism as a movement lacking theology, based only on the charisma of Rev. Moon and imply that its members were sure to imitate the devotees who followed Jim Jones in the 1978 mass suicide at Jonestown. Fundamentalist fearmongering reminded me of the scene in the 1936 film *Mr. Deeds Goes to Town*, where the elderly Faulkner sisters insist that everyone else is "pixelated" with potentially catastrophic results for Gary Cooper. In our case, too, there were serious human rights issues at stake—namely, freedom of religion. I was glad that we were able to offer a diverging opinion to the anti-cult propaganda. We would not have been able to do so effectively without the serendipitous—some might say divine—intervention of one Georgia peach of a secretary.

Curious as it sounds, CARP fundraising expeditions were not about making money. Nor was the intent to annoy people, though I knew some probably took offense at, or were afraid of, a somewhat frumpy-looking college student knocking on their door. I was frumpy not only because that was my natural style, but also because, in focusing on spiritual rather than material concerns, I wore ill-fitted hand-me-downs or clothing gifted to me off the rack at the five-and-dime. At one point, even my underwear was secondhand. ("Imagine no possessions / I wonder if you can"—I was translating in real life the ideals I heard in my head when John Lennon sang "Imagine.")

If someone did take offense at me calling at their door, I wished them well and moved right along. Far more often, however, I found that people wanted to look at the products we sold (flowers, nature domes, foil prints, toys). Even if they weren't interested in buying anything, they often wanted to talk. I met all sorts of otherwise isolated, lonely, bored, curious, friendly folks of various ages, races, nationalities, occupations, and income levels—all of them, as far as I was concerned, brothers and sisters, children of God, my siblings.

Internally, each fundraising "run"—a patch of town where I would go door to door until the van picked me up—provided me with an opportunity for an elongated prayer whereby I could put the Divine Principle to the test. While the internal goal could be to understand some spiritual lesson, I discovered the external result—like raising a specific number of funds for the center—would follow if I met my internal goal.

For example, say my internal goal were to be humble: my fundraising run would place me in situations where I could practice that attribute. Another internal goal might be to love all people as God's children, or to understand one's own position as a child of God. Reading the Bible, I might want to understand Jesus' heart at a particular point in his ministry. Beginning my fundraising run, then, I'd pray about my internal intention, and then remain mindful of my intent as I knocked on doors. When a door opened, after introducing myself, I would say, "I'm fundraising for CARP, a student group founded by Rev. Moon." If people were interested, I would show them the product and we'd talk. Some people would ask questions about CARP, or Rev. Moon, or how the product was made; others wanted to tell me their stories.

I experienced God in those fleeting conversations. Each person, it seemed to me, had wisdom to share or ignorance to reveal. As we exchanged words, I discovered a divine presence in many humble and unexpected places. I also received answers in nature, the way a leaf might wave a split second before I passed, or a bit of gravel might sparkle in the sun. I savored God's presence in each moment and encounter.

Externally, it was useful to make money of course. We used the proceeds for projects on campus, to pay our rent or the electric bill, or to buy food, clothing, or gasoline, and so forth. It was fun to travel and meet new people. I visited large and small towns across the lower forty-eight states working with various fundraising teams. The variety of places justified the acronym for this group of activists: MFT, which stood for Mobile Fundraising Team.

Walking door to door talking with people, I had a chance to see the "real" America—citizens at work, at home, or doing their laundry at the Wash-O-Matic. I met newlyweds and retired folks, military and government workers, people on welfare and corporate executives, strippers and surgeons, you name it. I talked to everyone on my route. I felt each person I encountered had been placed there by God to teach me something.

Fundraising could be challenging, but it was not a punishment. On a practical level, it provided me with the means to earn my keep. At the center, there was generally more than enough to eat. I never paid a water or grocery bill out of my own pocket. My fundraising efforts helped keep the center running and supported our various causes. Days when my result was small, someone else's might compensate for my lack of contribution, and vice versa. No one was rebuked, kicked out, or left unfed for lack of result. Each person's effort added to the spiritual value contained in the collective result. One person's mighty prayers could bring someone else's windfall. The internal purpose of fundraising was to grow our own spirits in relationship to God and make an unconditional offering, to seek understanding of the unseen wisdom of the universe in the world all around us. We supported each other. If someone were sick and stayed home, they were cared for like family.

On rare occasions, I had spiritual experiences while fundraising. Once, having paused behind a grocery store dumpster to pray, my paternal grandfather, long since passed away, appeared in front of me standing in a somewhat transparent form, shimmering in a flash of bright white light. As he smiled at me, I felt the warm embrace of deep love and comfort. At the time, I was in Kentucky on a new team and didn't know my brothers and sisters very well yet. This experience showed me that God knew me even if they didn't. That experience of love sustained me and gave me courage to persevere.

Another time I needed courage, I was somewhere in Florida on a traveling team. My run was in a gated condominium complex. The day had grown long, and the winter sky had darkened early. Rain fell. As I knocked, door after door remained shut tight behind deadbolts. Occasionally one cracked open just the length of a lock chain to reveal a dark sliver of interior, before the person on the other side muttered, "No thanks!" and slammed the door closed.

Rain pelted the white buildings, the black asphalt of the parking lot, and me. I felt sorry for God. I sensed an ache from beyond myself. I felt as if I were holding a telephone with God on the line longing to talk to these people like a parent desperate to share a moment with their beloved child, just to hear them breathe, to share a word or two, to hear their voice and know they were okay. My heart welled, yearning to reach these people, not because I wanted to be recognized, appreciated, dry, or even to make money. I simply hoped God's love could touch their hearts.

I felt this desire to love transcended class, penetrated doors, filled the air. Yet I failed to reach people's hearts, which is where this divine spirit wanted to dwell. As I soldiered on, I yearned to connect with them so that in some small way, through me, God's spirit could help enlighten America and heal our nation's historic spiritual wounds. Not my ego but this divine spirit I felt within me longed for this. At the time, I was unaware that Florida had been a Confederate state—at any rate, I wasn't thinking about that consciously. I was fundraising in a mostly white area. I felt the people had shut themselves off from God. I did not take their rejection personally. I simply felt they'd replaced divine love with material things.

My heart was breaking for America, how injustice demonstrated her lack of internal direction, how bereft of true love, this nation was cruel. Change seemed impossible. Overcome with sorrow, I fell to my knees, praying in tears, in the dark, in the rain. And, as it turned out, in a puddle. The rain, my tears, the puddle, and I were one in grief—a soggy scenario designed not by me but by the cosmos.

On the surface, this part of Florida was a paradise, bursting with flowers beneath the rustling fronds of palm trees and blessed with balmy weather. Though drenched, I wasn't cold. Sobbing, when I cupped my hands over my eyes holding my cheeks, I felt Father Moon's face, not my own, resting in my palms. His face was larger than mine, heavier, longer, had a different jaw. As I held Father's face in my hands, I felt him crying for America. We sobbed together, in gut-wrenching sorrow for God's broken heart, and we repented together that we were unable to reach the hearts of the people.

After my prayer, I arose from the puddle and knocked on several more doors, but to no avail. I completed my run without a single sale. As I was leaving the complex, a handyman in overalls came out of the shadows. He handed me a single white rose he had snipped from a nearby bush. "Here. This is for you," he said and walked away.

The depths of failure contained the seeds for the victory of love.

CHAPTER FOUR

WHILE I WAS MAKING
OTHER PLANS

Happy, working to establish world peace by bringing together people of different faiths, nationalities, and cultures, I hoped for a groundswell to change the world. It would be easy, once people understood, I reasoned. United by a common project, by breaking bread together and sharing about our families, we'd form natural bonds making all of us sisters and brothers, regardless of the happenstance of our birth. It was simple: everyone wanted to be loved and to give love.

Resolute with optimism, I went to Chattanooga, Tennessee to pioneer CARP on a different campus with three other Americans: two sisters, Claire and Celeste, and Paul, whom I'd first met in Chapel Hill. To leave one center and go to another was not to bid "adieu" to friends I'd come to know well. We were sure to see each other again. Though geographically dispersed, our international community gathered regularly on the national, regional, and local levels. Worldwide, we shared routines of prayer and reflection that created continuity as we read similar texts and sang familiar songs. Our philosophical discussions examined not just the how but the why of our commitment and lifestyle. Most considered it a calling or mission.

Wherever I went and with whomever I served, I sought to make an offering to God. Connecting with God wherever I was, I communed in a sort of a spiritual chat room with sisters and brothers. In this way, we remained close in heart even when apart. I felt this bond of love with my old friends and family, too.

Busy living in the moment, I wrote occasional postcards to friends and letters to my parents, but communication with people outside of the movement was rare due to logistics. Cell phones and the internet didn't exist. My daily life was full of activity, travels and prayer. Pursuing a contemplative life in the midst of the hustle bustle of the center was challenge enough. One of my very best friends was sure she had lost me forever to the Moonies. But to me, our lack of communication was like being away at summer camp. I knew we'd reconnect eventually.

Claire, Celeste, Paul, and I found a two-room sublet in a duplex near the University of Tennessee in Chattanooga. All three of us talked to people on campus about the Principle and invited them to an evening program at our home or center. In church lingo, this was called "witnessing." But to me it just made sense. Feeling as if I'd discovered that the world was round instead of flat, I wanted to share the news. Learning about God's love felt like that—so exciting. And since my old friends and family weren't interested, it was an adventure to find others who were.

Days ticked on without a soul wanting to hear about our ideas. Yet, each time I returned home, a mockingbird greeted me by the front door. Perched on a thin dogwood sapling, he invariably sang full throttle keeping his ground as my hand reached for the door. His cozy proximity and cheeky greeting, made my heart swell. I felt as if God was with us even though we had no fruit to show for our efforts.

Logic compelled me to think it would be better for us to live long-term in Chattanooga, take classes at the university and serve the community there in some practical way. However, to use Hebraic imagery, in the movement we were not yet living in an age of settlement; rather, we were still in the era of wandering in the wilderness. We contextualized our lives in biblical history, which we consciously emulated with the purpose of "restoration"—or hindsight—to do the right thing instead of re-enacting the same mistakes that had previously resulted in biblical catastrophes.

Accepting an assigned location was a choice we each made. We were all single. My two older sisters, Celeste and Claire, were "matched," or engaged, to brothers whom Rev. Moon had chosen for them. They both loved their respective fiancés very much but had been living celibate lives for years working in different missions and states. Claire's betrothed was from Germany, Celeste's from the UK. We sisters shared one room for our sleeping bags, while Paul slept in the other.

We prayed for Tennessee and for the nation. Racism endured in the greater community, segregation an assumed habit. Our goal was to love the people with God's love. It was difficult to love people blind to the value of their sisters and brothers of different skin color. Tears readily flowed when I prayed, especially in the seclusion of nature. Praying on Lookout Mountain one evening, a little apart from the others, I had a vision of Abraham Lincoln. His face appeared out of the dark before me, in a cloud, huge, compassionate. No stovepipe hat. Just his face, his eyes gleaming under a wayward forelock of hair.

This comforted me that somehow our prayers were heard, that maybe we could create a different spirit in this land, a spirit of true brotherhood and sisterhood. That same week, I had a second vision of Abe while praying in a meadow near campus in the twilight. It was so vivid I ran and asked the others if they'd seen it. When they said they hadn't, I was surprised. It was the same image I'd seen on Lookout Mountain, but instead of being enveloped in a cloud it glittered brightly. I felt his love for America there with us. His spirit, more than my brother and sisters, gave me strength to persevere in the face of our constant defeat. I trusted my visions and dreams in some ways more than other human beings. I had a hunch that God was guiding me even when I had misgivings about mortals.

To pay the rent, we fundraised with laser prints and large glossy photos of tranquil landscapes, cute animals, and inspirational quotes. One day, just we sisters went out to bring home the bacon. Fundraising mortified Paul so we left him at home to his own devices. We went shop to shop in town, as usual, entering each establishment. Ever the gadfly, I enjoyed explaining the founder's connection to our work to see what kind of reaction that would produce.

After taking a deep breath, I'd show the product and pipe up that I was fundraising for "a student movement founded by Rev. Moon to bring together people of different races, religions, and ideologies." If people chastised or cursed me, I prayed for the strength to love them, for God to bless them, and then I moved on.

Idealistic, I was determined to tell the truth and explain everything. After all, I joined the movement seeking not only God with a capital G, but truth with a capital T. I think Celeste and Claire, with their greater discretion, were probably the ones responsible for keeping us fed and with a roof over our heads. My fundraising results were far from stellar. However, I had some great conversations. One was with an English chap drinking plain Coke in a bar. After hearing my spiel, he offered me a Coke, too, which I declined. He confessed that he was lonely and isolated due to his line of work—he provided weather data for local airports and the news. His name was Peter. He wanted two laser prints but didn't have cash on hand.

He was so respectful and apologetic, and we were so desperately strapped, I thought that Celeste might agree that we could go to his house to receive his donation. (While there were suggested prices for items, CARP was at that time a non-profit organization, so proceeds were considered donations rather than income.) I went outside to meet the others while he paid for his Coke. Celeste and Claire hadn't had much luck fundraising either. Even though it was only late afternoon, they were ready to call it quits.

Peter emerged from the bar and into the daylight, blinking as his eyes adjusted. I'd had a good feeling about him even in the dark bar because he didn't seem jaded like everyone else. He had a bright spirit and, like us, shunned alcohol. Celeste further chatted him up to confirm he was legit. He gave her directions to his place. The plan was to follow his car in ours. Celeste drove with Claire riding shotgun and me in the back seat. Following him in our dusty brown Dodge sedan, fields engulfed us as we left town behind. Celeste caught my eye in the rearview mirror, and said, "I sure hope he likes laser prints."

Claire, who recoiled from her window at the sight of all those rolling fields said, "Me, too," twisting her hair around one finger. On the horizon, the road disappeared into never-ending countryside. Even I started to have second thoughts. But the sun was shining and the three of us were together. With God as a heavenly wild card, we totaled four in all. At last, Peter's car slowed as his left tail light blinked red indicating our final turn. Stone crunched beneath the tires as we drove up the long, gravel driveway that divided a deserted, flat plain. Fields of stubble yawned for miles in all directions crossed only with an occasional line of windbreaker trees. Atop a white pole, a faded red windsock puffed and exhaled in the breeze, its metal clasp *tink-tinking* against the pole. A broad asphalt runway ran past his front door and into the fields.

We followed Peter into his little white cottage. He explained to the others his daily routine flying an airplane with instrumentation to gauge the weather. He led an isolated life, like a lighthouse keeper. I noticed he was quite handsome with dark curly hair, long eye lashes and cute dimples—the kind of looks that could have made him popular with the ladies in a bigger city. His English accent was dreamy. I could have listened to him talk for hours but we CARP sisters had been trained to shun temptations of the flesh.

Of the three of us, I was the only one not engaged. When, looking embarrassed, he confessed that he used to be obese but had lost a lot of weight, his shy humility made me melt. But I stoically said something righteous about admiring the effort and discipline of his mind/ body unity. He picked out a coppery butterfly print that was one of my favorites because it had some relief that made it feel three-dimensional when you ran your fingers over it. He also chose the Serenity Prayer, which had a white background and some flourishing letters that caught the light—that one was a favorite of people in AA.

I could tell Celeste, ever mindful of the bottom line, was not happy. We had spent time and money on gas to follow Peter to his home, yet he had chosen two of the small prints—not a big glossy photo that would have meant more money for the CARP center. But I was happy because I thought that was his heart—free like the butterflies, serene like the prayer. He paid us in cash and said, "How would you like to go up in my plane?"

"Sure!" I said, looking to my sisters in hope that they would agree. I was almost too excited to pray, yet managed to squeeze in a silent, "Oh please, Heavenly Father, please, please, please!"

It was the end of our fundraising day. Celeste shrugged her shoulders, then smiled, giving me hope for a yes. Claire looked worried, "Gee, I don't know," she said, pushing a stray lock of hair behind her ear a couple of times, the way she always did when she was nervous.

However, Celeste convinced her. So, we filed out the back door to a small, yellowish hangar, with a corrugated tin roof behind the cottage. Peter slid up the hangar door, walked to the right side of his propeller plane and unlatched it. Celeste and Claire climbed in first and clicked on their seatbelts in the back seat. I followed and belted myself into the black bucket seat on the front passenger side. Peter, in the pilot seat to my left, turned on the engine and we rolled out of the hangar. The plane wheels bumped over the grass as we taxied to the runway. The late-afternoon sun was bright, but not the kind that blinded you through the windshield.

I'd last flown in a small prop plane with my dad in Colorado. Right after he received his instrument rating, he checked me out from my then hospital bed to take me up. Nurses plugged the tube from my IV needle, so I could be away for a couple of hours. I was thrilled to be out of bed and in the air. The flight made me green with nausea, though I didn't tell Dad. This time, I dutifully prayed that I wouldn't barf, and I felt lucky to sit in the front given that there were three of us. Looking out the main window helped my stomach settle.

Peter accelerated. Engine roaring, we zoomed earthbound down the runway. We kept zooming and bouncing in our seats as the plane shook. The trees at the end of the runway approached at an alarming rate. My heart lodged in my throat. The wheels beneath us churned on the asphalt. Just as we were about to careen into the windbreaker poplars, the bounce went smooth. The shaking stopped. Up we sailed into the blue, our wheels barely clearing the treetops.

We went higher and higher until the endless fields became tidy checkerboards below. The engine now hummed; it seemed happy to be up there too. "How would you like to steer her?" Peter asked.

"Really?" I said. "But I don't have a pilot's license!"

He said, "That's okay, I do. You're in the co-pilot seat."

I took the little wheel; so small it almost felt like a toy. He showed me how to push it down and pull it up so that the nose of the plane would go up or down. Left and right were obvious.

"So, it's okay if I turn the wheel?" I was worried about being in someone else's flight path.

"Sure. Other planes don't fly around here."

I saw a river over in the distance. I swung us hard to the left for a look-see. It felt like riding at a full gallop through the air. I could hardly wait to discover what we would find over there! I leaned into the turn, the left wing pointed earthward, the right wing pointed up. As the river came into view, I eased the left wing back up and the right wing down, steadying the plane on the horizontal axis. I imagine Claire and Celeste must have been saying a few prayers of their own at this point. Below, the tranquil blue serpentine water wound and stretched invitingly—I wanted to see where it went.

"Wow! This is great!" I said. "Shall we go down between the trees and fly up the creek?"

Peter said, "I'm not sure we're quite ready for that." He directed me back whence we had come above the fields. "Let's go over that way, but without turning quite so hard."

I did as he said, easing right as he explained more about how the plane's engine ran. "This is a breeze!" I thought.

We coasted along. He said something about a throttle, that oxygen was needed for the engine to perform. Then, the engine went silent.

"What happened?" I asked.

"What are you going to do?" Peter replied.

Acutely aware that we were in a tin can with stubby wings, lifeless propellers, and losing altitude, I ventured my best guess: "Pull up the nose to glide?"

I watched the red altitude indicator moving counter-clockwise. Peter decided this was the moment for an extended explanation of aerodynamics. He spoke of lift, air currents, rudders, wings.

"So that means?" I asked, as politely as possible. My zeal to correct the situation increased as our altitude decreased. Celeste and Claire were silent. I figured they could not see the altitude gauge arrow spinning counter-clockwise.

"Point the nose below the horizon," he said.

"You're kidding," I said, trying my best to imitate his calm tone. Meanwhile, my brain fired in every direction—*Do something! He's gone off his rocker! We're going to die! And it's my fault!*

We were still losing altitude. I started to wonder how rough the landing would be. I searched the patchwork below for a large swath of field with no trees. Then, I remembered skiing. To descend a mountain successfully, you lean away from mother earth, hang in space at ninety degrees above the surface, like a swan diver launching into the open sky, defying gravity, when every fiber of your being begs you to curl up into a fetal ball and whisper, "There's no place like home! There's no place like home! There's no place like home!" while clinging to the nearest tree.

The fear I felt skiing was immune to logic. I had to overcome the same sort of fear now. I told my rational self, the one that screamed for self-preservation, to be quiet and go sit in the corner. Then I nudged the nose of the plane down just a little, as Peter said to do, into what I felt to the depths of my soul was the wrong direction.

He reminded me to add full power to the engine. That appealed greatly to me. Full *anything* between our beloved mother earth and us at this point seemed like a good idea. Finally, after what felt like an eternity, the motor clicked over, and all was well with the world. The engine happily hummed. Peter told me to bring the nose back up to horizontal. It turned out he had stalled us on purpose and had things under control the whole time. I was too relieved and serious to be angry. I realized that I'd put us all in jeopardy by yanking us to the left to go check out that stream. He then talked me through landing the plane step-by-step. I did what he said as if our lives depended on it.

Claire and Celeste never said a word the entire flight. When I think back on it now, I know I was in the presence of saints. The plane should have stalled, the way I gamboled through the air toward the stream. Their silent prayers kept us aloft and at peace. Fortunately, it was a (non)crash course in learning how to accept the wisdom of a trusted advisor to handle a difficult situation beyond my expertise. Through Peter, God showed me both how much he trusted me, and how foolish I was. My "monkey mind" thought it had all the answers, when it did not. My enthusiasm was a strength, but also a liability without good counsel. The calm that prevailed and enabled me to make the right decision was due to my sisters' silent support.

After the plane ride, we said our goodbyes and loaded ourselves and the product in the car to head home. We thought we'd survived our brush with death that day, then discovered we didn't know anything. The next thing I remember was waking up in a hospital bed. I was propped upright, the headboard elevated. To my left was a window. In front of it, Claire sat up in a bed with the headboard tilted upright just like mine. She had a big bandage on her hand. From a chair at the foot of Claire's bed, Celeste looked on, focused. Her long blond hair framed her face, like a da Vinci angel—wise and holding back just enough sass to pass for serene as she took in everything that was happening. She seemed to be the only one who was not addled. We had had a car accident.

Peter was at my bedside. I did not know why or how he got there. Claire had a nasty gash on her finger. A nurse entered and checked her wound. Claire protested that she was fine but shouted "Ouch!" as the nurse fiddled with her bandage, now red with blood. It was so unlike her to raise her voice—she never complained.

"Really, I'm fine. We need to go," said Claire, resuming her composure.

"A doctor will have to determine if you need stitches," the nurse said.

Nothing seemed to be wrong with me, though I must have been woozy to be in the bed. I felt like I must have been in a dream because Peter took my hand and asked me to marry him then and there. I looked into his eyes full of wonder at the thought. Then came the clincher: he needed a green card, and he could pay. I looked over at Claire, as unsure of how to respond as I was of my whereabouts. Her eyes locked on mine from across the room.

"I don't think that would be a good idea," she said evenly, wincing as she repositioned her cut hand.

Claire's voice brought me back to reality. I didn't know Peter at all. How could I imagine such a thing? Celeste, running interference, came over and thanked Peter for helping us get to the hospital. I have neither recollection of the accident nor how Peter could have known about it, but surmised Celeste had asked him for help. He left before Claire got her stitches. The hospital discharged us to drive home in our dinged-up car, putting a rather abrupt end to flights of fancy on every level.

For several months after meeting Peter, who I never heard from again, we managed to scrape along with fundraising but had little success witnessing. During this time, one of the Korean leaders I loved the most, Rev. Chong Goo "Tiger" Park, came to visit us. Our apartment was sparsely furnished, a low coffee table in the living room, no beds in the sister's bedroom, as we used sleeping bags. Likewise, Paul slept on the floor in an adjacent apartment furnished only with a blackboard.

When Tiger Park arrived, he took off his shoes at our door. As he padded about talking with us in his black stocking feet, he made our humble center feel like a palace just by being there. He glowed with good cheer and optimism; he embodied CARP spirit to me. One of the early members, he loved Father, yet wasn't afraid to boldly disagree with him. Listening to Tiger Park's stories, it seemed to me that he offered his utmost humility to yield to God first, before yielding to any human. Like my own dad, and Father, he didn't need a middleman. He made me feel like anything with God was possible.

When it was time for supper, he happily sat on the floor with us at the low coffee table to share our meal. The previous tenants had left a limited selection of dishware and our only water glasses were wine goblets. Tiger Park laughed as he saw our table setting, "What is this, the Last Supper?"

I thought he was just teasing us. We didn't know it at the time, and he never let on, but he had cancer. Instead of staying home, he was careening about the region from Florida to Tennessee, driving long hours from center to center offering encouragement. It's the last time I would see him alive as he would succumb before the year's end.

Though buoyed by Tiger Park's visit, it was with great relief that we left Chattanooga to gather in Atlanta with the rest of the regional CARP chapters. A road trip was planned for the whole of Southeastern CARP to attend a workshop out West. The entire region of members was organizing to travel together by bus. After a little over a day in Atlanta, I found myself bound for Aspen, Colorado aboard a dated yellow school bus.

The plan was to save money by driving straight through from Atlanta to Aspen. As usual there were several guitar players among us. When we weren't talking, reading, or sleeping, we sang all manner of songs—the Beatles, Woody Guthrie, Irving Berlin, various spirituals and songs brothers and sisters had written. Debbie Anderson gave a rendition of "The Yellow Rose of Texas" that would knock your socks off.

My parents lived in southeast Denver, miles off our planned route. Since I joined, I'd written letters to them about my endeavors and inspiration—the old-fashioned kind—longhand on real paper and mailed in an envelope with a licked stamp. Occasionally I had made phone calls, but the phones were in constant use for center business. As in our days in France, using the phone was not a daily or even a weekly event for me. When I did call, my parents seemed withdrawn and annoyed. I couldn't understand why their enthusiasm for my lifestyle didn't match mine. Since our bus would pass near my old haunts, I thought that if they could meet my friends and we spoke in person, my parents would finally understand.

"Could we stop by my parents' house outside Denver?" I asked Dennis. He agreed. Once across the Colorado border from Kansas, rather than making a beeline west for the Rockies, we instead traveled south of Denver bumping over miles of dirt roads to my home from high school days. I was excited to see my folks and introduce them to everyone. I knew all the brothers and sisters aboard the bus. Through sun and rain, we had worked, camped, shared meals and bathrooms, done laundry, prayed, laughed, cried and sung songs together.

Chuffed that somehow the divine had arranged for me to bring all my friends from back east to meet Mom and Dad, I bounded into the old homestead. I expected a big hug from the folks. The visit seemed a miracle of synchronicity. Following me was a busload of people who'd been bouncing for thousands of miles on rather hard seats. Instead of reciprocating a warm hug, my parents were reserved and looked nonplussed. I thought we'd gone to a great deal of trouble just to say hello; they felt invaded by strangers. Even still, my mom maintained her southern composure. My dad, however, scowled with irritated disapproval. He felt we'd invaded his house, even though my fellow travelers were ever polite.

Our Japanese-dominated traditions meant people took off their shoes, were deferential, and soft-spoken.

Growing up, I'd always counted on my parents' welcoming attitude toward friends and acquaintances we met casually abroad. Opening doors to the stranger was a normal concept for me—it went back to Ingrid taking in my brother and me when the hotel in Aix was full. My parents' aloof reaction disappointed me, even if I was glad that we'd seen each other.

Not dawdling, everyone thanked them. Before climbing back aboard the school bus, I hugged Mom and Dad and gave them each a kiss. They waved from the front yard as we left. That seemed a small victory. Later, I would learn that in Hinduism this is called *darshan*, a glimpse of the divine. Beholding someone you love has that value. As a singleton still in my early twenties, I loved my folks, yet relished the adventure of travel and my new life. I was soon enjoying the scenery and even the way the bus chugged haltingly as we gained altitude.

Workshops inspired me not only for the ideas, but also for the energy, stories, and good company of CARP members from throughout the US and abroad that I met. The regularity of these sorts of gatherings made it possible to bond with people from all over the world. Workshops offered the opportunity to see someone whom you had befriended at a prior meeting. We communed listening to presentations together beneath a huge white tent, sleeping in dormitories (this time, on real beds—no sleeping bags), talking, eating, and singing. In the summer beauty of the woodlands outside Aspen, we nurtured our souls with prayer. At the workshop's end, we trundled into the bus and headed east with only one mechanical breakdown among the endless cornfields of Kansas. But before heading south to Atlanta, we stopped in New York City because a matching and blessing ceremony was to occur there.

Like us CARP members, hundreds of Unificationists from all branches of the movement descended upon Manhattan by bus from across America. Others flocked from around the world for the event soon to take place at the New Yorker. The lobby and hallways of the old hotel flowed with rivers of people burbling a goulash of languages. Over two thousand of us, from all nations, were there. Most were veteran Unificationists—some were already "matched" or engaged to a spouse Father Moon had chosen, like Claire and Celeste. They awaited the blessing ceremony that would bless them to start family life. Others had been celibate in the movement for years without a betrothed. They hoped Father would choose a spouse for them in the next few days.

I was not among those hopeful for either outcome. As a new member, I did not anticipate participating in the matching ceremony, let alone being blessed in marriage. I was still a "spiritual child," in Unification lingo—not fully fledged in the faith. Besides, I was not ready to settle down. Calm in the thought that the matching did not involve me, I anticipated an interesting wait observing as the others went through these rituals.

To pass the time, I worked as a gofer for a newly created administrative branch of the Unification movement called the Blessed Family Department. I was still a SE CARP member yet volunteered my services "on loan" while in Manhattan to stay busy. I photocopied and filed documents, answered the phone, cleaned hotel rooms, made coffee, whatever was needed. It was easy work, though the office was small. My coworkers' chitchat about blessings and babies seemed irrelevant to my own focus on saving the world.

Between chores one day, I wandered downstairs for some fresh air. Turning the corner from the elevators, I nearly bumped into Dennis, our CF at the Atlanta center, as well as a friend. Spotting a familiar face in the sea of mostly unknown sisters and brothers triggered a grateful smile across my face. "Hi Dennis!" I said.

"Father needs more sisters," he answered. "Do you want to prepare to go in?"—"in" being through the white door and into the ballroom where Father Moon was pairing up brothers and sisters to be engaged for marriage.

Marriage did not cross my mind. Rather, I wanted clarification. What did the word "prepare" mean? I wondered. I said to Dennis, "You mean *pray*?"

He laughed. With remnants of his North Carolina drawl and a crooked smile, he said, "No! Put on a dress!"

His directness took me by surprise at the time. I'd not expected to be matched. I looked like a boy from a Dickens novel in my herringbone knickerbockers and knee socks. And yet I took in his words and said, "Okay."

I felt a stunning calm, like being in the eye of a storm. I had no desire to actually be married yet figured the matching and blessing would be better than boring old conventional marriage. Still enthusiastic about the joy of agape love I was experiencing in the movement, I felt confident that the matching and blessing, though a challenge, would be doable. Like fundraising. It didn't occur to me to consider the reality of what could ensue with marriage, like children, a joint bank account, liability for the actions of another. I thought of it as a more fun version of my current lifestyle, with the added perk of having sex again—having friends and romance sounded like having my cake and eating it, too.

Gliding on a sort of spiritual high, I felt embraced by light and love as I took the elevator up past the thirtieth floor and exited to the one-bed hotel room I shared with half a dozen other sisters—most of them Japanese. There, against the wall, my bundle of belongings resembled all the others. After finding my blue sleeping bag and small duffel with my clothes, I pulled out my only dress. It was ginger in color, made in India, with elastic gathers about the waist. Putting it on transformed me from a nineteenth-century schoolboy into a girl again.

It was a long way back to the lobby. I had time to reflect both waiting for the elevator and on the ride down. None of the logistical aspects of marriage concerned me, not even the sex. I was only considering the spiritual context of my life. A clear thought penetrated my meditation: my seven-day fast had prepared me for this. Fasting was one of the requirements for the matching and blessing. At that point, I wondered if Akira, the CF who'd advised me to fast in Alabama, had known about the matching? Although I had fasted purely for my own spiritual journey, I knew then that technically this was a prerequisite for the matching, even if I hadn't anticipated pursuing this course.

I'd heard stories about how the matching worked from my elder sisters and brothers. Like the answers people received in prayer, each story seemed unique and tied to that person's own spiritual journey. On a practical level, I knew that Father Moon would look over people in the room and put together couples based on complimentary ancestry. Like a medium, he could perceive someone's ancestors even by looking at a photo. So, some people might be matched to another person in the room, while others who could not make the trip for whatever reason might submit a photo instead. The Japanese were perhaps most enthusiastic about submitting photographs.

In a matching, Father put together marital partners, a man and a woman, one at a time. He didn't match couples with an eye to individual compatibility; his concern was that they be complementary for the sake of their children, and in order to restore historical wrongs. Such reciprocal matches might see a Jew matched with a German, or a Japanese with an American, a Chinese with a Filipino, a Protestant with a Catholic, etc. The enemy nations of World War II, as well as other troubled histories between peoples—slavery, religious oppression, economic and class exploitation—and various individual crimes were to be "restored" by the marital couple's love for each other. Instead of treating each other with cruelty, thereby perpetuating the injustices of the past, they would atone through love. We understood the matching as an offering to God for the sake of the world, and that, by loving unconditionally within our couples, we would create the spiritual foundation for world peace.

Basing marriage on ancestral complementarity to restore relationships made sense to me. And I trusted that whoever my partner might be, that person would share my values and be prepared to work through differences, not only for our own sake but for the sake of history. Indeed, for many families, the matching worked. Say you were American with prejudiced parents from the World War II generation, and you were matched to someone from Japan. At first, your parents might not accept your spouse. However, over time, with love and service and ultimately grandchildren, your parents would come to embrace their daughter or son-in-law from their former enemy nation.

The people I'd met in the movement thus far were all good sports, willing, as I was, to try to work through obstacles of understanding with compassion and logic. Only one brother had irritated me. I had been on an ad hoc fundraising team with him in Atlanta. What had chiefly annoyed me about him, besides his moping reluctance to fundraise, was how he'd shied away from telling the truth about Father Moon being the founder of CARP. Fearing persecution, he claimed to be fundraising for his own college tuition instead of for the cause—an outright lie. I was big on truth, honesty.

So, as I rode down the elevator, I was considering my matching in abstract terms having to do with world peace—not as a precursor to marriage and family life. I thought of my potential partner as a long-term prayer buddy—not someone with whom I would be physically intimate, have children, and remain forever faithful. Other sisters and brothers had prayed and anticipated such a day for years. They'd worked in many centers and even different nations as un-betrothed celibates. By contrast, I felt that by saying "yes" to the matching, I was simply taking another chance to trust God and the universe. I trusted God more than people and an otherworldly calm remained with me. This was just another milestone in my spiritual journey.

Dennis saw me exit the elevators but waited for me to come to him. He smiled and asked, "Are you sure you're ready?"

I didn't have to go in. I could leave at any time. The Tick Tock diner was next door and I could go have a cup of coffee instead. But none of that crossed my mind. I felt that I could trust God no matter what Father might say, no matter who my match might be. And there was a chance I wouldn't be matched at all.

"Yes," I said, before taking two more steps toward the ballroom door.

Dennis silently pushed it open. My eyes swept across the sea of people seated cross-legged on the floor. Entering, I was the only person in the room standing up besides those in the distant center. It felt like a grand entrance. Being fashionably late to meet the Messiah was not cool. I wanted to melt into floor unnoticed in the back. But it was packed wall-to-wall with people and nowhere to sit. I froze. Helpful sisters started pushing me forward toward the center of the room. I tiptoed between knees and feet. Avoiding stepping on someone helped me forget my embarrassment as I kept my eyes to the ground. At last spotting a patch of floor, I squeezed between the sisters there. Looking up, I discovered that only a couple of rows separated me from where Father Moon and Colonel Bo Hi Pak, his translator, stood looking at a brother and sister. The couple bowed and went out.

There were about ten square feet of space around Father and Col. Pak. Brothers and sisters, sitting cross legged, crammed in knee to toe from the center to the far edges of the ballroom. Initially, I remained riveted on the scene playing out before me. Occasionally, though, I'd look about the room. Living in community, we were well versed in how not to consider anyone of the opposite sex as anything other than a sister or brother—not as a potential mate. Looking about at the pool of eligibles in the matching, I sought to gaze with indifferent eyes and avoided imagining whether or not one or another might suit. Father was so spiritually sensitive, as were many in the movement, that even the vibration of such thoughts would be perceived. To focus my mind and avoid speculation, I chanted silently "Glory to Heaven, Peace on Earth, I pray only to be grateful."

Father had several rows of brothers and sisters arise in one quadrant. They were all college graduates. He matched them off two by two. Each couple bowed and went to an alcove to discuss the match. If they agreed to it, they returned, bowed to Father, and left the room. If they did not accept the match, they resumed a place on the floor for Father to rematch them. I only saw this happen once or twice.

The hours clicked by. I rearranged my legs under me to keep them from going numb. Father asked if any American or European brothers wanted to be matched with Japanese sisters. I perked up to see how many brothers weren't racist. I remembered one brother who said he never wanted to be matched to a "Yoshi Chunkinora"—his made-up name for a fat Japanese sister. I thought he was a lazy, lying, gauche, racist fool and glad he didn't typify most brothers I'd met. The whole basis of the matching was supposed to be for true love and character, not what we looked like. Yet free will was fundamental to Father's entire teaching and he was a practical man, which is why he asked for brothers who wanted a Japanese wife. Father wanted to match up the whole world with interfaith, interracial, and international marriages to bring world peace. Yet like true love, a legitimate offering can't be forced. To be matched was an opportunity, not a commandment.

A large number of brothers stood up, which I found gratifying. Those matchings went on for quite a while. Then, Father started going around the room pointing at this person or that. The person pointed to stood up and remained standing until told to sit down. Sometimes several brothers and sisters would be standing at a time. Father was looking at their ancestors' compatibility. As if eliminating puzzle pieces that did not fit, he'd have some of them sit down. Then he'd put together pairs from the remaining few.

It was a curious and stamina-challenging process. You never knew with Father. The matching could last for all day and continue deep into the night if he was on a roll, and it could resume at dawn the next day. The initial novelty of the proceedings helped keep me awake, though hours of repetition took their toll. If God had not seen fit for me to be there, I reasoned, I would not have been there. Still, I silently prayed: "Glory to Heaven, Peace on Earth, I pray only to be grateful."

With this inward chant, I massaged the shoulders of the person beside or in front of me to stay awake. Others likewise massaged my shoulders, which helped to relieve the creeping soreness from sitting for hours on the floor. Chanting silently, my gaze wandering about the room, I didn't notice that Father had called for me to stand up. Several attentive sisters around me whispered something incomprehensible. One nudged me; I thought she needed more room for her feet, so I gathered my legs closer to make more space.

"Get up!" she hissed with a Japanese accent. "Father said, 'Stand up'!"

I clumsily rose to my half-numb feet and looked to the center of the room. Father and Col. Pak conferred in Korean. The way they stood blocked my view of the brother they seemed to be discussing. Col. Pak poured out a stream of Korean. I heard, "*Washington Times*," followed by more Korean. Father gestured to me to come forward with a brisk wave of his hand.

Navigating between the feet, knees, and hands of several rows of sisters, I picked my way over. My eyes riveted on Father and Col. Pak. I sensed someone was standing next to me, yet I did not look at his face. I heard him say, "Bow to Father!" with an American accent.

He spoke softly. I didn't recognize his voice. Used to being nudged about protocol, what he said made sense, so I bowed. Not until we left for the alcove did I glance at him. Having trained myself to avoid evaluating based on lust, I assessed him as a geometrical entity: someone taller than me with curly dark hair. We sat down in a pair of chairs arranged so we could face each other. Not knowing quite what to say, I broke the ice with, "Want to see my favorite picture of Father?"

I pulled out a little black-and-white photo of Father deep in prayer. He was sitting Indian-style, his eyes closed with Mother at his side, and half a dozen Korean elders in a semicircle, their eyes closed in prayer too. They were atop a bald granite mountaintop that resembled the holy ground in Central Park but was actually in Korea. My matching partner commented, "The photographer should not have taken that photo."

"Why not?" I asked.

"Because he should have been praying too," he said, looking down at it.

I took this as a good omen of my future mate's commitment to the Principle and decided, based on that one statement, that I could have faith enough to go through with this match. I don't know if he recognized me. More focused on Father than him, I still didn't recognize him.

"So, what do we do now?" I asked since he seemed to know.

"You want to go through with this?" he asked, somewhat amazed, he later told me, at his good fortune.

"Father decided, right?" I said, thinking, *He looks young.* "Yep," he replied.

"So, what's your name?" I asked. "Boris," he said.

Huh, I thought to myself, *he looks familiar*, but I was still in a spiritual bubble, not quite placing him. I told him my name as we both stood up.

We could have stayed to talk longer, but more newly matched couples kept appearing. They needed room to talk too. And after sitting on the floor for so long, I was ready for a bathroom break and something to eat. Besides, I figured we'd talk more later.

"So, see you later?" I said, thinking we were done. "Let's go back in," he said.

"Why?" I asked.

"To bow to Father," he replied.

We sorted out who needed to be on which side, walked back in, bowed, and were dismissed. Outside the ballroom, he said, "Meet me in the lobby by the central column at 2:30."

Later, returning to the lobby to meet my betrothed, I felt like I was entering a multi-species rookery. Hundreds of voices chattered at various decibels in multiple languages. My partner and I found each other. I thought we would exit the din to talk outside to get to know each other. Instead, he led me to a stairwell. I was surprised that Boris knew this back stairway. We walked up dozens of flights of stairs to visit a friend of his whose matching had not worked out. It seemed curious to me that Boris would choose this as it was not a particularly romantic gesture, nor a religious one.

The fellow we met was square built with a Dick Tracy jaw set. He seemed hardened by life. Even as we spoke, though I was polite, I thought inwardly, "Yikes! No wonder his wife left him!" He nattered on about his work, how he kept the boilers and elevators of the New Yorker running. My matching partner seemed to be showing me this brother as an example of someone with the kind of career success he hoped to achieve. I felt a little nauseated. Something didn't feel right.

It slowly dawned on me that the brother I was matched to was the very one who told me he dreaded being matched to Yoshi Chunkinora. From our fundraising days together, I recalled how he was the one who had lied repeatedly to avoid admitting he was associated with Rev. Moon. Raised a Unificationist, he wanted to fit into the world by accumulating wealth and status. In contrast, I had given up everything to join, including risking the wrath of my own parents and friends.

I wondered what kind of joke God was playing. Then, I learned that Boris had played keyboard in a band. That seemed promising. Leaving Dick Tracy, he next introduced me to several band members. They shook my hand vigorously. One said, "God BLESS you," with such earnest enthusiasm I started to wonder what I had gotten myself into.

"Glory to Heaven, Peace on Earth, I pray only to be grateful." My misgivings about my partner were looming. I remembered fundraising, how by fulfilling my internal goal, I would meet my external goal. I had prayed to be grateful. God was giving me a chance to be grateful no matter what my concepts were. For God's sake, I was willing to give it a shot. I truly loved God and was willing to have an open heart about whatever He might ask of me even if I didn't understand it at the time. There was no fear in my heart.

Behind the closed doors of the ballroom we'd exited, the matching ceremony carried on until the evening. At last, Father had matched all who were eligible, combining complimentary lineages. Those whose mate was not in the room in person or via photo would have to wait for the next matching. There was an announcement: everyone matched was eligible to be blessed straight away instead of waiting, as was customary.

The blessing involved a sacramental exchange of vows before God—not a government-sanctioned civil marriage. These vows would be given in Madison Square Garden the next day. Boris and I retired to our respective rooms to prepare. This time, I did interpret prepare to mean "pray."

I found the sisters' quarters packed tight as a box of pencils. More Japanese sisters had arrived with their sleeping bags and blessing paraphernalia. Most had awaited this day for years. They seemed to know what they were doing. I relied on faith far more than reason. They unpacked wedding dresses and veils; I had little beyond the dress I was matched in—my knickerbockers, a shirt or two, some underwear, socks and sneakers—and no money.

Out of nowhere, one sister found a spare wedding dress and gave it to me. Amazingly, it was exactly my size. Another handed me a spare veil, someone else gave me shoes, another gloves, and someone else white nylons. These items appeared for me though I was incapable of uttering a word of Japanese or Korean other than thank you—*Arigato* and *Kamsahamnida*.

A table downstairs in the lobby displayed "blessing rings," gold bands that resembled class rings, in various sizes. They had an insignia of the Unification symbol. The gold felt soft and smooth. I was fond of the symbol. Arrows indicated giving and receiving from above (God or the divine) and below (human beings or the earth). I liked the reciprocity in the relationship. The four-position foundation of origin, division into complementary subject and object, and their union was inherent in the design, as were twelve varieties of relationships this matrix depicted. To me, this was not a church symbol, but a mathematical one, like an atomic or molecular structure infused with divine love. This ring, I felt, symbolized my relationship with the divine—not necessarily my relationship with the matching partner with whom I had only a rude if not rudimentary acquaintance.

Figure 1: Unification symbol. The arrows indicate giving and receiving, an exchange between God or the divine and human beings or the earth.

The next day, our stuffed room was abuzz with Japanese sisters cooing, ironing, and primping. There was no time now to have second thoughts about my partner. It took a couple of sisters to wrap me in satin and attach an elbow-length veil atop my head. Having had an early morning dress rehearsal in street clothes, I met my blessing partner by the same rendezvous post where we'd met after the matching. We and 2,074 other couples walked up Eighth Avenue to Madison Square Garden—sisters in white lace wedding gowns with veils floating up in the breeze and all the brothers in dark suits and burgundy ties—ready for vows that were meant to last an eternity.

Unsure of my partner, I focused on my own personal experience with God. I felt divine spiritual presence as a living, breathing entity in my life, neither an amorphous spiritual dust cloud nor an old white man in a beard. This being enveloped me in love, but also in knowledge. I knew that arrogance could block true love. I was willing to sacrifice my own desire for love to fulfill something bigger than myself. I trusted God and the wider universe; trusted that events meant to be would transpire even if my monkey mind could find thousands of entangled excuses to prevent inner peace. On a human level, my partner seemed all wrong to me, but I was willing to give God the benefit of the doubt, that just maybe there was more to my matching than my limited perception.

In God's presence, a different set of criteria seemed to define possibilities and prohibitions. Was I centered on eternal existence or temporal priorities? Were my mind and heart pure or self-centered? Had I accurately defined and fulfilled my portion of responsibility? Would my actions, if replicated by many, produce outcomes that would serve to better the world or harm society over time? My experience had taught me that I could trust God more than any human being I had ever known. And so with my vows, I promised myself more to God, whom I loved, rather than to my partner.

CHAPTER FIVE

MATCHED, BLESSED, AND CELIBATE

Within days of the blessing, Boris and I left New York by train for Virginia. Exiting the station in Alexandria, my feet found the brick pavers comforting. Their warmth reminded me of the cobblestones and Roman ruins I used to clamber over in France—not soulless like contemporary American cement and steel. We walked to the circuit court, a small brick building with white framed windows where the justice of the peace had an office. It was Boris's idea to procure a marriage license. He was afraid my parents would try to deprogram me. Marriage provided legal protection for both our chaste union and my choice of religion. I wasn't eager to get legally hitched, but I liked the idea of protecting my freedom of choice. Given the antagonism toward the movement at that time, it seemed prudent.

In the early 1980s, more than a decade before the internet as we know it existed, even the term "multiculturalism" was relatively unknown in academic circles. It certainly wasn't common currency in the wider world, particularly in the southern Bible Belt. Christian bookstores, which generally promoted evangelical ideology, had entire sections devoted to "cult" awareness—they even went so far as to label Rev. Moon the Antichrist. Fear could sell books and newspapers. There was little objective investigative reporting about the movement and the media fanned the flames of fear to characterize it as sinister. To my dismay, my parents believed the newspapers more than me.

When I'd phoned to invite them to our blessing ceremony, they must have been shocked; though at the time, I thought they were merely disinterested. My mom, I felt, had always wanted me to marry a Kennedy, or at least someone from a respectable family in the suburbs. Dad's vision for me had never included marriage. Rather it seemed his hope for me was some combination of maiden warrior and business tycoon who would put empires on hold to run to him, rather than a spouse, when he whistled. I knew neither of them was enthusiastic about my joining movement.

At the time of the blessing, I'd also phoned an old high school chum, Jeanette, and invited her to the event. Unlike my parents at the time, Jeanette was a devout Catholic. I thought as a spiritual person she would understand what I was doing. But instead, she tried to dissuade me from attending the ceremony and encouraged me to leave the movement. Again, given media coverage of the movement at the time, her position was understandable. Years later, chatting by phone, Jeanette revealed to me that she'd had a dream of me at the time of my MSG blessing. I'd appeared to her in a bright light and said, "I am the vision of hope." This vision had so moved her that she never again sought to persuade me to leave the movement.

I felt peaceful resolve with my decision to legally marry. So when the clerk in the Virginia courthouse sent Boris and me for blood tests, I willingly obliged. We returned and presented proof from the nearby lab that neither of us had syphilis—a health concern that dated back to the early twentieth century. The clerk, who was round about the edges and filled her prim dress with quiet fortitude, dutifully read over the lab results. She then told us to wait as she called in the justice of the peace, a white-haired, southern gentleman. My betrothed explained that we could not kiss due to our religion, so after the "I do's," we bowed to each other Japanese style. The clerk, serving as witness to the event, restrained herself from rolling her eyes at this extreme dedication to purity. We had not yet fulfilled the requirements to have sex: according to Unificationist doctrine, we were to live in chastity and fulfill our spiritual duties first.

As I understood it at the time, our temporary chastity was an offering that we both made to apply the Divine Principle in our marriage. Before physically uniting with each other, we first sought to spiritually unite with God to bring divine love into our marital relationship. We'd both studied DP; therefore, I thought Boris and I shared a common definition of true love that factored in both purity of heart and body. Theologically, within our marriage, we were restoring the process of the original separation of humankind from the divine, also known as the fall of man, so that together we'd strive to reverse that process.

Unpacked, the fall of man was more than an amusing fable to me. Rather, it explained spiritual principles to guide both our attitudes and actions to realize true love by inviting God into our marriage. Love was not a matter of predestination, but a consequence of choice and effort. God was not an unstable, tyrannical dictator who banished the first human ancestors from the Garden of Eden in a fit of pique and eternal wrath due to their fruit selections after the cheese course.

As the story goes, the first human ancestors, Adam and Eve, were pure, innocent, naked and unashamed. I always thought that was fine. I didn't consider the human body shameful. Then, God gave the commandment not to eat of the fruit of the Tree of the Knowledge of Good and Evil. I resisted the idea of being "commanded;" furthermore, the idea that "disobedience" was the root of all evil didn't make sense to me.

The biblical story says the serpent tempts Eve to "eat of the fruit to be like God." After partaking of the fruit, she shares it with Adam, whereupon they both realize they are naked and hide from God. Subsequently, God kicks them out of the Garden of Eden. And I'm thinking God must be out of his mind. He put the fruit there so they ate it—duh!

Before eating a fruit, people were sinless but after eating it they were sinful? This is where I thought religion went bonkers. When I first heard DP, I braced myself for some fundamentalist wacko interpretation defining the world applying a set of bizarre rules. But DP suggested the story is allegorical. I liked that idea. A story with a talking serpent seemed more like a sci-fi encounter rather than a strictly literal moral guideline.

After eating the fruit, Adam and Eve hid their nether regions. The Divine Principle postulates that was because their shame at the fall involved the misuse of the sexual parts. I thought that was interesting. According to DP, the fruit Eve shared with the Serpent was sexual love. And I thought that was sort of kinky. But the Serpent in the story was not an actual snake any more than the fruit was a banana. Before the fall, the Serpent was known as Lucifer, the Angel of Light, God's right-hand man. It was only after the fall that God turned him into a snake by way of punishment.

Eve and Adam, like God and the angels, were spiritual beings, yet they had the extra bonus of physical bodies. Eve, therefore, could spiritually have relations with Lucifer. However, angels and humans are not the same species. So, this relationship was like a human having sex with a dog—possible, but not recommended for either the human or the angel. This story understood as an allegory literally fleshed out for me what the misuse of love looked like—a love triangle complicated by the spiritual implications.

The relationship between Eve and Lucifer entailed an exchange of spiritual elements that the DP explained in detail. This liaison put Eve's mind and heart akimbo. When she went to Adam, fearful, confused, and ashamed, she wanted redemption from the elements of her relationship with Lucifer that had passed on to her. However, neither Adam nor Eve were mature enough to bring the joy of agape love into their conjugal relationship. Instead, when Eve seduced Adam, he, too, experienced the negative emotions and spiritual problems that Eve and Lucifer's intimacy created—desire rooted in selfishness, envy, and fear rather than unconditional love.

The DP's explanation of the original misuse of sexual love was not to create shame about sex. Rather it established a pattern of redemption to experience the original true love God had always intended—that is, love with pure joy. True love was meant for all people to enjoy and to pass on naturally as parents loved their children unconditionally, modeling true love. It was easy to see that the children born to Eve and Adam inherited a spiritual stew of suffering instead of the intended joy and love. Their elder son Cain, filled with jealous rage toward their younger son Abel, committed the first murder in human history, and thus played out the inherited, dysfunctional spiritual content of their parents' false love relationships.

Because of this teaching, I wanted to right the historical wrong of the misuse of love by purifying my own heart to bring agape love into my marriage. I trusted that my spouse would do likewise for me. On that foundation, we'd share a fulfilling physical relationship driven by pure hearts of true love and absent fickle lust or self-centered egotism. By realizing unconditional love for each other, we'd defeat the false love that Lucifer's unprincipled intrigue had wedged between our original human ancestors. Instead of a false love triangle dominated by Lucifer's fears, cruelty and greed, we'd live bathed in love centered on God. Don't get me wrong, I thought sex would be fun. But my marriage was not merely for my own pleasure—rather, it would serve the noble purpose of righting a historical lapsus, thereby helping to change history.

Just as the chanting of Tibetan monks may not demonstrate worldly power, spiritually, its resonance serves as a catalyst for world peace, so too did we believe that our prayers and offerings could help improve the spiritual atmosphere and serve to shovel some of the karmic crap out of the Augean stables of history. And that history began, as I understood it, with me—with my own history, my own ancestors, and all our combined flaws. My seven-day fast in Auburn had been an offering; so was the matching, my praying, which felt as natural as breathing, and all the other little gestures I offered to God. People of many religious faiths have led this conscious way of life.

The US media portrayed the matching as an exotic ritual, however, in non-Western cultures, the practice of arranged marriage was common. Though I had not been raised in Asian culture, my matching partner had. Although American, he grew up in the Unification movement: his parents had joined when he was two years old. He was a cultural Unificationist, the way some people might be culturally Jewish or Catholic. Overall, he was non-practicing. He did not live in an intentional community but worked at a secular job to pay rent the conventional way.

Even still, Boris knew the traditions and their hypocritical violations. He was familiar with the character flaws of many venerated elders in the movement. And he maintained a deep compassion for and understanding of the intrinsic value of Father Moon's teachings. Some of Boris's subtle understandings went far beyond book learning. He was a movement "insider" in a way I never would be, not only for his own experience but also because his parents' position as founding members gave him the clout of inherited spiritual seniority. Within the movement, by luck of the matching, I'd "married up" to someone above my status.

After legally marrying, Boris and I parted ways. He returned to his job in reprographics at the *Washington Times* in D.C. I rode in a van back to Atlanta with some of the sisters and brothers I was living with at the center there. The journey was painful as the van only had padded bucket seats up front. I sat on a hard folding chair with a bruised bum for the entire trip back to Atlanta. The van was old and its shocks were shot. Each bump reminded me of the bruises I had from the "indemnity stick ceremony." Bumping along to Atlanta, I had time to reflect and relive that ritual. It was a surprise precursor to the blessing.

To atone for Adam and Eve's failure, we gathered, prayed and one by one were given a paddle. First the wife was to hit her future husband's backside three times; then the husband was to do likewise to his fiancée. If they didn't execute the paddling with sufficient vigor, the paddle would go to an elder church leader who, presumably, understood original sin with greater precision.

The symbolism of this ritual was to atone for the fall of Adam and Eve to create a clean slate for the marriage. It was more akin to a birthday spanking: an opportunity to be swatted for as many years as one has inhabited the planet plus one for good luck. The indemnity stick ceremony was not so much an act of violence or S&M as it was a familial Asian custom that required some degree of stoic resolve. It was a formal ritual and we were all fully clothed.

Unaccustomed to hitting anyone for any reason, I grasped the paddle with both hands and took aim as Boris bent over in humble submission. I wacked Boris's bottom three times with limited enthusiasm. A Japanese elder, therefore, took the paddle from me and gave him three whacks to remember. Then, it was Boris's turn. Like me, he lacked vigor in his delivery. So I too received the blessing of a Japanese elder whacking my bottom with a wooden paddle the way my dad used to do. The three whacks were given with sufficient enthusiasm to bring tears to my eyes as they had to Boris's.

A long lecture about the indemnity stick ceremony explained that as husband and wife we would never ever hit each other again. Having paid historical tribute to the fall of man, we stood as restored Adam and Eve, exonerated from original sin. On this foundation, we imbibed a shared thimbleful of holy wine to complete our change of spiritual blood lineage from fallen history so we could establish a new history without original sin. The upshot of all this holiness was I had a very sore bum.

Back in Atlanta, I continued my prior activities with CARP. Committed to my own spiritual growth, I prayed about this new person in my life. We were so different from each other. I spent long hours asking God about how to love my partner. Besides having sex and producing children, I wondered what I could do to fulfill my spiritual mission on earth.

I presumed that Boris, like me, felt fully dedicated to God. At this juncture, I was unaware that his "cultural" Unificationism was a good deal more liberal than my dedication at the time. My lifestyle didn't change at first despite having married. Plenty of activities kept my days full of incident. I lived in a bustling international community, fundraised and traveled, met people in all manner of work and lifestyles. Amidst all this, my dad informed me that he wanted to disown me. I wasn't sure what that meant, other than that he was seriously displeased with how I was living. He hadn't supported me financially since I'd left home, so money was not at issue.

In fact, my father's reaction perplexed me. I thought my engagement with the movement followed the very precepts my parents had instilled in me: to follow my heart and take the road less travelled. While to those unfamiliar with Asian culture, being matched, engaged, and married could seem loony, to me, it didn't seem any more unusual than my own parents' encounter. In his college days, my dad had obtained a blind date with Willy Ann, at the time my mother's roommate and nursing school classmate. When Willy Ann saw that she was several inches taller than him—apparently a deal-breaker in the fifties—they laughed. Willy Ann said, "I'll set you up with my roommate in the dorm, Connie—she's short!" My dad's disapproval therefore seemed illogical to me: sharing lifestyle choices and religious philosophy was less of a basis for marriage than height? I just didn't get it.

Yet I knew I didn't need my biological father's approval when I felt that my divine Father—God, that is, not Rev. Moon—was guiding my life. Father Moon was like a good coach; dear to me, someone who helped me see my own potential, and someone I listened to, admired, and with whom I could disagree. In the bigger ball field of life, my biological father's disapproval was but a jeer from one of many hecklers who would distract me from my own game plan. Though I loved dear old Dad, I wasn't going to let him ruin my life or dampen my enthusiasm for a new adventure.

And so I continued on my journey of witnessing and fundraising throughout much of the lower forty-eight states for the next couple of years. The streets educated me as I continued to meet people from every walk of life while living with a multilingual, international group of folks. I enjoyed the camaraderie with my fellow Unificationists. My prayers and engaging conversations with sisters, brothers, and strangers made me eager to learn more.

I especially wanted to explore my religious conviction with more academic rigor. It seemed there was nowhere better to do this than at the Unification Theological Seminary, founded by Father Moon in upstate New York. To matriculate, I needed an undergraduate degree. Having left college before graduation, "sacrificing my Isaac" for God, I wrote to UNC to inquire as to what classes I would need to complete my degree. Within a few weeks, I received a letter granting me a BA in economics. Transfer credits for coursework from Boulder, combined with my UNC classes, had qualified me to graduate. I felt that what I'd given up for God, God had given back to me, like Abraham finding the ram (coincidentally, UNC's mascot) when he'd been willing to offer Isaac.

With my BA in hand, I took a bus from Atlanta to the Port Authority bus depot in New York City, where I walked up 8th Avenue much less dramatically than my previous stroll to Madison Square Garden in a wedding dress. At Penn Station, I boarded a train for Barrytown, a small upstate village on the Hudson River. The grounds of the Unification Theological Seminary (UTS) formerly housed a Christian Brothers monastery. (Indeed, white statues of Catholic saints on pedestals still contemplated the inner, manicured grounds.) There was a pond and acres of woodlands where Teddy Roosevelt had once roamed as a boy; apple orchards hugged the periphery. Inside, the architecture focused the gaze upward to encourage individual introspection. Vertical lines of steep walls with tall windows rose high above narrow corridors imposing nineteenth-century institutional decorum rather than broad horizontal lines and open vistas.

To the north, Bard College hummed with academic vigor, while to the south stood the town of Redhook. Its predominantly white residents sometimes resented the large number of Japanese immigrants the seminary brought as each new class of enthusiasts would subject the town to their evangelistic zeal. These Japanese members, many of whom Father had sent to the US as missionaries, were often undaunted in their devotion and eager to persevere when rejected. Perhaps this was due to some internal discipline that Westerners lacked. Or perhaps, it was due to their more limited English, which prevented them from understanding the extent to which locals reacted negatively.

I ignored public opinion. I was too busy drinking in my studies in great gulps under the tutelage of diverse professors with whom we uncorked the history of liturgy, pastoral care, theology, and philosophy. Scholars at UTS included an

Eastern Orthodox priest who taught church history; a Methodist minister who gave a Protestant perspective; a former Catholic priest who taught group process; a Polish professor who taught philosophy; a Korean Buddhist who presented tenets of his faith; and a rabbi who taught the Hebrew Bible and its exegesis, or Mishnah, through a thick Israeli accent. An African American Baptist minister served as librarian. We immersed ourselves in an array of faith traditions and received inside perspectives from both scholars and practitioners.

I reveled in my studies and the discussions over meals at the round tables that dotted the dining hall, seating six to eight of us in animated conversations. We took turns giving the daily 5:00 a.m. morning service. Sometimes, we had guest speakers too. One morning a visiting Japanese scholar of Nietzsche commented on my enthusiastic follow-up at a post-sermon breakfast chat: "Is she always this engaged at this hour?" It was all of 7:00 a.m.

One paper I wrote addressed the inclusion of homosexuality in the ministry of pastoral care. At the time, this was unthinkable for cultural Unificationists. There was no pastoral approach for homosexuals because it was assumed that all people seeking God through Unificationism would be heterosexuals. Though my paper was viewed as avant-garde by Unificationists at the seminary, it was not so for non-Unificationist faculty.

Outside of their academic qualifications—for seminary was accredited—the main criterion for professors to teach at UTS was to have read the DP. That did not mean they had to agree with it. Nor did all faculty members see Father as their lord. For instance, faculty had staged a strike in the early years because, initially, Father did not admit women to the seminary. Father responded by allowing sisters as well as brothers to attend and thus the faculty agreed to teach.

Some Unificationists categorized such protest as akin to Moses challenging God on the commandments. However, in terms of DP, "give and take action"— the exchange of feedback and response through loving interaction—should occur between people occupying different hierarchical positions within an organizational structure. The Divine Principle modeled "give and take action," or more accurately "giving and receiving," as communication to exchange information back and forth. It did not model a one-directional chain of command.

Despite my intellectual engagement, I felt myself a small fry among the many movement leaders who happened to be in my seminary class. These people had sacrificed for years, living in poverty, chastity, and devoted prayer as missionaries and activists, some in dangerous situations in the Middle East, Africa, and behind the Iron Curtain. It was 1984, some five years before the Berlin Wall would come down, yet Father had long been calling for its removal and Tiger Park had led CARP demonstrations there with many in my seminary class.

My studies at UTS enthralled me yet I wrestled from afar with my relationship to Boris. Seeing other couples lovey-dovey together made my own blessing feel out of step. To figure out how to relate to this person with whom everyone seemed to expect me to have a family, I wrote letters. Boris occasionally called. The latter required going through the switchboard and then someone paging me to pick up the phone in the dining hall or at the top of the stairs in the sister's dorm.

Our lack of intellectual compatibility was off-putting to me—he read comic books; I was reading Teilhard de Chardin, Bonhoeffer, journals on pastoral counseling and comparative theology. While he knew church protocol and how to behave in group settings, I discovered that he didn't seem aware of or perhaps didn't care about the implications of various theological precepts I relished studying. What concerned me more, he seemed unaware of how to apply the Divine Principle and take responsibility for his own actions. Instead, he followed what his friends, parents, and peers expected of him as a cultural Unificationist. For me, these were shallow waters in which to realize a relationship of sincere emotional depth.

Walking the seminary grounds in all manner of weather, I prayed for many hours over my marriage and my studies. I spoke with God far more than I spoke with Boris. Exchanges with him, on the phone or by letter, felt increasingly as if I were talking with a child. Bound by duty to relate, I felt we lacked a bond of authentic friendship. We didn't even seem to share the same faith. Praying outside one day, I threw the thin wedding band he'd given me into the deep grass. I kept my Unification ring, though; I may not have felt well matched with my partner, but I wanted to work things out with God. The way a nun marries Jesus, I felt married to Father and to God.

I took solace in horseback riding and rode the same feisty barb chestnut mare that one of Father's sons, Heung Jin, often rode. Other times I rode a heavy-footed, draft, bay gelding that was as slow and uninteresting as my matching partner was. After a year and a half of marital limbo, I decided to leave UTS to live near my intended rather than remain and take the last three courses for my Masters in Religious Education. Although I loved my studies—learning about comparative religion and cultures delighted me—I was still in my twenties and didn't want the responsibility of pastoring a center. Despite my travels, answered prayers and spiritual experiences, I felt ill-equipped to counsel people with real problems like divorce, chronically ill children, and poverty.

My CF was David Kim, the president and spiritual leader of UTS. As requested, I'd written a letter explaining why I needed to leave the seminary. When I hand-delivered it to him in his office, he stood up from his desk to greet me with a warm handshake then sat down again to read the letter. I sat across from him as he read. In the letter, I cited my lack of maturity to lead and my desire to sort out my "blessing" as key reasons for wanting to leave the program.

He unfolded the pages with composure and started reading. Then, his eyes winced, his jaw tightened and his shoulders went slack. He drew in a slight breath as if to hold back a sigh. He arose with the straight back of a disciplined soldier. I was braced for him to be angry or to give me the brush off and dismiss me to resume work in the kitchen or perhaps tell me to focus on my studies as my mission and forget about my marriage for the time being. Instead, he granted me permission to leave. His face, usually bold and determined, looked resigned and compassionate. He said, "Okay, go then," as he stood up, shook my hand, then pushed open the office door.

I bowed and exited feeling relieved not to be chastised but also a little daunted by the unknown. A pang of sorrow tugged on my heart for President Kim as I recalled my studies, teachers, friends and walks with God in nature at UTS. I felt he granted my request not due to divine intervention or the reasons in my letter but because, unlike my own father, he respected me as an adult and my choice as a child of God. While I was drawn to world peace, family life was core to the goal of Unificationism. Perhaps, had I been a brother, President Kim might have protested more as a commitment to public life was expected of seminarians, even at the cost of putting one's own family second.

To raise travel money, I took the five dollars I had to my name and went to the Creative Originals warehouse, the seminary's source for fundraising product. When I asked for the cheapest item I could buy wholesale, the brother working there led me to the recesses of the warehouse. We walked past the globes with real butterflies posed on mossy bits of log, past laser foil prints of scenic landscapes and Jesus, past plush terriers that sat up and barked when you clapped, and deep into a back corner. There stood a forlorn collection of artificial sunflowers whose centers contained not black pistils but the faces of Cabbage Patch dolls. They were supremely ugly, but I knew they would be perfect. If God wanted me to leave seminary, I thought, surely selling these would be the miracle that would prove it.

Having no car, I walked into town with my bouquet of a dozen uglies, purchased for fifty cents each. I called them "Happy Flowers," and I proceeded to go shop to shop to fundraise for my ticket to Washington, D.C. to see my ostensible husband. Since I calculated the one-way fare to be thirty-five dollars, I had to make at least three dollars per flower. For the first sale, breaking my resolve, I sold two for five dollars at a gas station. No more compromising, I had to make thirty dollars for the remaining ten. Marching into a dentist's office, I made my pitch—"Happy Flowers for sale!"—and stuck to the price I needed. Miraculously, the dentist bought the remaining ten. Having fulfilled my goal for the train ticket, I walked the several miles back to seminary flush with my cash. With little to pack, I set off the next day.

My train pulled into D.C. and Boris met me at the station. We went back to his flat which he shared with another brother. He and his wife had not yet started family life either. Like us, they were recently matched and blessed in marriage and as yet ineligible to have sex. I stayed with Boris and his roommate for my first couple of weeks in New Carrollton, a suburb of D.C. at the end of the Orange Line. We managed to keep the sleeping situation chaste. Soon, I found work as a hostess at a church-owned Japanese restaurant and could commute by metro. Eventually, a bed freed up with sisters and brothers near Dupont Circle downtown and I moved in there.

Even months later, when Boris and I rented a place of our own, we remained chaste as sister and brother. We shared a cozy, older brick apartment in Hyattsville, Maryland, on a quiet, maple-lined street. I slept in the bedroom on the floor in my sleeping bag, he slept on the couch in the living room. The metro was far away, which made commuting a challenge for me so I found a new job within walking distance—working alongside educated immigrants in a modern building on a bustling roadway. We read documents and reported on their taxonomy for an enormous lawsuit. That job ended when a bomb scare forced us to evacuate to the sidewalks outside and the automated ceiling sprinklers drenched all the documents in response to a fire.

We had little money, despite my work and Boris's long-held job at the *Washington Times*. Luckily, he already owned a vintage VW Bug. The floorboard was so rusted out on the passenger side that I'd watch the asphalt speeding by beneath my feet as he drove. When that car expired, he found a used Fiat (as in "Fix It Again, Tony!") through friends. In it, we traveled on occasion to visit Boris's parents. Meanwhile, my dad's anger since he'd first threatened to disown me seemed to have cooled down and I spoke amicably with my parents by phone.

Sporadically, Boris and I attended the Unification church in downtown D.C. One Sunday morning, the pastor announced an opportunity to visit ministers of different faiths. We could teach them DP with video cassettes. My hand shot up. Boris volunteered too. I assumed we'd go together on this little adventure, but he was sent to Asheville, North Carolina, and I to Columbia, South Carolina, in the thick summer heat. Given the age of the Fiat, we took separate buses to our respective state centers.

Besides the CF, I was the only non-Asian at the Columbia center, which housed a bevy of Japanese and Korean sisters and brothers. For starters, I needed to fundraise to support myself. The center provided me with foil prints to sell for my expenses, but I fundraised on my own. Sometimes, I wore a swimsuit for underwear. That way, when sweat from the muggy heat drenched me, I could strip off my clothes and take a quick dip in the nearest condominium or hotel pool. While being yelled at, or worse, for trespassing was a risk, I felt invincible, as if enacting a movie script of my own life. Once refreshed, I put my clothes back on over the wet swimsuit and resumed fundraising. Before dark, I returned to the center for supper, prayer and a rest, my sleeping bag sardined next to the other sisters on the floor before arising to go out again the next day.

One evening the center hosted a program with Dr. Mose Durst. I was inspired to meet him. A former comparative literature professor, he'd joined the movement and risen through the ranks to serve as president of the Unification Church in the US. He and his Korean wife later founded a school in California. Sensible and kind, Dr. Durst gave me hope that there was a place for intellectuals like me in the movement and that despite the apparent odds, I might work things out with my intended one day. However, I didn't see how Boris and I could untangle the knots in our relationship long distance. Remaining in South Carolina didn't make sense for my marriage, despite the wishes of Boris's CF and assumed spiritual adviser—who insisted we live apart. My Japanese sisters wouldn't dream of questioning decisions leaders made. Stifled, I had to do something.

At the time of Dr. Durst's visit, I confided in an elder Korean sister. She was an itinerant counselor, passing through to offer spiritual support as Tiger Park had done, traveling center to center. Father had nicknamed her General Kim because she was tough. A large woman, with a square-set jaw and piercing eyes, I watched her dance with Dr. Durst after supper as we played music in the living room. She danced slowly, rotating like a sumo wrestler in a dress, except for her hands, which fluttered like butterflies.

The next morning, I found General Kim in a back room off the kitchen surrounded by billowing taffeta she was ironing for another blessing. She was preparing the fabric to sew who knows how many wedding dresses using the same Simplicity pattern that had produced mine and numerous others not long ago. I explained my dilemma, enunciating simple words in English I hoped she could understand. As a rare native English speaker, I naturally picked up Japanese and Korean intonation and inflection by ear the same way I'd learned French like a parrot as a child.

"My bless-ing," I stressed each syllable, "is so di-ffi-cult. We must talk. We must work things out. But my bless-ing part-ner, he is not here. His cen-tral fi-gure says 'NO! He can-not talk to me!' What can I do?"

I caught glimpses of her face and torso above the cloud of taffeta. From beneath the shimmering fabric, her hands reached out and clasped mine. Her keen brown eyes bore into my soul as she said, "Pray and act." She cut right through my insecurity. I'd felt embarrassed to pray because in a global context, my problems seemed far too small to bother the Almighty about. Her words convinced me that God could multitask and handle both macro and micro supplications.

My own mother had never looked at me with such intensity. I felt seen and understood. In her short syllables, I felt the power of General Kim's spirit. Her absolute confidence that God would guide me gave me confidence in myself. She didn't just have faith, she seemed to know God would answer my prayers and guide me the way I needed to go from within my own heart.

I prayed and caught a bus to Asheville the next day. By now it was autumn. Evening fell. The air went from nippy to frigid as I knocked on door after door, shivering as I looked for a place to sleep. At last, an elderly couple opened their door and hearing my plight offered me an unfurnished room. They ran a boarding house. I didn't have any money. They let me to stay for the night provided I paid in full by the end of the week.

Filled with hope now that I was at least in the same town as my spouse, I anticipated talking with him face to face. I walked to a gas station and put coins into a pay phone to call him. (Remember, no cell phones or laptops back then!) On the other end of the line, I heard him confer with his team leader who forbade us to meet. Boris refused to question this decision. I asked to speak directly with his team leader. The CF was adamant; he had his own concerns and mission to fulfill. I had come all this way, with hardly a cent in my pocket, only for this to be my answer?

The time my coins bought on the pay phone ran out. I trudged back up hill and let myself into the house, now dark as everyone else was asleep. After climbing the stairs, I curled up on the floor in a corner of my empty room. Tired, hungry, and cold, I cried softly so as not to disturb anyone. I felt as alone as the day I found myself pregnant in Cap d'Ail. Shivering, I couldn't sleep despite my exhaustion.

As I lay awake in the dark, a sparkling cloud of light appeared and glimmered in mid-air before me. From it emerged two figures, Father and Mother Moon, or True Parents as we called them in the day. They smiled at me and I felt embraced in love, comfort, and warmth. This reassured me that following my choice to pray and act as I had—taking the bus to Asheville despite being assigned to Columbia, despite the rejection of Boris's CF—was the right thing to have done. Praying and acting, as General Kim had advised, I felt I'd followed the spirit of the law, God's calling for me. Boris, afraid to appear blasphemous by countering his CF, seemed to prefer the letter of the law. I was unafraid to follow my intuition and own my actions before God with or without a CF, thanks to General Kim.

The next day I fundraised door-to-door. By going church-to-church, I managed to distribute sets of videos of the Divine Principle to several ministers. Throughout the day, I stopped at public pay phones to call Boris to no avail. After several days of this, his CF, alone, met me in person. When he insisted Boris and I stay apart, I felt angry that Boris refused to talk to me directly and explain his own point of view. I didn't need for my partner to agree with me, only to communicate and take responsibility for his own choices. I wanted to understand what he really thought. Unlike Boris, his CF seemed narrow and fundamentalist. He effectively blocked us from direct communication even though we were a legally married couple. I decided there was no point wasting my time. I wanted to serve God—that didn't seem promising in Asheville. I decided to return to D.C.

Fundraising for bus fare, I moved along the main road. Near Thomas Wolfe's former home, a car slowed to a stop next to me. The driver and only occupant leaned toward me until I could see his face as he lowered the passenger window. It was an old college boyfriend from Chapel Hill. We hadn't spoken in years, long before I joined the movement. Like meeting Emma and Christine in Aix, this seemed like a divine intervention.

While I'd dropped out of school to devote my life to God, he'd completed vet school in Colorado, married a fellow veterinarian, and returned to North Carolina to go into real estate like his mother. Brad and his wife raised llamas. Bending down to talk with him through the open window, I balanced my fundraising product on one hip as I told him briefly about my life. He wished me well and drove on. I wondered why God had sent him my way.

My success could not be measured by worldly things. And yet now, it didn't seem that the otherworldly side was pulling its full weight either. I had no degree from seminary; my marriage did not look promising; I owned next to nothing; and my biological family thought I'd gone nuts. I had given up everything for a vision of a world unseen—for the sake of spirit, not an institution. Yet the vision of True Parents from the night before had met me right where I was—in the midst of my splendid failure. I kept fundraising until I had bus fare.

Once back in D.C., for lodging, friends directed me to a church dormitory and center near Catholic University called Capitol Gardens. The place bustled with sisters and brothers in various missions and life stages. Meals appeared at regular intervals in the public dining room and a kindly cook could find you a little something if you came home late and missed dinner. There were meeting rooms and quiet nooks—the dorm rooms even had real beds. I wasn't sure how my marriage would go but this seemed like a good place to sort things out.

In the US capital city, part of Father's vision was to offer an alternative to what he saw as a mostly left-wing press. In 1982, not long after the *Washington Star* folded, he founded the daily *Washington Times*. In 1985, he founded a weekly magazine, *Insight*, which was to rival *Time* magazine. And with characteristic gumption, the following year he launched a glossy, full-color, four-hundred-page monthly magazine, *The World & I (WAI)*, just as I arrived at Capitol Gardens.

The timing of my return to D.C., as we used to say in the movement, seemed "providential." I was hired to work in editorial production for the monthly tome. It was the combined equivalent of eight specialty magazines: each section had its own style set and font for text and captions as well as a distinctive tone based on subject matter. Two of us proofread and copyedited the entire publication from drafts to galleys the first two months. Within a year, *WAI*'s editorial production expanded to a staff of six, three of whom had PhDs, to do the same job.

I commuted by Metro to Judiciary Square, where the magazine had its first office. At night, I read and wrote. Besides my letters to Boris, I wrote a long, plaintive appeal to Brad, the former boyfriend I'd met in Asheville. I pleaded for him to sign on with the church so my nominal spouse and I could "start family"— in other words, have sex. Nature called and we could not consummate our marriage without our "spiritual children," i.e. people willing to sign on as supportive of the movement. I never heard a word back from him.

All blessing partners needed three spiritual children each to qualify to start family life. A spiritual child was a person that one introduced to Unification teachings and for whom one took responsibility in terms of pastoral care and service. On the one hand, I didn't expect people to accept the church's theology. I figured people had different faith traditions for a vast number of reasons that often had little to do with logic. On the other hand, the Divine Principle made sense within itself, yet increasingly, there were addendums that arose out of what was a more shamanistic church tradition. And I didn't necessarily agree with the more Catholic or hierarchical infrastructure that Boris obeyed with a childlike trust that seemed like passing the buck to me. More of a goat than a sheep, I felt accountable for my decisions when I united with leaders out of my free will. I didn't consider the leaders spiritually responsible for the choices I made. Perhaps my self-sufficient attitude went back to childhood when I saw first-hand that my own parents were not infallible. Conflicted over our different theological views, I still wanted work things out in my marriage.

Church directives must have changed since Boris followed me to D.C. from Asheville several months later. I helped him find work at the *WAI* magazine in reprographics—his previous job at the *Washington Times*. Together at last, we rented a flat in Takoma Park and took the Metro to the *WAI* office. I enjoyed the liveliness of work and the articles I read. They varied from highly academic pieces on philosophy and science to current events, art, and culture. However, I remained restless; my marriage felt unsatisfying and, more importantly, bereft of real love. Our relationship was one of stoic duty with a side order of expedient, if limited, intimacy. My vapid home life felt stifling despite living in the nation's capital and working with bright, intellectually inquisitive people.

I took the GRE and applied to graduate school. When UNC offered me a full scholarship and a position as a teaching assistant, I moved to Chapel Hill. Boris soon joined me and together we rented a duplex in the nearby village of Carrboro. While I studied for my master's degree in French with a Russian minor, he found work in reprographics at the then Chapel Hill newspaper (it would later move to Durham). Even with my T.A. stipend, it was tough to make ends meet. I took extra work, first at the Trail Shop (a hiking outfitter) and then at the Intimate Bookshop, owned by Wallace Kuralt, brother of Charles. There, I eventually became a night manager. Boris took extra work washing dishes at Spanky's Restaurant (a Chapel Hill fixture for forty years, it closed in 2018).

Studying, teaching, and working kept me busy day and night. Boris and I had little to discuss in common. Computer games like Tetris and Pac-Man amused him for hours. I brought home a pair of doves from a pet shop for company. Sinbad was pure white and Lucille was gray and lavender, a classic ringneck like her cousins in the wild. Though they didn't seem to match, their cooing was soothing. I let them fly free in my home office while I prepared for classes and graded papers. Unlike Boris and me, the nesting doves were soon so prolifically amorous that I sold the chicks back to the pet shop on a regular basis.

After Christmas, as winter settled in earnest, I began to receive regular phone calls from my father. He called late at night, sloshed, attempting to resume the old habit of confiding in me rather than my mother about his problems. My grandmother wanted him to come to her deathbed. He refused. He tried drunkenly to justify his position to me, his confidante. I was also receiving calls from his sister and brother-in-law pleading with me to get my father to his mother's bedside. But the man would not be budged. He did, however, attend her funeral, as did I. It was all very proper, with Pachelbel's *Canon in D*, little silver butter knives, and individual salt and pepper shakers in all the right places, just as his mother would have wished.

Despite my personal trials with my blessing partner, my parents' reluctance to accept him as legitimate annoyed me. His good points were that he was a musician and, being tall, he could reach things on high shelves. Besides, he was not an alcoholic. Boris and I planned a trip to Colorado to visit my parents. We hoped that face-to-face conversations would help dispel the wretched PR and downright lies promulgated in the newspapers about Father Moon and people, like us, that they pejoratively labeled "Moonies."

I did not see myself as a follower so much as an activist. As a student, I'd participated in demonstrations and spoken up in conferences before joining the movement. Over the years, I'd debated and examined various interpretations of the Divine Principle with scholars, theologians, heads of state, rogues, ruffians and people far saintlier than me. My seminary studies had enriched what I felt was a reasonably broad religious perspective. I sought to learn from Father's life lessons and the principles he taught, yet I didn't see my life as a direct mirror image of his. Afterall, he'd studied electrical engineering; I pursued literature in graduate school. I was intrigued by philosophy and theology but challenged dogmatic interpretations that appealed to some fundamentalist members. Prioritizing Father the man over his teachings, Boris, raised in the movement, could be doctrinaire when unsure of himself. He felt at odds with what people in the movement often referred to as "the fallen world." In the fallen world, people would lie, steal, and be careless with your heart. Such folk did not understand the value of true love. They also did not treat my partner with kid gloves when he was inept.

When I was between semesters, Boris took off from work so we could make the pilgrimage by car from Chapel Hill to Denver to see my folks. Upon our arrival, Mom put us in a single bedroom. Boris surprised me as he protested this sleeping arrangement. He was so committed to the idea that we remain chaste until we had collected our spiritual children, that he insisted that we had to sleep in separate bedrooms. However much my parents disliked my marriage, it seemed my mother hated breaking with convention even more.

Raised in the South, Mom so rarely raised her voice I couldn't remember ever hearing her speak loud enough to be heard over a lawnmower. But in this instance, Mom's cheeks turned crimson as she scolded with all the bluster that Dixie could muster, "Why, you two are now married! You surely are to share a room! I will not have it otherwise in my house!"

Her furious declaration—spoken loud enough to be heard over several lawnmowers—did not faze Boris. Not terribly wise in the ways of women, he maintained that it was imperative for us to sleep in separate quarters. *I have a mother in major meltdown and he thinks his opinion matters?* I thought. *What is wrong with this man?* I needed to convince him that my mother freaking out was more important than his principles. Besides, couldn't he sleep on the floor while I slept in the single canopy bed of my childhood? I managed to convey my compromise as a holy duty to share the room to better serve my parents. I'm not sure I managed this without rolling my eyes.

In this way we navigated that first night with my parents. It was hard work. I hoped that our effort—taking time off to travel across the country for a couple days of conversation—would prove to Mom and Dad that I loved them and that I was not out of my mind. The next day, Dad invited Boris to go off with him for a while, which I thought was promising. I later came downstairs to the dining room. Sitting at the table was my high school boyfriend—the very one who'd impregnated me then purchased a motorcycle instead of coming to see me in France. Having been out of touch for years, I had no desire to rekindle our former acquaintance.

In the kitchen beside us, Mom bustled, baking something. She was focused and a little flushed in her cheerful, cherry-print apron. Only the occasional ping of the wooden spoon on the metal mixing bowl revealed the full extent of her unadulterated joy. It dawned on me that Dad taking Boris out was a setup to get me alone with the old boyfriend, who served as a pawn for my parents' machinations. My prim mother wanted me to divorce the person I'd just married, or at least have a tryst and be done with my newfound religion.

I hadn't seen the father of my aborted fetus for nearly a decade. It felt longer. I had done, seen, and changed so very much. As soon as he spoke, I felt that he had changed so very little since high school—apart from the apparent prosperity of regular employment. I felt embarrassed that I'd ever been involved with him. And I felt embarrassed that my parents had roped him into their scheme. I drew upon some of the southern upbringing I'd gleaned from Mom. We had coffee and tea seated across from each other at the family table. We made talk so small that to this day I cannot recollect its content.

However, I do recall that before he left, he knew my principles were different than they'd been before I joined the movement. Furthermore, he got a taste of my activist side. My dedication to my marriage, unconventional as it was, remained intact. I tried to buffer my rejection of him by expressing that I could nonetheless, in the agape sense, love him as a child of God and as my brother, but not as a romantic partner. At last, he sensed his visit was a dead end and politely left. The rosy glow left Mother's cheeks as she shoved the steel pan into the oven, scraping it across the oven rack metal on metal. The oven door made a high-pitched whine as it slammed shut.

Mom and I had never shared deep heart-to-heart confidences. Maybe that's why she didn't know how I felt about that old boyfriend. I was surprised that she would a) try a scheme like this and b) think I was so docile that it would work. However, my father's collusion in this trickery galled me to the core. I thought our chummy, though admittedly dysfunctional, rapport was deeper than that, especially given the many, many conversations we'd shared during his late-night, alcohol-infused rants. Though my parents' scheme hurt my feelings, it seemed we had no real relationship left to damage. Their attempted manipulation of me sadly confirmed that they did not relate to me as the adult I was but only as an effigy of the daughter they wanted me to be.

My dad's response made me mad. I'd hoped for his support in attempting something as conventional as marriage even if I'd approached it in an unconventional way. After all, he'd never approved of any of my boyfriends. I figured he'd think it was peachy keen if I was hitched—that it might help keep me out of trouble. When he returned with Boris, I lamented loud enough to be heard over fifty lawnmowers, "Dad, how could you do this? Trying to set me up with an old boyfriend? I'm a married woman for God's sake!"

Perhaps it was the woman part he refused to accept. One of his mantras was, "Parents never forget changing their children's diapers—no matter how old they are." I took this as his way of saying he would never respect me as an adult capable of making my own choices. And yet on this visit with Boris I discovered that, however much he may have disliked my choices, Dad had nevertheless taken a stand on my behalf.

He revealed to me how, not long after the 1982 blessing in Madison Square Garden, my spiritual father Paul had called him and offered to deprogram me. I was unaware of this—though I knew from *People* magazine that Paul had become disenchanted with the movement after his parents had him deprogrammed, a procedure that was denounced by the ACLU at the time.

Deprogramming could include kidnapping and coercion to force a person to abandon their religious beliefs. People who experienced this often became deprogrammers themselves. When Paul called my father, he offered to deprogram me for a fee of fifteen hundred dollars. To his credit, my father had refused. The mere recollection of it made him livid, as Dad explained it to me, "Much as I hated the Moonies, I hated an apostate even more!"

Besides the money—for my father was a frugal man—the real obstacle to deprogramming was that it violated his lawyerly adage: "Your rights end where my nose begins." Dad may not have respected me as an adult capable of making my own decisions with legitimate reasoning, but his rights did not extend to my person or my personal choices as an adult. Perhaps it was the idealist in me that imagined him honoring an ideal of law that privileged sacred reverence for principles. Deprogramming, at its core, violated the concept of free will and respecting the self-evident truth of human rights and individual freedom. Its coercion and presumption of control opposed the basis of democracy itself: that "we the people" are endowed by our Creator with inalienable rights. To me, those rights included religious freedom of choice, the freedom to decide how I wanted to spend my time and with whom I wanted to spend it.

As Boris and I drove back to North Carolina from Colorado, I found irritated comfort in his simplicity. I still felt alone in our marriage. And sexually frustrated. But I sensed the spirit of God in the wider world watching over me. Mid-journey, in Kansas, running low on both money and petrol, we stopped at a gas station amidst endless cornfields.

Between us, Boris and I did not have enough cash to fill the tank. On a whim, we bought a lottery ticket. Such an outrageous purchase had never tempted me in the past for two reasons. First, like my father, I found it ridiculous to subsidize gambling under the pretense of supporting education (the proceeds from the sale of lottery tickets were earmarked to fund public schools). Second, the probability of winning was so remote, burning the cash spent made about as much sense to me. However, when we won just exactly enough money to fill the gas tank, I interpreted the windfall as divine approbation of our visit to my parents. This filled me with hope—not for future gambling ventures, but for God's knowledge of and very real intervention in my life.

— CHAPTER SIX —

CONFESSIONAL

Back in Carrboro, above our little brick duplex, clouds hovered. They cast steel-gray shadows through the living room window. My blessing partner's hulking frame took up most of the kitchen as he stood in front of the open refrigerator looking for something to eat. Small stains sprinkled down the front his shirt—a little trail from his past feedings. The buttons couldn't quite hold the edges together over his beer gut: it puckered open before rippling into loose folds, which he partially tucked into his lint-flecked pants. His leather belt was distressed from use. I wanted to disappear. I wanted him to disappear. I wanted the past six years of my life to disappear.

Even after visiting my parents, later traveling to Florida together, and sharing routines at home, Boris and I still lived on two different planets. Determined to remain optimistic, what seemed to me an unequal yoke must be for a reason, I kept telling myself. What was I meant to learn? My journey with God had asked me to handle this. "I am here," said Isaiah (Isaiah 6:1–8) and Samuel (1 Samuel 3:1–10) to God. How could I do less? I had the blessing of so much more information and help.

I'd experienced the reality of the spirit made flesh in the form of answered prayers, wisdom from total strangers, and healing when all I could feel was pain. I called upon my mind to focus my heart to seek God first, no matter what, to look beyond external circumstances to seek what was at stake on an internal, spiritual level. Now, however, Boris's external repulsiveness registered with a new internal repugnance. "Boris, I found this in the bathroom," I said, my voice flat with disbelief as I confronted reality.

I held out a well-worn pornographic magazine, its corners upturned from repeated use. It far exceeded the pin-up-calendar type of women in bikinis—not that I endorsed that sort of objectification either. It was hard-core porn for serious voyeurs, with a glossy cover photo of group sex, everyone's private parts center-stage.

Still deep in the refrigerator, he looked over the door, "What? Oh," he said, "That."

"Uh, we need to talk about this," I said.

"Oh. Okay," he said, taking a last longing look at the sandwich meat he would have to abandon as he slowly shut the refrigerator door.

Father's commission to me in marriage, I felt, was to strive to love my partner "from God's point of view." That meant first of all to see him as God's son and focus on the potential of his internal character rather than my misgivings about his external form. His habit was to shirk responsibility for his own actions, I thought. Look at the way he used credit cards like limitless pots of gold that never had to be repaid. Perhaps that was ignorance and he just didn't know better. But when his internal character appeared deviant and inconsistent with the very teachings that were supposed to unite us, my noble ideals fizzled. I was left with a pornography consumer. I tossed the rag face down so a cigarette ad showed instead of the obscene photos. Already in teacher mode, I didn't want his attention distracted while we talked. My heart froze in my chest as my logical mind switched into gear.

As Ice Queen, I had no expectations of him. He was a stranger to me. I recalled how he avoided difficult discussions about Father and CARP when we'd been on the fundraising team together. Maybe he didn't even care about DP, a teaching so precious and compelling to me that I'd sacrificed my friends, family and worldly respect to follow it even to the point of marrying him. I'd devoted years of my life working to "transcend" my own point of view since we were matched to love him as a partner, not just "a brother". Relentless in my desire to serve God, I'd taken refuge in spirit to escape him even when we were together. In my mind, I sought to overcome frustration by sinking myself into divine, all-forgiving love, to overlook everything about him that repulsed me. I couldn't do that now. Truth had priority.

Revulsion sat like a toad in the pit of my stomach. My suppressed frustrations with him flooded my emotional circuits. Yet I knew I was confronting a child in a man's body, so I maintained my cool-under-pressure schoolteacher approach with him.

We sat down on the white wicker living room chairs beneath the print of Winslow Homer's *Snap the Whip*. The chairs creaked as the woven rattan adjusted to holding bodies. We rarely used this "formal" living room space. Having returned to UNC, I'd decorated the place in a vintage style redolent of graduate-school hope: hope for a fresh start; hope for something beyond eking by, studying, teaching, and working at Pizza Hut (my job after the bookstore hours weren't enough), while Boris washed dishes at Spanky's, having lost his job at the newspaper.

Boris's face registered uncharacteristic cognizance as his eyes met mine. There was no one else in our two-bedroom flat he could accuse of having purchased the rag. He acknowledged it was his. Putting his elbows on his thighs, he hunched over, his shoulders sagging and said, "There's something I have to tell you."

"What?"

"I've been using that magazine for a while."

"So I gathered."

"But there's more. When my mother was sent out as a missionary, my dad took care of my little brothers and me."

"Right, and your sister."

"Yeah. Well, because my mother was away and I was in college things got out of hand."

"What do you mean?"

"Because my mother was gone and I was helping my dad take care of the kids, things got out of hand."

"What does 'out of hand' mean?" I asked.

"Because my mother was gone, I had to help my dad take care of the kids and I made Rebecca have oral sex with me."

"What?" I pictured his sister, still only thirteen or so, just a kid. "How old was she?"

"Six to eight years old."

"You mean, you don't know? How long did this go on?"

"For years."

"What? Four years?"

"Two years."

He went into detail. Where. When. How. He was this huge guy, eighteen to twenty years old. She was a tiny little girl—even now, I could easily hold her spindly wrist between my thumb and forefinger. He had her come to him as he sat in a chair off the kitchen, his pants unzipped. That's where her bedroom was . . . I'd stayed in it. The toad in my stomach went bilious; I felt nauseated.

Not only was she a little girl, she'd been entrusted to his family's care. I was there when Boris's mother had legally adopted her in the backwoods of the rural south. The girl's mother had joined the church pregnant. When called to sing in a choir traveling around the world, Maud, Boris's mom, had taken Rebecca as a baby. She grew up with Boris's family of three big brothers at home, of whom Boris was the eldest—the two eldest half-brothers were usually away.

I thought of the Divine Principle, of true love, peace, goodness, everything I lived for, everything Father had taught us about the value of maintaining purity, the beautiful innocence of childhood. My emotional circuits were blown. This was the exact opposite of what Father taught us—indeed, it embodied the very things he decried about society:

> What about the glut of pornography littering your society? Some twenty-five thousand children disappear or are abandoned every year in America. Many come to brutal ends to satisfy the appetites of child pornographers, for the sake of lust and money. The tone of your national entertainment media reflects this rapid disappearance of moral sense from America. American society has degenerated to such an extent that it is making Sodom and Gomorrah look trivial.[5]

"Did she get help?" I asked.

"Nobody knows."

"What?"

"Nobody knows it happened. I threatened her so she wouldn't tell."

"How could you?"

"It was because my mom went away. It was because she was gone."

"Why didn't you ever tell me this before?"

"It was in the past. But now we've started family."

He was referring to the fact that we'd finally consummated our marriage after six years of living platonically—well, more or less. In the last year, heavy petting, short of intercourse, allowed us to while away some time without having to talk too much and be reminded of how little we had in common. Furthermore, when we did first have sex or "started family," I'd used birth control. The last thing I had wanted to do was procreate.

I was trying to live what Father had taught us by "uniting" with my matching partner. We shared little common ground, save for connecting sexually. But I felt like a prostitute. The physical parts fit—just not the mind and spirit. Before learning of his sexual predation of his little sister, I considered my physical relationship with Boris—my marriage—to be a sort of penance or "indemnity" I would pay to "restore" something for history.

Yet I had also thought that this person with whom I was bound shared with me—at the very least—a common theology and interpretation of the Divine Principle. As individuals, we each had a personal responsibility to establish our own mind-body unity centered on God prior to marriage. That was the teaching of the Divine Principle. That was why so many people spent years in the

---

[5] From "God's Warning to the World: Reverend Moon's Message from Prison," available at https://www.unification.net/gwarn1/gwar1-4.htm

movement celibate before being matched. How could he possibly have thought child molestation fit that paradigm? Thoughts fired through my mind in every direction as I tried to make sense of this, of my life, of what had happened to Rebecca. I felt cold and removed with sickening abhorrence as the truth of what he said took hold.

It did not occur to me to call the police and report him. It did not even occur to me that this was a criminal act. It was a family tragedy and I was drowning; I didn't know what to do. I decided to call his mother for help. I couldn't turn to other people in the church because Boris's family, as founding members, held a position far above me in Confucian terms. Comparatively, I was a nobody. I couldn't turn to my own parents because they hated Father and the church. I hoped Maud, Boris's mother, would be an ally to help the little girl.

Boris's family lived like a lot of poor white folk in the rural countryside south of the Mason-Dixon line. There was chicken shit on the front porch, empty beer cans and trash covering the kitchen counters, the TV was always on running soap operas or football. Conversation was confined to Kmart sales prices, who was having a baby, fixing cars, and a mention or two of God on Sundays. I said Pledge[6] with them one time in the living room with the TV on mute, but I thought they may have done so because I was there.

George, Boris's dad, worked long hours in the freezer of a church fishing business. This was a tough job. I was used to living a public life in the CARP center where we constantly did outreach. Boris's family focused on survival rather than evangelism—how could they live otherwise? I failed to see how they were devoted to saving the world. I didn't see how they could save themselves. They were not overt racial bigots, but they reflected their non-cosmopolitan surroundings in other ways.

The children went to poor schools yet aspired to find good jobs when they finished. Maud and George could hardly make ends meet on low church wages. George had shellacked a cow pie and hung it on the wall for art. It was a humorous statement intended to defy all the snooty, educated rich people that seemed in charge of the world. They marshaled their energy to get up in the morning— George to work, the kids to school—and to put food on the table, gas in the car, and keep the kids in clothes and shoes. There was no time to get rid of the chicken shit on the porch. Besides, who cared?

---

[6] Pledge, like the Apostle's Creed, was a promise we made before God to uphold our ideas on the individual, family, national, and world level. Rev. Moon changed it over time when he declared the Providence itself had progressed. The one we recited from 1968 to 1994 is available at http://www.unification.net/misc/oldpledge.html.

When I called Maud and told her what happened, she didn't seem surprised, but instead retreated into a readymade speech that sounded born-again and Southern Baptist to my ear: "It was spiritual, not my boy's doing. God will take care of it."

The absurdity of this reminded me of comedian Flip Wilson's iconic phrase, "The devil made me do it." Where was a mother's heart for her daughter in this? And then I remembered: the daughter was adopted. Boris was Maud's biological son and the first of her brood to be blessed. He was the love child from when she and George first ran off together. I don't know if she was in shock or denial, but she didn't believe that her son could do wrong.

"But Maud," I said, "you need to talk to Rebecca and make sure she's okay. Maybe get her some counseling. This is so wrong!"

"Don't worry. It's no problem. It's all in God's hands," she said before hanging up.

I slowly put the phone back in its cradle on the kitchen wall. "What did she say?" Boris asked.

"It's all in God's hands," I replied.

"I told you. It happened because she left home to go be a missionary," he said confidently.

I was still shocked by the revelation, and aghast at Boris's lack of contrition and stunned by his mother's reaction.

"You can't blame this on your mother! This is something *you* did, not her!" I said vehemently. I couldn't believe I was standing up for his ignorant mother. Yet this was not about me or what I felt about his family. It was something so much bigger. He'd stolen the sexual innocence of a child. It was rape. I could not fathom that he'd actually done this.

He repeated, "It was spiritual."

"It was also physical," I replied, not believing I had to say this. Boris and Maud's logic registered with me like something from a science fiction universe without the Principle, without consequences, without reason, law, or love. I could not believe that neither Boris nor his mother found these years of sexual abuse serious.

"Did you confess this before the matching?" I asked. We were supposed to have cleared any sexual impurities like past relationships before being matched.

"No."

"So, nobody knew about this."

"Nope." He had been eager to go to the blessing and, given his family's position, perhaps he was not vetted as much as others were.

Numb, but having work to do, I retreated to my office to grade papers and put my books in order for the next day. That night, I slept in a sleeping bag on my office floor. The pair of doves, Sinbad and Lucille, remained quiet in their cage through the night.

The following morning, I rode my bicycle to school and taught. Riding helped me sort things out. I had to do something. This situation was unacceptable. I called the president of the church in Washington, Doris Orme. She had joined with Maud back in the early days. Doris was English, no-nonsense and to the point. More importantly, she was of Maud's generation. We'd met once when the Ormes used to live near Maud and George.

By some miracle, the church switchboard clicked me directly to Doris, who answered the phone. I told her what happened and made my case that the little girl needed support, love, and help. Still feeling like I was dealing with aliens, I emphasized that what had happened should not be passed over as a mere "spiritual" aberration—that it was a real psychological trauma and physical violation that had to be addressed. Doris seemed to understand and assured me that she would visit Maud personally to make headway with her.

But another aspect of the issue remained unresolved. Even if the girl got help, what was I to do with the marital commitment I'd made? I never wanted to marry and have children; I went through the blessing to forward my own spiritual course by uniting with a partner of similar dedication. This abhorrent deviation contradicted my basis for both spiritual marriage and physical consummation. The person I married was not merely immature, but a sexual predator. I told God that this was far more than I could handle in the way of restoration. I'd prepared to accept someone with flaws, maybe habits I didn't care for, like picking his teeth clean with a knife at the table—nothing of this magnitude.

I'd tried to embrace Boris's family as simple folks, perhaps rustic. I didn't want to be an elitist snob. They just hadn't had the same opportunities or inclinations as me, I used to say to myself. They hadn't lived abroad and experienced the wider world. They didn't understand the Principle the way I did. In their favor, they too liked Tiger Park—the CARP pastor dear to me whom I thought most closely resembled Father in spirit and truth. But George and Maud didn't connect the Principle with actual praxis the way Tiger Park did. They didn't see taking initiative as a self-directed mission, centered on the Principle, the way I did in CARP. They didn't even connect CARP—by definition a college student organization—with actually attending college or see value in education more broadly. Or maybe just not for women, who were supposed to make babies and follow a husband.

I struggled to understand my in-laws. How could Maud define child molestation as a "spiritual" event? This absolutely violated the Principle that had "revirginized" me—eliciting a life of celibacy and a concept of the sacred with regards to sex. How could any thinking person claim a relationship with God and ignore that Boris had molested a child? Perhaps they were used to being given a pass on meeting the standards expected of others. Maud and George were founding members of the movement in America, one of the original three founding members. Dr. Young Oon Kim, one of my professors of theology at UTS and one of the first missionaries to America, had brought Boris's mother to the church. Maud had always said she was led by the "spirit" to join rather than drawn by the Principle. Maybe she didn't even know the Principle. Yet even the rule of law, the logic of man, prohibits molesting children. Why didn't her maternal instinct revolt against this?

My spiritual world was caving in around me. Still, I continued teaching, studying, working at Pizza Hut, and sleeping in my office the rest of the week. And I prayed. To dissolve the marriage was to dissolve my relationship with the church. In the eyes of the movement, there was no such thing as divorce at the time. I couldn't sleep with Boris. I never had been able to share much intellectually with him. What was the point? What did God want of me?

The weekend arrived. Boris and I went for a walk arriving at the base of a hill with a shale pathway. I told him, "Please wait here."

"Why?"

"I have to talk to God. Alone."

I walked up the hill praying about this situation. The blue Carolina sky offered no miraculous answers or visions. It seemed like God himself was holding his breath, waiting to see what I would do. I'd spent half a dozen years celibate during my roaring, hormonal twenties devoted to the idea that a true love relationship had to be built on far more than sex. According to the Principle, pure devotion to God preceded fidelity and trust within marriage. All three elements were supposed to be the foundation to share the marital bed. I remembered the advice General Kim had given me years ago in Columbia, "Pray, then act."

I didn't want to let God down. What if God had chosen me to help Boris correct his behavior? If I took a pass, who would challenge him? After I returned down the hill, we rode home in silence. Later that evening I asked him, "So do you think you would ever do this again?"

"What do you mean?"

"What if we had a little girl some day? Would you molest her?"

"I can't promise I wouldn't."

"Would you be willing to get counseling for this?"

"No. It's spiritual."

"It may or may not have a spiritual cause. But this action of yours is a behavior. You must take responsibility for your actions."

"I told you it happened because my mother was gone."

"Then we must separate. I cannot remain married to you under these conditions."

I'd entered a zone of cool logic, pure and simple. I had to cut off from him. Now. He had confirmed that he was unwilling to recognize this event as something he had caused. I found a lawyer to see how to go about separation and divorce—an act then considered blasphemous and meriting excommunication. Divorce did not officially exist in the Unification movement, only "restoration." Our blessing promise was to reverse historic evil to restore the Kingdom of Heaven. To divorce was tantamount to leaving the movement and, for Unificationists at the time, betraying God.

As we prepared to part ways, I gave Boris nearly everything. I wanted nothing from this marriage but my books, my files, and my papers. And the Winslow Homer. One cloudy morning, I took my pair of doves to the park and let them go free. Lucille flew to a nearby branch. Sinbad plopped onto the ground with a sickening thump. I waited until he, too, flew up to a branch. It was warm and there was plenty of food around. As I walked away, I saw them fly off in different directions.

Boris took the little red Toyota pick-up truck loaded to the gills—including the now empty dove cage. From the doorway, I watched him drive off. Assured he was really gone, I turned to write a letter in the house now emptied of Boris. Finding a blue ballpoint pen, I wrote in deliberate loops and swirls using my best schoolgirl script on perforated college-ruled notebook paper. Remembering how President Kim wanted something in writing when I left seminary, I felt my relationship with Father merited at least as much.

"Dear Mother and Father," I wrote, eschewing the titles True Father and True Mother. I felt both a deeper sense of intimacy than these titles accorded and an urgency to go beyond formalities, given the very personal nature of what I was about to share. "Though I will always love you and the Principle, I cannot go on with my blessing . . ." I don't recall the full wording. I told them the truth about the child molestation and how it was more than I could handle. What I didn't say was that I didn't want to remain a nun forever. I knew that anything less would not be tolerated in the church.

Placing the letter into a small envelope, I addressed it in the same blue ink to Rev. Moon at 4 West 43rd St., New York, NY, the church's headquarters in Manhattan at the time. Papers awaited grading on my desk as night closed in with reassuring darkness. I affixed a stamp and put the letter on the windowsill by the door to post it the next day.

— CHAPTER SEVEN —

PERESTROIKA

Russia had first brought me to Chapel Hill, before I met the Unification movement. After my second year of college in Boulder, my aunt and uncle invited me to join them in Moscow as a nanny for their toddler, my little cousin. To prepare for my gap year of employment abroad, I needed to learn Russian. The University of North Carolina offered an intensive summer program. I immersed myself in the language and culture—one I had last encountered teaching Russian immigrants English in Colorado. Their boisterous camaraderie and colossal pathos fascinated me.

"At shopping, with cart," one of my students lamented, "no one in line talks! They are, how you say? Automatons! Why no talk?"

I still shared my student's sense of alienation in America's serene capitalism, where public restrooms had ample toilet paper and department store shelves held a dizzying array of consumer products, but where a person could die at home alone and not be noticed for days. I wanted to bundle myself up in the Russian language—its tactile grammar embraced me and the passion of its literature fed my soul. Though my original reason to study Russian had evaporated when my aunt and uncle cancelled their, and hence my trip, I clung to Chapel Hill like a Russian peasant to the land. Something in Chapel Hill's clay dirt drew me to stay the way the earth's core attracts a seedling's roots to nourishment. The creative community there both nurtured and inspired me. For money, I held various odd jobs, waiting tables, working retail, and later as a secretary for a real estate agent. For my soul, I attended workshops on theater, listened to live music, read poetry at open mics, and performed in an avant-garde play in French.

The playwright was a visiting scholar at UNC at the time. The plot deconstructed love to shatter assumptions. In a series of scenes, men visited a brothel to have their fantasies recounted to them. At the conclusion, a couple artfully made love behind a screen wearing body suits to appear nude. I alone was cast as someone out of the seventeenth century and wore an ankle-length dress with ample petticoats. My scant lines reflected the pastoral innocence of a Fragonard painting. "Bonjour, Jean des près," I said, greeting my would-be client as though he were an innocent shepherd and I a shepherdess. Prim decorum was absent in the rest of the play, where actors dressed, spoke, and touched one another in a gritty, sensual, contemporary fashion.

My character was in the play but not "of it," similar to how I had inhabited my contemporary world. Imagining an eighteenth-century French salon, I invited fellow cast members and friends for a party at my shared cinder-block house to share music, poetry, and revelry. To my astonishment, more and more people arrived, including the Russian poet Andrei Voznesensky, who happened to be visiting our little corner of the world.

My own inadequacy overwhelmed me. Not knowing how to host the party, beyond embarrassed for my lack of talent in such company, I hid in my bedroom. It was furnished with a cast-off desk from Goodwill and a twenty-five-dollar set of boards bolted together that contained a waterbed mattress upon which I took a nap to escape it all. My guests carried on just fine without me. At last, I heard moments of silence lengthening between bursts of conversation as people, to my relief, departed.

Then, there was a knock at my bedroom door. Thinking it to be one of my friends, I called out, "Come on in!" without rising. In walked Voznesensky. The waterbed sloshed as I stood up next to his towering frame. He thanked me for a lovely evening as though I'd attended to his every whim. Everyone else had gone. He alone had stopped by to bid me farewell.

In Russian, I blurted out a phrase from one of his poems, "Вы настоящий человек" (*You are a real man*). He gave me a great bear hug and left with a wink at the door. "Thank you, again," he said, before pulling my bedroom door shut behind him.

This internationally renowned poet who had spoken before stadiums of people was such a gentleman, he made me feel as though I'd not behaved like a frightened imbecile. He treated me like royalty—better yet, like family.

The party taught me that I was ill-equipped to be a torchbearer of the intelligentsia—never mind the hip art scene. I felt much safer as a mousey academic, dressing rudimentary French grammar in literature to entice students more interested in each other than verb conjugations.

These memories made Chapel Hill a comfortable nest in which to remain to finish my MA and work after Boris's departure.

In some ways, I felt that my world-changing days were over. Though I'd left the movement, I hadn't abandoned the ideology. Intellectually and emotionally, the existence of the divine remained real and important to me. I wanted to legitimize theistic space as a perspective whence to interpret literature. I didn't care about church politics or seek retribution for the decay of my marriage. Yet I still wanted to serve God and follow the Principle according to my own intuitive path.

When I first had heard the Divine Principle, I chafed if ignorant critiques of communism swiped at the culture of Pushkin, Lermontov, and Tolstoy. I loved the passion and precision of these authors—the verve of the language in which they wrote, whose grammatical structure held a sensual physicality that rubbed words and meanings against one another. While I was already adept in French, Russian fascinated me. I felt myself living the literature I studied. In moments of self-scoffing, I saw myself as Flaubert's Emma Bovary, married to the lumpen Charles, and wondered if, like her, I'd been corrupted by literature except for the heinous reality of my ex-spouse's crime.

Reading *Anna Karenina* in Russian, I could not help comparing her to Emma Bovary—and just as I loved Tolstoy's prose over that of Flaubert's, so, too, did I come to love Anna more than her French counterpart. However unfair it may have been to compare the two, I did. And I felt myself vulnerable to the unruly passion of Anna (though preferring to avoid her tragic end) while I vehemently rejected the pedestrian silliness of Emma. And as if bringing literature to life, a Russian lover found me. His family had fled Saint Petersburg before the Russian revolution. Vincent was everything my "Charles" was not—refined, soft-spoken, and intellectual. He kept *Popular Mechanics* beneath his couch rather than *Hustler*. He'd been Boris's boss. While married, I was devoutly faithful—once legally separated, I no longer felt bound. Vincent seemed to read my heart and appreciate my mind not just my body. With him, conversation felt easy and endlessly interesting as he engaged in the wider world.

I was restructuring my life outside the Unification movement. My own reconfiguration seemed akin to what was happening in the Soviet Union under Gorbachev. The USSR's internal reformation involved a move toward greater transparency—or what was referred to as *glasnost*—and a reconfiguration of the political and economic models—known as *perestroika*. I had tried to encourage some *glasnost* within the Unification movement and had met with resistance. Not only did the parents of the girl violated choose to remain silent, but it seemed the leadership did too. As the whistle-blower and person leaving my marriage, I became an instant pariah while Boris was soon "rematched."

I'd participated in the movement for the better part of a decade—nearly a third of my life. I still had a personal and ongoing spiritual conviction that Father and CARP had kindled—not controlled. I valued the practice and wisdom of unselfish love in service to family, community, the world, and God. I felt it a force of good that could change history. Out of my own conviction to submit myself to God, I'd allowed myself to submit to a leader's decisions. Yet if a leader were to make an unethical or amoral choice, I had no problem protesting vocally or with my actions. God remained a spiritual force, uncontained by any institution or hierarchy.

For me, being in relationship with God meant I owned my thoughts and my actions. I couldn't control the world around me, only myself. My portion of responsibility before heaven and earth resided in how I directed my free will in response to outside events and circumstances. While some who were deprogrammed blamed the movement for their experiences, I refused to see myself as a victim.

Boris's behavior was an anomaly, not the fruit of Unificationist theology. His misjudgments were of his own making. Taking responsibility in my own marriage, I did not expect the movement to supply my happiness. Nor did I feel that it was Father's fault that Boris was a sexual predator.

Before Boris left, as we were separating, a Japanese sister had called and said, "You must come to Washington, D.C. for forgiveness [*sic*] ceremony."

In this era before email, a church phone chain often notified us of upcoming events. And yet, this particular request was unfamiliar: it seemed odd to me that people were supposed to confess their sins in public. I asked the sister, "Why?"

She provided a classic Japanese response: "Father say."

Given my own relationship with God, the Principle, Father, and trusted pastors in the movement, I wondered, "Why would I want someone I didn't even know to forgive me?"

The person purported to bequeath forgiveness was an African brother nicknamed "Black Heung Jin Nim" because he claimed to channel the spirit of Father Moon's deceased son, Heung Jin Nim. Out of blind faith, many complied with this request, including Boris. He caught a bus to D.C. to follow the church directive. I chose not to participate. I didn't see this event as coming from Father directly. It seemed odd to me.

"Black Heung Jin Nim" was from Zimbabwe and his actual name was Cleophas Kundioni. Photos from the time show him as clean-shaven, wearing a Western-style suit, short hair, and the type of aviator glasses so popular in the 1980s. He spoke in English strongly inflected with a cadence from his native land. Claiming the dead son of Father Moon spoke through him, he gave sermons and assigned penance with equal enthusiasm.

With a full teaching schedule, working extra hours at Pizza Hut, and my own studies, on top of dealing with my pending separation from Boris, I had no desire to waste my time with a charlatan. Reincarnation was not part of the Divine Principle. I relied upon my personal, intuitive sense of Father's guidance from my own prayers. Furthermore, I had seen the original Heung Jin Nim regularly when I attended seminary—I used to ride the same horse he rode.[7]

Despite church leaders' directives to attend this ceremony, I chose not to go. I was confident because the Divine Principle had taught me that each one of us could access the divine through our own prayer. Yet I had received no revelation that Mr. Kundioni, not knowing me from Eve, was meant to be my father confessor. It seemed to me the movement was changing from one that responded to the intimate heart of God to being a massive organization with impersonal protocols.

I thought grimly how important the practice of mind-body unity was. In Unification teachings, mind-body unity did not include institutionalized superstitious behavior. Right action carried the blessing of vitality, good will, and enhanced compassion with practical beneficial outcomes. I strove to fulfill my responsibilities in this world rather than worrying over possible punishments in the afterlife. In fact, fearmongering about eternity was contrary to what I understood Father Moon, as a reformer of traditional Christianity, taught.

Members with a hierarchical or absolutist view trusted Mr. Kundioni as if he were a spokesperson for Father. I did not. Father taught principles that clicked for me with mathematical logic, yet he fleshed them out with parables that demonstrated finesse and allowed for fluid applications that could adapt to specific circumstances. The essence of the Divine Principle for me was True Love and the reality of God as a being of love. From what I gathered, Mr. Kundioni was not in a position to pass along that love to me.

Boris returned from the ceremony happy to report that he was in the good graces of the church leadership. He had presumably confessed his sexual predation and agreed to do a seven-day fast as a form of penance. But despite his fast and public repentance to the church hierarchy, he refused counseling. I was not convinced he would treat a daughter—or any girl for that matter— appropriately. A public display of ritual without a private change of behavior was meaningless.

Therefore, at the end of my marriage with Boris, I found myself in an awkward position of embracing the theology of the church, yet disagreeing with the church organization's interpretation of its own theology. I still cherished aspects of Unification ideology like building community based on agape love, but

---

[7] I had my own experience with Heung Jin before his fateful drive, as told in Chapter 32: Normal Is Just a Setting on the Washing Machine.

I rejected misinterpretations based on blind faith. I did not feel bound by monastic vows of poverty, chastity, and blind obedience.

This is not to say that I became an eager entrepreneur determined to become rich, or a sexual swinger seeking casual hookups, or an anarchist bent on destabilizing convention with violence. For the most part, my life was over-determined. I had my graduate work, a thesis to write, classes to teach and an outside job—in short, plenty to keep me busy. My own restructuring involved accountability to myself in direct relationship to God. In the movement, I had been in constant negotiation with a manmade organization. My goal remained, however, to fulfill what I felt to be my spiritual calling, to remain responsive to God's voice in my life.

As I left my marriage, others had diverse interpretations of my actions. My parents thought I was exiting a reprehensible organization. Church members, not knowing my story, thought I was being an unfaithful wife. To leave my marriage was tantamount to leaving the movement. There was no such thing as divorce in the church at that time. Thus, Boris was "good" because he obeyed orders to perform a forgiveness penance whether or not he changed his behavior. I was "evil" for I looked beyond the church for solutions to real problems.

I still sought a relationship with God and felt this divine presence to be essential in my life. I felt Father Moon regularly consulted God too. But I had eliminated a large quantity of noisy middlepersons standing between God and me—namely my ex–matching partner and the church leadership. I had to find new networks to explore my devotional sensibilities.

Breaking with church tradition through divorce, I lost an extensive social network of friends in the movement who rejected my choice as an unfaithful act. Divorce broke with the institutionalized ideal of eternal marriage. My letter of resignation from the movement confirmed me as an unfaithful unbeliever. This cast my ex-spouse as the wounded, faithful husband who had atoned for his sins. If someone's spouse left the church, the remaining faithful spouse could be rematched and given a clean slate—like a Catholic marriage annulment. Boris quickly availed himself of this option. Soon after we divorced, he was rematched and remarried. Even had this been an option for me, I had no desire to be rematched.

After nearly a decade of celibacy and marital commitment, I felt estranged from others my age involved in secular relationships. Few people besides monks and nuns fully give themselves over in chaste service to God to live in spiritual community. However, I did not fit in with monks and nuns either since they do not marry in the flesh. Furthermore, I was at odds with those who left the movement through deprogramming. They believed they had been brainwashed, while I refused to abdicate my portion of responsibility for my own actions.

Within the movement, I had experienced more than the mess of being blessed. I enjoyed traveling, meeting new people, and having the freedom to develop my own relationship with God. I knew that human relationships were, by definition, challenging. In retrospect, my experiences in CARP were not as onerous as those of friends in more strictly evangelical or shamanistic branches of the movement. Overall, there was a dearth of leaders. Young, over-zealous or rigid team captains, carried away with their own dedication, could impose standards of sacrifice upon others that lacked compassion as well as reason.

The membership of the Unification movement was socially and culturally diverse, but communication among this international group was filtered through a Confucian-inflected hierarchy. This organizational style placed veneration of the elder, or a person's position, over their behavior. Loyalty was so extreme and the desire to please Father so great that leaders would not reveal the problems they were having.[8] Striving to meet nearly impossible goals, they would misrepresent facts in order to please Father. I believe that many who did these things genuinely felt they were making an honorable choice, not a politically expedient one. However, the net result was that Father was often the last to know of problems.

My *perestroika* after the divorce had to do with reclaiming my voice—both as an individual engaged with the world and trying to master practical skills, yet also as a daughter of God with intrinsic value apart from my ex-partner. To this end, I invested in my studies and explored the relationship between Unification Thought and the wars of religion during the Renaissance. Like many of the humanists of that era, I could not reconcile how people could murder one another in the name of Jesus.

For my master's thesis, I studied the work of the Huguenot poet Agrippa d'Aubigné. I examined a satirical chapter, "Princes," from his larger work *Les Tragiques,* which addressed the abuses of political power and the religious wars. Nonetheless, I had not lost my love for Russian from years prior as an undergraduate. So I kept it as my minor while doing graduate work.

---

[8] This was true in the case of Mr. Kundioni's treatment of members, for example. Other examples existed in the area of business, where church leaders misused money without telling Father. Spearheading new projects, Father focused on the future and restoring the past. Leaders had their own free-will portion of responsibility to fulfill. In the bigger scheme of things, Father was not always in a position to micromanage the choices that leaders made, even when such choices were made out of greed, fear, or excessive zeal.

Once legally separated and well on my way to divorce, I visited Vincent's shop one evening to fetch a printer cartridge. We ended up chatting. Thereafter, when in the neighborhood, I would stop by and we would talk as he repaired computers. I learned that he was a descendant of Russian Trotskyites. Pale from working indoors, he was wiry, strong, tall, and thin, with a trim moustache. His hair curled about his head in loose waves that contrasted the tension he carried in his body. He never seemed at ease unless intent upon a project.

Vincent had the self-possession of a Russian aristocrat without speaking Russian. He ordered his shirts custom-made in New York's Chinatown and had them monogrammed with his initials. Their cuffs had little holes that required real cufflinks. The ones he wore were old fashioned, of polished gold, handed down from his father. Vincent had a European sense of family—they were his world, even though they lived across the US in Oregon.

Despite his fussiness about clothes, he wasn't prissy. During our chats, which often migrated to the parking lot, I watched him work bare handed on cars in cold, rainy weather. He did not hesitate to plunge into greasy machinery as the situation required. He owned the computer store, or rather, the store owned him. He worked all hours to assure that his clients' machines would hum along and behave as intended. Customers would call Vincent on the telephone ignoring store hours. Holding the receiver to their computer at home, they would say, "Listen, Vincent! What's wrong with it?"

They expected him to telepathically diagnose and resolve their computer crises over the phone. Sometimes, he could. Often, he would end up making a house call. Gathering his toolbox, he would travel to see his electronic patient like an old-fashioned doctor. And we would part ways in the parking lot.

Vincent and I fell into a routine of dining together after working late. One evening walking down a quiet lane toward his flat, we saw shooting stars above the trees in the night sky. He put his arm around me and said, "I've always wanted to see one of them fall." Then he kissed me. In the moment, I couldn't help but take in the scene, and his words, as though I'd been swept into a Russian novel. Over the ensuing weeks, our intimacy evolved accordingly. A month before my thesis defense, my rent went up. Boris had been gone about a year. Vincent invited me to move in with him.

Keeping my desk, clothes, books, and the Winslow Homer, I sold what remained of my belongings at a garage sale that was surprisingly brisk. People began ringing my doorbell at six in the morning. When I opened the door for the official start at nine, they dashed inside and pulled pots, pans, plates, and cutlery from cupboards and drawers. Strangers helped themselves to pictures right off the wall. They asked, "How much for this?" for things I had not originally intended to sell.

Putting my nose to the spiritual winds, I decided it was time to let go of the past, to start fresh. It seemed Providence was pushing me to make a clean break. I joined Vincent at his one-bedroom condominium, studied, taught, and finished my thesis. I added working for Vincent at Dataway to my schedule, answering the phone instead of taking orders at Pizza Hut.

My life was being restructured in ways I'd not anticipated. Vincent and I both kept long hours at work. Late into the night, he hovered over broken computers, correcting software and refurbishing hardware. As he worked, I wrote my thesis on a computer that served as a display model during the day. I thrived around Vincent's intense stoicism. It felt as if his focus added acuity to my own.

Like me, he did not count the hours spent on a project but instead tracked whether or not the problem was solved. I admired his intuitive sense with computers and that he seemed to live for the sake of others. He pushed himself constantly, hardly ate during the day, and spoke in a fine, low baritone voice that was reassuring and patient as customers—many of them academics—would come into the shop with the latest computer disaster that was ruining their lives. In the way he lived and in his opposition to communism—though not a Unificationist—I felt he was "walking the talk" of the Divine Principle far more than my ex-husband.

My master's degree was hard won as I fought for theistic space in literary analysis. Few professors in a secular institution were willing to work with me on such a project. Luckily, I'd found Professor George B. Daniel, a kindred spirit with an irrepressible sense of humor and an open mind regarding a variety of literary approaches. He was my lone champion as I swam in what felt like a sea of solitude.

In academia, naive theistic approaches—based more on faith and convenient, literal interpretations than research—could be ridiculed as ignorant or religiously partisan. My approach, enhanced by Unificationism, attempted to provide a neutral language for theistic interpretation. Meanwhile, I no longer claimed to be a Unificationist. I felt isolated for having divorced Boris even though by any rational measure it was logical. Vincent's bright mind, friendship and passion offered me solace in my solitude. The only other person that made me feel human was Dr. Daniel. His encouragement of my academic work meant the world to me.

A year into the program, I discovered that a different professor had lobbied to keep me out because of my former religious affiliation. She told me so to my face. Rather than challenge her over religious bigotry, I worked twice as hard in her classes and visited her during office hours to understand what she wanted me to learn.

With coursework completed, I had exams and a thesis defense to pass. When I drew this seemly antagonistic professor as an examiner by lottery, I had some trepidation. Her understated evaluation, "Clear and well-considered responses," made my heart swell. My other examiners also approved of my essays, so I continued to the oral defense of my thesis, hopeful but tense before my committee. When they signed their approval of my research and interpretation, I was thrilled. Passion for my studies and faith despite divorce had carried me through years of work and professional training. Following my thesis defense, I was eager to continue my studies in real life.

Unsure whether I would pass or not, I had pre-arranged a trip to the Soviet Union for a summer language program. Having read Lermontov, Pushkin, and Tolstoy in Russian, I owed these authors a visit in their land, the one that begat their mother tongue. My connection with French had taught me that. Poets, dreamers, artists, and schemers called forth to life the mysterious concoction of language and culture from the very soil. To speak another language without visiting the place that gave it birth seemed like reading musical notes on paper without playing the song on an actual instrument. And so, the day after defending my master's thesis, I boarded a plane for New York; from there I would travel to Geneva and then on to Moscow. (Russian planes were forbidden to fly directly to or from the US.)

Though elated to go on an adventure, relieved to have passed both my exams and defense, I hated to leave Vincent. His support of my academic career objectives and of my upcoming trip made even one summer apart bittersweet. Yet beyond my passion to understand Russian culture and language, I also needed an emotional sorbet. The trip would cleanse my palate after years of intense academic work. Thus refreshed, I planned to tuck into the next round of employment and studies.

It was 1989. Even in the US there was no internet superhighway. People used landline telephones, read printed newspapers, and got their news from the radio or television. I had never lived in a world without a Cold War. The Iron Curtain cloaked Russia and the Eastern Bloc nations from easy access to the outside world. Traveling to the Soviet Union felt exotic and daring enough to keep me alert.

At JFK airport in New York, I met fellow students of Russian to fly to Switzerland. In Geneva, we boarded an Aeroflot propeller plane. The Russian passengers ignored conventions like wearing seat belts or remaining seated during takeoff. They bustled in the aisles and chatted with Slavic gusto. We Americans obediently followed the "Fasten Seat Belt" signs. Once airborne, we puttered higher and higher above the Swiss Alps. Suddenly, one of the propellers stopped working. The plane began to descend. Even the Russians fastened their seat belts and grew quiet. I wondered where we could make an emergency landing given the mountain peaks below us. Just as suddenly as it had stopped, the propeller sputtered back into rotation.

I thought we would head back to Geneva for another plane, but onward we flew. I recalled that someone once said Russian pilots had to be the best in the world because their planes were the worst. I hoped our pilot was up to the challenge. Eventually we touched down amidst a birch forest outside Moscow, bumping with rubber-burning grace onto the runway.

Everyone on the plane broke into applause and loud cheers. This was my introduction to Russia. In Moscow, we stayed in a hotel that provided cucumber, tomatoes, and sausage on a regular basis—luxuries that the locals could scarcely obtain. The water from the aging pipes in the hotel spewed forth as brown as Yoo-Hoo Chocolate Soda. As an experiment, I left a glass of water overnight so the impurities could settle. The next morning, I found a good two inches of brown metallic sludge in the bottom of the glass. Locals from nearby high rises with broken elevators lugged water jugs to fill at a solitary fountain that offered potable water.

Money, I learned, was best exchanged on the black market, and officially "there was no alcoholism" in Russia because paddy wagons quickly collected the bodies of those passed out in the gutter. After visiting sundry museums and padlocked churches, a state-of-the art computer center, the Kremlin, Lenin's tomb, and various back alleys and parks of Moscow, we moved on to Tver,[9] a town beloved by Pushkin, where we would spend the summer.

Cable car tracks and overhead wires crisscrossed the streets of Tver. The hotel where we stayed kept our passports, which felt disconcerting. Still, I wandered about town and met a couple of local women: Tanya and her friend Mina. We wound up running into each other on a regular basis.

With them, I found myself riding on a glass-bottom hydroplane boat on the Volga and sailing with their gentleman friend Ivan, who sported a chest full of gray and black hair, a deep tan, and a small Speedo as he offered his hand to help us all aboard. I felt like I was learning more Russian skipping class to hang out with my new friends than I did sitting in the large gray classrooms where I was

---

[9] Tver was renamed "Kalinin" in 1931 for one of Stalin's henchmen. Its original name was not restored until 1990. When I was there in 1989, it was officially known as Kalinin, but the locals preferred to call it Tver.

supposed to join the other American students singing the Russian national anthem and listing rigorous syntactic rules.

Time sped by, yet impressions remain. To my left, the Volga River, dark and calm, to my right, Pushkin's life-sized, top-hatted statue as I passed jogging on the footpath. Tangible connections superseded the academic lexicon I was supposed to be learning. Breathing the air along the river, feeling the sun through the birch trees, watching school children in the park in their tidy rows, the girls with big flouncy ribbons in their hair and the little boys in tidy shorts, listening to Russian people speak rather than my fellow Americans reading classroom dialogs, gave me a visceral sense of the language. Still, cutting class was unlike me—an avowed nerd since kindergarten.

Perhaps it was the unofficial culture rubbing off on me. I felt an increased reliance on intuition over academic logic. Being in a country with a language, culture, and political system foreign to me resembled my situation in the Unification movement, where I'd learned to adapt to Korean and Japanese ways. Lacking both deep cultural knowledge and language proficiency in either Korean or Japanese, I'd adapted by imitating others in my living environment and trying to sense their heart. I did this the way a blind person uses a cane to feel their way through the obstacles of an unknown city. In like manner, I tapped my spiritual cane in Russia, finding my way by intuition rather than maps.

Accepting an invitation from Tanya, I skipped class and boarded a train with her to escape to the countryside and visit her family's *dacha*, a simple wooden cottage, without an indoor toilet. She showed me handmade lace, a traditional art in her family. A portrait of Lenin in a small round frame hung on the wall above the refrigerator.

Portraits of Lenin dominated public buildings as well as homes. Indeed, every building my classmates and I entered—offices, museums, shops, the preschool classroom we visited—had large portraits of Lenin, often with an altar beneath them. I took snapshots of other ephemera on my disposable camera: handwritten "in search of housing" signs in Russian glued on brick walls about town; ghetto housing we weren't supposed to see reflected in the windows of abandoned buildings; a horse grazing by the stoop of a church, its door fastened with a lock the size of an infant's head. The church, a seventeenth-century wooden monument, seem to defy the government and embody both the ingenuity and resilience of faith. The entire structure was in pristine condition and held strong, toggled together entirely by handmade wooden wedges rather than metal nails.

I shared a sense of compatriotism with Russians oppressed by their society. I felt oppressed by both capitalism's superficiality and the oversimplification of Bible Belt religiosity. Yet I wanted to challenge the Marxist scaffolding that shaped most US literary criticism of the late eighties.

I played hooky more than once to explore the environs with Tanya, but I didn't miss school excursions to travel further afield. Visiting a Byzantine church, for instance, I wandered off from the group and found a young Russian woman in the vicinity. She told me that she could sell me a black-market Russian Bible for two hundred American dollars—a sum that my grad-student income could ill afford.

The clandestine availability of religious information and the official oppression of religion during the revolution was a topic native Russians seemed eager to share with me. Such was the repression at the time, that speaking of government acts of religious desecration and destruction as undesirable occurred only in clandestine conversations. As for overt critiques of the current government? Fuhgeddaboudit. One of our guides called me aside after a tour. She furtively pressed into my hand a packet of postcards depicting Moscow's skyline before the revolution. Tears filled her eyes as she quickly told me how the government had destroyed most of the churches pictured in the collection.

While my master's thesis was on Baroque seventeenth-century French literature, I had found resonance with my own passions in nineteenth-century Russian literature. The more I read the Russian Romantic poets in Tver, the more I missed Vincent. The characters in his family fascinated me like those of my Russian novels. His paternal uncle had been on the *Carpathia*, the ship that rescued the survivors from the *Titanic*. Another uncle had engaged in cannibalism after he was left adrift for months at sea. A paternal grandmother had given birth on a train fleeing the revolution. His family stories enthralled me.

In the US, a dial-up, DOS version of the internet existed. A few people had car phones, but most did not. In the Soviet Union, however, the internet seemed unknown and even landlines a luxury. I had no contact with the US from the Soviet Union. A letter I sent by post would not arrive stateside until more than a full month and a half had passed. I began to have a recurring dream of Vincent. In it, he lurched, put forth his hand upon a counter to steady himself and stop midway a fall to the ground. I could see he suffered and seemed unable to battle some dark forces at Dataway. I sensed that his store, his life, seemed to be falling into confusion. I felt that he needed me and compelled to help him.

The persistent spiritual SOS of this dream caused me sufficient concern that I determined to leave the program early and return to the US. Like cutting class, departing early was uncharacteristic for me. When it came to my studies, I was driven. Besides that, I'd already paid for the program and it was not yet over. Yet, feeling summoned from beyond to return, I focused on what I had to do to leave Russia, which was not as simple as it sounds.

Retrieving my passport from its captivity at the hotel's front desk was only step one, as I learned after a taxi whisked me to the airport. There, I joined hordes of Romanians seeking asylum from the chaos and hunger that prevailed under Ceausescu's Communist dictatorship. I knew little of their situation other than their visible desperation and destitution. Escaping the crowd into a small airport shop, I had my hair cut with the last of my soon-to-be worthless rubles—having my scalp scrubbed clean would be my final luxury.

Rejoining the masses, I would eat little but some leftover crackers and a rare, boiled egg for the next three days. We all slept leaning against one another mingling the odors of our sweat-perfumed bodies that defined us as airport refugees. No fans, open windows, or ventilation provided respite. I gave myself over to being slow-cooked, mashed between extended families that huddled together in the crowd.

Hours and days passed as I became human flotsam. When the crowd surged toward the airline ticket counter, I drifted there too, caught in its tide. By the third day, I had managed to maneuver inch by inch to the front of the mob. At last, I met the eyes of a uniformed employee at the ticket booth. I sensed the enormous distance between the employees' world and that of the refugees and me. Unlike us, the airport personnel had showered and eaten within recent memory. There is a kind of confidence that a full belly and a uniform provide that enables people to deny the humanity of the smelly creatures before them.

I proclaimed my US citizenship several times, requested a revised ticket to travel, and showed my valid visa that granted me permission to do so. The ticket clerks ignored my evidence and dismissed me with a wave of their hands. I was out of category, unclassifiable, and therefore could not exist or be within their realm of concern.

Stunned and hungry, I sought escape. The other refugees had one another for comfort. I was alone. I noticed a set of metal doors tucked away in a corner. Their small upper windows of thick glass revealed a hidden stairway.

Putting my shoulder to the door, I squeezed the handle latch and shoved. To my relief it gave way without protest. I ventured up the stairs. Had my fellow refugees found the stairwell, they would have swarmed to colonize the area. Unlike the stifling linoleum halls where we slept and stood, this refuge had plush carpet. Cool air conditioning tickled my nose and made me sneeze. At the top of the stairs, I found a pristine restroom. With both hands, I splashed water over the grime on my face. Bending low, my dry lips eagerly slurped water from my hands cupped beneath the faucet. I swished and spat out a couple of mouthfuls to rinse off the acrid taste of unwashed teeth. Thus emboldened, I proceeded to explore the maze of glass-encased offices, hoping to find signs of life in this hidden sanctuary.

Around a corner, I found an office inhabited by a receptionist. She smiled at me from beneath her tidy helmet of brunette hair, coiffed with hairspray. Coordinated costume jewelry was pinned to her ears and peered from beneath the Peter Pan collar of her starched white shirt. Her bright red suit was ironed to perfection. In Russian, I said hello and asked if she spoke English. Smiling she said, "Of course. How can I help you?"

Unlike my Romanian comrades, I had accessed another world. Here, the airport personnel treated me like a human being whose questions deserved answers. I explained the snafu. Still smiling, she took me to her boss and introduced me as though I was an important guest they'd invited to an exclusive function. A gray-haired gentleman in a fine, freshly pressed suit that draped with tailored grace over his elegant frame reached for my hand in greeting.

As his long fingers reached for mine, I noticed his manicured nails. The skin of his hand felt soft as he shook mine. Greeting me, he made small talk, excused himself to answer the phone on his desk; unavoidably eavesdropping, I heard him speak several languages with casual ease. He introduced me to his superior, a more rotund, slightly shorter version of himself with a handlebar moustache and twinkling eyes. This man loved "Amer—ee—ka" and did not fear to say so.

We had a friendly chat about where he had visited in the States and where I was going. As though it were no problem at all, he handed me a ticket that confirmed I would be on the next plane to JFK. We shook hands, smiled, and laughed over some nonsense about how crazy bureaucracy could be. After descending the secret stairs, I pulled open one of the heavy doors and reentered chaos—it was like leaving Shangri-La to return to the Inferno.

My excursion felt like a dream—apart from the real ticket my hand clenched. It was not the ticket alone that gave me peace of mind. My office visit, a grail quest into unknown and forbidden territory, had reconfigured into a pilgrimage.

Prior to finding this upper room, I did not even merit the repugnance a refugee experienced; because my situation was baffling, airport personnel had dismissed me as though I did not exist at all. In these secret chambers, I had been seen with welcoming eyes. It was akin to darshan, an encounter with the Divine. Inner bliss softened me and made me resilient. As my fellow refugees compressed me in a human sandwich, their elbows jabbed me like meat mallets. I let myself go, yielding my body as my mind retained hope.

Several hours later, I reached a brocade rope. It separated those who would reach the tarmac from those who would spend another night on the airport floor. Light-headed from lack of sleep and food, I stood in line and watched the clock hands tick closer to the hour of departure. Only ten minutes remained before my coveted plane would sail into the sky without me. I felt panic rise, choking my throat, at the thought of missing my plane. Then, I let go of fear, of anticipation, or planning strategies to deal with consequences.

I disassociated from the babble of voices, the crowd pushing me, and the tension of uncertainty. As I stood swaying, dumb with fatigue, hope and hopelessness washed over me. An official unhooked the rope. He permitted me alone to enter the gate area. Behind me, he replaced the rope that held back the bulging crowd. The plane was fully boarded except for me. Only a few minutes remained before takeoff. Nearly delirious with happiness and relief, I skipped a few steps and leaned back against the weight of my duffel bag, swinging it around me like a square dance partner.

I'd tasted a scant few days of the protracted futility and powerlessness refugees regularly face. The promise of leaving overwhelmed me with a delight made sweeter still by the fact that exiting had for some days seemed an impossible dream. As my spirit took flight, my body rejoiced. I could not help but dance a little jig. Yet determined not to miss my plane, I quickly bore down on the gate entry.

In retrospect, twirling round and round must have appeared bizarre given the militaristic solemnity of the security guards. Then again, this was Russia, where people regularly laughed, cried, and sang with the help of not a little vodka, albeit not in front of officials. Like my fellow refugees, I was wary of those in control. I danced in a release of joy, not a mockery of those I was leaving behind. I did not look back as my swinging bag propelled me toward freedom. I imagined the others would have done the same.

I faced what looked like a horse-race starting gate—a series of chutes. Instead of a horse, each chute contained a conveyer belt topped with an x-ray machine. Passing through a chute to x-ray my bag was all that separated me from the exit door, beyond which my plane idled. Behind each x-ray machine, a uniformed attendant scrutinized the contents of bags and the remaining passengers' tickets as they passed through the narrow adjacent aisles. Everyone else had passed their bags through security and had their tickets examined without incident. My peripheral vision caught the image of the last passenger before me filing through the exit door that led to the plane.

"The last shall be first, the first shall be last," I gloated as I twirled and cavorted to the only aisle with attendants lingering to clear my bag and ticket. It was the chute nearest the exit. I could hear the engine of my plane roaring, preparing to taxi onto the runway. It beckoned to me the way a dinner gong calls home the famished.

I released my bag onto the conveyor belt to pass through the x-ray machine, operated by two well-groomed women. They each wore a crisp navy-blue uniform and a little triangular cap anchored with bobby pins to their tidy hairdos. I approached grinning like a gargoyle, thinking I was as good as home. The woman on the right said bye to her comrade and quit her post to board the plane. It was getting down to the wire. The personnel were boarding. Adrenaline shot through my system. My dreamy giddiness vanished. I snapped to the task of answering whatever questions might be posed to secure my place onboard.

The woman official I faced glared at me with cool authority and said, "*Nyet.*" She was part of the ground crew and not boarding the plane. She turned to flirt with Sergei, the male baggage clerk. She had crooned his name several times as he gathered the final bags to load before departure.

Wait a minute! I thought, "*Nyet?*" *Are you out of your mind?* There was no way I was returning to refugee land.

Sergei said in Russian to the woman official, "Are there any more bags?"

I knew this was my only chance and yelled as loudly as my dry, unwashed throat would rally, "Да! Ещё один!" (Yes! There is one more!)

I picked my bag up off the conveyer belt and threw it to him. He caught it.

The woman glowered. I pointed to my bag boarding the plane with Sergei, and then pointed to my ticket. In Russian, I said, "I must go with my bag."

Sergei, with his big, brown eyes, smiled at the official over his shoulder. She blushed and smiled back at him. Hardening her face to me, she unlatched the final barrier, which allowed me to squeeze through. I darted past her and followed Sergei toward the sound of the whirring plane engines.

Blasted with air and sun on the tarmac, I mounted the ladder leaning against the plane's belly. Squeezing down the aisle, past row after row of occupied seats, at the very back by the kitchen, I found a small, hard, non-reclining chair. I strapped on the seatbelt and promptly fell asleep. I remained in sound slumber all the way to Switzerland, making up for multiple sleepless nights on the floor of the Moscow airport.

Back in New York, I called Vincent from a payphone after clearing customs at JFK. He met me at the RDU airport and we drove back to Carrboro. En route, we talked. He told me about his business problems. I learned that his computer shop Dataway had gone bankrupt and that he was facing no end of financial woes. I wasn't aware of these facts before leaving, and we hadn't communicated at all while I was in Russia. The dream that had compelled me to return seemed to have been spot on.

Twilight settled as we entered the condo on Fidelity Street. Leaving my bag in the living room, we went to the bedroom, closed the blinds against the lengthening sunrays, and tumbled to the floor to make love under the window. That night I had a dream of a little boy with Dutch blond hair who appeared from between my legs as I gave birth among the birch trees outside the Moscow airport. Animals walked past two by two as I delivered—giraffes, elephants, orangutans, a doe and stag, while a pair of butterflies fluttered in the sun.

As restructuring went, my post-Unificationist life with Vincent was romantically and intellectually engaging though he was an engineer and I favored the humanities. We complemented each other. He was an avid science fiction reader and fond of Ayn Rand; I was steeped in classical literature and theology, but we shared a love of film, music and an appreciation of cultural observations. Our intellectual compatibility alone was an enormous relief after years of having to dumb myself down in my previous marriage. Vincent was tender and kind with an intuitive awareness and sensitivity that filled my heart and made me long for him when we were apart.

Our relationship liberated me from two lifestyle constraints: both those of my parents, especially my dad, who wanted me to be exclusively a career woman and those of the church that would not have approved of our romantic alliance. Together we were free to construct our own independent paradigm of love and family. Our ongoing romance saw us through the painful process of losing Dataway and Vincent finding work in Alabama. I remained in Carrboro to work locally as a secretary while he commuted back to visit until we were sure the new job would work out. Meanwhile I discovered I was pregnant.

My spiritual experience at the start of my pregnancy was that of an otherworldly force. I sensed a warm light beaming out of my belly when I had first called Vincent confirming the new life we had unintentionally conceived. Though the embryonic body was not yet fully formed, I felt a presence emanating from within my uterus—it felt substantial and distinctive. The gush of sheer will to live came from this being inside me. I was not its source, but a mere witness. As certain as I'd been about my teenage abortion being sanctified by God, this time I felt to my very core that this child was meant to be born. But what was for me the hand of God being made manifest, seemed for Vincent more of an inconvenient mess given the recent bankruptcy of his company and the uncertainty of his new job.

We decided to visit his family in Oregon, whom I hadn't yet met. While there, Vincent surprised me with a day trip to visit a justice of the peace in nearby Washington State. Once back home in North Carolina from our holiday travels, we attended birthing classes together. In class and at home, Vincent was attentive and solicitous. We were both first time parents-to-be and read *What to Expect When You're Expecting* with inquisitive reverence. Yet as the actual event approached, Vincent seemed distracted, ignoring me when I needed him most. I felt disappointed, especially since I had first-hand experience of the phenomenal willpower of this—our—child, when he was just weeks old in the womb.

To be fair, for the birth, Vincent drove straight from Birmingham, Alabama, where he was working and now house hunting for us. We'd planned for me to join him there once the baby arrived and luckily his company would pay for the move. I'd continued working up until a few days before delivery. Since my return from the Soviet Union, I'd worked as a secretary and sometimes translated medical journal articles from French working at the Department of Genetics and Metabolism at the UNC Hospital. This made me privy to more information about potential birth defects than a first-time mother should ever contemplate.

Listening to autistic kids play in the room next door, I typed up the clinical reports of doctors and sociologists at the clinic. My job provided steady income and insurance to cover my prenatal care and childbirth. The department felt like a warm family. To my surprise, they showered me with baby supplies, including a much-needed child seat that we could scarcely afford.

Nine months after my return from the Soviet Union and my dream of giving birth, I forced air through my lips, "Hee-hee-who! Hee-hee-who! Hee-hee-who!" as I paced in my hospital gown, dragging an IV pole on rollers back and forth across the floor alongside me.

Vincent sat in the birthing room, avoiding eye contact with me, as he chatted on the phone with his lawyer friend back in Oregon. Ever practical, he'd replaced the hospital wall phone with an office phone from home because it had a "hold" button—that way he could put a call on hold while muting the receiver. As I went into labor, I begged him to help me breathe through my contractions. He'd put his friend on hold, and then return to his conversation as soon as my pain spasms receded.

As for my personal perestroika, nothing quite prepared me for the total revamping of my life that a child would bring. I was least prepared for the overwhelming sense of love I felt and sheer joy for the little Buddha boy who joined our lives. I performed a Unification ceremony out of my personal understanding of the Principle and my own dedication to God, not to an institution, when I offered little Vincent Alexander to God. My prayer followed the intent behind the tradition of the Eight Day Ceremony. I prayed in gratitude for God's love made manifest and offered Alex to God as his true parent. I saw myself as his earthly caregiver on behalf of God. I didn't invite his father, Vincent, to join me in this prayer. We shared many things, but not prayer. Besides, he seemed preoccupied. I decided it was the nature of his work, the new job and the pressure of first-time parenthood that kept him distant.

Without forewarning, a couple of days later, the doorbell rang. It was my Uncle Bill, a Methodist minister. He'd driven with my aunt from Pinehurst to christen our boy right there in the condo. We hadn't been in touch or seen one another in over a decade. His visit was not for earthly reasons; rather, it confirmed for me that God had received my prayer and that the spirit of God was with us even though I was no longer involved with the Unification movement. God was bigger than that.

My uncle sprinkled holy water on Vincent Alexander's head and recited prayers. Then he and my aunt sped off as quickly as they'd arrived. Just as efficiently, Vincent soon sped off in his car for Birmingham to resume work. My mother flew in from Colorado to help me and little Alex, as we called him, make the move to Alabama.

My redefinition of self now included motherhood. With my life forever changed, no longer affiliated with the Unification movement—or so I thought—it seemed my perestroika was complete.

— CHAPTER EIGHT —

ALABAMA

Holding Alex in my arms, I felt my way down the metal steps from the plane onto the tarmac at the Birmingham airport. The whir of engines had settled to a raucous hum. Alex remained quiet, still lulled in his milky snooze from feeding during the descent, the sucking timed to soothe the air pressure on his tiny ears. I hugged him to me. Labor had reactivated an old back injury from carrying heavy product while fundraising. The back brace from the chiropractor held my spine in place and straight enough so I could walk without sciatic pains shooting down my hamstring. All that mattered to me was the little snuffling bundle I held close to me.

A gracious fellow passenger, a southern gentleman with gray hair and kind eyes, grabbed the baby seat and carried it for me with a, "Let me help you, there, little lady." As baggage jostled into carts and mechanical noises clanked from trucks, lifts and other jets, people called out with deep southern accents. These sounds dropped into the background; all I heard was the soothing in-and-out breath of my little Buddha boy clasped to my heart.

Vincent was standing to the side of the other greeters, who were waving and smiling behind a red velvet rope. His eyes seemed to be focused on the floor. He paced in small semicircles, with occasional surreptitious glances toward the crowd. I knew that he was sacrificing valuable work time in order to meet us.

"Hello, Vincent," I said softly so as not to startle him.

"Bé girl!" he said (his nickname for me—short for "Baby Girl"). He smiled as he looked up and gave me a shy, awkward hug. He was always self-conscious in crowds. "Hi, Alex!" he said, his eyes crinkling in the corners as he tickled Alex under the chin. Taking the baby seat and collecting my bulky suitcase from baggage claim, Vincent loaded up the car.

Behind the wheel, his public persona descended into steely determination. I know that my mother driving the car down from North Carolina for me caused him stress. In classic libertarian fashion, he would have preferred me to be sufficiently independent to have driven Alex, by then scarcely two weeks old, by myself. I felt sorry to have let him down, yet relieved to have flown. Alex's round-the-clock feeding schedule and the pressure of moving had left me little time to recover from childbirth.

I appreciated that Vincent had found a place for us to live. He'd been living in motels while working and found a house to rent in his spare time. From the airport, he drove us into a tree-lined suburb of Birmingham, aptly named Gardendale. From there, he had a quick commute to the metro garbage dump. Gardendale had a quirky used bookstore, a pediatrician's office, and some strip malls with all the usual banks and shops. We passed a Catholic church and a KinderCare on Main Street before turning onto a windy road that ended in a cul-de-sac. Within it, nestled into the hillock, sat a small, white, and pretty ranch-style house with black shutters we would call home. Vincent parked in front of the deep two-car garage. He had already colonized it as a work area to process boxes and wrapping paper from the move. Out back, a chain-link fence encircled the yard. On either side of us, neighbors had houses of various designs and with similar mowed lawns.

I had scarcely settled Alex when my mother arrived. Within a couple of hours, having stocked our larder with groceries, she whisked herself off to the airport in a taxi. She was nonplussed by Vincent's demeanor, which was polite but preoccupied. Between always being on-call with his new job and dealing with the recent move, he felt keenly the responsibility of having a family to provide for. Mom's smile drew thin and terse as she left. Her southern charm and grandmotherly indulgence had grown weary from the long drive and our hectic lives. I was grateful for her help, yet faced the unpacking chores ahead and knew she would give a negative report to my dad about Vincent. At thirty-one, I was grateful for my parents to be in my life, but I didn't rely upon their approval for my happiness.

Vincent's company had provided for our move—including the packing. Stacks of boxes had to be unpacked. Each one contained items individually wrapped in newsprint. As we unboxed, shoulder-high mounds of rumpled paper rose in the garage. Ever frugal, Vincent saved every single piece of packing paper by spending endless hours smoothing them into wrinkle-free perfection. Once flat, he would align each sheet with engineered precision into a tidy, growing pile on the garage floor. I wondered why but didn't dare ask him.

He tended his sheets of packing paper with the focus of a Hindu temple devotee pressing garments to dress the gods. I embraced his behavior as his form of prayer. Yet silently, I grieved that he should prefer to spend the bulk of his after-work leisure time in the garage smoothing paper rather than doing something with Alex and me.

But I was a new mom, adjusting to a new place, and not yet back in the workforce. I couldn't expect him to have the same social needs I did given that he had colleagues and a demanding schedule at the plant. Perhaps straightening the paper was his form of Zen. Besides tending Alex, my energy went into understanding our new environs.

The Deep South differs from your moderately southern states like North Carolina. Here in "Alabanana," as one radio DJ termed it, local culture revolved around church and football, and not necessarily in that order. And "church" in these parts meant the Baptist Church.

Wanting to be neighborly, I set forth to make friendly overtures with those nearby, beginning with the Catholic church up the road, a rarity in the region. When I, a non-Catholic, peeked into the sanctuary, I received an uncommonly hospitable welcome. The priest was a shaggy-haired Irishman with a fondness for beer that was outmatched only by his zeal for God, which he proved by abstaining from alcohol each year during Lent.

Father Clancy O'Hara's congregation was mighty small. For Wednesday morning communion, it consisted of Edith, an elderly widow from New York, and a rosy-cheeked German housewife. Technically, only bona fide Catholics could take communion. But Alabama, with its Baptist hegemony, was the equivalent of an untamed frontier for Catholicism. Father Clancy and his congregants had known the kind of persecution I'd encountered directed against Unification movement. Thus, we shared an uncommon alliance. Furthermore, by including me, the Gardendale congregation increased by a full third, so when I arrived, they invited me straightaway to take communion with them. Father Clancy had another church in a nearby town with a bigger turnout and more developed adult study and Sunday school. He soon invited me to study Catechism with him there. I agreed and attended one evening class each week. By way of exchange, he agreed to weekly study of the Divine Principle too. For several months, we met semiweekly to exchange theological perspectives.

I still had a set of the tapes that introduced DP to ministers from my mission days in Asheville. Father Clancy and I met in the fellowship hall of the Gardendale church. After he flicked on the TV and chunked the videocassette into the VCR, we watched as an American brother of Irish descent, Tom McDevitt, gently moved through the whole of the Unification Principles. Tom presented DP in an old-school style, with a whiteboard and markers. At the end of each segment, Father Clancy clicked off the TV and we discussed the content, comparing notes.

My seminary training came in handy here, as did my love for Rabelais. I found in Father Clancy more of a Pantagruelian priest than a rigid doctrinaire Jesuit. We had much to discuss given his rigorous training for the priesthood and my years of celibacy, graduate school, and seminary. In the bleak cultural landscape of football, hush puppies, and Baptist fundamentalism, we shared lush discussions on all manner of ethics and theological tendencies, from Aquinas to Barthes and current interpretive theories.

I attended his Sunday sermons in Gardendale with the faithful Catholics and received communion in friendship as well as wafers. When the congregation recited the Nicene Creed, I was grateful that Father Clancy recognized the recitation as a political decision regarding canon reflective of a particular point in history. I recited only what I believed to be true, and remained silent for the bits I thought incorrect, like Jesus being God and Mary a virgin. By the time we reached the completion of our theological exchanges, I heard a new zeal in Father Clancy's sermons. He incorporated elements from the Divine Principle that brought Bible stories and his Catholic interpretations to life.

I experienced the spirit of God in our exchanges. Father Clancy's renewed enthusiasm fed my own living relationship with the Divine. I gained a new appreciation for aspects of the Catholic faith tradition rooted in sincere devotion, and our vivid discussions inspired me. Father Clancy seriously loved the Divine without taking himself too seriously.

Meanwhile, Vincent took his work and himself quite seriously. I fully supported his cause. I saw the extraction of usable gas from methane as an environmental crusade to reduce pollution and provide renewable energy. Indeed, his work at the plant was more than a job—it was a mission. He kept a beeper on our bedside table by night. Inevitably, the plant would shut down during storms. Even after a 6 a.m. to 7 p.m. shift, if the beeper went off at 2 a.m., Vincent would leap from bed, pull on jeans and a T-shirt, and drive through sleet, fog, or rain to the plant.

There, he'd scramble up scaffolding pipes three stories high, even during thunderstorms, to take a wrench or a ratchet to whatever needed tending. He'd cling to the metal scaffolding soaked through to the skin, holding a flashlight in his teeth, balancing on narrow bars as lightning threatened to electrocute him. He never complained and dashed off with the urgency of a doctor saving a patient from certain death. And like a doctor, Vincent worked at all hours, every day of the week. It was a start-up venture. We knew it would be difficult to launch. Therefore, I felt I had no right to think of myself when such a great cause was at stake. However, we didn't know that his paychecks would become unreliable. At first, they arrived late with an apology. Then, late without explanation. Next, late and short the full amount. Soon, they arrived only sporadically.

I needed to work to make ends meet. When Alex turned six weeks old, I began my job search in earnest. The KinderCare at the end of the road had a bevy of kind staff. One of them, an earth mother with hugs to spare, took Alex under her wing. She loved him like one of her own children, which gave me peace of mind.

I hand delivered my résumé to colleges within commuting distance. At Birmingham-Southern College, the director asked me to return with a thesis sample for an interview. I did and she hired me to teach a couple of intermediate French courses. A neighbor told me that Ramsey High School needed a French teacher, so I drove into downtown Birmingham to apply there too.

Immediately, I was sent to talk with the drama teacher who had been fielding the French classes. She was eager to sign me on. At the last minute, the French PhD they'd originally hired had declined to work at an inner-city school. I found myself with two college courses and a full-time high school French curriculum to teach within a week. It seemed to be the hand of Providence.

I counted it as the divine in our lives providing for our needs with the blessing of work. With divine presence, there was always room for more love. Vincent found Black Kitty in the drainage ditch just out the front door. A miniature Sylvester look-alike, he wore a jet-black tuxedo with white paws, a bib, and a snippet on his nose. "Dat's dem Kays," Vincent would croon in baby talk cradling the kitten.

As Black Kitty grew strong and sinewy, Alex outgrew lying in place and took to rolling around and squiggling. Vincent would sometimes take him to work in a hand basket. He nearly crowed when his coworkers commented on Alex, "Well, he's simply the best baby in the world." Vincent had grown from reluctant parent to proud Papa. I was pleased with the transformation.

As the days shortened and Christmas approached, I heard a mewing at the front door—it came from the drainage ditch again. This time a miniature tiger with fox-brown ears appeared. It was love at first sight for me as I picked her up and showed her to Vincent who was, as usual, at work in the garage. I showed him the fox-eared kitten, whose whole body sat comfortably in my palm. Vincent said, "No. We already have a kitty."

I made the case that she wouldn't add too much to the burden of cat care, but he was staunch. Reluctantly, I put her back outside by the gutter, where I hoped she would find her mother. I felt that uniting with Vincent was more important than my own desires. Having first seen his wrath as his company fell apart and knowing that his new position entailed its fair share of stress, I feared opposing him, even about a kitty.

And so with a heavy heart I resumed grading papers, when all of a sudden Vincent came up the stairs from the garage cuddling the kitten to his chest. "Merry Christmas," he said.

The plucky feline had done what I didn't dare: she vocalized dissent with Vincent's decree. After I'd put her outside, she went around the house and down the hill to where Vincent was working in the garage to mew at him directly.

As his paychecks waned, despite Vincent's dedication and long hours working far beyond overtime, his stoic countenance began to fracture. Holding himself in constant control, his face used to be serene, set firm in concentration. Now, insignificant events caused little eruptions of outrage: the way a juice carton was labeled; the way a cupboard was designed; the angle at which the trash collectors left the garbage can at the curb.

Vincent didn't talk about it, yet I knew that he felt hurt, shamed, unappreciated, and ultimately betrayed by people that he'd trusted—his employers. The increasing irregularity of his paychecks, while financially trying, caused psychological harm too. Vincent prided himself on his excellent job performance. His parents valued old world artisanship, honor, and integrity, for wealth required integrity to manage it properly. Vincent comported himself with decorum, as if he were wealthy. He wanted to be "above" working for a paycheck. Rather, he worked for the sake of aesthetics, the realization of a perfectly engineered system, and the joy of creating something that served a purpose. The reality, however, was that we were broke without his income before mine kicked in.

"Did you pick up the mail?" I called from the front door one day, before entering the living room. We took our shoes off at the door. I wondered if I needed to keep mine on to saunter down to the mailbox at the end of the driveway. Vincent was around the corner, in the dining room. I felt happy. It was a sunny day. We'd been let go early from work.

Vincent thundered into the living room like a freight train. I wondered what caused such panic. Maybe there was some fuel spilling in the driveway. He had a wild-eyed look that frightened me. His face was hard, furious. Growling profanities through clenched teeth, he rampaged through the living room and threw an armchair to the floor. Then, his eyes fixed on me. He barked, "You! You whore! You bitch!" He lunged toward me. His fists flew landing on my side and back as I twisted away.

I was so perplexed at first that I forgot to be shocked by his outrage. Even as I tried to escape his blows, my mind raced to comprehend his motives. Did he think that by pulverizing me, his problems would diminish? Though trembling with fear, some other part of me sought a higher spiritual perspective on the moment.

As this sort of unexpected and unexplained event became routine, I learned to cower and cover my face. As if possessed, his rages exploded, it seemed, out of nowhere, and would end just as abruptly. Like someone who'd blacked out, he'd seem oblivious to his prior fury. There was no apology or explanation—it was as if it never happened. I learned to be fearful because his anger and physical power could be relentless. As I made myself very small, he loomed larger and stronger. This was a battle he could win every time. In truth, I was terrified—both by his physical strength, which seemed to become superhuman with rage, and by his accusations of my worthlessness and incompetence.

On the surface, as long as I hid my face from his blows, I could keep the black and blue marks on the other parts of my body hidden beneath my clothes. But the fear and doubt I felt about my own value remained. Most of all, I feared losing his love, for once he had loved me. Yet, as I saw it, he was unraveling into anger from his own disappointments. When that mood possessed him, he no longer saw me as the person he had once cherished.

Perhaps today people might explore explanations like "bipolar" but that wasn't common currency at the time. I blamed myself when in his eyes, I was no longer good enough for him. I felt dumb, numb with simple thoughts. All I wanted was to be a happy family. To have some professional success. To see Vincent happy. My own inadequacies loomed before me. I felt ashamed by his outbursts and blamed myself for his unhappiness. I pleaded with him for us to get counseling, said that it was strange to have him hit me, then to sleep with him. However, he didn't want anyone to know about his personal life. For him, it would be a form of betrayal to confide in a therapist. He framed it as his ideological position, his right to privacy.

While at work, I had to be competent, strong, logical, and sure. At home, I experienced constant trepidation. I never knew what, as yet undiscovered foible of mine would trigger an episode of rage. My love for Alex made me irrationally determined to take every burden in stride. Pacing the floor with Alex late at night, lulling his colicky sobs to a quiet as he nestled against my neck, I felt that with God's help, love could overcome anything.

I was a college-educated woman with a master's degree and more than full-time employment. I had this beautiful boy, a place to live and work to put food on the table. How could I be anything but grateful? It didn't occur to me to consider myself a victim of abuse. Vincent had his own unique relationship with God to sort out, as I saw it. I had the power to change myself, not him. Scrambling to survive daily, I didn't see how I could add one more thing to my overfull schedule to create change.

Home in Gardendale, I still went to the Catholic church solo to see Father O'Hara and the neighbors, yet I told them nothing of Vincent's anger. We gathered each month at someone's home for pot-luck dinner followed by board games. When off from work Vincent would attend these sorts of social events with me. One evening, we all went to a gathering at a grange. The beer flowed. Everyone danced the hokey pokey—even the priest. I didn't drink alcohol in those days. Vincent, self-possessed and ever stoic in public, would not drink more than a single beer. Among friends, we presented ourselves as a "happy family." Driving back from the grange, I hoped that our public performance, the taste of casual peace, might be realized at home. But his rages only continued to worsen. In response, I tip-toed around him with Alex and focused on my own substantial workload of college and high-school teaching, course preparation, office hours, faculty meetings and grading.

Late one afternoon, after a long day of teaching and meetings, I was driving home from downtown Birmingham in rush-hour traffic. I switched on the radio to a rock-and-roll station and following the cars in front of me, slowed to a crawl. Behind me, the driver of a utility truck failed to notice the shift in traffic speed. Going more than sixty-five miles per hour, he slammed into my two-door Pontiac. The jolt scrunched my car into an accordion as it smashed into the rear of the sedan in front. I exited by cranking down the passenger side window and slithering through it.

Dazed, I walked forward to check on the driver in front of me. She emerged the regular way, through her door, and said she was fine. Police cars and ambulances arrived. The pile-up of vehicles stretched to the horizon. Amidst the confusion of stopped cars, sirens, and blinking lights, my Pontiac sat wrecked on the highway. Police and ambulance drivers wanted me to go to the hospital. I declined their help. I couldn't afford it: we were broke and without insurance— Vincent would be furious were I to spend the money. And besides, there was no time for a hospital visit; I had to pick up Alex.

Vincent's wrath was foremost in my mind. I knew he would insist upon fixing the car himself, regardless of the damage. I rode with the tow-truck driver who agreed to give me a ride and tow my wrecked Pontiac to the garbage dump where Vincent worked. A winding gravel road snaked its way up the hill to our destination. Every pothole and large rock we bumped over sent zings of pain through my injured body. Vincent wasn't there. We turned around and bumped our way back on the gravel road, over the same rocks and potholes. The driver kindly agreed to tow the car home to Gardendale. As we pulled up to the house, I was in a daze of pain and fatigue. Worried about picking up Alex, I feared delivering the car to the wrong place, as that would irritate Vincent.

My house keys dangled from a key ring hanging from the ignition of what used to be my car now mounted high on the tow truck. I walked to the front door of the house like a zombie and found it locked, even though Vincent's white

Coupe de Ville was parked in the driveway. I knocked. No answer. Then I rang the bell. Still no answer. I had to ring again. Vincent must have been sleeping. He scowled and snapped "What do you want" between clenched teeth as if I were a stranger. I knew he was furious that I had awakened him. I explained what happened, how we had to get Alex or be charged a late fee at KinderCare and I apologized for the ruined car.

He looked at the Pontiac, asked the driver to wait, got Alex from KinderCare at the end of our block, and left him with me. The next thing I knew, Vincent and the tow-truck driver left. Vincent wanted the car dropped back at the garbage dump. Exhausted, I stretched out on the couch after tending Alex.

Night fell. I fed Alex again and tucked him into bed. Still no Vincent. I called the plant. No answer.

The pain in my body was symphonic. Mentally, I ignored it, hoping I could reduce the pain to white noise with my own will power. Adrenaline-infused fear for what might have happened to Vincent made me alert as a live, loose electric wire. Was he injured in a car accident? In hospital somewhere? Had the car fallen on him while he was working under it? I was ready to phone the police, except that would have infuriated Vincent. He hated the police.

It was about 11 p.m. when the telephone rang. Vincent was calling me from a payphone in a prison hallway. They'd moved him from the county jail to a prison for dangerous felons. He would remain locked up with these scary individuals for cellmates unless I could make the hundred-thousand-dollar bail. In our financial situation, it might as well have been a million.

I thought that in the Deep South, having a Yankee attitude would be frowned upon, and that it was entirely likely that Vincent was simply an innocent victim of regional politics. When I asked him why he was in prison and in such tight security, he said tersely, "They're idiots!" as though that explained everything. "They should have put the tow-truck driver in prison for trying to steal from me!" he ranted.

Safe from his fists, I silently wondered how that could be. The tow-truck driver had seemed like a nice person, kind enough to go far out of his way on the garbage dump detour before driving me all the way home to Gardendale and then, after dropping me off, hauling the car back to the dump with Vincent. Meanwhile, my body ached all over, with fatigue and injury. I had not yet sought medical attention for myself.

It was too late to call anyone. I cried, prayed, and eventually fell asleep. The next day, I talked to Father O'Hara, who called the two church ladies. Edith, from New York, said she would post bail by using her house as collateral. The shock of her generosity piled atop the shock sustained from my accident, discovering Vincent was in jail, and the amount of bail. I floated in a sea of conflicting emotions—gratitude, confusion, and worry alongside the demands of an infant at home and a full-time job to tend.

After the churchwomen insisted I get medical attention, I went to a day clinic. The doctor fitted me with an IV for dehydration, a neck brace for whiplash, and a pain prescription when I left the office.

I wouldn't hear from Vincent again until the following night. To my surprise, he said his cellmates were okay—though most were detained there for serious crimes like murder, assault, and arson. They played cards together, he said, making it sound like boys away at summer camp. I had the responsibility to get him out of jail, tend Alex, cope with my own physical state, and perform my full and part-time jobs, while Vincent, at last, had a holiday from constantly being on-call at the plant. He deserved a holiday, but not like this, I thought. I still didn't understand why he was in jail. I was afraid to press demands upon him for more information during our brief conversations. If I angered him, he might not call at all, I thought.

Adrenaline kicked in to deal with daily life as every waking moment was filled with activity. Bypassing analysis of the situation, I just did the next thing I had to do. Pray and act: there was time for little else. I tended Alex, took him to daycare in the morning; prepared and taught classes, attended faculty and student meetings during the day; fetched and cared for Alex in the evening; graded papers and planned lessons by night. Vincent had to remain in jail for the better part of the week as officials reviewed his case and processed bail.

It surprised me how much easier it was to get through the day while Vincent was gone. I could come and go as I pleased without fearing an encounter with his fists or his anger from some unanticipated cause. Relieved from these stresses, Alex and I had a fine time. Experiencing the kindness of the churchwomen, I privately recalled how little Vincent had cared about my pain after the accident; how he had not acknowledged my efforts to bring the car to the plant in the first place. I remembered how he had practically ignored my labor and delivery of Alex, remaining on the phone with his lawyer friend until I begged him to help me breathe as I went through contractions without anesthesia.

My neck started to heal from the whiplash. And without the threat of Vincent's reprisal, for it would have been a betrayal for me to question his authority, I dared to wonder what had actually happened to land him in jail. His story—that the tow-truck driver tried to rob him—did not seem to match the incarceration he received. Without him berating me, I felt secretly relieved that someone had understood his temper. I was grateful to be protected from him without revealing my own story to authorities. Had I done so, that would have infuriated Vincent. All this conflicted with a sense of panic I felt that Vincent might be injured in jail. I felt guilty for enjoying his absence. I still cherished the tender moments we had shared, glimpses of kindness from before Alex was born of our original love.

I hadn't realized how great was the shadow of fear that had dominated my daily life. It receded as if a nightmare. In the light of day, hope for renewing the ideal that we had lived before the rages rekindled within me. When he got out of jail, I thought he would be different, that our lives would be different. Having my suspicions yet wanting to believe his story, out of loyalty, I wanted to believe that he was wrongly incarcerated. One day, I was sure, we would be a happy family.

While it didn't occur to me at the time, my ability to deny wrongdoing went back to childhood. My mother's resilient optimism, her stopping the car to yell at me, tears flying from her eyes: "Don't you ever say that again about your father!" when I had said he was an alcoholic and needed help. I learned to accept only the positive, deny the negative in my home life. And God forbid the neighbors or anyone else know that we were struggling.

On the day when Vincent would finally be released on bail, I took a personal day from school. Alex was safely at daycare when I answered the doorbell. It was Edith, from church, who had arrived to pick me up in her Lincoln. Her hands grasped the wheel strong and sure as a veteran sailor steering a long, black barge. As we drove to the jail, moments flashed through my mind: Vincent smiling at Alex; dangling a string for Black Kitty; wishing me "Merry Christmas," as the fox-eared kitten won his heart when I could not. We parked at the jailhouse in a desolate part of Birmingham beneath a cloverleaf of highways, surrounded by bleak factory buildings.

We met with officials as stolid as the windowless cement building where they worked. Taking charge, Edith, a real New Yorker, filled out the paperwork. She'd put her house up for collateral; my hand shook as I signed the documents. I was glad Edith had driven. I still didn't understand why Vincent was in jail, and was too exhausted from stress, work, and lack of sleep to challenge the officials. Feeling like an expat in Alabama, I accepted Vincent's vehement declarations of injustice. I believed him when he said he was innocent of any wrongdoing. I wondered if at any moment any of us might not be in his shoes.

The bailiff brought out papers that seemed oddly amateur compared to the seriousness of the situation. There was no fine-grained paper, nor official seals nor embossed headers denoting the majesty of government documentation. The papers were faded Xerox copies. They had multiple questions, lines, and boxes for numbers, like a tax-factoring worksheet.

Edith filled out the columns with all the numbers they needed for the collateral, signed it, and showed her driver's license. However, ten percent of the bail bond remained for me to produce—some ten thousand dollars cash for Vincent's release. The collateral was on top of the cash, in the event he failed to show at court. I did not have that kind of money. So, Edith and I left without Vincent. I didn't think to question the amount of his bail, fearing any challenge on my part might simply raise the sum needed. Like Alice behind the looking glass, I expected changes to occur based on some arbitrary logic understood only by officials in the Deep South.

Days passed. Even behind bars, Vincent controlled me. I caught daily rides with the principal of the school to commute to class as our house was on his way into Birmingham. I never mentioned that my husband was in jail—only that my car was out of commission. The principal dressed like the successful family man that he was: a churchgoing Baptist, husband, and father. His idea of extravagance was a beer at the Fourth of July family barbecue or perhaps a whiskey with the gentlemen in the parlor while the womenfolk tended the kids and food at Christmas. I kept my conversation with him focused on how much I loved teaching and the weather.

Vincent would call late at night when he had access to the public phone in the jail hallway. I could always hear his fellow inmates talking in the background as they waited for their turn at the phone. Their impatience increased the brevity of our conversations. Vincent assured me that he was getting along fine with his cellmates, that the card games were ongoing. I imagined his cellmates as large, strong, inarticulate men who might listen in on our conversations for a reason to beat him up.

Vincent's court appointed lawyer called me one day after school while I was juggling the kitties, Alex, and a stack of grading. "We need a character witness," he said.

I thought, who better than Father O'Hara? The good man agreed as a kindness to me, having only met Vincent a few times at the monthly socials and once when we'd invited him to our house for spaghetti dinner.

The day of the hearing, Edith drove Father Clancy and me to the courthouse. Before the proceedings, we were to meet Vincent briefly in a waiting room. When he entered, I noted that his ashen gray complexion from the long, unpredictable hours at the plant hadn't changed during his stint in prison. As usual, I worried about his health and how he was feeling emotionally. Decked out for the hearing, complete with his official backward collar, Father Clancy was professional and calm. Edith's presence, with her New York attitude and matronly compassion, was also reassuring. After Vincent greeted them both, they waited on the other side of the room while Vincent and I conferred in the far corner.

At last I'd hear what I thought was the full story of why he was arrested. According to Vincent, when he and the tow-truck driver had returned to the plant, the driver had charged $125.00 for the tow instead of the anticipated $100. Vincent, who only had $100, was short on cash. The driver refused to release the car without the full amount. This sounded like more of a misunderstanding than a jail-worthy disagreement. I felt relieved to finally hear what happened.

I knew better than to ask Vincent why he didn't write a check for the full amount. To avoid a paper trail the IRS could track, he only dealt in cash. To avoid his anger, I didn't question why he felt so strongly about this. I favored rendering unto Caesar what was Caesar's. It was easier. Moreover, telling the truth meant you didn't have to worry about matching up your lies. Besides, we lived way below any level of income that the IRS would care to investigate. However, Vincent disdained big government—repudiated it as though it could steal his soul. When we married, he didn't want me to take his name for that reason. Initially, when Alex was born, he didn't want his son to bear his name either, though he later acquiesced. He was proud of his family and his name but dedicated himself to secrecy to avoid the government gathering information about him.

Looking at him preparing to go into the courtroom, I thought, "How far this high-security prison is from the hills of Oregon and the Willamette River." The whole event felt surreal. Added to the layer of absurdity was the fact that I was still hiding Vincent's violent outbursts from Edith and Father Clancy, the very people there to help him get out of jail. Until his imprisonment, I thought I had successfully hidden this problem from everyone.

Instead of my bruises, the face I showed the world was that I loved Alex and my husband; I enjoyed my friends at church and at school; and I was doing my best working full-time at the high school and teaching at the university. With the energy of youth, I also attended Alliance Française meetings, driving into Birmingham on occasion when Vincent could watch Alex. At one of these gatherings, the department director for French at the University of Alabama, Birmingham asked me to apply for the tenure-track position at their downtown campus. I was grateful for the offer as it confirmed my own desire to teach at university full-time and return to research.

However, thinking it through, I decided, "If I can get a tenure-track offer in Birmingham with only a master's degree, imagine what I could do with a PhD? I could teach university pretty much anywhere, and that would please Vincent." I knew he didn't want to stay in Alabama. A tenure-track job for me in Birmingham wouldn't put a smile on his face, therefore it couldn't be the right choice for our family. So, I set my sights on a doctorate. To prepare for it, I enrolled in two courses at the University of Alabama in Tuscaloosa: intensive Latin and French literature. The Spanish teacher at my high school, who was also attending summer classes there, offered to carpool with me from Birmingham. Saving money on gas sounded like a good idea. Besides, I wouldn't mind the collegial companionship.

These cheery plans coalesced while Vincent was contained in jail. But as I contemplated his release, I worried that his behavior could jeopardize my academic performance. Vincent's imprisonment had provided me with the respite and luxury of feeling safe. I nonetheless pushed aside the thought that this wouldn't last once he was out of jail. Instead, I prayed constantly about my decision to return to school and hoped that Vincent would be able to accept it when he would be released from prison. I fervently hoped God would work a miracle.

When it was time for the proceedings, Vincent left to join his attorney. Edith, Father Clancy, and I entered the courtroom and sat upon benches that resembled church pews. Vincent sat down with his attorney near the judge.

The prosecuting attorney said, "Your Honor, permission to identify Exhibit A."

"Granted"

"Mr. Buckley, is this your pistol?"

"Yes."

"Is it true that on the night of . . ."

My heart had stopped. I was unaware that Vincent owned a pistol. ". . . this was in your glove compartment?"

WHAT? I thought to myself. This cannot be happening. My ragdoll self, worried sick over poor Vincent, gained a backbone of steel as I learned in the courtroom that Vincent had used a gun to threaten the young, cherub-faced tow-truck driver when he insisted the tow cost $125.00.

There was a pause in the proceedings. We had to exit and remain in an isolated room, out of earshot from the rest of the hearing. I was stunned by what I'd just learned.

A bailiff came to call Father O'Hara to testify. Edith and I waited for his return. When he did, the three of us waited for the verdict.

Next, Vincent entered the room and said his attorney had negotiated a plea bargain. If he admitted to having committed a felony (threatening assault with a deadly weapon), he would be released with one year of probation. Father O'Hara's character testimony had made this outcome possible. Vincent was aggravated that the government would be able to pin the label of felon upon him, yet pursuing litigation not only posed the risk of having a felony charge, but also serious jail time and a fine.

Emboldened that he would not hit me in these circumstances, I dared to express my opinion. "Why not take the plea bargain?" I said to him. "But I will support whatever decision you think best."

I feared he would blame me somehow for his felony charge down the road. That would surely result in a violent outburst. Besides, I wanted to be a loyal wife. I wanted to believe in the innocence of my man, despite Exhibit A, an object that hitherto I had no idea he possessed, never mind threatened to use.

His plea bargain accepted, Vincent was released on probation in his street clothes. Edith, her generous bail collateral never called upon, drove Father Clancy back. I was too stunned by what I'd just learned to wonder how their conversation went. I drove Vincent home in his car now released from impoundment. As we drove, he complained about not getting his gun back. Inwardly, I resisted taking his side in the matter, yet said nothing. We picked up Alex from daycare. Vincent thought his verdict was a gross injustice on the part of Big Brother government. Still stunned by the existence of the gun and the threat made to the tow-truck driver, I remained silent and numb to his commentary and hoped he would not turn his frustration toward me. I felt a new trepidation alone with Vincent. That he was capable of threatening someone with a weapon unnerved me. Yet I felt a renewed sense of purpose to fulfill my academic calling. The appeal was not exclusively vocational, to better support my family, but also held intellectual appeal and beckoned to my soul.

In high school, I'd read Sartre's *Being and Nothingness* during a family beach holiday. This book had planted a seed of determination within me. As a gangly teenager, I decided that existentialism was the way to go. Every moment we face death, therefore each act we commit must be deliberate, the result of personal conviction, as though it would be our final gesture and historic legacy. I called upon this determination to defy my fear and crawl under the sheets next to Vincent that night.

I continued to pray. Yet something had ruptured between Vincent and me. Now I knew he could—and had—lied to me. He'd threatened the life of another and could do so again. He resumed work at the plant as though nothing had happened. The chronic gaps in his paychecks continued apace as my two jobs supported us.

Vincent was humiliated when he discovered that reporting to the probation officer also meant he had to submit to drug tests. The Russian aristocrat with monogrammed shirts and real cufflinks found himself with drug dealers, thieves, and other assailants dressed in jeans and high-top sneakers talking jive in the grimy probation office waiting room. Those days I made a point of being extra careful not to cross him. Yet, after visiting his probation officer, he seemed to return home more subdued, which made me feel safer with him.

It still hadn't occurred to me to tell anyone about his violent behavior with me. I remained baffled that he was capable of such a thorough personality change when he his random rages occurred. I yearned for the amiable, Jekyll side of his nature to remain in charge. I interpreted his shift in character, from mild to furious, as a sort of possession or spiritual transformation, so completely did it overtake him. Spiritual unrest was not the realm of reason, but one of faith. I was sure that if my prayers were earnest enough, divine intervention would change the spirit world around us and make our home safe, trusting and loving. I may not have trusted Vincent, yet I absolutely trusted God.

As summer arrived, I immersed myself in my university courses in Tuscaloosa, excited to prepare for my doctoral studies in the fall. I received a full scholarship, a stipend, and insurance to support the family. As planned, I met with Señor Reeves, the Spanish teacher in the class next to mine at the high school and we shared the commute expenses. He drove a little VW Rabbit whose horn was so weak it seemed to bleat, "'Scuse please!" when activated. We would laugh over its feeble voice, but at home, when I faced Vincent's wrath, I felt just as ridiculously miniscule as that wee horn against an oncoming semi.

Still, I told no one about my precarious home life. I was sure that within Vincent smoldered a brilliant soul that just needed an outlet to prove itself, to innovate freely, work, and deliver. He was an engineer to the bone. The most finicky mechanical problems could not withstand his scrutiny for he would labor over them until they succumbed to his bidding. He had no off switch when it came to mechanical puzzles. He would work until he solved the problem, no matter how late the hour or how belated his supper.

I felt this was God's gift to him, this uncanny drive, persistence, and ingenuity to fix machines, motors, and gadgets of all sorts. For him, the mechanical world had rules that made sense, while emotional bias corrupted the human world. Seeing his potential, I endured his ongoing rages and abuse. He did not harm Alex as an infant; it was me he came after when angry. My adrenaline flowing, I would corral my fear and churn the derived energy into my own version of stoic productivity.

Pursuing my doctorate to one day support my family, I was in my element at the university, chatting with colleagues and professors, digging through bibliographies like an archaeologist, and devouring scholarship with the gusto of a farmhand at breakfast. Safe within the ivory tower, I was free to speak my mind fearlessly. At home, the smallest of household decisions took on the delicacy of a hostage negotiation. So when Vincent agreed to move to Tuscaloosa, still within commuting distance of his work, it was an answer to desperate prayers. I would have a full course load in addition to my teaching, which was supporting us, so being near campus was essential to integrate work and family time.

We found a small ranch house to rent near the VA hospital that had a golf course and a trail around the grounds where I could walk Alex in the stroller. I researched daycares and found a suitable one nearby. We moved without company help, packing and loading our office, clothing, dishes, art, and toddler paraphernalia into boxes ourselves. The garage still teemed with towers of packed boxes that had remained untouched. We hauled them with us too.

The new house had a carport, but no garage, so the box towers moved into the house with us. Vincent wanted to keep them out of the Alabama heat and humidity. What was in all the boxes? Remains from Dataway: cables, computer pieces, tools. Vincent's collections of antique tube lights. All manner of oddments he collected crow-like in his mania for everything retro. Like the ring to Gollum, Vincent's possessions possessed him. He scrutinized their well-being more than he noticed the human creatures around him. I hid the ubiquitous cardboard brown beneath scraps of Indic cloth—sari silks in bright patterns. They fluttered softly over the box towers like fragile butterflies sunning atop sturdy monoliths.

School was in full swing soon after we moved. At the same time, Vincent's paychecks dwindled until they didn't appear at all. He applied for and received unemployment compensation. It was not vast, but it helped. After a few months, he also began queuing up for food stamps at deep cost to his self-esteem. We managed to pay for childcare, rent, and food on this, my stipend, and some small student loans. I saw it all as God's grace.

The house we left behind in Gardendale was bigger and more amply furnished than the one we rented in Tuscaloosa. We no longer had dressers or nightstands and lived out of the moving boxes. Vincent lined the walls of every room except the kitchen with teetering towers of them. Between the cardboard columns, he left narrow passages for foot traffic, like between the couch and the boxes that held the VCR. A now old-fashioned square CRT computer monitor sat atop the VCR for a screen. On occasion at night, we might watch a movie on the CRT screen. Then, the world would fall away while we spent some ninety minutes in a story.

Our rental house was just this side of a mobile home. It had a cinder-block foundation, a kitchen without a fridge, and a bathroom with a tub. A large grille on the floor outside the bathroom was the intake for air conditioning—crucial to survive the Alabama summer. Vincent and I slept upon a mattress on the floor between boxes in one bedroom. The other bedroom served as our joint office and contained desks, a printer, office supplies, and desktop computers. Alex's crib was in the living room.

Vincent found an abandoned refrigerator at the dump and brought it home. He often made forays to dumps for car parts and would bring home other treasures like a real potter's wheel and a kiln, both of which took up residence in the carport.

Neither of us used the wheel or kiln, yet Vincent smiled when he spoke of their potential, imagining a life of leisure and art instead of unemployment lines and food stamps. He repaired the wheel and kiln until they worked as designed. Their place among his other scrapyard finds beneath the carport was totemic. They held the same promise as Christmas ornaments in an attic box—at once a holiday memory and a hope of respite from the whirl of surviving.

I found curtains at a thrift store to hang over the windows facing the street. Vincent manhandled the fridge into place in the kitchen. The kitties explored their new home. They settled in atop the sari throws, perching themselves high on various box towers, or nestled into the Goodwill couch. I was grateful we lived close to campus, where I needed to put in long hours in class studying and teaching.

On a typical day, my alarm would go off at five. I would be out the door by six, leaving a sleeping Vincent and Alex. Evenings, I would pick up Alex from daycare and head home. There, Vincent or I would make ramen noodle and hotdog soup for supper. We were in our mid-thirties and living, I thought, a classic married-graduate-student lifestyle.

At two or three some mornings, "Wahhhhhhhhrrr! Wahhhhhhr! Wahhhhhhhrrr!" would reverberate through the house followed by high-pitched squeals. Toddler Alex had night terrors. It terrified me the first time I heard him. I ran to hold him, yet he seemed oblivious. He was yelling at the top of his lungs while in deep sleep. I wanted to walk him as I did when he had colic. Vincent slapped him across the face to wake him up. After that, at the first peep from Alex, I would rush to him, try to gently wake him, rock, and walk him until he fell back asleep. Then I'd tuck him back into his crib.

To exercise while entertaining Alex, I popped him into the stroller and jogged laps around the VA hospital. As he grew, I took him on woodland walks and to the park to swing and play on the jungle gym, teeter-totter, and springy hobbyhorses. Now with a full set of teeth, his gleaming smile and cherubic cheeks made my heart sing as the lazy Alabama sun brightened his hair into a golden halo. He was my beamish boy and always ready for adventure.

The first full-fledged word he ever spoke was *voiture!* (car) because I often spoke to him in French. I laughed with some remorse that a chugging, motorized vehicle, rather than, say, "Momma" or "Dada," would be his first word. Yet cars were Vincent's obsession too. Like his father before him, he was devoted to vintage Cadillacs.

Returning home from a sunny stroll one afternoon, filled with satisfaction from classes taught and taken and an outing with Alex, we two burst through the front door into the house dark with boxes. We called out to greet "Dada!"

Vincent had his back to us. He quickly whirled around hunched over; I thought he was going to initiate a game with Alex until I saw his face was twisted into a sneer of hatred and disdain. "You Goddamn bitch! You whore! You don't deserve to live!"

The fury of his profanity blew into a raging storm cloud that grew with each insult. It accumulated enough velocity to blow the roof right off our little house. I was sure the neighbors for blocks around could hear his bellows. In a rampage, he went for my holy books, words of inspiration I had from Father, and ripped them apart.

Next, he lunged toward me. I knew that icy look in his eyes meant no mercy. I hid my face from his fists, ran to the office, and locked the door just before he arrived behind me. As he slammed into the door, it bulged in from the hinges. I prayed they and the flimsy doorknob lock would hold, hoped his rage would blind him to picking the lock. This time, a new phrase entered the volley of his derisive lexicon: "I'll kill you!" he said.

I was familiar with him saying I did not deserve to live, but he'd never before offered to exterminate me on behalf of the demons in his universe.

"I'll kill you, you fucking bitch!" he said. "I have a gun! It's here in the grate! I'm getting it out!"

The door pounding paused. I could hear Vincent shuffling through his tools for a screwdriver. The ventilation intake grille, with a gun, evidently, beneath it, was just outside the door. I prayed for a miracle and wondered how to escape with Alex, who was still belted into his stroller and now crying. Hearing the metallic squeak of the screwdriver loosening screws, I opened the bedroom door, dodged past Vincent, grabbed the stroller with Alex, careened out the front door pushing the stroller, and ran toward the VA hospital.

In public, with nearly a mile between home and us, I slowed to a walk. Exhausted from crying and lulled by the movement of the stroller, Alex slept, his head tilted to the side and his light blue overalls soft and dry. I pushed the stroller for over an hour while I decided what to do. He would need a diaper change at some point and food too.

"If I tell anybody about this, Vincent will literally kill me," I thought. As I kept pushing the stroller, we passed the house of one of the assistant professors in the department. Instead of confiding in her, I prayed she hadn't heard Vincent yelling from a block and a half away. I walked until exhausted. As the sun began to set, it was getting cold. Alex began to stir. I went home.

Vincent's car was gone. I changed Alex and fed him. When Vincent returned, he brought home two Little Caesar pizzas. We ate and watched *The Deer Hunter* as Alex dozed between us. At the end, I put Alex to bed. Vincent and I retired to bed as though nothing had happened.

When I look back on that time now, it floats in a hazy cloud of fear and faith. I relied on God alone as though facing death each day, which sometimes I was. With danger acute and unpredictable, few were the moments in the day when I was not in active or subliminal prayer. I kept Vincent's outbursts secret for fear of his reaction if I told anyone. I coped by defining the situation as temporary, like a bad dream. I watched myself live my life and coped with mortal fear the way I had learned to transcend pain as a child.

I knew God was aware of my situation. My portion of responsibility was to cling to the principles of true love and persevere. I was confident that God would intervene, if not today, then tomorrow; if not tomorrow, the next day. Despite the danger and illogic of staying in my marriage, I believed that divine love could overcome any obstacle. I knew I couldn't control Vincent. But I could control myself.

For the sake of Alex, God, and Vincent, I wanted to be a good wife and mother. I focused on keeping God first in my heart. I wanted to stay true to my mission and calling, which I felt was to find and reveal the divine in literature. I was sure that if I did these things, and fulfilled my portion of responsibility, then God would take care of the rest. Only God, I felt, could help Vincent find peace and love in his heart again.

I lived through literature. To survive my emotional isolation, I tried to place my surrealistic life within the proper story. I wondered if I had Evgeny Onegin syndrome. Neither Anna Karenina nor Madame Bovary, but Tanya would be my model. Poor Anna besotted with Vronsky. I was not her. Nor, I reasoned, was I Emma Bovary, seeking some quick fix from Rodolphe for a difficult situation.

Vincent and I shared the same values, I thought. I felt Tanya's passion for Onegin and later suspected Vincent had Onegin's casual disdain for me. He would play the Russian aristocrat to my barbaric ignorance of his family's prestige, fortune, and enduring legend in Oregon. Yet I did not care about his family's would-be status. I only cared for my studies, for Alex, for loving in the here and now, for what we could create for the future, not for what had been in the past.

With determined optimism, I continued to justify his behavior. I imagined it due to some failure on my part; or, that his rage resulted from some mysterious circumstance that would pass. I saw his violence as something temporal and worldly that divine love alone could overcome.

One night I had a dream where I appeared before Father Moon, who was sitting on a throne in an auditorium. We were alone. I didn't speak; I approached and stood before him, glad to be near him. It was as though he'd read my Akashic record and knew everything. He looked at me tenderly: the trappings of the throne did not divide us—he could have been on a wooden bench. In his gruff and gravelly Korean accent, he said, "Go! Pray with the women!" and gestured flicking the back of his hand toward the rear of the room to dismiss me.

It didn't feel like banishment, but a direction given with love. So warm was his look into my eyes, I knew that had I kept standing there, he would not have been able to suppress his tears. He knew everything I'd been through. I bowed, went to the back of the auditorium, and parted a black velvet curtain that was there. It opened unto a bright, sunny meadow that smelled of fresh earth and new grass. The sun made me squint as the light warmed my eyes. I heard birdsong and saw before me a green hillock dotted with daisies, and on the grass sat a circle of sisters with Mother Moon in a pink *hanbok*—a traditional Korean dress.

Before venturing outside with them, I looked back into the auditorium at Father. I saw that Vincent now stood humbly before him, his head downcast. Father was blasting Vincent with a volley of guttural Korean syllables. Vincent looked down as the words fell upon him. Father's hands were open and swept up and down, left and right, his gestures aligning the spirit world. Before Father caught my eye looking back, I ducked past the curtain and walked outside into the clearing to sit by Mother. I didn't want Father to scold me for peeking at his private audience with Vincent. Yet I knew he'd felt my gaze upon him and I was secretly glad.

Peaceful calm surrounded me with the women, yet I knew battles remained to fight. I felt called to be not just Father's daughter, but his ally. At the same moment, I understood that Vincent's anger was beyond my control, that it would take someone bigger than me to help him and that spiritually, Father could do what I alone could not. This dream would give me courage for years to come to cope with challenges I could not yet imagine. It showed me that there was a limit to my responsibility and that big problems require help.

The French Department in Tuscaloosa was tight-knit with several native speakers among the graduate students, in addition to the faculty. Perhaps the less-academic surrounding area made our little university enclave that much closer. Moreover, I felt a kindred spirit in my advisor, Greg de Rocher. Like me, he had attended seminary and, furthermore, he'd studied for the priesthood before marrying a French woman. He understood Rabelais from the inside out, like me, from a faith perspective of an unconventional theistic peregrination.

Though American, besides speaking impeccable French, Prof. de Rocher had been recognized by French scholars for his research on humor as it related to Rabelais. They had given him an actual medal, which he showed to me during his office hours one afternoon. It dangled heavy with aplomb from a blue satin ribbon, an impressive thing, bigger than an Olympic medallion, and justifiably so given the magnificence of the honor. Not only did de Rocher understand Rabelais—the greatest writer of French civilization, if not the Western world—he understood Rabelais' heart, making him the perfect advisor for me.

Come spring, the university decided to outfit the football team but cut funding to sissy graduate studies like Romance languages. We began counting down the days for an announcement confirming the death of our program. Some graduate students were willing to chance a last-minute turnaround—not me. Not with the ticking time bomb I had at home. I had to be sure to have income to support the family.

I applied to programs with application deadlines later in the year: in Boulder at the University of Colorado, another at Rutgers, which had a Renaissance scholar my advisor highly recommended. Both universities responded with teaching opportunities, paid tuition, and stipends. Rutgers offered me a better stipend and insurance package besides having a renowned Rabelais scholar, so I accepted their offer and told my UA mentor of my decision. He wept as only a fellow Rabelaisian surrounded by the cultural incoherence of everything outside literature could. In a farewell note to him, I recalled Gargantua's laughter and tears at the birth of his son and the death of his wife, for my advisor had a heart full of Pantagruelism and I knew he wished me well on my journey. Neither he nor anyone else knew of the bruises I'd hidden beneath the bulky sweaters I wore year-round.

Terror and unpredictable circumstances at home had driven me to focused intensity at the university. There, I relished being in a world without fear, with comforting deadlines and clear definitions of what I needed to do to fulfill my responsibility as a student and teacher. At home, there was no way of knowing when I had done enough to earn respect, or at least enough to be spared violence.

But I stubbornly clung to my theory that Vincent's outbursts were due to a series of bad breaks. In rapid succession, he'd lost his company, his dream job at the plant fell apart, and then there was the loss of status from being on welfare. Inspired to leave Alabama for Rutgers, I was sure the move north would provide both of us with more opportunities for success. I bought a copy of the *New York Times* and gave it to Vincent, hoping he'd read the Want Ads and see for himself how much his skills were in demand. He never managed to look inside the paper, which I thought was odd. I didn't dare question his lack of interest—he had to do things on his own terms.

The stress of Vincent's unpredictable rages, combined with the demands of teaching and graduate school, put me on an unintentional, semi-anorexic diet of tension, coffee, and scant food: a sausage biscuit at dawn, a diet coke for lunch, and peanut butter or Ramen noodles and hot dog for supper. By the time I arrived at Rutgers, I had not only lost all the pregnancy weight, but was down to ninety-five pounds—not enough for my five-foot, four-inch frame. Alex was well fed at daycare. I still supplemented his all-natural baby food with soy formula. Vincent seemed to live on air and anger.

It was a godsend that the preparations for moving preoccupied him with concrete objectives. His own demons seemed to let him alone when he worked. He spent hours under the shade of a live oak, working on the cars to ready them for our upcoming journey; he welded a hitch to tow a flatbed with his car and fixed the interior clock on the dashboard of mine. The former entailed multiple trips to the dump to acquire the flatbed and rig it out. The latter project roused his passion, for it involved restoring the vehicle to its original condition. He had to remove the entire dashboard—a day's labor in itself—to replace the clock's tiny ticking mechanism, an exercise in perseverance to attain perfection.

With Vincent busy preparing and packing with his elaborate precision, I was free to work. I took summer employment evaluating freshmen to place them in the appropriate French classes at orientation and judging a high school French contest. On the side, I tutored undergraduate students from home. One day, one of my students visited me to discuss her final grade in my course. Looking around the boxes strewn with fabric and the dearth of furnishings, she offered helpfully, "I could pay you well if you change my grade. No one would know."

A sense of parental calm settled over me and I had to hold back a smile. "No," I said firmly, "I would know," and escorted her to the door.

Somehow, no matter how many arrows of misfortune came my way, I felt God's love shield me. Even when Vincent raged, Alex wailed, the car sputtered on the brink of failure, and mountains of student work awaited grading, I felt that God knew my situation and loved me. I knew His suffering was worse than any I might experience.

My prayer life, driven by acute circumstances, delivered me from the shadow of death on a regular basis. It was an intense way to live and probably not good for the adrenal system. However, at the time, my faith and experience of spiritual presence overrode the logical terror I could feel. In its stead, I felt an embrace of supernatural peace. I was sure I could embrace Alex in that same peace and keep him from harm. I couldn't predict Vincent's temper, the weather, or where I would next find money to keep us afloat. Yet I felt certain that with prayer and effort, I could take on any problem and, with God's grace, resolve it.

— CHAPTER NINE —
NEW JERSEY

Driving north to New Brunswick, in the middle of the night, my engine malfunctioned along a pass in the Blue Ridge Mountains. The breakdown seemed an omen of things to come. We had traveled a long way from the innocence of Alex's conception, through my teaching in Birmingham, and the past two years of graduate school in Tuscaloosa. My delight in being immersed in academic life and caring for Alex was as beautiful as the mountain scenery—and like that scenery, invisible in the dark. What was going on at home was bound to inhibit my journey. I was tuckered out from moving, long-distance driving, and navigating around Vincent's moods. The breakdown offered a welcome excuse to stop.

As Vincent and I caravanned, we communicated by walkie-talkie. We switched off having Alex or the kitties as passengers. "Vincent, my check engine light is on. There's a funny noise from under the hood. Over."

I felt safe because he was in a different car. Besides, he would believe the check engine lights more than me. He asked me a couple of questions, and I followed his car as he exited the highway and pulled into a repair shop near the exit ramp. It was, of course, closed.

My twenty-plus-year-old Caddy sputtered to a stop. It refused to revive, forcing us to await morning for a mechanic to fix it. God's grace, I thought. Sleep-deprived, I was ready to nod off behind the wheel. My body ached with fatigue. Had the car not malfunctioned, Vincent would have pressed on, challenging me to continue. To my surprise, he did not blow up at me. His equanimity given this setback validated my hope that our move north was already proving successful.

We arranged kitties and Alex in Vincent's car. Nearby, through the dark, the word "Motel" blazed in red neon. Vincent drove us there—just past a McDonald's. While he checked us in, I fed Alex a Happy Meal then played with him as he darted and slid through the toddler-sized gerbil tunnels. The next morning, once the car was fixed, we continued our caravan to New Brunswick.

Vincent's good mood seemed to be holding and all felt right with the world.

Preparing for our move north, I had already researched childcare opportunities for Alex. I was excited to be studying in a strong program and looked forward to my classes. Vincent would have a fresh start—New Jersey and all of New York City were accessible to find work. Remembering the endless want ads for computer technicians listed in the *New York Times*, he was certain to find employment in his field. New surroundings would transform his steely resentment and icy anger into joy; I was sure of it: it was already happening.

The Alabama landscape would never let him forget standing in line for food stamps, his time in jail, his dashed hopes of making his fortune at the plant, and the loss of face after an entire year of submitting himself to regular visits with his probation officer. His frustration and anger for the past two years we had spent in Tuscaloosa confirmed for me that Alabama was the problem. I believed that up North, he could reinvent and rediscover himself however he desired. He could resume his persona as a member of the Russian gentry and tech wizard. We'd paid our dues and happiness awaited. As we crossed the state line into New Jersey, I felt we were entering the Promised Land.

Our little caravan, my gray boat of a Sedan de Ville and Vincent's white Caddy coupe pulling the flatbed loaded with the kiln, the potter's wheel, a rocking chair, and endless boxes under a tarp, chugged onto the Rutgers, New Brunswick campus. We would find a place to rent after I got my class schedule. The sun rested low in the late-afternoon sky, its light softer than in Alabama. We wended our way behind a quad, where we found a shady place to park by a white-spired chapel. Beyond it sat the undergraduate library in solid red brick, to the left, green soccer fields stretched beneath a low stone wall.

I unbuckled Alex from his car seat to play, leaving him under Vincent's watch. Then, I traversed the oak-lined quad to the Ruth Adams Building to retrieve my employment and registration papers from the French Department. When I returned, Alex was playing alone in the quad. He cheerily greeted me, "Look Mama! Look!" showing me his treasures—rocks, acorns, and acorn hats.

I saw that Vincent had not moved from his position behind the steering wheel. He was keeping an eye on Alex through the rearview mirror. I no longer thought it strange that he would let Alex play on his own. Had I questioned Vincent, it would only arouse his fury and insistence that he had everything under control. I strolled over to Alex, who had dashed off to hunt for more treasures. He toddled with merry insouciance under the oaks, collecting more acorns, his diaper wiggling as he gadded about barefoot. He was always my nature boy.

I took Alex's hand and we returned to the car where Vincent sat immobile, staring straight ahead over the steering wheel. He hadn't moved since we'd arrived—not even while Alex and I frolicked on the sun-dappled grass. Eyes riveted forward, without looking at me, he said flatly, "I can't stay here. I'm going to Oregon."

My mind went numb. I felt the blood drain from my face. I managed to project a smile to Alex as he brought me another acorn hat. I knew better than to question Vincent, but my brain could not process this last-minute change in plans. Like a person drowning, I relived our lives for the past year, running through all the events leading up to our long-awaited departure from Alabama.

I reviewed all his gestures and statements—they all seemed to point toward his eagerness to leave Alabama. The hours he'd spent hunched over the cars in the driveway, fixing every knob, glitch, and quirk in our vintage vehicles. Surely, his punctilious preparation was a sign of his readiness to leave. Why, he'd been so busy, he had not had time to look at the *New York Times* ads. Then, my heart stopped. It was not that he'd lacked the time—he lacked the desire. He never intended to move to New Jersey yet hadn't told me so.

Slowly, I registered that he'd planned to go back to Oregon all along. Vincent's probation period was over. He was free. And he wanted to lick his wounds in the comfort of his childhood home. I watched my visions for our fresh start, like so many fragile bubbles, pop and vanish: our new home, Alex's new daycare, Vincent's new job, our happy home life, my workshops, classes, students, research . . .

The contract I had just signed flapped against my hand in the breeze, along with the tissue-thin copy of my class schedule. This was real. Not a bubble. I had income and insurance for the family. It would be expensive, but I could tutor besides attending classes and teaching. Alex and I could settle here while Vincent went to Oregon for a visit, I reasoned.

Vincent said, "We don't have money for childcare. Besides, I don't want Alex in daycare." He was adamant about that. "Rita," he said—his mother, whom he always called by her first name—"can take care of Alex." He added, "I have friends in Beaverton and can find work. I have to go home. Come to Corbett with us."

Alex! My heart pounded. I couldn't bear to be apart from him. Yet Corbett seemed bereft of opportunity for me. It was a small town outside Portland. Isolated in the countryside, I would have no means to support our family out there. Nor did Vincent have a job contract like I did. In New Jersey, I countered, I could find childcare and keep Alex with me. But Vincent preferred that a family member help raise him. His mother was capable, willing, and above all, free of charge.

I thought I'd left behind the problems of Alabama. But hearing the steeliness of Vincent's voice, I knew there was no crossing him. I feared him clobbering me within view of my new employers' window, right where we were supposed to start living our happily-ever-after.

Vincent's mother did love Alex. And I knew that in New Jersey my family time would be limited and my paycheck thin, too thin for the kind of daycare Vincent wanted me to provide. Yet my opportunity at Rutgers was precious, not only for me personally, but so I could better provide for our family and Alex's welfare in the long run.

Instead of looking for housing for us three, we followed Vincent's plan and found housing for one—me. Vincent would take Alex with him to Oregon, where his mother could babysit for us. By reviving his old consulting contacts, Vincent would find work. We would save money because Alex and Vincent could live at home with his parents and grandmother. When I had vacation time, I would commute to Oregon. Eventually, after saving up some money, perhaps Vincent and Alex could rejoin me in New Jersey.

Of course, Vincent presented this plan—a dramatic new direction to me—as if it were a fait accompli. I felt like the target of a knife-throwing demonstration. Each point was a knife that just missed my heart, my shoulder, and my head. Each one pinned me—trapped, I was unable to move without his approval.

Vincent offered me release if I would forego my studies, my life, my hope for the future, and return to Oregon with him and Alex. Here was a supreme test. The contract in one hand, my son playing under the oaks—my very heart incarnate. How could I bear to be apart from him? Closing the window against the storm in Cap d'Ail flashed in my mind. Then, I chose career over conception. Now, I seemed to be choosing my career over my son. Only this time, the storm that raged was my longing to be with Alex. Like many new mothers, I'd had the experience of a child calling out in a grocery store, not even my own, and my breasts spurting milk, turning the front of my T-shirt into a soggy mess. It was a visceral reaction, that maternal feeling.

Still, with absolute clarity, I felt a sense of mission, an undeniable calling to fulfill; I was sure of it. That calling was to be something more than an abused homemaker and mother. I knew in my bones that God needed something more from me and that I had to pursue higher studies to get there. My spiritual drive gained traction with the Principle as I strove to perceive my life not from its temporal perspective, but from an eternal one. I saw the sacrifice of being without Alex, no matter how painful, would be temporary. Perhaps having lived in France apart from my dad as a child made the proposition of temporary separation seem less extraordinary.

Nevertheless, it frustrated me that Vincent refused to stay in New Jersey. I had been the main breadwinner for years—not only for Boris, but also supporting Vincent and Alex. I'd given my word and held a signed a contract with my employer. My graduate teaching job not only paid for my schooling, but it was also our family's meal ticket and would cover Alex's insurance. Combined with student loans, I could keep our family off welfare. Although a woman, I was making decisions, some would say, like a man. I chose to assure my employment to take care of the family.

Yet even in public, Vincent terrified me and I was afraid to cross him; I feared for my life if I did. I remembered uniting with his wishes and foregoing my own about the kitten in Gardendale, the one that mewed in defiance of Vincent. My argument would fail if it came from me. *Deus ex machina*, the kitten could contradict Vincent—though I could not—and change his heart. God seemed to answer my prayers in these unlikely ways. Foregoing my own will could result in a happy surprise. I hoped for such divine intervention now, that my yielding could allow for the space and time for God to somehow change Vincent's mind.

Considering my problem in terms of the Divine Principle, if I sacrificed being with Alex for the short term, I reasoned, it would be as an offering, the way Abraham offered Isaac. It would not be without pain, but I hoped that in trusting God, He could bless my offering. Perhaps this exacted suffering could serve some higher purpose; a purpose of which I might at the moment be unaware. I absolutely trusted God, more than Rita, to protect Alex and I dared to hope God would soften Vincent's heart to bring him and Alex back to me in New Jersey.

I had to cling to my faith in divine love to pay the price of being apart from my son and remain without him at Rutgers; it was not a mere economic or intellectual choice. Yet I would have the unexpected consequence of relief from Vincent's violence. I still blamed myself for his outbursts. Living with him, I turned the other cheek, imagining each rage would be his last.

My love for Alex made me overlook his father's cruelty toward me. I saw in our son proof of God's love and remained convinced that God would resolve what then seemed to me incoherent violence inflicted out of the blue—as if it arose from mysterious and dark spiritual forces over which Vincent had no agency. I was still in denial and doggedly focused on making the right spiritual conditions for a positive outcome. I had absolute faith that if my prayers were strong enough, something would change. But as soon as the car pulled away without me—the black kitty and belongings in tow while I kept the fox-eared kitty for company— I felt the high cost of Vincent taking Alex.

Despite daily phone conversations with Alex, night after night, I could sleep only after my relentless, uncontrollable sobs of longing to be near my son exhausted themselves. I sent handwritten letters using markers and my best blocky, colorful penmanship. Illustrating the words with silly cartoons and photos, I hoped to encourage him to read. I concentrated on ways to keep Alex cheerful and thriving for his happiness assuaged my own sorrow as I dug into my studies and teaching.

CHAPTER TEN

A TREE FALLING IN THE FOREST

The French Department at Rutgers soon felt like family. A compassionate crew, many of my colleagues—grad students and professors alike—had children, and they understood the emotional demands of familial separation. One faculty member parented singlehandedly during the week until his spouse commuted by plane from her tenure track position in Florida for long weekends. Everyone recognized the kind of sacrifice graduate school demanded and that geographical proximity did not determine the power of love.

Due to all the offspring, whenever there was a departmental party or lengthy meeting, the French Department provided babysitters and child-centered events like pumpkin painting, Disney movies, food, and games. These reminders stirred to overwhelming my already poignant desire to be with my son. But I couldn't allow myself to miss Alex at work. It was like fasting when serving food to others—I dialed down my own emotions to focus on the happiness of others.

The professors were as brilliant as they were affable, and I flourished in this intellectual environment. Liberated from Vincent's daily outbursts, I made friends with my colleagues. Though I missed Alex fiercely, I knew from past conversations with Vincent's mother, Rita, that she loved him and, with her husband's backing, she could handle her own son too. I was confident that she, not Vincent alone, was the one tending Alex, so I felt he was safe.

Taking prayer walks, I combined exercise and spirituality. To this I added Taekwondo practice. My class instructor, Master Choi, was Korean. The *dojang* felt comforting, safe, predictable, and homey. Upon entering, we left our shoes at the door, bowed, and honored the wisdom and discipline of our elders. Practicing mind-body unity, I felt an internal bond with my fellow students. We shared the common suffering of sweat and sit-ups as we strove to harness within ourselves to a higher power to challenge our physical limitations.

Despite my studies, friends, and Taekwondo, I eagerly anticipated the prolonged Christmas holiday as a chance to reconnect with Alex. Each day, Vincent would put me on the phone with our growing toddler. Yet I felt Alex struggled to stay interested in my disembodied voice. After grading final exams, I flew back to Oregon, excited to rejoin my little family. I couldn't wait for a hug. However, as soon as I arrived, I felt a new sense of alienation.

In my absence, Vincent and his mother had created their own routines with Alex. Their ways of raising him didn't include me. I was an outsider looking at *their* family unit, which was centered on *my* little boy.

Rita told me how Alex had continually walked around the house the first few months crying, "Mama! Mama!"

I believed that her intention in telling me this was to confirm that Alex had missed me too. Yet I also sensed that she, a homemaker of the WWII generation, wondered how I could put career before family life. And like many a daughter-in-law, I couldn't help but feel that she disapproved of my mothering skills. Still, I was grateful for the love and support she gave to Alex in my absence. Had she not been there to help tend him, I never could have let Alex leave with Vincent. I thought God had provided the means for us to endure the challenge of separation.

I had to adjust to understand Vincent and Rita's routines with Alex and reacquaint myself with my son. My little nature boy had grown. I watched him dart outside, his thick, golden hair tousled like wild hay as he ran with long strides and swooped up a tree as if returning to his native habitat. He was growing quickly and becoming attached to Oregon. Yet, his ease being there was due to more than familiarity with the people and places he frequented.

Rita had found new purpose and meaning in her own life with Alex. She was not only babysitting in my absence but enthralled to make Oregon Alex's home rather than encouraging him to invest his heart in his absent mother. However, my tacit understanding with Vincent remained: he and Alex would join me in New Jersey, eventually, when Vincent had saved up some money.

Vincent's mother had found a new source of entertainment, prestige, and love in Alex as her grandson. She now had a reason to visit neighbors with children. She connected with younger mothers at the local daycare. Her life, it seemed, revolved around Alex. Before his arrival, her world had been much smaller, as she was the primary caregiver for her mother, who lived with them and had Alzheimer's.

Before her mother's decline, Rita was involved in her community of extended family and neighbors. She used to throw parties and play piano at the concert level—her repertoire encompassing the likes of Rachmaninoff. She'd taught piano and taken classes herself in oil painting and Spanish. Alex renewed her hope not only that the family name would continue, but that her status as a grandmother was assured within the clan. Besides, she loved doting on him and spoiling him with toys and expensive toddler togs.

On Christmas Eve, in Russian tradition, we set forth by car to make the rounds of all the extended family. Vincent, Alex, and I sat in the back seat. Vincent's father took the wheel and "Grandma," as Alex called her, sat in the front passenger seat. We made small talk. I leaned my head against the cool glass of the rain-streaked car window, watching hazy streetlights approach and recede as we drove through the storm into downtown Portland. I noted the mustard yellow of a streetlight and Vincent, at odds with the festive occasion said, "No! It's red!"

Thinking it a minor difference of opinion and seeing no other light in the vicinity, I said, "I really think it looks yellow."

Vincent's fist suddenly met my right eye, clunking the other side of my head against the car window. Alex, who was between us, began crying. I leaned over him, trying to protect him and my face from further punches as Vincent snarled through clenched teeth, "You stupid bitch!" and punched my back as I scrambled to undo seatbelts and change places with Alex. I managed to put him by the window in a seatbelt, leaving me in the middle to take the punches while trying to protect both Alex and my face.

Vincent's mother yelled, "Vincent! What's gotten into you?"

His father kept driving through the rainstorm, past the hazy lights, until he could find a place to pull over. Leaning in the dark over Alex, my head pounding, I heard the car tires slow on gravel and the distant sound of Vincent's father telling him to stop. He did. As the car pulled off the gravel and back onto the road, I slowly raised up my head to peer out the window.

With each beat of my heart, I felt my head pound, yet I wanted to divert Alex from what had just happened inside the car. I had to think up a game that allowed me not to look at Vincent. Looking out the window, I remembered how I would encourage Alex on our woodland walks by giving him a goal to run toward, like the next mushroom, or the next tree stump. I searched in the night for some identifiable object outside the car and said cheerfully, "What do you see beyond that tree, Alex?"

"A house!"

"That's right! What do you see in the parking lot?"

"A truck!"

We arrived at the cousin's house near Reed College. Vincent grabbed Alex by the hand to escort him in. Vincent and his father waltzed through the door smiling as though they had entered a Currier and Ives Christmas Eve lithograph. From the street, I could see through the open door an enormous fir tree sparkling with real candles. Beneath its great boughs laden with ornaments rose piles of gifts in Victortian wrapping paper and topped with fantastic bows. As I approached the door, I made out gaily dressed relatives, coiffed in high style. I could hear them clink crystal glasses and burble over Alex. Having walked from the car in the icy-cold, my rigid body, numb from the shock of the sudden attack, went limp. Without adrenaline to keep me resolved and focused, my knees went wobbly and tears fled my eyes to escape the disdain I felt from Vincent, my shame and physical pain. The relatives hushed as I entered the room. Out of the crowd, the hostess emerged—Vincent's divorced cousin. She whisked me into a side room. Her ample form was elegant and festive in a red velvet gown with a faux-emerald Christmas tree brooch. It sparkled on her bosom as she took a breath, steadying herself for this unwelcome surprise. She spoke with Vincent's mother out of my hearing, but soon a huge, clammy, red steak appeared for me to put on my eye. *Who will want to eat this after I use it?* I wondered at the extravagance—not only that a big, juicy steak was so conveniently available, but that I should use it on my face rather than some hungry person eat it.

In the next room, the party chatter had resumed. Through the door that rested ajar as the hostess and Grandma left, I saw Vincent back in character as the soft-spoken charmer, clinking glasses and showing off Alex while his father, slightly less jovial than usual, bypassed the eggnog to make his way straight for the hard liquor with Vincent's mother at his heels.

Outside the bedroom, where I pressed the cold steak against my eye, my pain did not exist. In their world, there was nothing awry. As soon as possible, I was expected to socialize around the tree with the cheerful countenance befitting such a holiday. After about fifteen minutes, the steak was growing warm. I went to the sink in the bathroom to wash the steak blood off my face. A mark remained around my eye. I tried to cover it by parting my hair on the side. Drawing a deep breath, I straightened my clothes, and then reentered their world. I forced a smile across my face, which continued to ache.

Driving back to his parents' house, Vincent did not apologize or even acknowledge what happened. When his mother asked whether he had been "on something," he launched into invectives as to my incompetence and impertinence. Vincent's father, still fired up on vodka, told his son, "Cut it out!" After putting Alex to bed upstairs, shouts exploded in the living room between Vincent and his folks. On my way down the spiral staircase, I paused, out of reach of Vincent's fists, while they had at it. When they were done, Vincent and I retired to his mother's bedroom, where we were to sleep. I shuddered in fear to sleep alongside him, yet I crawled in keeping as far to my side of the bed as I could. I feared reprisal if I didn't slip under the covers. I whimpered myself to the edge of sleep, praying for a cloak of silence and measured the length of his every breath until it calmed in the steady rise and fall of peaceful slumber.

For all social purposes, the next day, the incident was forgotten. So much alcohol was consumed, I was not sure if either of his parents could have remembered. Besides being fully cognizant of what had happened in the car, I found Vincent's rage publicly inscribed on my face. Yet, from Rita's determined cheerfulness and Vincent's nonchalance, I gathered that the incident had been dismissed and was not to be discussed. For Alex's sake, it was incumbent upon me to maintain Christmas cheer and let it go.

I was foreign both to Vincent's household and to his friends. Though I felt bound to Alex by flesh and blood, our love intrinsic, I was extrinsic—unessential—to the people that surrounded him. Alex was my life, but to those he lived with now, I was an accessory rather than a vital part of his world. I tried to overcome their attitude with logic. "It just takes time to adjust," I told myself.

Yet a nagging philosophical concern persisted, "If a tree falls in a forest and no one *acknowledges* hearing it, does it make a sound?" In this case, I was the one felled, unacknowledged. And I had no ally apart from God that I could talk to about it. *→ there are human allies in domestic violence clusters/shelters*

One afternoon, Rita invited me to accompany her to pick up Alex from a playdate she had arranged for him. She confided in me that her husband was also an engineer. She intimated, with a look deep from under her brows, that this explained everything. Engineers, she went on, were a type not known for their people skills. The woman whose son was playing with Alex, her spouse was an engineer too. It slowly dawned on me that this was all code for abusive behavior. Abuse that was taken for granted and accepted because that was what women did in exchange for being "kept" by powerful men.

Did she not know that I was the one who had supported the family? Was she unaware that I had married Vincent thinking he had only a condominium mortgage debt and a company going into bankruptcy to his name? Wordless and unable to respond, I looked at her as she drove; she had the same focus Vincent had on the road, chin bent down, eyes like laser beams set on forward. She'd confided in me. I was thus granted access to the mysteries of the inner sanctum of womanhood. What pestered me, though, was that these were not at all the terms by which I wanted to live my life. Nor were these the values I wanted Alex to absorb.

Days later, returning to Rutgers, I remained in denial about the physical abuse, despite my still-blackened eye. It was as if all that happened to someone in a movie—not to me. I kept the bruise hidden with my hair and gingerly put

→ How does the framework of our problem-solving apparatus shape possible solutions?

makeup over it until the soreness and purple faded away. I felt ashamed and at fault as though I had failed at the job of "wife." Rather than admit I was afraid that my husband would hurt me, I disassociated this fear from its logical cause—Vincent. Like a floppy spray of goose grass, once freed from one host, fear affixed itself wherever it could grab hold in other parts of my life. For instance, I feared losing my job at Rutgers if people knew about the physical abuse. The sticky tendrils of fear blinded my reason and made me think I was unworthy to teach if I had this sort of home life.

And so I fought an internal battle to corral my family life in one part of my brain, to disassociate myself from the pain of longing and betrayal I felt in order to prevent family concerns from interfering with my career. I knew women were often handicapped in ways men weren't when it came to professional evaluations of career potential and parenting. My circumstances left me with few choices. Locked in step preparing for my degree, I had little money or practical means to extract Alex from Oregon. I nurtured the fantasy that Vincent would change if he were happy and found work. Meanwhile, I threw myself into teaching, studying, and preparing for my doctoral exams.

Spring semester passed and I again boarded a plane for Oregon—this time, to live there for the summer. At once, I reveled at the thought of seeing Alex and worried over how I would navigate Vincent's fury. To counteract my fear, I summoned faith and hoped that perhaps he would no longer have a temper. "Live in the moment," I told myself. "People can change."

Vincent picked me up at the airport. The ride to his parents' house challenged my blissful hopes. I forced myself into a deeply prayerful trance not to panic. His driving, it seemed, had only become more reckless, or perhaps I was more aware of the risks he took. He drove like a test pilot trying to break the sound barrier. After activating his Fuzzbuster on the dash, he gripped the wheel, set his jaw, and launched the car forward at dizzying speeds, dodging and weaving between other vehicles with only a foot or so to spare. He relied fully on his own instinct and reflexes. To question the soundness of this logic was to risk the fury of his derision and abuse. As he instigated and avoided near-accident after near-accident, I could only pray.

While I was at Rutgers, Vincent's mother drove Alex back and forth to childcare and was his main caretaker. Once I arrived in Oregon, Vincent resumed more of a parenting role together with me. We soon moved from his parents' house in the country to a tract house Vincent owned in a suburb near Martin Luther King Boulevard, close to gas stations, machine shops, and other light industry. The neighborhood had its quirks, like the house next door where a broad assortment of cats lived—they slithered through the boarded-up windows unfazed by the partially caved-in roof. Other neighboring houses had car or motorcycle parts scattered across their front lawns, still others had roses that must have been tended by loving grannies.

The interior of Vincent's house was like a 1940s movie set—complete with old-fashioned cradle telephones; a Formica-and-aluminum kitchen table; a leather-tufted sofa with nail-head trim; a working railway potbelly stove; and a framed topographic map of an uninhabited island. I was surprised to learn that he owned a house. He'd bought it long before we ever met and before he'd first moved to North Carolina. He never rented it out because he didn't want strangers to disturb his space. I thought it curious that he hadn't mentioned something like owning a house and got the feeling that perhaps Vincent didn't tell me a lot of things.

He'd painted the walls and ceilings of his home in various shades of white. Strewn about in each room were white shag carpets—a nightmare décor for a busy family with a toddler and active indoor-outdoor kitties during mud season. In contrast to the 1940s theme, he'd installed a hot tub in the basement—the epitome of 1960s California mellowness and, in attitude, diametrically opposed to the severe cleaning regimens he maintained.

Our first day in the Portland house, Vincent initiated a cleaning project, combining chlorine and bleach to render the aged white shower tub spotless. The acrid chemical fumes burned as they shot through my nostrils and down my throat; it was like inhaling a blowtorch. I tied a kerchief to mask my nose to keep scrubbing. The room was stuffy and windowless. Without protecting his lungs, Vincent cleaned with relentless determination. I wondered if he used the pain from breathing the infernal air to spur his vigor.

The cause at hand—restoring a pristine white tub—overrode his own health and well-being, as well as anyone else's that got in the way of this goal. His fastidiousness was a kind of obsession. In his house, I learned to fear seeing the slightest speck of dirt fall to the floor. Fearing any possible trigger of Vincent's wrath, I maintained a state of strained, hypervigilance, aware of each wayward molecule Alex might distribute. Not only could I be a klutz, but I knew Alex could spill juice or cereal wherever he went. Living here required constant caution and navigational strategies.

To get us both safely out of the house for much of the day, I enrolled Alex in a French immersion pre-school to attend while I studied German at a local community college. When not studying or in class, I went to the Multnomah Public Library and became chummy with the inter-library loan desk. My summer research included all manner of books in French written in and about satire across the centuries. Evenings, I picked up Alex and jogged about the neighborhood with him in the stroller. Vincent stayed busy with regular consulting work. Thus occupied, he seemed happier—yet his anger simmered just below the surface. Except, it seemed, when he was with his friends instead of me.

We traveled to eastern Washington State to visit a close friend of his, a libertarian who had married an Amerindian. Their kids were grown, but they socialized with an extensive libertarian community in that area. His friend had built and maintained a fully stocked bomb shelter. When we arrived, I saw more than half a dozen men sitting in a semicircle around a campfire. They were cleaning their rifles as they drank beer and smoked pot. Afterwards, they would shoot clay pigeons. Their wives or girlfriends had gathered in the kitchen and their kids ran loose around the compound.

The adults' casual attitude about kids meandering among the beer, the pot, and the guns alarmed me. I kept Alex close to me inside the cabin, where I helped wash dishes and tried to make friends with the women. One, our Amerindian hostess, worked as a house cleaner. She'd completed the eighth grade. An orphan, she had graduated *cum laude* from the school of hard knocks. I felt an easy camaraderie with her. The others joked among themselves. Several had matching bottled, brassy blond hair. They popped gum and beer bottle caps with equal ease and maintained an enthusiasm for American football I could not fathom.

I felt as if I'd dropped in from Mars with little to add to conversations about nail polish, recipes, and people they knew that I didn't. I kept Alex busy with crayons and paper while trying to blend in washing dishes, stirring the spaghetti, and not speaking. It seemed I was revisiting the sticks and hicks of Colorado when I'd first returned from France in high school. Only now, they were grown up with children of their own, voted libertarian, and identified with retro sexist values. Vincent seemed so eager to fit in among them, which left me baffled.

One of Vincent's closest friends, the one he virtually crooned to daily, either in person or on the phone (including on the day I was in labor), was a lawyer. His wife was Filipino. I looked forward to meeting her and getting to know him better when we were invited to dinner at their house. I knew people in the movement from the Philippines and hoped for a new friendship. But I soon learned that the lawyer spoke patronizingly of his wife using the third person in her presence. In return for lodging, money for groceries, and clothes, she provided house cleaning, sex, and food preparation with no expectation of equal status with her provider.

Over dinner, if I joined in the conversation, the two men would glare in silence or provide a backhanded verbal snub. Meanwhile, the lawyer's wife silently served food or retreated to the kitchen, where I was unwelcome. In the countryside or back in town, on Vincent's turf, I felt extraneous—merely Alex's historical birth mother. Neither my studies nor livelihood had value in the world of Vincent and his friends.

When I returned to New Brunswick, Alex moved back up to Corbett with his grandparents. I was relieved not to have the stress of dealing with Vincent's moods, his parents' tacit support of his inconsistency, and above all his friends, who were clearly no friends of mine. I missed Alex, but we had enjoyed a good summer together playing and reading, talking in French and English, and visiting museums and parks. I cherished the little mundane moments of everyday life we'd shared, a Cheerio breakfast, letting a kitty in or out the door, hugs and tickles, pushes on a swing, bath-time splashes, and bedtime stories. I hoped that with age, he could understand that my being away did not change my love for him. Heart-wrenching as it was to leave him, I forced myself to cut from my own emotion, determined to make an offering to God, offering my "Isaac" for what I hoped would be a greater cause.

I knew my suffering was minute compared to God's. I saw God not as an unmoved mover but as my original parent and source of parental love. As such, he agonized over his/her children and how they mistreated one another. In my little world, in some small way, I had experienced the heartlessness that God encountered every day, not only on the family level, but also on the community and national level. In my complicity with the historical Abraham and Isaac—due to my understanding of this iconic story—I hoped that somehow, I was growing my heart to better relate to God. In sacrificing what I loved most, Alex, but releasing this pain as a form of offering to God, I was convinced there would be long-term benefits, not for me, but for the restoration of America.

Though I was no longer in a marriage arranged by Rev. Moon, I had forgotten neither the dream message I'd received in Russia about Vincent being in trouble, nor the vivid dream of Alex before he was born. I interpreted any experience of kindness as God's grace. When I experienced hardship, I thought of Job, or Abraham and Isaac, or Daniel in the lion's den. I viewed my life as part of a broad historical timeline where I connected my choices to a purpose bigger than myself.

I still felt called to fulfill a mission. I was sure that persevering with Vincent and enduring the pain of being apart from Alex somehow served God's Providence. Although no longer involved with the Unification movement, I remained committed to a bigger reality of True Love on a global level. I wanted to help realize this by bearing my own burdens so that spiritually I could help establish a foundation to put an end to war, starvation, and injustice. My tribulations paled compared to what other people in the world suffered. Yet through the act of offering my daily heartache up to God, I hoped to alleviate the pain of others.

— CHAPTER ELEVEN —
RESEARCH AND REALIZATIONS

To be closer to campus, I rented a room in downtown New Brunswick on Commercial Avenue. Mary Shaw, a professor of nineteenth-century French literature, helped me move from the boarding house in the suburbs. She borrowed a pickup truck to haul my desk, the dozens of milk crates that held my files, my computer, printer, and boxes of books. Her upbeat helpfulness and conversation felt warm and safe—a stark contrast to the constant tension I'd endured through the summer in Oregon. I'd forgotten what "normal" felt like. Back at Rutgers, I was a human being again and part of a community where I belonged.

The upside of my new home was that I could walk a block east to the French Department on Douglass campus in under ten minutes. The downside, at this time before gentrification, was a drug-dealing neighborhood a block to the west; two blocks to the north was the bar where local prostitutes met their clients. However, these external threats seemed less dangerous to me than living with Vincent. And besides, I was glad to be much closer to the department and, to my mind, where the action was—at the library and at my computer.

I shared the place with four others—a woman and three men, a mix of students and professionals—each in our own bedroom. My cozy corner room held my desk, single daybed, cinder-block bookshelves and two six-foot towers of stacked milk crates filled with research notes and photocopied articles painstakingly culled from obscure journals. The fox-eared kitty seemed happy, too. She settled into the room, flea free and peaceful, playing with my papers if I left them on the floor.

I worked long hours with relentless drive. Research compelled and delighted me like the warm scent of a tasty mouse luring a hungry predator. I immersed myself in teaching and relished every new tidbit I learned in my graduate courses on the Renaissance, poetics, rhetoric, and theory.

Although downtown, if I crossed the street, and traversed campus past the pond, I found myself in a bucolic farmland scene. The agricultural college of Cook campus was an easy walk. Despite living in urban Central Jersey, I could stroll among cows and horses in the evening.

Leaving memories of Vincent's driving and the car parked, I no longer had to pray to get from point A to point B alive. I felt spiritual guidance in my studies that drew me forward in my research, and into inspired conversations laden with the happy coincidence of shared interests. I relished the cool, quiet tranquility of the library stacks. They felt as cozy to me as the catacombs—a place where I could commune with the dead.

One day, collecting primary and secondary sources of French literature from the PQ section in the basement of Douglass library, I noticed a stray book on the desk of an otherwise empty carrel. This was not an unusual sight, but I seldom relinquished focus from my own quest. This day was different and I felt drawn to look at the abandoned book.

Flipping it open, I found it was a psychological self-help book on physical abuse. I looked right and left to see if someone nearby might have left it there. No one. I had a clear sense that it was left there for me to find. I plunked down in the chair and devoured it cover to cover in a couple of hours. As I read about the symptoms and patterns of abuse, I noticed an uncanny resonance with my experience. In eerie detail, the book described Vincent's behavior, my response, and Vincent's reaction. "Check, check, check," I thought to myself as I read each description.

I had assumed that the dysfunction in our relationship was unique. We had, I thought, a peculiar, nineteenth-century sort of Romantic rapport. I thought Vincent was a tortured genius who was vulnerable to spiritual possession, that our relationship was strained due to the complexity of love in the modern world and the interference of evil spirits. What I read was that I was a textbook case of an abused woman. Me! A college graduate. I couldn't believe it. Though I took this gift of insight as a sign, I still didn't know how to process the information. Questions I'd refused to consider raced pell-mell through my mind. If Vincent was abusive, wasn't Alex in danger?

There was so much at stake that I could not control. Shouldn't I get Alex, for starters? How could I work out this dilemma across such a long distance? How could I approach Vincent about this without him beating me up? How could I afford to do anything if I didn't keep steady on with my job and coursework? How would I keep our family intact emotionally while Vincent got counseling? I still didn't give up on the idea that love would conquer all, that I could find help to save my marriage. Yet how could I keep paying the emotional and financial price for it all? I had a new perspective, but no clear plan for what to do next. And so I continued to tread water, studying, teaching, and talking to Alex in the evening as though nothing had changed with my newfound insight.

Then, one afternoon, while writing a paper in my bedroom lair, a cloud of love suddenly descended and hugged me from every angle in a soft, spiritual embrace. My pen clattered on the wood floor and my papers glided to earth in pursuit, yet I didn't care. Bursting into sobs, I wailed uncontrollably like a wounded animal, so loud that my conscious mind noted that my housemates might hear. But the uncontainable release overrode social propriety. There must have been no one home, because if there were, surely one of my flat mates would have run to my door to inquire after me.

This spiritual cloud embraced me with such perfect love that I felt completely free to be honest instead of honorable, truthful instead of truth loving. The absolute embrace endured until slowly my sobs slowed to sniffles and amazement with this sensation. I felt utterly known to my core and accepted exactly as I was. I felt two fingers of a spirit softly touch my lips. The spirit that brought this love knew everything about me. I hadn't told anyone about the abuse (though Vincent's parents had witnessed his anger, they remained in denial) and he—for the spirit was a "he"—knew this.

When the being touched the front of my lips with his fingers, I understood at last that I must tell someone. I didn't question the being. I didn't question the experience. It was more real, more knowing than anything I'd experienced in the activity-filled life I'd led up to that moment. My sobs ceased as this being of light continued to embrace me.

My literary homework could wait—I didn't want this feeling to stop; I had to do something. I rose from my desk, left the blinking orange cursor on the computer screen, went down the stairs and out the door to walk in nature at Cook College following the late afternoon sun. I paused to look both ways before crossing Commercial Avenue and thought to myself how peculiar it was to wait for traffic in the midst of a cosmic experience.

As I walked through campus my feet seemed to float off the ground as the cloud of love and I passed trees that lined the path, the pond, and approached the fields dotted with cows and sheep. All the while, I felt this being holding me in an embrace, letting me know that true love was real. That what happened on the earthly plane was known in the beyond. That I mattered. That someone—an actual person who happened to be in the spiritual realm—cared.

Boundless love embraced me in warmth from deep within and walked with me, held me with every step. While we walked, my mind still tried to fathom what it meant, even though I just wanted to feel the embrace. My noisy intellect pounded at the door of my heart. It wanted to ask practical questions, but it was silenced by the overwhelming supremacy of a greater truth, the truth of absolute, enduring love. I felt liberated, as though granted permission from beyond to admit to my own mortality, to my own weakness and vulnerability, to receive instead of being strong alone.

As we walked, I pondered the simple yet challenging revelation that I needed to tell a three-dimensional human being that I needed help. I felt a new sense of resilience arise within me as I determined to tell someone about the abuse, to break the pact of secrecy that Vincent had exacted of me—though I didn't know whom to tell.

It was not until I resolved to follow through on my decision that I felt the being move away. He'd stayed with me until he'd completed what he needed to do. Just like when I joined the movement and had seen the vision in the clouds, I sensed the refrain, "Okay, I've given you the love: now it's your turn to act." I didn't feel abandoned, only strengthened and with a clear sense of direction and hope that I would talk to the right people.

I held the embrace of this visitation within myself for the night. Having deadlines, I had to finish my paper. But the next day, after Taekwondo class, I broke my silence and confided in a black belt and former New Yorker, a feisty hot-pepper, and down to earth sister. Though we had spoken only briefly—in the locker room and in the *dojang* practicing forms, stretching, and sparring—I felt I could count on her for straight, no-nonsense advice.

She listened as I explained first the spiritual experience, then the abuse. She took me seriously without judging any of it. I intuitively knew she would understand the spiritual aspect. That was what worried me most in approaching the secular-humanist world with my story. She advised me to see a counselor, get some help to heal, and to make a game plan.

So, I did. I went to counseling. At one point, the counselor had me imagine Vincent sitting in a chair right in front of me. What would I say to him if he could not hurt me? Tears flew from the corners of my eyes, I thundered with the guttural force of a Taekwondo kyah, "You have no right to treat me this way! I am a Daughter of God!"

The counselor appeared pleased. Whether or not he bought the theological tenor of my declaration, I did not care. I felt that I was on the right track. I still had to come up with a plan of what to do. Living with Vincent without stopping the abuse put me at mortal risk. And I had to have a plan for Alex.

— CHAPTER TWELVE —
LIKE KITTIES

Thanksgiving break approached but I had no plans to travel to Oregon until Christmas. Swamped with writing and grading my students' midterms, I booked the time off to keep pace with my work. On top of regular class exams, I needed to prepare for language-proficiency exams in Spanish and German. The PhD program required proof of my reading ability in two languages beyond English and French. Rutgers hosted these nationally recognized exams twice a year. I'd registered and paid to take them the week after Thanksgiving.

Meanwhile, Vincent had a temporary consulting job on the East Coast. He called and said he wanted to stop by without Alex. I told him about my nonstop work schedule: could he please, please, please visit another time? Of course, he came anyway. Perhaps he suspected that something within me had changed.

It felt like the perfect storm was brewing: his demands, my teaching deadlines, graduate coursework, language exams, and the realization that I couldn't be his punching bag anymore. I prayed for strength and focus. I alerted my housemates to Vincent's arrival. Breaking my silence again, I confided in more detail to one of my elder flatmates, Tom, about the abuse. He'd been kind to me and had even driven me to surgery when I had my wisdom teeth out. He worked as a nurse and was like an elder brother. He passed word to the others.

Like Vincent, Tom was tall and thin with a soothing voice, though he had a soft manner. With age, his pale skin had gently begun to loosen from his skeleton. His hair had gone white decades before its time when he lost his wife and children in a California mudslide. Now it lay upon his head in frail, sparse rows, like my grandfather's once did. Ever humble, Tom seemed to glide across space in a spiritual bubble, looking into the distance through his thick, round glasses. He appeared mild, but I knew that if Vincent did anything to me, Tom could act quickly, and he was stronger than he appeared. He nursed the severely disabled and could deadlift full-grown, uncooperative patients.

When Vincent arrived, Tom opened the main door downstairs and escorted him to my bedroom by the kitchen. I heard knuckles rap on my bedroom door and a familiar voice on the other side: "Hello, it's Vincent."

I unlocked and opened the door, gave Vincent a brief hug, then gestured toward the daybed as the only spot besides my desk chair to sit. Tom lingered a bit at the threshold, making small talk and his presence known to Vincent. This helped to calm me. Hearing Vincent respond with civility, Tom receded into the dark hallway. I saw a small flash of light reflect from his glasses as he nodded before leaving. Shutting the door, I steeled myself to deal with Vincent alone.

He sat unusually relaxed on the edge of the daybed, his shoulders rounding his wiry frame into an uncommitted capital C. Settling into my desk chair, I swiveled around to face him. I felt the strength of the bookcases behind me. Their shelves were laden with texts I'd scoured for meaning, underlining, highlighting, and scribbling notes in the margins. They bore witness, as did the windowpanes that looked down on the grit of Commercial Avenue, with its prostitutes, pimps, and drug dealers below.

After chatting about our jobs, his trip, and Alex, I knew I had to tell Vincent the truth—our relationship needed work. I'd pleaded with him before about counseling. He couldn't tolerate the thought of revealing anything personal to outsiders. Counseling would reveal facts he wanted kept private.

Emboldened by my familiar surroundings and sympathetic housemates, I told Vincent that I found it strange that he could become so furious as to hit me, and that I would seek comfort from him—the very person who had hit me. "This isn't a normal relationship," I said. "I think we can do better and we definitely need some marriage counseling."

I'd anticipated an angry outburst, profanity, and a beating. But for the first time, I saw a flicker of regret pass across Vincent's eyes. "It's like the kitties, can't hurt the bé kitties," he said using baby talk and the affectionate tones he reserved to address cats. He was comparing me to the kittens, which he loved. I liked the comparison in terms of their innocence and his gentle demeanor with them, but not in terms of our human potential for a full reciprocal relationship. Never before had he recognized his actions as unsuitable. Now, he seemed to comprehend that beating me black and blue was wrong.

For my part, it was the first time I told him that my pattern of returning to him bleating for mercy, then seeking consolation after he cooled down, was also wrong. The pattern of his violence and my submission was as endemic to our relationship's dysfunction as relentless drama is to Wagnerian opera. My courage to discuss this with Vincent—I would not have dared use the term "confront" with him—resided from knowing that my flatmates were close by in their respective bedrooms. Tom, Elsie, Jim, and Morris all knew Vincent was there with me. They were ready to come running if they heard sounds of an attack.

True to form, Vincent replied, "Well *you* get counseling if you need it, but I'm not."

"Vincent, this isn't normal; it's not right. We need to work it out together. But I can't sort it all out today or this week. I have exams. This is a working holiday for me."

He wanted to stay the night, but I told him he couldn't under these conditions, repeating the pressure I was under from teaching and my classes, reiterating the counseling we needed. Instead of glaring at me with his icy stare, he looked dejected. He focused on his hands in his lap, like a little boy reprimanded. He repeated, "I understand. It's like the kitties. You can't hit the kitties."

"Right," I said, amazed that he seemed to understand, even if his words did reduce me to animal status.

He stared into space a moment, then rose to leave. We'd discussed the fox-eared kitty before his arrival. Vincent had agreed she'd be happier with more space in Oregon. He was prepared to take her back with him on the plane. I gave Vincent another hug, which he stiffly tolerated. Then, he picked up the kitty, put her in the carrier, opened the door, and left without saying goodbye or turning to take a last glance my way.

As he walked down the hall to the stairs, he dangled the kitty carrier at his side like a bulky briefcase. I felt conflicted about how he left and longed for the love we'd once shared, remembering how the plucky, once-feral kitten had mewed at him until he relented and gave her a home with us for Christmas. Yet I drew a deep breath of relief that I didn't have to dodge blows or endure Vincent's furious cursing and belittlement. His docile departure stunned me. I wrenched myself away to resume working.

The next day, while studying, I heard a brisk knock on the apartment's front door. It was an unusual sound, as visitors were rare. I scrambled down the stairs and opened the door to a chunky, middle-aged white fellow standing on the stoop with a manila envelope. "I have a delivery for Ms. Claxton," he said.

It was odd to hear my maiden name spoken in such a formal fashion from the lips of a stranger. It was a Sunday afternoon, not the usual time for mail, I thought.

The man wore regular street clothes and remained at attention with a dour fortitude the regular mail carrier did not share. He said he was a sheriff. What? I hadn't been speeding, nor did I have any overdue parking tickets. I couldn't imagine why he was there. He said he was serving me with divorce papers. My trembled as I opened the envelope. Documents confirmed Vincent Lawrence Buckley, Petitioner and Pamela Ann Claxton, Respondent.

Immersed in Renaissance French literature and German vocabulary, I read the strange words in English summoning me to a court in Oregon. The more I read, the more aghast I felt. Still, my rational mind took over; after all, the sheriff was still standing there. I looked up at him, scared, ignorant, trusting, and confused all at once, "What do I do?" I asked him.

"You sign them to agree or not if you disagree. Ask your lawyer."

"But I don't have a lawyer," I said.

"I can't advise you. You need to consult your lawyer," he repeated.

I leaned against the doorframe and skimmed through the documents. Divorce? So quickly? Conflicted, I felt relief that Vincent had chosen for us to part ways. It removed from me the onus of having to decide. But then I read that he was petitioning for full custody of Alex. What? He didn't even take care of Alex, his mother did! No! This body blow made my heart stop.

"You can sign here," the sheriff said as he held up a clipboard with a piece of paper with lines on it, "to show you received the papers. Then contact your attorney to respond to the summons to appear in court."

My life-shattering event was someone else's delivery job. I felt stupid and confused. "What does it mean if I sign? I don't have a lawyer" I repeated.

The sheriff assured me several more times that my signature only confirmed that I received the papers, not that I agreed to Vincent's terms for complete custody of Alex. I signed; he tucked the clipboard under his arm and strode away before I could ask any more questions. I wanted to howl, "What do I do now?"

My mind went into a backward tailspin. How could these papers have arrived on the heels of Vincent's visit? They must have been prepared in advance. Yet during our chat, the word "divorce" had never arisen between us, nor had it ever.

Despite the shock, I made plans fueled by adrenalin. For Alex to join me, I had to find another place to live, one suitable for a child. I'd also need daycare to keep working. But first, I had to get Alex. Moreover, I had to find enough money to fly to across the continent to Oregon. And money for an attorney. My research papers and exams demanded attention, too. Overwhelmed, my knees crumpled beneath me as soon as I shut the front door. Holding the divorce papers, I hunched into a ball in the tiny foyer at the bottom of the stairwell and sobbed.

— CHAPTER THIRTEEN —

FREEFALLING INTO FOLLY

Still crumpled on the floor, I heard Tom's discreet footsteps. They paused on the landing to give me time to save face. I took the opportunity to brush away my tears. His nonchalant amble soon resumed down the stairs.

"I've been served with divorce papers," I said, looking up at him. "He wants full custody of Alex."

Tom said nothing, but his blue eyes filled with compassion behind his thick glasses.

"You're not surprised?" I said.

"You denied him sex?" Tom asked, raising his eyebrows and firming his lips.

I looked away, embarrassed and exasperated.

"That may have been the deciding factor," he said, bobbing his head ruefully.

"How could I be intimate with someone who cared so little for me?"

"He was your husband," Tom replied, as though that explained everything.

Men! I thought to myself, my composure restored by irritation. As Tom exited the front door, I climbed the stairs back up to my room and telephoned Alex just to hear his voice.

"Alex!" his grandmother called. I could picture her calling to him across the den, her voice carrying above the elephant pedestal intricately carved with ivory tusks, across the heavy antique furniture, the rare coin collection on the shelf, copies of *National Review, National Geographic,* and financial newsletters on a side table. Outside, their acres of land would sustain hay, horses, and the corpses of vintage cars pillaged for parts.

I looked across my little room. The kitty's liveliness gone, my books comforted me, as did the shrine of my computer hutch. Taekwondo and grad school made for a simplified, disciplined life. My clothes easily fit into a closet designed in the nineteenth century for someone who owned only two sets—working garments and Sunday best.

At last, through the receiver, I heard Alex run into the room, "What Grandma?"

"Telephone. It's your mother."

I didn't have a name, I was "the mother," not even "Mom." But I didn't care. I longed for his voice to reach my ear through the telephone receiver.

Hearing him breathe in quick puffs from running I knew he held the receiver. "Hi Sweetie! What have you been up to?" I said in my cheeriest voice.

"Climbing trees! I am going to see friend Alex."

Friend Alex was another little boy his age with the same name. We chatted until he was ready to move on to the next thing—ice cream. Perennially stashed in the freezer of Grandma's fridge was ice cream—as if it were part of the food pyramid to be consumed daily by every youngster. I could ill-afford such luxuries. Alex lived in a palace, and I wanted to bring him to a hovel just to be near him, to hear him breathe and hum as he noodled with his Matchbox cars. I told him I loved him before he begged off to go play. Listening to his high-pitched nattering had bolstered my spirits.

Still reeling from receiving the divorce papers, hearing Alex emboldened me not to hide in shame. Instead, I called each confidant I knew with systematic determination to ascertain my next steps. The spirit that had touched my lips wanted me to talk, and now words cascaded to friends and family. The threat of losing Alex crystallized within me a new resilience. I stopped fearing to tell the truth about the violence we'd survived. No longer in denial, I related the cursing, threats, and blows, as a torrent of images and places came forth; they dated from when Alex and I joined Vincent in Gardendale, to our time in Tuscaloosa, to Vincent's fist on my face in the car with his parents on Christmas Eve.

My father, an attorney in Aurora, Colorado, offered to help me find a lawyer in Oregon, where the divorce proceedings would occur. By the following week, Dad was on a first-name basis with a partner of a high-ranking law firm in Portland, who had assured him he would find the right person to represent me.

The following day, when I called Alex, I could tell things had changed at Grandma and Grandpa's house. Now that the divorce papers had been served, the state of antagonism was official. I detected that they scrutinized the motive and content of every phone call I made to Alex and, without my knowledge at the time, recorded the conversations.

Even worse, Alex was now rarely available to talk. Unbeknownst to me at the time, Vincent had to be there to assure the call was taped. Every interaction became a wooing contest—me from New Jersey with talk, cards, and letters; Vincent and his mother in Oregon with bribes of friends, outings, and ice cream.

I couldn't believe the betrayal of Vincent's mother, who had witnessed him hitting me. Vincent wanted the divorce—of that I was already aware. But slowly it dawned on me: it was his mother who wanted Alex.

After passing my midterms and proficiency exams in German and Spanish and administering midterms to my own students, I flew into a hyperspace of activity. I scoured affordable rental options near Rutgers, researched childcare support, sought counseling for myself, prepared for travel across the country, and secured student loans. I needed to find a safe place to stay in Portland to see my son. All this time I had to try my best to freeze my heart so as not to make decisions based on feelings. I needed to rely on logic if I was to advance my course.

But as usual, faith carried me more than reason. The probability of me retrieving Alex was slim; he was a resident of Oregon now and I lived across the continent in a strange place he couldn't recall ever visiting. He supposedly had a loving home. Vincent and his parents would portray me as a ruthless careerist who had chosen self-advancement over parenting.

While my dad had found a law firm in Portland for me to consult, producing the funds to retain the attorney, traveling to and staying in Oregon were financial obligations I had to meet on grad-student wages. Vincent, however, would have infinite funds from his supportive parents, in addition to the home-state advantage. Moreover, I would soon learn from my attorney that mothers were not favored over fathers as the custodial parent under Oregon law at that time. Ignoring the odds, I prepared for Alex to join me. Stage one was to find a place to live to accommodate a toddler. Commercial Avenue was not that place.

A friend, a fellow graduate student, told me about an apartment available in her complex. It was upstairs, with a fire escape and window off a tiny kitchen overlooking an asphalt playground—a far cry from the country estate Alex enjoyed with Grandma and Grandpa. It nonetheless seemed safe and cozy there, even though in the building across the way, according to recent news headlines, someone had been hacked to death with a machete, the result of a domestic dispute.

There is a reason police respond to domestic disputes in pairs. Domestic conflicts are known to be volatile and dangerous. Unlike war, where presumably there are rules of engagement like the Geneva Conventions (limiting attacks on civilians and allowing for safe passage of the Red Cross, for instance), domestic violence has a quality of anarchy about it. In states of officially declared war, combatants on both sides typically prepare for battle with the proper attire, foxholes, and hearty supplies of Spam. But conflicts of passion respect no such rules.

There is a euphemistic if not oxymoronic quality to the term "domestic violence." Domesticity connotes blissful predictability, harmony, and perhaps even boredom. Violence rudely opposes this bucolic state. In the case of my erstwhile neighbors, one of whom was eliminated by machete, the issue, unlike mine, involved a love triangle. The offended husband saw fit to cut off the liaison—into, apparently, many pieces.

How could I feel safe when such a grisly attack occurred only steps from my building? It involved people who knew each other. My own experience had shown me that it is those with whom we are closest who may inflict the most pain. Strangers were often kind. Besides, I had friends nearby and Vincent was on the other side of the country.

I mounted shelves above my computer desk and bought a sleeper sofa. I put a freshwater aquarium on a stand by the door and populated it with angel fish, guppies, and a peaceful catfish. During the day, my studio looked like a living-room office. By night, it converted into a bedroom.

When Christmas break arrived, I flew to Oregon. At the airport, I rented a car and drove to Portland to meet my attorney at her downtown high-rise office. I entered the building, then crossed the threshold of the elevator, the interior of which gleamed with brass and mirrors. It was bigger than my kitchen back home.

I pushed the button for the sixteenth floor. Beneath my feet a mechanical surge sent the floor upwards. The launch nearly popped my ears. Lights blinked as my spaceship rose past the lower levels. Soon, the doors parted with hydraulic efficiency. They revealed the law firm's reception lobby complete with a shiny, chrome-and-brass drinking fountain. Beyond the fountain stood plush offices with polished mahogany desks. Large windows framed a 360-degree view of downtown Portland. *This is not going to be cheap*, I thought.

Lack of sleep, the six-hour plane ride, and a somewhat harrowing parking experience had left me lightheaded and drained. I was wearing my only pair of trousers that were not of blue denim. They were stain-resistant but stale from the journey. An acute awareness overwhelmed me as I perceived each molecule of debris, invisible to the untrained eye, coating every square inch of me, from my scuffed clogs to my wrinkled teaching jacket. I was an abominable snowman of dirt invading a pristine corporate mothership. Here, tidy vacuum trails made equidistant parallel lines across sumptuous, gray carpet, creating a sea of precision. While my off-the-rack duds approximately fit, the garbage cans were outfitted in *soignée*, perfectly tailored plastic liners.

As the room began to spin, my knees went soft. I grabbed the water fountain to steady myself and flinched encountering the bite of cold metal. I dreaded the fingerprint marks I would leave on its brassy surface. Still, I leaned over to take a sip and pray for strength.

Sure enough, the water was freezing cold and filtered. Moreover, the fountain had multiple spray height settings. This customization feature enabled me to squirt myself in the eye. Water spluttered down my face, over my chin and its icy tendrils glued my once white, now graying, oxford shirt to my chest.

I rubbed the dribbles off my chin with the back of my wrist, yanked the withered lapel of my jacket a couple of times in a vain attempt to hide the water splotch, and took a deep breath. I thought it was a wry gesture on God's part to remind me of my mortal status and that my fate was not in my hands. I forced my legs to hold me up and walk down the corridor.

Relying on faith, I strode into the cool, computer-conditioned air and viewed all the dressed-for-success people briskly walking with important papers, talking with serious expressions on phones, or sitting with regal mastery before their keyboards and monitors. From my days in the Unification movement, I recalled a long-ago fundraising stop in the pouring rain at an upscale Connecticut enterprise. Crossing the elegant eighteenth-century threshold, every step of my sneakers yielded frog-worthy squishes. The first person I spoke to, an older gentleman, it turned out, was the corporate president. He had soggy me, in my five-and-dime, polyester skirt and hand-me-down blouse, sit in his vintage leather Gainsborough chair.

He then gathered employees around his desk and had me explain to the entire company why I was fundraising. My hair dripped puddles onto the glass that covered his cherry-wood desktop. I don't remember what knickknacks I was selling, only the feeling that what had carried me into the office of the firm's president was faith, not my clothes, knowledge, or the products I had in my bag.

The boss seemed to take genuine interest in my words. He bought my trinkets, as did his employees; I imagine they did so more out of respect for his example rather than my presentation. But at the time, I took it as an act of divine intervention. The contrast between my grand fundraising result and my humble appearance was too vast to explain.

Swaying and light-headed, in the office of Portland's own Brown, Miller and Wilson, I knew that I had to call upon that faith again to stay focused on why I was there and what I was doing.

A perky receptionist with sculpted, blown-dry hair and airbrushed good looks led me to a room to wait for the lawyer my dad had found. A well-fed, silver-haired man wearing a gray tweed herringbone suit, clasped tie, and a warm smile soon entered. He introduced me to Pearl, the attorney he believed most suitable for my case. After commenting on how he enjoyed talking to my dad, he left. Pearl looked young, about my age, yet fresh and focused. She wore a skirt and crisp shirt. She was clear and direct, which I appreciated.

"How was your trip?" she asked.

"Exhausting. But I'm running on adrenaline anyway, so . . ." It was early December and I had wrapped up my fall classes to visit Alex and deal with the divorce over winter break.

Pearl asked me the essentials, firmly pressed the needed Kleenex into my hand to deal with the tears, and gave me a questionnaire to fill in details. She seemed well versed not only in family law but also in its emotional ramifications. She briefed me quickly on her background and gave an overview of what we would need to do.

As I told her my story, I didn't consider my desire for my son an attempt to own him, nor even as an exercise of my "right" as a parent. Though logic would suggest that a child reside with the non-abusive parent, I couldn't indulge in that sensibility. Pearl informed me that Oregon law at that time did not consider an abusive spouse a threat to the child of the union.

While the instinct to cherish and be with my son surged within me as a mother, I had to amputate that emotion from myself to process the logic of the court case. To not go crazy from the emotional pain, I went "vertical" and looked to a higher power to transcend my own situation through prayer and connect with the divine. To survive this process, I could trust neither logic nor my own feelings as a parent. I decided to rely upon faith.

Internally, I reframed my every effort and my entire existence to consider only what would be best for Alex. Was God asking me to offer my Isaac, my beloved boy? I scrutinized my heart to be sure I was not seeking custody out of some selfish motive. I had to ask myself whether Alex would have been better off with Vincent and his parents. They had much more in the way of material goods—that was true. They could buy his way into the best education. They had a stable place to live and acres of land where he could roam. But did they have true love?

Various images ran through my mind as I told Pearl some of my story. Images of Vincent in a rage, hitting Alex when he was crying from nightmares; rapping Alex's knuckles with a screwdriver for playing with nuts and bolts he left scattered on the ground; Vincent hurling accusations, swearing, throwing furniture, his eyes steely cold with fury until a glint appeared and he threatened to kill me. This side of Vincent was callous and unpredictable; this was not the soft-spoken, solicitous man I thought I married.

My mind churned over the pros and cons of battling for Alex, replaying arguments for (to offer him a home with unconditional love; to teach him about God's love for him; to protect him from violence) and against (I had little money, they had much; I had a small apartment, they had a grand home; I would have to fly from New Jersey to Oregon for the court case and take Alex away from friends). The answer that came to me was not based on my human rationalizations: I had to go with God and fight for God's right to love Alex, His own son.

It was not that I was perfect or God incarnate, yet I knew that with everything in my heart, I would strive to embrace Alex with God's love and truth. I would find mentors that could embrace him. I would do my utmost to help him have his own relationship with God by honoring his unique self. Of course, I said none of this to Pearl as I strained to understand how the law defined what would be in Alex's best interest. I was new to this legal business. During the initial greeting and debriefing with Pearl, the receptionist brought me coffee with powdered cream, which helped me to follow Pearl's detailed advice. Sensing that she had successfully begun to align my expectations with what the process entailed, she produced a form for the initial deposit of well over two thousand dollars toward the retainer fee that I needed to sign.

My skin froze in the corporate spaceship air; my breathing stopped. I lived hand to mouth on Ramen noodles and frozen burritos. I wore underwear older than Alex—some of my bras still bore milk stains from Gardendale days when he was a baby. I only made $833.00 per month in gross wages.

Evidently used to dealing with shocked clients, Pearl put the retainer into context for me. The whole case could amount to twenty to forty grand, easily. This was a drop in the bucket toward what was forthcoming. Besides, she said cheerfully, "We take credit cards."

The figures to me were absurd, astronomical. I felt as though I'd been thrown onstage to improvise some unscripted, surreal play. I could only trust God. Freefalling into folly, I pulled out my credit card for the retainer. In the gleaming corporate context, it appeared to be a trifling sum.

With the paperwork thus cleared, Pearl explained how the first procedure would be a hearing to declare that I also wanted custody. She would handle that. Somewhere, I had heard the saying that a good lawyer knows the law, a great lawyer knows the judge. Pearl was both.

The hearing was held and the judge granted me visitation rights while I was in Oregon. This was a key victory. Already Vincent and his parents were trying to keep Alex from me; now I had a legal document ensuring my right to see my own son. Since filing for divorce months prior, Vincent, although permitting occasional phone contact from New Jersey, was not eager to cooperate with me seeing Alex in Oregon.

Beyond desperate, I clung to gratitude. I was grateful that Pearl would advocate for me. Drawing on my Unificationist contacts, I connected with the Baggins, a family no longer active with the movement. They lived in Vancouver, Washington, under ten miles from Portland, and generously took me in for

Christmas. They offered me a haven to rest and a safe place to have visitation with Alex in a normal home setting. I was grateful, too, for their warm, cozy family routines. They had created their own traditions and spiritual space apart from the church. Living with them and their four kids felt natural and comforting.

On days that I couldn't see Alex, it was a welcome relief to grocery shop, help prepare and clean up after meals, and read bedtime stories to the Baggins kids. Their parents, Victoria and Mark, were smart, creative, artistic, and never at a loss for words. With them I enjoyed good conversation and company. I felt God had provided for me in the warmth of their family. As the court case progressed, grounding myself in the everyday homeliness of their routines became my lifeline to serenity.

When I learned that the first hearing had been a success, I rejoiced for it meant that I could see Alex. But this was only the first hurdle of a long, difficult obstacle course, one in which I would be challenged each step of the way. For starters, Vincent and his lawyer vetted my personal life to the very limits of the law. Likewise, we vetted Vincent.

Innocent of battles to come, I enjoyed a snug Christmas Eve with the Baggins. Mark read the Christmas story from the Bible. We gathered to sing carols as Victoria, a good Jewish girl by birth, played piano and eldest daughter, Evelind, accompanied on flute. I missed Alex yet felt hopeful for I had obtained permission to visit with him on Christmas day.

Christmas morning, the Baggins kids pounced and wrestled with each other like tiger cubs in their PJs as they scrambled beneath pine boughs and hunted for their gifts. Breathing in the moment, I relished their joy and tried to divert my mind from my heart's longing for the little yellow-haired boy who wasn't with me. After a late breakfast, we stacked plates still sticky with maple syrup and pancake remnants by the sink to wash later. Victoria and I set off to fetch Alex.

It is odd how the mind assumes that a current experience is an eternal one. As we drove, memories shared with Alex flickered like movie stills: picking blackberries with him in diapers, watching him walk in shoes for the first time, pushing him in a swing up, up into the sunshine—countless moments when it never occurred to me that I could lose him, lose the ability and even the legal right to be with him. Custody was no longer a dispassionate description on childcare forms—it was a hostile foreign country. And it required legal papers to secure safe passage to dislodge him from enemy territory.

"Love the enemy. Turn the other cheek. Give and forget that you've given." How does that work when your own child's well-being is at stake? I remembered a Russian tale of one of Vincent's great grandmothers. Before the Revolution, she'd married into an aristocratic family that lacked an heir. She produced one, but soon they had no use for her—a commoner—as the child's father had by that point moved on to other conquests.

The child's paternal grandmother got hold of the child and denounced the mother during the Revolution so she had to leave the country to avoid being killed. After emigrating and finding refuge, she sent for her little one, but the grandmother refused to let the child go. The mother tried repeatedly to retrieve her child to no avail. She went on to remarry and have other children, but she never saw her firstborn again. Vincent's father had told me that story after supper and quite a bit of vodka one evening years ago. I put the fearful outcome of losing one's child forever to an antagonistic and wealthy mother-in-law out of my mind.

We drove in prayerful silence. I recalled Vincent's joking praise of his cousin's divorce as a model for marriage. They led thoroughly independent lives in separate houses on the same street so the kids could visit either parent with ease. It was all very aristocratic and logical and sounded heartless to me. "I hope I'm never *that* sophisticated," I remembered thinking at the time. For me, true love was cuddly and kind and included honoring the divine in one another. *How could being apart be good for family hugs?* I wondered. I still believed in the ideals of marriage and family even though the imminent divorce reduced them to a fleeting anachronism.

As we wound through the Willamette Valley, past Corbett, to the estate of Vincent's parents, I felt like Daniel entering the lion's den. Vincent could attack me and no one would be the wiser, as any cries for help would be long lost in the trees before they reached the nearest neighbors. Though Victoria would be there in the van, she was a petite, mild-mannered mom, not strong and armed like Vincent. Vincent's parents, meanwhile, hadn't prevented him from hitting me in the past, so their presence was of little comfort. Besides, I imagined, they were already tucking into the hard liquor.

In New Jersey, after responding to the divorce summons, on the advice of my attorney, I filed papers to obtain a restraining order to protect me from Vincent. Until the divorce was final, without the restraining order he could enter my home and hurt me. However, according to New Jersey law, if I went to Vincent's house, I would annul the restraining order. The logic was that if the victim decides they're no longer in danger by ignoring the protection the restraining order provides, the law cannot be enforced and the restraining order no longer holds. I wanted a restraining order for protection—not only due to my experience, but because the divorce situation added an extra layer of tension that could provoke Vincent.

The judge in Oregon did not perceive my vulnerability. He overruled the New Jersey restraining order. He said that if I wanted to visit Alex, I had to go fetch him myself from Vincent's house. This was part of Vincent's home-state advantage. I felt that my life was in jeopardy following the directions of the Oregon court. But violating my own restraining order was the only way I could see Alex.

Compared to New Jersey, Oregon seemed like the Wild West, a place where you were supposed to carry your own gun to protect yourself. I felt safer in New Jersey, where civic order seemed to provide a natural protective buffer. But my yearning to see Alex overrode my own safety. I decided that, like Daniel, I would have to rely on faith to protect me.

As Victoria turned the van onto the familiar asphalt driveway, my heart thumped in my chest. Here, from the base of the hill below the house, my eyes scanned the pastures on either side looking for the horses to comfort me with their natural beauty and unadorned grace. I found them in the distance. They huddled by the fence at the far end near the house and their respective barns: the mares and gelding in the pasture to the left and the stallion alone in the pasture to the right. As the van slowly climbed up the hill, we passed between them. Reaching the top, Victoria pulled to a stop in front of the garage. Just beyond it, up a walkway, stood the house.

I had to approach the back door alone. The air was cold, gray, and still. I paused by the garage to breathe and pray. *Heavenly Father, not my will but thy will. Please help me to love them from your point of view.*

To the left of the garage, I could see looming in the distance the familiar steel airplane hangar. It housed an old B-52 Vincent's father was forever restoring. The rusty silhouettes of vintage cars in various states of decay were still strewn around the hanger. Beyond the car graveyard, I could make out the patch of scarred earth where they burned their trash. Beyond that stretched acres of yellow stubble. The dormant wheat fields curved up to the horizon and met the shadow of blue-gray mountains in the distance.

A horse snorted down below, bringing me back to focus on my task. It was time to summon courage to approach the door. My eyes searched in vain for even a forlorn crow to break the sky's bleak, overcast scowl. Still in need of courage, I returned to my old fundraising prayer, *Glory to Heaven, Peace on Earth, I pray for the success of True Parents' mission.*

That mission now seemed so far away. The mission of True Parents was to establish ideal families of True Love centered on God where spouses loved each other, their children, and their extended family with fidelity, absolute devotion, and tender care while serving their community, nation, and world as an extension of their family. Clearly, this was not happening in my case. However, I prayed for it anyway. Prayed out of habit. Prayed out of longing for the ideal itself. Prayed to call upon that greater spirit of peace and love that seemed to arrive in the direst of circumstances if I could transcend my own petty angst and perspective.

I inched up the flagstone path that curved to the back-porch door. Slick, gray ice coated the walkway, muting the mosaic of gray and brown to reflect the saber-rattling sky. Prayer or no prayer, this didn't look auspicious. I slid and stepped across the icy stones. Landing on the porch, my eyes found the familiar black-and-white sign hanging in the shadow beneath the low eave. "Never mind the dog, beware of wife," it read above the black silhouette of a rifle.

My knuckles tapped on the door I used to enter freely without a knock or hesitation. I was a stranger now. Still, I had always felt out of place. Now a legal outsider, my new classification simply matched the disdain and denial I used to experience yet had refused to acknowledge. Still, part of me still wanted to love them for their quirky ways and exotic tales. *Trust God; love the enemy*, I thought. Moreover, Alex called this place home. I wanted to understand him and his life now.

When Rita opened the door, her face was hard and businesslike. But it was Christmas. Their extravaganza was extra elaborate this year. Soaring to the living room ceiling, a great pine laden with ornaments glowed over the expensive gifts for Alex that lay scattered over plush Oriental rugs and red leather furnishings. The black-lacquer grand piano Rita played stood in the alcove beyond the glimmering tree; guns regularly used stood grouped in cabinets of beveled glass while antique rifles rested horizontally on the wall across from the marble fireplace with its shiny brass andirons and tools.

The Christmas décor in the living room glowed red while the kitchen was still retro avocado green and harvest gold. Its dated, casual style reminded me of how awkward formal meals in the dining room felt; how Vincent hated his mother's cooking; and how I'd always dreaded the dinner hour for the way Alex was expected not to squirm.

Rita insisted I follow her through the kitchen into the living room to see the tree. She beamed over her handiwork—the oodles of toys and games she'd bought for Alex that I could never afford. I felt sorry for her. Sorry that she felt she had to buy her way into Alex's heart. It was all she knew. I couldn't help feeling that in this isolated paradise of riches, the real spirit of Christmas, of loving and being loved just as you are, was skewed. The lavish, exclusive display lacked the easygoing affection of the Bagginses' cheery mess.

I asked for Alex. Rita called to Vincent, who appeared from the back bedroom, Alex in tow. Vincent's face was wan and dour, his steps jerky and stiff. By his side, Alex's entire body capered freestyle except for his right arm, which Vincent held aloft, straight and rigid in a firm grasp. Vincent's clenched jaw matched the tight grip he had on Alex's wrist. Seeing me, Alex broke free from the solemn march. His face lit up with a big smile as he charged into my arms: "Mommy!" he shouted, "I'm so glad to see you!"

I closed my eyes and held onto his squirmy body in a hug that made all my fear and anxiety melt away. He grabbed my hand and pulled me into the living room to show me his Christmas gifts. For his sake, I admired them. While he played with a truck, I went over to Rita and handed her an antique ring, studded with diamonds, once hers, which Vincent had given me. "Oh, you keep it," she said. "I have lots of jewelry."

"No. It isn't right," I said firmly, pressing it into her hand.

I didn't marry for diamonds or money and it was without either that I would need to fight for Alex in the upcoming court case we were all overlooking at the moment. Pearl would later tell me, "You should have kept it and sold it to help pay for the legal fees!"

When it came to matters of the heart, I couldn't think like an attorney. My dad used to say, "You can't legislate morality." I knew you couldn't legislate love either. I never regretted returning the ring; it was a family heirloom. And I was no longer part of that family.

"We're going to visit the Baggins!" I told Alex brightly as he played in the living room.

Rita stepped in to ready him with a backpack of clothes and some toys for the road. I walked over to Vincent, who had paced out of sight into the far end of the kitchen. I gave him a can of Almond Roca wrapped in blue paper with stars, snowmen, and children in snowsuits, smiling and sledding down an imaginary mountain. It was Christmas after all, and that was his favorite.

My default idealism was such that I wanted to believe in love that once was and in the man with whom I had started family. Only later would I learn that in the case of physical and emotional abuse, it was common for the abuser to hit the victim legally after hitting physically.

Vincent looked embarrassed. I hugged him, putting my head against his chest so he wouldn't see the tears spilling out of my eyes, "How did it ever come to this?" I stammered.

As I retreated, composure returned like a slap in the face: he was not my friend; he was trying to take Alex from me. I had to remember that. And yet how little I knew then about how very much Vincent was not my friend.

Rita returned with Alex bundled in a snowsuit, shoes, and socks, carrying a blue backpack. As we made our way to the kitchen door, Vincent handed me an unwrapped package of Werther's Original caramel hard candies. He mumbled, "Merry Christmas," looking at the floor.

Alex was ready to charge out the door, but I told him to first give his grandma and dad a hug. When we exited, I saw that Victoria was waiting outside the van. She slid open the rear door for Alex and helped buckle him in as I put his backpack in place. I buckled myself back in on the passenger side, my heart thumping. I feared some reprisal until we were completely off and away. We made small talk as we headed down the driveway back to the Bagginses' home in Vancouver. My body sighed into the seat once we reached the open road and were out of gunshot range.

At the Bagginses', Alex and I played free from worry about damaging antiques or spilling juice on expensive carpets. We were now surrounded by people without antagonistic courtroom agendas, let alone guns. We walked to the local playground, joined in preparing, eating, and cleaning up after family-style meals. We spent evenings working on puzzles, playing games, or watching movies and munching popcorn with our hosts. The Baggins kids all packed into one bedroom so Alex and I could have one to ourselves.

The visit sped by, and when it was over, Victoria again trundled us in the van so we could meet Vincent at a Burger King to deliver Alex. Pearl had by then secured a restraining order for me in Oregon. She had also successfully negotiated for a neutral public place for all custody exchanges. No more trips to the lion's den.

CHAPTER FOURTEEN

LOGIC HAS NO POWER HERE

As Christmas vacation ended, so, too, did my visitation with Alex. I flew back to New Jersey and a teeming schedule of graduate coursework, research, teaching, and preparation for a complex divorce. Contested custody meant that I had to convince a judge that my studio apartment was as appealing for a soon-to-be four-year-old as the country estate he now enjoyed. I photographed my apartment and documented how I'd provide for Alex, including specifics regarding daycare, a pediatrician, and what afterschool activities I could offer. When the semester ended, I returned to Oregon for the divorce and the Baggins took me in yet again.

As the proceedings dragged on, the court case grew uglier and more complicated. After Vincent's legal paper trail emerged, I discovered that his history of anger mismanagement did not originate with me. Meanwhile, my visits with Alex required formal legal negotiating and removing him from his routines. He felt the tension. Neither party was to alienate Alex's affection from the other. I took that to heart—it was in Alex's best interest. Vincent's household, however, did not share that opinion. I took a long-stay motel room in downtown Vancouver, Washington, across the Columbia River from Portland.

Eventually, the proceedings required an evaluation of our respective parenting skills. I went to my appointment by bus. The social worker's office was the size of a walk-in closet. She wore a black-and-white polyester dress splattered with bright, red poppies and carried herself like an aged turnip, upright but sort of soft around the edges. Besides her social-work license and diploma, on the wall hung a sign that read, "When I am an old woman, I shall wear purple."

"I like that poem," I said.

She looked at me somewhat cross: "I plan to retire soon."

The way she scowled, I surmised that she thought I was up to no good.

"Do you have children?" I asked, trying to get to know this person who was about to probe into my personal life with gynecological intimacy.

"No. But we are here to interview you, not me," she snapped before swiveling briskly toward me in her desk chair.

"Okay," I said, shrugging my shoulders to indicate it was no worry and to help me relax. I sat in a wooden interrogation seat, jammed between a table slathered in documents and the door.

When she got around to asking about my apartment, I pulled out my photos, glad to have done my homework. *She ought to like this*, I thought to myself. I felt prepared, responsible, and confident that the photos proved that I had a good place for Alex. It was obvious that I'd thought through how to provide for him and that I knew my son's needs.

I showed her photo after photo—the office wall of my studio apartment with a shelf to keep papers out of toddler reach; the comfy sofa to lounge; the place for Alex's bed; the kitchen, the bathroom, and the view out the fire escape overlooking the woods. I described the child-friendly sociability of the French Department. Relieved that I'd made a good case for Alex's new home, I looked up at her for some sign of approval. Frowning, she said, "It looks too neat."

Too neat? Are you serious? I groaned silently; the wind knocked out of my chest. Aloud, I blathered, "I tidied up to take the photo."

I wanted to scream, "Do you expect me to be a slob? I have shelves to keep my stuff organized; I am a full-time graduate student and teacher! I must be organized to do my job!"

She looked on, frowning.

"Is that bad? Really?" I asked.

"A child makes a mess," she said the way a zookeeper might refer to a monkey in a cage.

"I'm ready for him; I can handle a mess. I know my son! I have to keep fragile things out of reach, but there's plenty of space for his toys," I said.

"Humph," she answered, turning her back to me as she swiveled away on her chair. She began filling out papers on her desk.

Still sitting in the little wooden chair, I asked, "Are we done?"

"Yes, you pay the receptionist on your way out," she said without looking up from her papers.

I looked at the clock; it was past 4:30 p.m. I concluded that she must have been angry that my appointment had kept her overtime. "Bye, then," I said, trying to stay cheerful as I mustered my resolve to enter the endless gray hallway.

The corridor eventually led to a bulletproof window. There, I had to cough up a hundred and eighty dollars—cash or check—for my share of the legal custodial evaluation. Besides the financial sting, I felt as though I'd miserably failed an absurd test of my character as a parent. A social worker who'd never parented had concocted mysterious criteria by which to evaluate me relying upon theoretical, potentially dated statistics and textbook descriptions. In particular, she was clueless about my Alex, his personality, our life together, and the depth of our relationship.

As the court date approached, the absurdity of the process seemed only to increase. I was away from home; camping in a motel; trying to have a "normal" rapport with Alex; having to negotiate with people who avidly disliked me in order to see him while being scrutinized from every angle—financial, psychological, and historical. Furthermore, I was expected to be "on stage" in the courthouse, replete with the appropriate attire.

I had court-sanctioned visits with Alex on alternate weeks. Unable to afford a rental car, I rode the city bus from my Vancouver motel into downtown Portland, roughly ten miles each way, for hearings and meetings. I longed for home in New Jersey. I missed my regular routines, my work and friends. There, I wasn't a stranger from back east under constant scrutiny and suspicion.

Divorce examinations, cross-examinations, official paper filing, and written statements filled my days, with meetings and calls to Pearl in between. Only the bus trips from Vancouver into Portland provided respite. Unable to read or write without getting carsick, I watched the scenery pass, my forehead planted against the cool glass of the bus window as I imagined myself on horseback racing the bus.

I could feel my steed's muscles rippling beneath my calves, hear him snort in rhythm to his hoof beats as we leapt fences and ditches; we galloped flat out through open grass or navigated tight quarters like seasoned barrel racers dodging trash dumpsters and fire hydrants, leaving the bus, and the court case, far behind.

My money was running out. I was an alien in Oregon—no roots, no job, no friends but the Baggins. My body chugged along like a car running on fumes. I focused my mind for strength to override my external circumstances by arising early in the morning to pray and prepare. When I prayed and really stopped to talk to God, the spiritual atmosphere around me changed; it was like the way the notes of a song can create a mood that takes you to a different emotional place. I felt heard—my words received—when I prayed, then I'd wait for God's response. The answer could come hours or years later. God could be sneaky about answering prayers and the form of His reply could be unexpected.

The probability of me winning custody was slim. Confirming my fears, Pearl said the social worker favored the grandmother as Alex's custodian. But the case was not between Rita and me; it was between Vincent and me. How would the judge interpret the law? I couldn't bear to consider the real consequences of losing. Yet winning remained an unrealistic possibility given the odds against me. Putting logic on hold, I relied on faith.

The court date arrived. My hands shook as I dressed and stifled sobs. I couldn't indulge in tears when I had to prepare and be presentable. The tears emerged in the form of sweat on my hands that fumbled the simple task of fastening buttons. I was sure this day would be an ordeal. I told myself, *I've done everything I could do as an offering. Now, it's in God's hands.*

As my hand closed over the doorknob to exit my motel room, the phone rang. It was Pearl.

"At the eleventh hour, Vincent's parents have filed for custody," she said, her clipped tone clearly furious that they did this at the last minute.

"What does this mean?" I asked

"If Vincent fails to get custody, they want to apply for custody of Alex as backup. I'm filing for a continuance. We need more time to prepare."

"Pearl, I need to get back to New Jersey. I have a non-refundable plane reservation and I'm out of money."

"No. You need to stay here and visit with Alex as much as possible. Since this was unplanned, the grandparents will have to pay for your continued stay at the hotel." She made sure I understood that the judge was not fond of either Vincent or me. It was the judge's job to be impartial. So when the court had ruled that the grandparents would have to pay for my hotel, I was relieved but knew it was not a sign that the court favored my position.

Okay, God, so this is the deal, I thought to myself as I put the hotel phone back in its cradle. If it was in God's hands, then I could relax and be grateful to see more of Alex. In keeping with that agenda, the first thing I did was change out of my court duds—the outfit I normally reserved for teaching—and back into jeans. I needed to ground myself. Goliath had grown by a factor of four: the two grandparents, their limitless supply of money, plus another attorney.

From the absurdity of having to justify myself as Alex's mother, to the astronomical legal fees, to the surreal experience of explaining to someone who'd never had kids that I could deal with my son's messes, I was now facing a court battle that looked impossible for me to win. In addition, I was having a sartorial crisis: I needed "girl clothes" but had very little money.

Pearl had pointed out that appearing in more feminine clothes—skirted suits instead of pants and a jacket—might make me look more appealing. So, on top of everything else, my appearance was an issue. Fancy clothes hadn't made my list of what I knew Alex needed from me: hugs, food, stories, playdates, schooling, and walks in the woods. Boy care required sweatshirts and sneakers, mud and glop. However, to "win" him, I had to convince strangers who needed to see me perform on the courthouse stage. Pearl had to spend the better part of an hour convincing me that my clothes mattered.

I thought a court case was like doing a calculus proof: you matched statements with theorems and their derivatives, showed corollaries and defined it all so it integrated perfectly with legal precedent, and voilà—"truth" and a lawful outcome. But there was so much more. Instead of lucid, rhythmical sine and cosine waves of logical progression, it seemed the process of going to court resembled the berserk lines of a toddler's drawing.

Amidst all that was stressful and wrong, luck winked at me. Walking back to the motel from the bus stop, I stumbled upon a thrift shop. There, for less than twenty dollars, I found a couple of outmoded skirted suits in passé pastels and polyester that fit perfectly. I hoped they would help me fit in better with the local culture. I thanked God for what others might call serendipity; I saw it as God's grace.

Mundane logic lost its power over me. Had I allowed it to control me, I would have had to give up. Exhausted from tension, my bank account drained, I longed to be with Alex. *God must have a plan in all this,* I thought, floating on faith to relieve my distress.

I had Alex with me July Fourth. We climbed stairs to the motel rooftop. Beneath the expanse of night sky two giant black snakes glistened below—the Willamette and Columbia Rivers. The fireworks doubled in size as they reflected off the water. From our perch, Alex and I watched multiple displays burst from the riverbanks. As the one closest to us exploded into chrysanthemums, circles of stars, random screamers, and streaming comets, "The Ride of the Valkyries" played over loudspeakers. For a moment, the music carried Alex and me far, far away, to some benign place where love was always strong, evil vanquished, and I could abandon myself to fate with a heart full of confidence.

Our day in court arrived. I entered the courthouse with Pearl, who towed a dolly laden with boxes of documents. We sat down at a wooden table, on the left facing the bench. On the right sat Vincent, his attorney, and his parents and their attorney. We all rose as the judge entered the room and the games began. It didn't take long for the difference of opinion regarding custody to indicate the case was contentious. Accusations accompanied by cross-examinations proliferated.

I needed to find witnesses to testify on my behalf. Vincent and his attorney seemed to have put me in the position of having to prove my innocence before their warped interpretations. My faithful friend Victoria—a social worker by day who by night managed the needs of her household of kids and her spouse as only a Jewish mother does—took the stand on my behalf. She looked so small and pale under her cloud of fluffy black hair. I felt wretched subjecting her to this courtroom trauma. But she spoke with aplomb and motherly kindness about my parenting.

The wife of one of Vincent's employers, a Mormon, under oath on the stand admitted that Vincent's driving was so crazy that "I would never let my children ride with him." She was a "hostile" witness. She didn't want to take the stand at all since her husband and Vincent were good friends. Afterwards, outside the courtroom, she came up to me, flushed with fear and confusion as her husband and Vincent conferred on the far side of the lobby. She gave my hand a quick squeeze, and then spot-checked the men across the way before glancing into my eyes. We'd met over dinner long ago and had enjoyed each other's company. All that was changed now.

I reached out to hug her. Looking down at the floor, she shied away and hunched her shoulders. We chatted a little. When I thanked her, she gave a quick nod. Then, eyes glued to the floor, she fled back across the lobby to her husband's side.

To save money, Pearl had me research precedents in books at her office and in documents down at the courthouse. I found more evidence that supported our case, prior incidents recorded in Vincent's Oregon police record. His case history, though a surprise to me, turned out to be substantial. Pearl's experience in family court and clerking for various judges had given her insight into the law and the court presentation. I appreciated her expertise, wanted to soak it up to understand, but was far from mastering what she knew despite my motivated attentiveness. My legal sleuthing, meetings, interviews, and visitation coordinating with Alex's schedule kept me in constant motion, even when the judge took a couple of weeks off in the middle of the case.

Upon the judge's return, as the trial dragged on day after day, the judge voiced her frustration over how long the proceedings were taking. She said that a custody disagreement should have concluded in a single day, or two tops. But this case had stretched into two, three, then four days in court. By day five, her scowl had deepened from resignation to resentment, which was tempered only by the higher calling of the law itself.

Then, day six arrived, and with it the *pièce de résistance*: Vincent's attorney took on my affiliation with the Unification movement, saying that I was not a fit parent because I was "a Moonie."

Pearl objected to this derogatory term. It was sustained. I had to explain that within the movement we called each other "Moonies" with affection, but that the correct term was Unificationist.

At this time, controversy continued to swirl around the movement. "Moonies are brainwashed" was still common thinking. Psychologists who specialized in faith-breaking called themselves "deprogrammers." They made fantastic sums of money kidnapping Unificationists (and others), isolating them in hotel rooms, and subjecting them to hour upon hour of false accusations, as well as legitimate critiques of the movement. Deprogrammers used emotional manipulation to coerce adults to renounce a faith community they had voluntarily joined.

These strong-arm tactics could be effective. Those "deprogrammed" often went into the deprogramming business themselves. The movement, despite enthusiastic adherents, didn't use such tactics. People made choices based on their own free will and they were free to leave at any time. Many did just that without deprogramming as an impetus.

Faith can produce profound will power. I would argue that people in faith communities are a self-selected group of stubborn wretches. Think of the Israelites who wandered in the wilderness for forty years, or the Christians willing to be fed to the lions, or the pacifists who risked and gave their lives to march with Gandhi. To choose to live a life prioritizing humility, chastity, and obedience to an ethical code may have been unusual, even radical, but it wasn't illegal.

However, it was not only deprogramming that jeopardized my court case. Bad press and ignorance, added to the deliberate misinformation from deprogrammers creating erroneous preconceptions about the movement that stirred fear. There had been extensive prejudice against the church long before Father Moon was accused of tax evasion in the mid-eighties. By the early nineties, in divorce cases in other states, members of the Unification Church had been denied custody because of their faith.

The legal enforcement of suspicion was a violation that went beyond name-calling. On top of what was in Alex's best interest and my ability to parent, I wondered whether my constitutional right regarding freedom of religion could be at stake. Pearl didn't think so. Even though I no longer considered myself a member of the Unification Church, this issue hounded me as Vincent's attorney was making it an issue.

Mulling over all this, I decided to consult Rodger, an old friend from seminary and CARP. He was now the Unificationist pastor in Washington State, right next to Oregon. Besides being the locus of my court case, Oregon was also where Father had sent the first missionaries to America from Korea. This piece of "providential history" gave me reason to believe that my case served a bigger purpose, one that related to Father on a spiritual level.

My spiritual hunch was not due to happenstance. Key spiritual events in my life had shaped my thinking: the dreams I had in Russia and upon my return prior to Alex's conception; the dream I had about Father and Vincent; the spiritual being of love that had come to me and told me to reveal the truth about the abuse I'd experienced. My spiritual antennae tingled and I felt a sense of higher calling, that this court case involved more on a spiritual plane than what met the eye.

There were also some unusual coincidences that made me feel my case in some ways continued the history of the Unification movement in America. I had personally known both of the first missionaries to the US: David S.C. Kim, who was the president of UTS when I attended there, and Dr. Young Oon Kim (no relation to David), who researched and taught at the seminary. I saw her as a mentor for she was both an academic author and professor. I'd read her books and taken classes with her but I had another bond with her at that time: Boris, my ex-blessing partner, was her spiritual grandson—she had introduced his parents to the church.

All this led me to feel responsible, not only to myself, to God, and to country, but to the history of restoration in America. It seemed my life had intertwined with key figures that made me personally involved. I felt Rodger would understand all that. We'd first met in CARP days, when he was a leader and I was but a mouse. Since then, we had attended seminary together so I felt much more his peer, or sister, rather than an underling.

Though I didn't know exactly what the opposing attorneys would ask, I knew they'd question me about my faith on the stand. I also knew that testifying to my beliefs could jeopardize my chance to win custody. Rodger, though a pastor, was a dad himself as well as a friend. I trusted his opinion.

I was temporarily staying at the Baggins again when Rodger returned my phone call. To speak in private, I used the phone in Victoria and Mark's bedroom. Clutching the receiver to my ear, I sat on my knees in front of a nightstand by their bed. In the hallway, the rubber ducky voices of kids playing rose and fell between giggles. Through the window I heard the wind rustle through the trees. I was a live wire, sizzling with stress and eager to grasp Rodger's every word.

Yet even though I listened with rapt attention to my old classmate, I felt an answer arise within me quite apart from his voice. I thought to myself how strange it was to seek advice about a situation I'd never imagined encountering. First, I'd never imagined myself married, yet I was going through my second divorce. Second, I'd never imagined myself a mother, but once I had Alex, I couldn't imagine life without him. Finally, I'd never imagined being interrogated on the witness stand in court regarding my relationship with Rev. Moon, and this at the risk of losing my beloved son—particularly after having left the movement. Despite or due to my atypical spiritual journey, I felt the Principle was true the way karma is true whether or not you practice Hinduism. I knew God had seen me through all manner of adventures that no one else really fathomed.

Given legal precedents and public misconception about the church at that time, the risk I faced avowing affiliation with the movement was not some melodrama of my own imagination. Rodger understood the consequences. He knew Unification Thought and the Principle, yet he was pragmatic and an engaged spouse and parent with his wife and children. Having worked in business and the communication industry for years, he knew the court, like popular culture, held a bias against the movement. Above all, he understood what it was like to both love your own child and God with all your heart. And I knew he would pray for me that God's will be done.

Beyond courtrooms and legal strategies, I loved Alex and I loved God. Rodger advised me to do the practical thing, saying, "Forget the church. Say what you have to in order to get your son!"

I felt relieved. As a pastor, he'd given me permission to deny the church. Yet I knew in my heart, however much of a blessing I felt his advice to be and however well intentioned, I had to follow my own conscience as I was responsible for my own choices. We both knew Father's example. He'd sacrificed everything for God. Though an innocent man, in refusing to deny his faith, he'd repeatedly survived wrongful, life-threatening imprisonment under the Japanese occupation of Korea in 1944, and later under the North Korean regime of Kim Il Sung in 1946.

My church loyalty wasn't an issue for I'd always been unorthodox. The crux was my own conscience, my own relationship with God. Would I speak the truth? Would I be true to my own heart and my own relationship with the divine presence I felt all around me? Was I Abraham and was God asking me to sacrifice Isaac? For me, the church and Father were two distinct entities. For those committed to the movement, the line of separation was blurry. I listened to Rodger's advice and appreciated his wisdom. Yet I knew the odds remained so stacked against me in court that I could rely only on God, not human logic. I had one advantage over Abraham, however: I knew the outcome of his story. Abraham struggled; he delayed; but in the end, he followed through and Isaac lived. God didn't need Isaac's blood. He needed a human being to trust Him.

As I settled the phone in its cradle after talking with Rodger, I felt calmer. Not only because he's given me candid advice, but because I appreciated having a friend and, beyond that, felt confident that God knew what He was doing even if I didn't know what I was doing. The next thing I did was pray to entrust Alex to God. Years prior, I'd offered him to Heaven after his birth, following Unification tradition. Alex, I felt, belonged to God, not to me.

Tears gushed at the thought of losing Alex, but I decided to trust God. The skies didn't part and I wasn't filled with confidence.

The next day, taking transcripts by phone, we completed several hearings at the law office rather than in court. Father O'Hara, the priest in Gardendale, and Ann, the neighboring parishioner who'd posted bail for Vincent, testified by phone to my ability to parent.

Proving one's innocence took this strange twist—people I'd asked to vouch for Vincent's character to get him out of jail in Birmingham, I now asked to testify to mine for our divorce. They knew me and mercifully agreed. The probing questions of the attorneys remained focused on the divorce, so the old felony charge never came up during these proceedings.

Vincent's attorney had subpoenaed my photo albums, including candid close-ups of Mother and Father Moon—Mother looking up in prayer and Father looking paternal through his spectacles. These were precious photos Paul Russo, a professional photographer and my spiritual parent or mentor, had taken before he was deprogrammed. Now they were submitted as evidence that I was a brainwashed Moonie, incapable of thinking for myself or caring properly for Alex. I would never see the photos again.

My sister flew in from Alaska to provide moral support. She could only stay a short while but wanted to attend at least one day of the proceedings. She'd saved letters I'd written to her about Alex—silly natterings about our daily life. These provided key evidence of my engagement with my son. Victoria, in nearby Vancouver, was also be called to the witness stand to testify about my parenting. She'd seen me interact with Alex first-hand, was a local citizen in good standing, and a parent herself. All this was to build a case for me, an outsider from New Jersey, to be understood by the court as a normal parent.

By day seven in court, we were all so familiar with each other that it would have seemed strange to be anywhere else. Together, we stood when the judge entered. Protocol united us in the law even though our preferences for the legal outcome diverged. The bailiff called me to the stand for the first time. I crossed the divide from where I sat next to my attorney, Pearl, and walked past the judge's bench to the wooden chair to her left, the witness stand. Once seated there, I felt very small. The judge's bench was on a platform and so she sat above me. Even though I sat stiff and straight from tension, I had to look up to see her face.

I scanned the audience at the back of the courtroom but recognized only Pearl, Vincent, and his parents at the counsel tables in front. Behind them, a bar separated the gallery from the public seating area. The other onlookers remained a blur. Besides my sister and Victoria, who I knew sat somewhere in the audience, the rest were strangers—people who I assumed felt unsympathetic to my cause and who couldn't possibly know or care what I was feeling as I prepared to bare my soul to fight for my son. In my mind, they blurred into an impressionist painting of gray faces; this helped me to stave off utter stage fright. The thought of speaking in front of antagonistic strangers only added to the stress.

"Do you swear to tell the truth, the whole truth?" the bailiff asked.

"I do," I answered, eyes riveted on his as I placed my hand upon the worn cover of the Bible he held in front of me.

Scanning the courtroom again, my eyes noted my in-laws and their attorney sitting next to Vincent and his attorney. Their faces had various grim expressions as they looked at me from their table on the left. I didn't allow my eyes to dwell on them or take in the threat of their demeanor. Instead, for confidence, my eyes searched out my only ally, Pearl, who was sitting at the table to the right.

Vincent's attorney approached me and with a gleam of restrained triumph in his eye he asked, "Do you believe Rev. Moon is the Messiah?"

I felt a hush descend over the court. I didn't expect such a blunt question. Nor had I rehearsed any answers in kind. Silently, all I could pray was *Heavenly Father, not my will but thy will.*

But suddenly I felt a spirit of clarity and calm. No longer intimidated by the attorney who could take my son from me, I answered firmly, meeting his eyes, "Yes, I do."

After a brief pause, I continued, "And Judge Brown, Rev. Moon says that you should be a messiah too."

I spoke looking up at her black cloaked figure to my right. "And so should you and you and you," I said, pointing around the courtroom with my right hand. "We all need to be messiahs to help God on earth."

My voice was strong, confident. I felt ready for the next question, any question. I glanced at Judge Brown: she was watching Vincent's attorney. He said, "No more questions, Your Honor."

His triumphant look turned resolute. He had made his point. I was a Moonie. The attorney of Vincent's parents had no questions for me. Dismissed from the stand, I stepped down and sat next to Pearl. I was glad that she seemed so collected, shiny, clean, and put together compared to frumpy me, in my serviceable but dated Goodwill suit. She leaned a little toward me. Her face held a professional, understated smile beneath adroitly applied peach blush and lip gloss. She said, "You did fine."

This reassured me, but as the proceedings continued, my confidence dismantled. The other side played phone conversations between Alex and me that Vincent had secretly recorded. My plaintive "Alex? Alex are you there?" dangled in the gray courtroom air.

The opposing attorneys twisted the call to show that I didn't know how to engage Alex. On the witness stand, the social worker who had never had kids said that in her professional opinion, the grandmother should be Alex's parent.

Pearl presented the evidence of Vincent's past anger-management problems. He affirmed that armed guards had escorted him from a previous place of employment. There were back-and-forths over that, evidence that it was more than mere protocol, evidence that his superiors had concerns about his anger. Vincent more than bristled at this, speaking out of turn. The judge reprimanded him.

After that day's cross-examinations, the two opposing attorneys presented their closing arguments. Pearl summarized our position. There was no jury, so the recap seemed more a formality than anything else. The judge would deliberate on the entire eight days of arguments in terms of "the best interests of the child," Oregon law, and legal precedent. We had to wait until the following day for her decision.

My sister flew back to Alaska to resume work. Alex was staying with Vincent and his parents. Hydroplaning on spiritual energy, held upright by invisible forces, I returned to the hotel. Every ounce of my physical and emotional vitality had drained away during the proceedings. Without Alex, I felt withered, a feeble November leaf in a December wind. I prayed, sitting Japanese-style on the floor, holding sacred space around me, then showered, and turned on the hotel television for company as I waited to hear what would come of this day and all the days before.

The only sure thing I knew was that my testimony that Father was the Messiah, Father's teaching about how God needs all of us, would be in the court annals for history. While that offering may have been a providential victory, my human side, the side that would die a thousand deaths if they kept Alex in Oregon, was a shattered mess. The odds were so clearly against us.

The next day, after rising early to pray, I dressed for court with a morbid calm. I felt surrounded with the heavy air of inevitability that directed me like a prisoner on death row going to my execution. My life had been publicly torn apart and misinterpreted for weeks. I was an outsider in Oregon, now a stranger to my former in-laws. And if I believed the attorneys for the opposition, I was a stranger to my own son.

Vincent's abuse was not admissible as evidence. Allowing Alex to live with an abusive parent would show poor parenting judgment on my part even though I was trusting Vincent's mother, not Vincent, to oversee raising Alex while they lived in Oregon. My restraining orders existed for my protection but remained legally irrelevant for determining custody. How could I possibly be given the right to parent my own flesh and blood?

I faced losing everything of earthly value: Alex and my career—for I would have to stay in Oregon to fight for visitation rights. To top it off, paying the legal fees from this protracted battle looked hopeless. I'd risked everything. I clung to God as my one true witness. I braced myself for emotional devastation. If I lost Alex, all I would have is God.

"All rise," said the bailiff. We did. Then we sat as Judge Brown rendered the verdict. "After extensive deliberating on this one-day custody case, which has extended to an unprecedented eight days, I grant full custody of Alex to the mother with visitation to . . ."

I could hear that she was outlining specifics but the words "full custody" had momentarily stopped my heart. Certain that I'd lost, I thought Vincent and his parents had received full custody. Then Pearl explained, and it began to sink in: I was granted full custody. I drew in a breath of air of a depth I'd not dared attempt since receiving the divorce papers that called for Alex's custody to be taken from me those eight months ago. Now, I started to reconstruct myself. I could dare to imagine a world where I could freely be with my son, where I was not publicly accused of being an incompetent mother, a brainwashed Moonie, and a cold-hearted careerist. Inwardly, I shot God a silent prayer of thanks, but there was no time for extensive internal reflection, tears, or rejoicing. The mantle of information and responsibilities that cloaked me weighed heavy with solemnity.

— CHAPTER FIFTEEN —
RECONFIGURING

Sitting in my little studio apartment back in New Jersey, I assessed the reality of what "divorced" meant for me. Alex was too young to fly alone. The judge decreed that the parent receiving Alex for visitation needed to accompany him on the cross-country flight. Vincent would fly to New Jersey to collect Alex for his visitations; I'd fly to Oregon to bring him home. We were to alternate Christmas and Easter breaks with him.

The court ordeal left me stunned and daunted by my share of the cost for the cross-continental holiday commutes. Yet I was grateful for how simple it'd been to disentangle our finances by simply letting go. We had no shared assets and we'd each kept our own credit cards and their accompanying debts in our own names. I didn't seek half of Vincent's property (his house in Portland, cars, investments) in the settlement; my only concern was Alex.

It was both thrilling and hectic to prepare for his arrival before school started in August. My professors recommended the daycare at Rutgers. It was close to the French Department and had parking—a campus rarity. Taking lunch at a nearby cafeteria, I watched the activities of the little place. The teachers were attentive and the curriculum looked enriching. Their healthy meals and snacks boded well, too. Alex's medical records in hand, I stopped in to enroll him. The cheery receptionist briskly photocopied my papers. She then gave me a tour that confirmed the hearty recommendations I'd heard. Pen in hand, I was eager to sign him up. Reading the heart-stopping faculty-salary price, I asked about a graduate-student discount.

"Certainly!" said the receptionist brightly as she furnished another set of figures. *What a relief*, I thought as I resumed breathing. Then she dropped the bombshell, "The waiting list is fourteen months."

Panic encouraged me to focus since Alex's arrival was as imminent as my classes. I hit the streets of New Brunswick nose to the ground to flush out affordable, educational, and loving daycare. All three qualities seemed nonexistent. Affordable and loving went hand in glove but included videos and Sesame Street reruns for activities. Educational and affordable were rare and often had the starchy atmosphere of West Point instead of a place where a kid would get a hug if he skinned his knee.

Patrolling on foot, I followed a sign into the basement of a red-brick church in downtown New Brunswick. Talking with the attentive teachers, I could tell that they took relationships as seriously as the ABCs. The church stood close to the swanky end of Livingston Avenue, with its seventeenth- and eighteenth-century manors. Around the corner stretched the neighborhood where those who formerly tended the historic homes once lived: maids, gardeners, and construction workers. Their row houses dated from the same era as the mansions but had aluminum siding instead of brick and wood. Alex would be one of two Caucasian kids at the daycare. Its diversity, I thought, would be a good change from his life in pasty-faced Oregon.

Discovering a daycare haven for Alex felt like another gift from God. I liked its daily program of activities, regular meals and snacks, as well as exercise for the kids. One of the caregivers, when I told her what'd happened with Vincent, said to me, "It seems hard now. But give it time. You will heal." She spoke from experience.

I burst into tears upon hearing this, and she hugged me. It was such a relief to feel understood. The personal side of my life was alien to my students at Rutgers, and for the most part, my colleagues too. I wanted to maintain a professional public face devoted to academic excellence, both in my studies and teaching. Yet on an emotional level, I felt my experience was closer to that of folks on welfare coping with the real perils of inner-city violence. They knew the harsh choices between love and death; they understood mortal danger and how poverty didn't define character.

What I'd survived seemed distant from the experience of childless, unrumpled academicians debating esoteric theories. In academic circles, the greatest mortal threat appeared to be mockery—for instance, the reprisal of a disdainful sneer should one choose an inferior vintage of wine to accompany appetizers at a faculty function. My department wasn't snooty, but I did feel as if I'd infiltrated paradise from a hell unknown to my colleagues.

My student loans helped to pay my credit card debt for the roundtrip flights to Oregon and the retainer fee for my attorney. My parents had chipped in a thousand dollars toward the fees—a generous amount for them given that they owed me nothing. But the total bill was close to $65,000—a sum I couldn't begin to accommodate. Thanks to Pearl, and the encouragement of one of my housemates on Commercial Avenue, I was able to arrange for initial monthly payments of $25.00. At the time, my annual salary was $10,000, plus tuition and health coverage.

While I continued to take prayer walks and reflect, once Alex arrived, my life as a single parent became a living, breathing prayer amid action. Our routine was to leave the "Mommy apartment," as Alex called it, in the dark to arrive at daycare by six in the morning so I could go to work. I picked him up by six in the evening, as the sun went down. He ate breakfast, lunch, and snacks at school and had dinner with me on weekdays. After picking him up from daycare, we'd often get burgers or other drive-through take-out, then head for the park to picnic, play on the swings, and stroll on the trail that meandered around a duck pond in South River. On one such outing, a pint-sized Alex turned to me and said with a ship captain's fortitude, "I want to get married and to have ten children."

"Wow, Alex!" I said. "Who will take care of the children?" "My wife," he answered with complete confidence.

I said a prayer for her.

My teaching assistantship salary was insufficient to sustain single parenting. To afford daycare and other expenses, I tutored on the side. One day, I received a telephone call from one Michael Moffatt, a professor of anthropology. His high-school-aged foster son needed tutoring. He added, "The head of the language program said that you'd be just the person for me—someone older, a veteran teacher and no-nonsense." I wondered how much older he thought I was, but I agreed to meet with his foster son, Ivan. I gave Michael directions to my apartment and arranged to tutor while Alex was in daycare. Thus, into my world of sixteenth-century bedfellows and outings with Alex in the park entered Michael, a man of the current era yet deeply drawn to history, literature, and nature. I first saw his lanky frame as he walked with Ivan across the courtyard to my building. Michael had the two arms of his sweater draped over either shoulder, European-style. Ivan, too, was reed-like: his oversized skateboarder's T-shirt fell long over his jeans as he ambled at Michael's side, matching his stride.

I was set to work with Ivan, expecting his guardian to drop him off, and then leave. But Michael seemed congenial and quite talkative with me, which I found curious. As he lingered, he asked me anthropological questions to situate me in my kinship group and chatted about birding—a passion he and Ivan shared. Michael was single and lived in Highland Park, like many professors. Unlike most, however, he volunteered to serve as a foster parent for Ivan, whose mother lived in a disadvantaged neighborhood. By living with Michael, Ivan could attend high school in a good school district.

At the next lesson's end, more friendly chat ensued. After Ivan exited into the stairwell, Michael remained at the threshold and said, "Would you like to go out with me sometime? I wanted to ask you last time but thought I should get to know you a bit first."

"Well, I'm not sure I know how to date. I've, I've, um, been married," I stammered. "Though I'm divorced now," I added.

The word "divorce" still felt strange in my mouth, though the rupture with my ex was definitive. We left it at that. As Michael remained amiable, I recruited some other women to go out with him. Maybe God wanted me to match him, I thought. He seemed like a nice enough chap.

One graduate student friend agreed to exchange email with him, but nothing came of it. She said, "I decided that since Michael really likes you, he probably wouldn't like me seeing as you and I are so different."

I was flattered by the "really likes you" comment but remained undaunted in my effort to match him with someone else. I tried to set him up with a feminist who was on my dissertation committee. She'd made frequent reference to her single status and said she was looking for a man. Plus, she had a good sense of humor. I blushed when she said she thought he was too old for her. Michael was pushing fifty to my thirty-five, but he looked like a forty-year-old.

My tutoring Ivan was not the result of Michael's or Ivan's extreme interest in French, but due to Ivan's mother, Yulia. She, a dissident Russian artist, insisted that Ivan have classical training, and this included French. For Michael to keep me on as a tutor, he needed to obtain her approval. He telephoned for permission to bring Yulia to meet me. I agreed, though Alex would be home.

The day of their visit, I heard a knock at the door. I opened it to Michael and a middle-aged woman of medium height, muscular yet graceful, with piercing blue eyes like her son and fair hair, faded but not gray, flying out of its loosely fitted clips. Everything moved around her—the scarf around her neck, the fabric of her jacket. Her hands seemed to cavort apart from her arms. They flew about as she spoke; her eyes darting this way and that. Syllables hung in the air and whirled around her vehement and bold Russian accent.

Michael had told me that he and Yulia did not get on well. There had been at least one instance of dishes flying from her hand across the kitchen in response to some disagreement. Yulia and inhibition were entirely unacquainted. Whereas Michael had been raised in Protestant New England, where buttoned-down repression was a way of life, Yulia was tempestuous even at rest. Nothing about her hinted at moderation—every moment was a sublime opportunity for self-expression. She was always "on."

She said a few short words to Alex and then shook my hand. After nodding her approval of me, she flew out the door with Michael in obedient pursuit; he was to transport her to the train back to Jersey City. Michael later called to tell me that I'd passed the Yulia test. In fact, she'd reproached Michael: "You must be good to her. She has SoFFF-ered."

I hadn't told Michael anything about Vincent. We had a professional relationship with me serving as a tutor for his foster son. But somehow this Russian intervention seemed more than coincidental. My main activity was not tutoring, however, but research, teaching, and single parenting. So when Michael and Ivan left to travel the world on Semester at Sea, I didn't seek other students to tutor.

Every other holiday and part of the summer, Alex had to fly to Oregon and I would have to fly there to pick him up. Scrimping to pay airfare, my schedule was full as I attended classes, taught, and prepared my thesis proposal. The latter entailed reading French works on satire across all the centuries, as well as primary and secondary works on satire in the sixteenth century.

Researching classical Roman satire and my sixteenth-century authors absorbed me as I prepared to defend my dissertation proposal to my committee. I wanted to investigate both the satire of war and satire as war. Like the theistic humanists of the time, I found it appalling that both Catholics and Protestants would kill one another in the name of Jesus during the wars of religion. Though satire served to cloak critiques of political and theocratic policies, satirists wagered their lives by writing. Small violations of religious doctrine could send an author to burn at the stake. The Inquisition had substantial power and influence as the Catholic Church and the state sorted out the divine right of kings, often with the sword. Yet, as sixteenth-century society emerged from the feudal system, linguistic vernacular took hold and the advent of the printing press helped democratize access to literature, much as the nascent internet was beginning to in my era. These juxtapositions fascinated me.

Furthermore, satirists critiquing war often waged stylistic wars on poetic and literary tradition. Thus, form and function, literature and culture, were in full flux in the Renaissance, making it feel contemporary. The pugilistic attitude and wit of satire appealed to me too, given the battles I'd fought in my own life—not only theologically, but personally, simply to live a life of peace and relative calm. Wounded by religious bigotry, I found comfort in the broadminded, theistic compassion of Rabelais, Erasmus and other sixteenth-century humanists.

My sense of mission was keen. I reveled in the theistic strains of my satirists' voices and detected spiritual components in each one I read. Their lived experience with war resonated with me. Aided by the theologically neutral language of Unification Thought, I wanted to show the relevance of their wisdom to the current era.

My connection with each author was palpable. I followed Erasmus' advice to "make of Christ a friend" by reading scripture—only my scripture was sixteenth-century French satire. I sensed a visceral spiritual rapport with the authors I read so doggedly. D'Aubigné remained ever close to my heart from my master's degree days. His baroque and fearless poetry inspired me to stand up for religious principles even in the face of persecution. I credit him with giving me the fortitude to defend a theistic approach to literature, even as his spirit had inspired me to speak my own truth in court.

However, as I continued my studies, I discovered alternatives to d'Aubigné's purely Huguenot vision. Rabelais' humanist-tempered Catholicism beguiled me. The more I read of his work, the more certain I felt that he held the key for reconciliation between Protestantism and Catholicism, and by extension any who found enmity due to dogma. In the process of my research, as I connected emotionally with my authors, spiritually I felt their desperation and urgency to establish peace. I shed countless tears. Their longing surpassed the words I read. From the spiritual world, I sensed their yearning to see God's ideal fulfilled on earth. Their zeal was so powerful, their desire for peace so great, their horror at injustice and stupid bigotry so vast, that purely intellectualizing their ideas was insufficient. I felt that somehow there had to be a spiritual explanation of how and why these authors wrote.

My own life course fueled my excitement for my topic. I'd been persecuted for my beliefs at UNC and refused entry to the PhD program there because of them. At the time, I took it as routine bigotry. How could I expect less when Father Moon himself had been unjustly imprisoned for his faith? Furthermore, when Vincent went ballistic, he'd destroyed holy books and photos that I held dear, in addition to decrying my faith and using it as a reason to deny me custody during the protracted divorce proceedings. I had actual experience of how false beliefs— like Vincent's interpretations when he was enraged, and ignorant religious bigotry—could, in practice, cause real suffering.

To stay focused, I continued to study martial arts. It had a spiritual or "otherworldly" aspect to it. I witnessed first-hand how the most advanced martial art masters at the *dojang* had a shaman's control of themselves and chi energy. They maintained a spiritual discipline that aligned with their physical control. Practicing Taekwondo, I experienced the value of self-discipline and inner mastery. It was the lack of self-reflection and internal discipline, it seemed to me, that my satirists lamented most in the excesses of the wars of religion.

My hours were filled with Alex, my studies, Taekwondo, and tutoring I wedged in anew. Whenever Michael brought Ivan for tutoring, however, he seemed to have all the time in the world. I thought of him simply as Ivan's parent and an academic. It was only later that I realized he was somewhat of a celebrity among the Rutgers community for his ethnography of college dormitory life, *Coming of Age in New Jersey*, which I immediately read after meeting him.

Just as I'd researched the publications of my professors, I naturally looked up Michael's work at the library. His ethnography of undergraduates describes how and what he learned about the "real" life of students through anonymous written questionnaires and by interviewing them while disguised as a fellow student. His youthful looks had enabled him to infiltrate their world by posing as a slightly older undergraduate living in the campus dormitory.

For me, Michael was not a hotshot professor, but simply an involved dad of one of my students. We shared a relaxed attitude about clothes—more "casual Friday" than uptown chic—and this reflected our down-to-earth approaches to life. He shared my fondness for nature and recounted family and birding stories during our little chats when he dropped off Ivan. I felt an easy camaraderie with him as a kindred spirit. Indeed, many people did, for he was approachable and honest in expressing his opinions. With Michael, it was not necessary to impress and guess where you stood politically or socially: he took an anthropological interest in people from all walks of life. He seemed at ease with well-to-do and brilliant people or simple folk without a dime because he was unpretentious. And there was nothing about me he seemed to reject, including my humble Mommy apartment.

I saw him and Ivan regularly, both before and after they returned from Semester at Sea. One day, I mentioned that my dissertation topic had been approved. Michael jumped in to suggest he take me out for dinner to celebrate that Friday night. Surprised, but a little excited, I agreed. No one else was in my life to share the significance of the event. My brother, sister, and parents were not involved with my intellectual life. My graduate student friends led busy lives and many hadn't yet arrived at that point in their studies, so I didn't want to flaunt my victory lest it seem like boasting. However, with Michael,I enjoyed intellectual freedom. As he noted in *Coming of Age*, sharing one's intellectual delectations could be more intimate than sharing stories of sexual exploits; that was one hidden agenda of the college dorm—the freedom to share intellectually.

Our chats were fluid, wandering from muddy kids to intellectual discourse with ease. He asked me questions about why I thought this or that, what interested me in how a particular author interpreted something, or how the historical context played into the design of my thesis. He was, it seemed, fascinated by the alterity of the Renaissance and, in particular, by my interpretive twist that tiptoed around the dominant theories that seemed to embrace either orthodox Protestant or Catholic theology or the inherent atheism of literary theory. This was another area where we colluded—he was by no means driven by theological constructs, but he had his own critiques of deconstructionist and other postmodernist claims on analysis. And I deeply appreciated that we could converse on this level.

However enticing our intellectual compatibility, there remained for me the issue of spiritual direction, of God's blessing. Part of my hesitancy in getting to know Michael was my desire to stay pure, to do God's will. Two husbands later, it seemed that perhaps I was just another serial monogamist. But in truth, with both spouses, I'd desperately sought God's guidance in my life. I was interested in Michael, but resisted, waiting for some sign from God about how to relate to him.

Never much of a chef, I'd uncharacteristically prepared spaghetti for Alex the night Michael and I went out to dinner. I wanted Alex's meal to feel homey, but it was planned. Perhaps I wanted to appear a little more domestic than I really was. Though I'd not made the sauce from scratch, I'd heated it in an actual pot on the stove instead of using the microwave. And I'd boiled the noodles myself. I served Alex at the little table in the corner where we rarely ate. Having already seen him in and out of the bath, I was able to leave him for a couple of hours with toys to play with and a sitter for company.

Michael came to the door to get me, and after we left my apartment, he opened the passenger door of his Isuzu Trooper so I could climb up into the bucket seat. Before shutting the door behind me, he approached my side, reached down and pulled up my seatbelt for me. I blushed into the lengthening evening shadows. I felt the heat from his body beneath his ever-present wool sweater, then the warmth of his breath near my face as he pulled the shoulder strap across my chest and snapped the buckle by my left hip. My heart fluttered to rest as I saw his hands fully occupied with the manual shift as he drove.

Heading north, Michael took a turn into a residential area and became thoroughly lost. Or so he said. He'd been looking at me quite a bit and talking nonstop. We meandered back and forth through side streets and houses as he maintained he was innocent of our whereabouts. As the shadows eased into darkness, he leaned increasingly close to me as he spoke. I got the feeling that he might be interested in skipping dinner altogether and just finding a place to park. Slightly alarmed by the prospect, I said curtly, "If we run out of gas, I'm not pushing!"

My emphasis came from recalling one cross-country rideshare trip from Chapel Hill to Denver wherein I'd enjoyed the pleasure of jumpstarting a van by pushing from behind each time we stopped for gas or food. The van's owner was a tall, thin artist going to New Mexico to visit his girlfriend. I was along strictly to help pay for the gas. After a pitstop, my rideshare partner would sit impatiently behind the steering wheel while I pushed from the rear—sometimes gravity assisted me if we'd parked at the top of a hill the van could coast down, other times kindly bystanders took pity on me and helped. By the time we arrived in Albuquerque, I felt as though I'd pushed my way across the United States.

To this day, I don't know whether Michael was coming on to me or if he'd genuinely lost his bearings in the suburbs. Nevertheless, we finally arrived and dined at a restaurant aptly named the Renaissance. It served up haute cuisine with décor to match. We sat at a table with a starched white linen tablecloth, shiny silver cutlery and bell-tuned crystal-stemmed glasses where we made our way through a lavish, multi-course meal with wine, cheese, and dessert.

Afterwards, he suggested we go to the jazz club next door. Before agreeing, I went to the pay phone in the back, by the cloakroom, to check on Alex. The sitter assured me he was fine, so Michael and I strolled under the stars to our next venue and took a small table in the back. There, our conversation continued in a more intimate vein. Michael was clearly interested in being more than a platonic friend. But seeped in sixteenth-century poets like Maurice Scève and Marguerite de Navarre, I was singing the praises of Platonism. I was determined that our relationship be something wonderfully spiritual, particularly as he seemed to appreciate my intellectual bent.

He presented me with a full exposé of all the other women friends with whom he was decidedly horizontal. He met them through classifieds in the *New York Review of Books*. Concerning a lawyer in New York City, for instance, he divulged in some detail how they'd jointly begun shucking their clothes on the landing outside her flat before continuing thus to the bedroom. Another woman he was seeing simultaneously had an older lover but took in Michael to practice tantric sex to see how long they could make their mutual pleasure endure.

Since his wife had left him, initially for other men, but ultimately to move in with a lesbian lover, I imagined Michael might have been making up for hurt feelings and lost time. But I didn't quite know how to react to his litany of adventures. As a woman, I felt daunted and apprehensive that, were he to involve himself with me, he'd find me terribly boring. And of course, there were diseases to consider. But from a priestly perspective, garnered from my years of Unificationist practice and awareness of pastoral care, I felt compassion and gratitude for his candor as an expression of trust.

His eagerness to tell me everything, combined with his obvious interest in me, left me bemused by his exploits. Yet I didn't want to end up as just another story to tell at someone else's dinner party. And so I said to him, "I'm happy to be in a platonic relationship with you. I enjoy your company and friendship. But if you want something more than that with me, it must be exclusive. No other woman in the romance department."

"I clearly need to spend more time vertical," he replied to my surprise. My answer regarding dating him didn't align with the randy stories he'd collected from the dorms and I thought he was a bit crestfallen by my response. But in the honesty of our exchange, I dared to imagine we shared an intellectual compatibility. We respected each other's ideas even when we disagreed. Honesty, however brutal, forged our relationship.

He managed not to get lost one little bit on the way back. In his rush to be off, he didn't even open the car door for me when he dropped me off at my apartment. I took that to mean we'd remain platonic friends at best, and that I probably wouldn't see him again until Ivan resumed his tutorials.

I was wrong. The next day, he called to invite me to a dinner party in Princeton. A sociologist friend of his whose wife was in town from Berkeley, where she had tenure, was hosting. Other faculty would be there. I was jittery about seeing Michael again, but facing a room full of senior faculty didn't faze me. My Unificationist background had given me a broad base of experiences to relate to all sorts of people. Fundraising, I'd had long talks with corporate executives and winos giving plasma, the inhabitants of multi-million-dollar mansions in Dallas and prostitutes in downtown Los Angeles. All people were God's children as far as I was concerned. Besides, my experience living abroad and with the international membership of the church meant that I was equally at home using a series of forks to eat high French cuisine or sitting on a mat to eat sushi with chopsticks.

Little did I know, however, this second date was Michael's "test" for me: he wanted to see if I could fit into his circle of friends. Apparently I passed, because upon delivering me home he kissed me good-night and then he did help me unbuckle my seatbelt. By this time, apart from the rupture from Semester at Sea, we'd seen, spoken, and emailed one another weekly for over a year.

That night he walked me up to my apartment. Alex was already asleep in his little car bed. When the sitter left, we went into the kitchen. The black and white silk wall hanging of Jesus praying in the garden of Gethsemane I'd found at a flea market in Alabama was mounted in a frame to the left of the stove.

Michael and I sat beneath that picture and talked late into the night. Forever after, he'd chuckle over his pleasurable association with that image of Jesus; in his mind it had more to do with virility than vows of chastity. That was when he determined absolutely that he preferred to be vertical with me and he left behind the other women for good.

We saw each other more often from then on, and between visits Michael regularly emailed me. We still had a blinking orange cursor and a dial-up connection that would sputter, screech, and squeal in several rhythmic atonal notes before the connection secured with the welcome, gravelly sound of sandpaper static: beep, beep, beep, bong, bong, bonk, kshhhhhh, shhhhhhk, khssssssshhhhhh—and you were "in." The sound was so rude and different from a smooth, computer-generated voice crooning, "You've got mail." Connecting to the web had a tension to it like skydiving. You wondered whether you'd land where intended. Whenever I received an email from Michael, I responded with a quip right back. His response would be immediate. This seemed to go on, back and forth, all day—it's a wonder we got any work done. But we did. Lots of it.

During this period, I was of course still deeply invested in my dissertation and class preparations. For his part, Michael's research included assessing ethnographic studies for the Annual Review, teaching, and constantly studying the latest anthropological theorists rather than playing safe with the classical theorists of his training in Chicago and Oxford. Michael's curiosity and intellect were insatiable. This was endearing to me because it also meant he acknowledged that there were things I knew more about than he did. I think being in two different fields didn't hurt.

But beyond all that, one day I had an undeniable spiritual experience with him. He was across town in his office at Rutgers, and I, at home. Having just emailed back and forth, I felt his spirit come to me. It was undeniably Michael. His emotional self manifested as a spiritual body whose presence I could feel with my spiritual sense of touch. His spirit body embraced me.

As our souls came together, the impact arrested time and weakened my body to the point where I couldn't hold myself upright in the chair. I was no longer breathing air but love. My body was of the earth and an empty shell; my spirit hovered just beyond my physical form, commingling with Michael's spirit. Overpowered, I abandoned my desk chair and wobbled onto the couch. As my physical body succumbed to the primacy of spirit, I fell back on to the couch, almost in a physical faint, yet with spiritual lucidity.

I lay down on the couch and felt Michael's spirit man make love to me, though his physical body was on the other side of town. I felt his emotion, intellect, and will embodied in an energetic field. In a rapture of love, I sensed the divine had blessed our union. There was an absolute quality of love, of ordination, and of sanctity in our unity. Our two spirits formed a single entity of peace and strength that surpassed our capacity and strength as individuals alone.

I'd never had such an experience with another human being before. And I knew afterwards that there was more to our involvement than intellectual banter or platonic friendship. I felt the spirit of God there between us, with us. This experience—rather than a central figure arranging our union—convinced me that this relationship was God's will, not just my own dream or desire.

CHAPTER SIXTEEN

A Proposal Full of
Mutual Surprises

Thanksgiving approached. My friend Jackie from the Comparative Literature department had invited Alex and me to stay and celebrate with her and her kin. Funny how university culture classifies people by academic department, as though that explains everything: Jackie from Comp Lit, Michael from Anthro, me from French. I suppose if we were in corporate culture, we would talk about so and so from accounting, legal, or marketing. In academia, though, the classification practically describes kinship ties. You knew where people lived intellectually; you knew the other personalities in their department, and you knew the political gossip and scholarly accolades.

Jackie and I discovered our kinship standing in line for the women's restroom at a conference. Being in different disciplines, we wouldn't have met otherwise. We were both grad students immersed in our respective fields, but we shared an appreciation for Russian literature, unconventional people, and literary approaches that resisted ardent deconstructionism. We established all this while waiting in line—divine intervention often seemed to take the form of temporal inconvenience or discomfort.

We also discovered that we shared a living faith, anathema to the academy at the time. Belief in God, one professor once confided to me, was so extraordinary that were one to admit it before other academics, it would be as shocking as urinating on the floor at the podium. Good thing we met in a restroom on the off chance anyone heard our heretical conversation.

Jackie was then in a mixed marriage to a non-academic—a boisterous barkeep and restaurateur with an extended Irish-Catholic family, all of whom had converged upon their little apartment. They lived less than two hours from Rutgers, above his tavern in Nyack, New York, where we would all end up gathering to eat. Jackie gave Alex and me a bedroom behind French doors that opened to the living room, where half a dozen people chatted and laughed as children pushed toys about on the floor.

Nestled to the side stood an oval, three-footed mahogany table that quietly displayed a collection of icons. Among them was the Theotokos of Vladimir—an infant Jesus with an elongated neck gazing into his mother's eyes, Saint Nicholas with his long forehead and short whiskers looking rather somber, and the Archangel Michael in a brilliant scarlet robe. Jackie had roomed with Russian Orthodox nuns and still sang in their choir. In her decor, Slavic reds mingled freely with Celtic greens, the whole of it harmonizing into a cozy, bright, and comfortable atmosphere. The wine flowed as kids played and adults chattered. I helped skin garlic cloves for Jackie's specialty—roasted garlic, that was delicious plain or spread on toast.

When the phone rang, she handed it to me. Puzzled as to who would call, I heard Michael's voice asking how we were. He recounted his woodland expedition with the young "cousins" with whom he was staying for Thanksgiving, and said he missed Alex, whom he thought would enjoy it up there in Glastonbury, Connecticut. "Well, maybe another time," I said casually as I felt my heart fill with warmth that only Michael seemed to light within me. My reaction surprised me. Years later, I would recall how cozy his voice felt that evening, a warm hug over the phone.

Later, I would introduce Jackie to Michael and I was pleased that she enjoyed Michael's intellect as I did. He inspired us grad students with hope that there were people with tenure who did not worship at the altar of contemporary criticism. Although secularly grounded, Michael did not belittle either of us for our respective faith traditions. While Jackie and I did not have the exact same theology, and Michael was a self-professed Darwinist, we three shared a rebel streak. For a course he taught on contemporary theory, Michael wrote a glossary of theoretical terminology—a wickedly humorous and scathing satire. He planned to submit it to the aptly named Prickly Pear Press, though I don't know that the project ever bore fruit.

After Thanksgiving, Michael, Alex, and I were often together. Michael arranged for me to have workspace at the table in his home office. I wrote and prepared for classes there when Alex was at daycare. In the evening, Alex and I would frequent Michael's for supper and do sleepovers on the weekends.

Ivan sometimes joined us as well, but I could sense that he was not entirely pleased. He had enjoyed Michael's undivided attention for years; Alex and I were intruding on his territory. Ivan did not say he was bothered—he would have been above that sort of thing. He was a bright young man and as confident as a nineteenth-century Russian dandy in his prospects for success. He could fashion himself a fishing pole with a stick and some line to catch his own supper, or market his mother's paintings for her. He had mastered social charm and street savvy by fending for himself and his mother during the pre-Michael years.

Living with Michael, Ivan had attended a better public school than the one available near his mother's neighborhood. I understood Michael's "foster parent" status as more like a volunteer "big brother." According to Michael, he and Yulia did not and never had gotten along. Though I never heard Ivan say so, I imagined he must have held hope that Michael and Yulia might have worked out their differences. Alex and I coming into Michael's life must have added to his annoyance, but Ivan and his mother remained very close, so he took to commuting home to Jersey City more often on the weekends.

One such weekend, when Ivan was away, I was grading papers at my end of the table in the office. The phone rang and Michael picked up. "Hello, Mom," he said. "Uhhmmm. Uhhhmmm. Well, actually I'm not seeing her anymore."

I submerged myself in paperwork, determined not to eavesdrop. Michael had not told his family about me as yet. Apparently, his mother thought he was still seeing several other women. As I did not keep my folks apprised of my every move, I did not find this unusual.

Clunking the receiver into its cradle, he said sheepishly, "She thought my having sex with the lawyer in New York would be good exercise for me."

I was both amused she would track his health and social engagements with such precision and stunned to imagine her cheering his sexual exploits.

Michael added, "I had to set her straight on that."

"I thought you came from repressed New England Protestants. Wasn't your dad the son of a missionary in India?"

"Yes, but Mom has other ideas," he said.

Unsure of how to respond, I resumed work, focused on the computer screen, papers, and books before me. While he had been on the phone, I had managed to tune out the conversation, but whatever he had shared with his mother zipped through the family grapevine. Within an hour, Michael's brother-in-law Leon called. He noted that at thirty-five, I was nearly three-quarters Michael's age and therefore rather old to be a mere mistress. I didn't quite follow it at the time, but there may have been some reference to Ben Franklin's advice to a young man. The upshot was that we had entered his family's spotlight.

Our first Christmas together, Michael and I had Alex for only a part of the holiday. I wanted to make my Mommy apartment as festive as possible but had little money. Michael bought a Christmas tree for us and insisted on purchasing ornaments and lights too. We put up the tree and decorated it for Alex. Then, Michael invited me to decorate the tree at his house too.

"Are you free this Christmas Eve? My parents are coming down from Glastonbury and I want you to meet them," he said. I was reaching for the perfect spot to nestle a tiny ceramic elf careening downhill on a sled. The elf's cap lay frozen, blowing backward in an imaginary wind. I paused midair and drew a deep breath, the sled swaying back and forth at a jaunty angle from the end of its ribbon loop. "Well . . ." I said, fishing for time and looking for reassurance in the recesses of the tree.

Emotions swirled inside me. Alex's holiday absence loomed. I would have to take him to the airport to meet his father for his trip to Oregon before Christmas. I would not be able to bring Alex back home until well after the New Year. I dreaded pining for him and could not repress worries for his safety. Added to this, the thought of meeting Michael's parents made me feel all of five years old.

I was sure they wouldn't think me a good enough match for Michael. Like the elf ornament, with his cap whooshing backwards, I felt fear blow over me. It seemed like my feet were dangling, helpless without the earth. I was sure Michael's parents could excise me from Michael's life with their disapproval. The thought of losing him made it hard to breathe. I realized how much I had come to fully trust Michael and his presence, not only in my life but Alex's too.

Perhaps reliving my not-too-distant court experience, I thought of parents as scary creatures. If I did not make the right impression, it felt as if my life would be set to self-destruct. I would never know happiness again. Adding to my fear over what seemed a momentous event in our relationship was the recent phone call from Michael's mother, who had recently suggested he relieve amorous tension with some other woman in New York. I felt dispensable. These fears formed fingers around my throat, cutting short my breath and squeezing my voice into a pipsqueak yelp. I looked at Michael and let slip a choked, "Okay."

For Michael, introducing another woman to his family was no big deal. Many of his women friends had met his parents in the past. Former paramours sometimes spent holidays with them even when he could not. Despite my own fears, I imagined that Michael's mother and father, Kay and Stan, must have been at least somewhat kind—after all, they'd raised a wonderful son. I hoped they would approve of me enough for us to have a pleasant dinner together. I practiced meeting them in my mind. After I visualized a reasonably successful encounter a few times, I was able to swallow my heart back down into my chest. Perhaps my awkwardness and inadequacy would not be too obvious, I hoped.

Christmas Eve arrived. Michael introduced another little twist to my meeting with his parents. We would not meet them in Highland Park. We would drive to meet them in Jersey City.

"Why Jersey City?" I asked.

"Yulia invited us to dinner," Michael replied. "Oh. You mean Ivan's mother?"

"Right, she likes to cook. She and Ivan have been to Glastonbury quite a few times for Thanksgiving and Christmas so she offered to host us this year."

This was news to me. I did not realize how intimately Yulia and Ivan were involved in Michael's life. I thought Ivan had been more of an amiable boarder, a young charge taken under Michael's wing in an avuncular and somewhat impartial fashion. I did not realize how intertwined both he and Yulia were with Michael's extended family.

"I don't know if feel comfortable with this," I said. "Yulia invited you," Michael assured me.

I was sure she knew that I was more than Ivan's tutor.

"She said that after supper we are to go to her church. It's Russian Orthodox," added Michael, as though that normalized the situation.

In some ways it did. I felt at home with God in general, and it was easy enough for me to adapt to a variety of religious venues. And my friendship with Jackie had deepened my appreciation of Russian Orthodox traditions. I envisioned a church service like an emotional oasis, a neutral territory with fewer messy mortal complications. Spiritual phenomena made sense to me—people did not.

Michael came with me to take Alex to the airport. The exchange with Vincent was reasonably uneventful. He was in good spirits picking up Alex. Christmas was a prized holiday to share with Alex back in Oregon and Michael's presence helped allay anger that Vincent might've directed otherwise toward me.

Several days later, as Michael and I drove to Jersey City, I plied him for more details to prepare myself to meet his parents and Yulia. After some initial hesitation, Michael revealed more to me about the already simmering social stew I was about to enter. I'd been led to believe that he'd taken on Ivan as a kindness, and that Yulia was a distant acquaintance. The longer we drove and talked, though, the clearer Michael's past history became to me.

Kay and Stan had not merely met Ivan and Yulia but had known them quite well for several years. Michael had dated many people after his wife left him. Yulia was one of them. Their relationship had been very "brief," said Michael, so brief he did not describe it as at all amorous. It had sounded to me as if they'd simply gone out for tea.

I knew that after his ex-wife and ex-stepson had moved out and on with their lives, Michael had gone into a depression. Friends had provided emotional support. A couple of neighbors had invited him to their place in the Catskills, where he met Yulia and Ivan, who were also visiting. Michael loved being a dad and missed his ex-stepson. Ivan, in some respects, served as a replacement. And this was a mutually agreeable relationship—Ivan benefitting from Michael's parenting in a way his ex-stepson had spurned.

Impressed with how bright Ivan was, Michael wanted to give the boy a chance for success. Thus, he committed to fostering Ivan through high school to provide access to Highland Park's academically focused school system. In Jersey City, artistic decadence and urban edginess took precedence over college prep and suburban safety. While Michael and Yulia had quickly decided they were not suitable partners for one another, they nevertheless soldiered on like a bitter old couple for the sake of Ivan's education—a cause Michael championed.

I was glad for the dinner diversion—I was always anxious when Alex was away—and glad that Michael wanted me to meet his parents. Still, it was a delicate situation from my perspective.

My tension mounted as I envisioned all our disparate personalities and agendas converging on Yulia's Jersey City apartment for Christmas Eve dinner. They'd all known each other for years. Somewhat exasperated by having had to pry loose this information from Michael, I decided to pray. Looking out the window as we passed clumps of leafless trees, warehouses, and truck yards, I took a deep breath, in silence, I asked God to help me see things from a broader perspective. Right then, there was no place I wanted to be more than in my Mommy apartment, curled into a fetal ball, in bed, with a large supply of chocolate. The last thing I wanted to do was meet a group of strangers who had more history with Michael than I did. I missed Alex. He was my only real family.

In a railroad yard, I saw a truck body lifted onto the flatcar of a train. Alex would love to see that, I thought, and imagined what he would think about this trip. He would be delighted to be with Michael and me, I decided. He wouldn't care whether Yulia had known Michael before or not. He would be happy just to eat.

As I silently prayed, imagining Alex with me, it dawned on me that Yulia's invitation was her way of giving her blessing to Michael and me. Like me, she understood what it was like to be a single parent. Ivan was the Russian nickname for Alexander—our sons, though different ages, had the same first name. As mothers, we had quite a bit in common. Letting go of my own psychobabbling brain and relying on faith, I could rise above my mortal fears and feel touched by her hospitality.

My thoughts turned to Michael's parents. His dad was the son of a missionary, his mom was evidently liberal. I felt embarrassed to meet both of them: his dad because our relationship bore little semblance to the conservative, no-sex-before-marriage paradigm I'd spent years trying to live in the movement; his mom because I didn't want to be compared to all of Michael's previous girlfriends. I asked God for strength to deal with the situation and felt a sense of peace begin to settle upon me as I tried to let go of my own scripts. I resolved to face events as they unfolded without my analytical preconceptions.

Yulia's tiny, two-bedroom apartment was on an upper floor of a public housing high-rise in a gray, scruffy neighborhood. I mulled over how she had been a part of Michael's "horizontal" past as we rode up the elevator. Though hurt that Michael hadn't told me the whole truth about his relationship with her, the story of Ivan's father tugged at my heart.

As a political dissident in the Soviet Union, he'd been incarcerated on politically invented psychiatric grounds. In prison, authorities had administered drugs to him that reduced him to such incoherence that he remained the rest of his life in an asylum. Yulia had managed to hardscrabble her way to the US with Ivan, their only child. As he explained all this, Michael convinced me that it was out of paternal care that he committed to seeing Ivan through high school in Highland Park, not love for Yulia. He served as a foster father even though he and Yulia "were history," he said emphatically.

The doors to the elevator opened, and we walked down the hall and knocked on Yulia's door. As it slowly wedged open to the end of its chain lock an eyeball assessed us through the gap; the warm scent of roast duck, sweet potatoes, and mincemeat pies swirled into the hall—the aroma so thick you could taste it. Having identified us as friends, not foes, Ivan opened the door just wide enough for us to enter. As we squeezed over the threshold, the savory scents of garlic, onion, and cinnamon commingled with the musk of old world antiques. Yulia called a greeting from the kitchen and invited us to make ourselves at home. We had arrived before Michael's parents. It was a little awkward making small talk with Ivan. I usually had a lesson plan.

"So, your mom is an artist?" I asked.

"Yes, would you like to see her some of her work?"

"Only if she says it's okay," I answered.

Yulia called out from the kitchen, "Sure, take them back to my studio!"

Ivan nodded and we followed him. There were two back rooms to the apartment: one served as a bedchamber, the other housed her paintings. Like a curator at Sotheby's, Ivan gestured with the back of his hand. I followed him into a room where several canvases loomed over us, standing nearly as broad and tall as the walls that held up the ceiling. Yulia's style tended toward the naïve, with a loose technique. Sepia-to-brown strokes created decisive movement and alluded to form with verve while vibrant splashes of ruby, magenta, and plum seeped into the golden, green, and blue backgrounds. I put myself in museum mode, as I had learned from childhood, taking it all in.

Ivan blushed beneath his freckles but maintained an expression of grandiloquence and smug nonchalance as my eyes came to rest upon a smaller painting. Yulia had proudly displayed it center stage: a frontal nude of a figure that, despite its rough-hewn form—more like Braque than Renoir—one could make out to be Michael, in his Beatle haircut. All his manhood was in full view as he sat erect in a wooden chair—the very chair that displayed the canvas. Nearby was another Michael nude—a rear view of him reclining. I noticed that although most of the painting approximated sharp, geometric abstract lines, she captured one intimate detail—the almost feminine softness of the curve above his hip.

Michael and Yulia were history, that's for sure. And here was the proof of that history, if the state of his manhood was any indication. I struggled to keep my poker face in front of Ivan's by now bemused expression, but felt unnerved, even though Michael standing near me was somewhat comforting. I still felt betrayed that he'd omitted to tell me about these little souvenirs. I wondered if his parents knew about them. I felt naive entering their world, ignorant of things they took for granted, and like more of an outsider than ever.

Since Michael had driven, I had no way home without him. I was expected to eat dinner and chat up his parents and impress them in front of his ex-paramour. To me, it was more than a test; it was a blow to my heart.

I exited the boudoir of nudes and went to the kitchen, where Yulia stirred various bubbling pots. She asked me to help dress the table. I was glad for something to do. Her cranberry sauce laced with liqueur glittered in its gilded Russian porcelain *saucière*. As I set it upon the table, I heard Ivan greet Kay and Stan at the door. The duck was carved and ready to serve so they washed up and came directly to eat. I was grateful their art tour was at least temporarily postponed and relieved our first meeting took place standing next to their fully clothed son.

We clinked glasses of wine, ate, and admired Yulia's gourmet artistry while making small talk about our lives. Kay had short white hair and dimply, fragile skin—the kind that crumples about the eyelids and softens cheek apples. Her eyes had the early blue glaze of cataracts, which made her appear as if she were in a constant state of wonder. You had to repeat yourself rather loudly if you spoke into her left ear. She burbled and effused grandmotherly interest in my teaching, writing, and Alex's wellbeing. Meanwhile Stan told Michael about his latest scheme to keep their early Colonial house functional. While Kay was more of a round shape on all sides, Stan was chiseled and New England strong. He spoke with a gravelly growl and hunched over his elbows splayed out on the table propping his chin in a perfect triangle.

Yulia was a masterful host. She kept the wine flowing as course after course appeared. By the time the plum pudding arrived and the samovar was lit, she had feted us with all the elegance of nineteenth-century gentry in a Tolstoy novel. At meal's end, she refused help to clean up, for we needed to make a brisk dash to the church. Only hard wooden pews in the balcony remained by the time we arrived. We sat for some three hours as a black-cloaked priest droned chants interspersed with scripture readings in Old Church Slavonic. One lone sing-along carol served to break the monotony. We all smiled at the end and thanked Yulia before scuttling back to Highland Park, where Kay and Stan would be staying with Michael.

On the return trip, I made Protestant laments to Michael of the Orthodox service where "only the priest has access to the holy of holies."

We agreed that it seemed more of a Christmas eulogy than a celebration and thus Michael invited me to what would be the first of many visits to the Reformed Church of Highland Park. Kay and Stan, having driven separately, reconvened with Michael and me. They declined the offer to attend yet another church service. Instead, they settled into the living room chairs before bedding down. As we made our way toward the door, Kay called out, with a twinkle in her eye, "Have a good evening, you two!"

I blushed as we left for the midnight service.

It seemed far sexier to enter a church together than it did a restaurant or faculty dinner. The heavens themselves seemed to look down upon us as we ascended the outer stairs to the massive wooden front doors. I felt breathless and warm despite the cold, star-lit air. We entered the sanctuary walking side by side.

This service was entirely musical, without a word of preaching. We knew nearly all the songs and sight-read the unfamiliar ones from the hymnal. Michael, I discovered, could not only read notes but also sing baritone and some tenor harmony. I melted into the sound of our voices as they blended with the soaring strains. The music program back then in Highland Park was admirable, and the choir—planted among the congregation—helped assure that the lot of us found notes somewhere within the vicinity of the actual melody of the carols.

The spirit of the evening felt intoxicating. When the sanctuary lights were extinguished, we lit little candles and passed the flame from one person to the next. After singing by the glow of candlelight, we retreated to my apartment for the night, where Michael made his own wordless personal amends for what had been a trying day.

Winter break, an ostensible vacation between semesters, was actually an opportunity to advance one's writing, research, and attend conferences. Given the abundant work I needed to resume after the holiday, I focused on my research, interspersed with telephone calls to Alex. At the end of break, I flew to Portland to bring my little one home.

Vincent and I would meet for the exchange at the airport. I counted myself lucky if it was quick and simple. This one was. During the plane ride back, Alex and I talked and dozed our way back into cozy familiarity.

On through the spring semester, teaching and research continued apace, as did regular outings with Alex. Michael and I further blended our two households. Once Rutgers had finished the spring semester in May, Ivan graduated and moved back permanently with Yulia in Jersey City. With Ivan's departure, Alex and I gradually migrated over to Michael's house in Highland Park.

Although we did things together as a couple, we weren't established like our friends and colleagues—most of them had been married for years. However, when my apartment lease was up that summer, rather than renew my contract, Michael suggested that Alex and I move in with him in Highland Park. He helped me haul my sofa bed out for the taking by the dumpster. We crammed Alex's and my remaining belongings into a few boxes, packed them into my 1971 Sedan de Ville and drove to Michael's with a tangle of plants jammed into the nooks between boxes. Upon arrival, I put books on shelves, plants in the windowsill, and Alex settled into a bed of his own.

Michael and I maintained our respective work schedules and coordinated outings, both with Alex and each other. Living in tempo was easier living together. We got an Irish Water Spaniel puppy and named her Sadie. We were becoming a family.

When my menses were late, however, I told Michael nothing about my suspicions. He had told me that he had medical evidence that he was incapable of having his own biological children. When he and his ex-wife had been unable to conceive, a doctor had evaluated Michael's sperm count and informed him that it was too low for conception to occur—a tragedy given how he loved kids. Assured I wouldn't conceive, we made no attempt to prevent pregnancy. Unsure how I could be pregnant, I decided to test myself first lest something beyond stress were amiss.

We were both in the throes of a busy semester. Michael had a full course load; I was teaching and finishing my dissertation; we had Alex to care for and our new puppy was now much bigger and more demanding. There was plenty of love to go around, but mornings were beyond hectic, more like a mad scramble.

Before collecting Alex to dash out the door, I remembered to pee on the little strip. It revealed two little pink bars rather than one. I took this information as one more thing on my to-do list, rather than a life-changing event. In the back of my mind, I had already calculated how my insurance could pay for the delivery. It would be challenging, but doable to add another member to the household.

Racing through my mental to-dos, I had nearly mapped out how to get the child through kindergarten before telling Michael of this new life in our lives. It had not occurred to me that he might not be prepared to receive the news. Despite his passion for parenting and desire for children, he was sure he was shooting blanks.

Pressed to get out the door on time, I had barely managed to throw my hair into a barrette and dress myself tidily enough to teach. I still had to drop Alex at daycare on my way to class. As I emerged from the bathroom, the floorboards creaked. I poked my head across the threshold of the bedroom where Michael was still dressing. "Got some news—I'm pregnant," I said, as though informing him it was trash day and could he please put the bin by the street.

Michael's face registered shock, as he looked up from buttoning his shirt. *Bad timing*, I thought to myself.

He did not look pleased. Neither of us had time for a long discussion at that moment. Robust hormones had been active within me for several weeks. My body was aware of the pregnancy even though my logical mind was not. Thus, grounded with an irrational confidence, I was more advanced in my planning about what to do next than Michael, for whom the news was a complete surprise. It was life-changing, if not heart-stopping—and he hadn't even had his morning coffee.

Shuffling some Lego bricks to the side with my foot, I seized Alex's hand and with a cheery smile said, "Let's go!" As Alex and I made our way downstairs, I took a last look up at Michael. He looked grim, his lips pulled tight, his face ashen as he gripped the top railing and watched us leave. His shirt was half buttoned and not yet tucked into his belted trousers.

Reading his face, I dreaded that he, like Vincent, would want me to have an abortion. "Whether you are on board or not, I'm having this child," I said. I quickly pulled my eyes from his face. What I saw there did not reassure me; what did was the solid mass in my belly and Alex's small hand in mine. We three would have to go it alone, I thought. As I navigated the stairs with Alex, sixty pounds of happy dog squiggled against me. She seemed to be hoping for an outing.

"Not now, Sadie girl!" I said.

Our happy event was unexpected, a surprise miracle, really. Yet I feared Michael was not ready to have a baby. As I thought about all the work I had to do, I felt daunted. At thirty-six, I had no plans to get pregnant again. I had an invisible tattoo on my forehead that read, "Tenure or Bust." Michael had a good heart, he loved Alex, Sadie and me, but he was also fully invested in a demanding academic career. An infant would overhaul our lives.

Despite all worldly logic, I was awash in maternal gushiness. Nurturing this new life inside me was no mere moral imperative—it felt as urgent to me as breathing. I already loved this child. Besides, Alex had always wanted a sibling.

I evaluated the pros and cons from every angle. In Unificationist teachings, there was no taboo against abortion. Theologically, the first living breath outside the womb was considered the moment when the spirit entered the child. Or, at least, that was my understanding at the time. But loving this little life inside me was not a question of theology. While it was a free-will choice, rooted in spirit and emotion, I also felt some inexplicable sense of destiny. Michael was free to choose to parent with me or not. I would ready myself to parent both children alone if it came to that.

After a brief pause, Alex and I continued our descent. Michael's stony silence and shocked face had already left their imprint. Raging hormones compelled me to protect my baby and survive my pregnancy. My mind whirred as I planned how to handle pregnancy, childbirth, and parenting alone.

It was a familiar feeling: stepping off a cliff, relying on faith. I knew it would be difficult, but I could handle difficult. *I've done it before, I can do it again*, I thought, casting my eyes down to watch our footing.

My memory flashed to my pregnancy six years prior, when I'd felt a similar sense of calling. I had felt the visceral force of Alex's will to live exude from my womb when, technically, he was the same age as the child I was now carrying—only a mass of cells. Besides the dream that had prefigured Alex's birth, I'd had a spiritual experience of his embryonic, self-determining force. It had jolted through me—a beam of sheer potential and raw character. Then, I had responded to that feeling by calling Vincent from a pay phone at work to tell him I would not go through with an abortion.

With this new pregnancy, I felt the same substantial life force, an incarnation blossoming within me. There was simply no question of annulling this little sprout for the sake of "practical" convenience. Love surrounded me and the being in my womb. I felt called to carry this child to term and take responsibility for him or her, even if it jeopardized my relationship with Michael.

I buckled Alex into his car seat in back, handed him his Matchbox cars, and tossed the rest of the cargo onto the passenger seat next tome. As I drove to daycare, I went over logistics: my insurance from school would fully cover having the baby; I could move back to my old apartment complex; Alex would be thrilled to have a sibling; perhaps the French Department could help me find more work—in short, I could trust God.

Amidst the flurry of plans, an irrational calm settled upon me. Although uncertain of Michael's commitment and certain of my limited income, I felt no fear. Somehow, I felt God was blessing us, watching over us. I knew Alex was born for a reason that went beyond worldly appearance. The same would be true of this new life within me.

When I returned home from work after having collected Alex from daycare, I found Michael more relaxed. What I had read as rejection on his part was in fact utter amazement. He'd always wanted to father a child despite doctors assuring him it was impossible. While I was gone, he had time to recover from the shock of the news and he had cooked dinner—a love offering of creamed chicken curry, my favorite. Despite having steeled myself at the prospect of solo parenting, as we ate, he held me in the embrace of his warm brown eyes.

"I want this child to have a father," I said. He took my words in silence as we looked into each other's eyes. At this point, all my worries melted away: I knew then that he was fully on board. Michael had a way with kids that I admired and trusted. He brought out their inquisitive side and sense of adventure; he knew how to have fun with them. And children loved him. Especially Alex. He needed Michael's parenting as much as our unborn child did.

Though the full glow of pregnancy would not settle upon me until morning sickness passed, it roosted upon Michael immediately. He was ebullient. After supper, Michael called his friends with the news. Asking around, he found a good obstetrician and was eager for us to arrange our first appointment. I was grateful that Michael was helping me figure things out by talking with actual people. I was weary of figuring things out alone with God.

Within a week, we met Dr. Graybell. Chatty, with more than a handful of his own kids, he was not a huge fan of the American Medical Association. He was amenable to alternative therapies and wasn't judgmental about our lack of marital certification. With academics, most of whom were liberal, there was no stigma in being pregnant and unmarried—at least not in the French Department. Dr. Graybell shared this open-minded approach; he was all about babies, and was delighted to assure a happy, healthy birth. Armed with a prescription for horse-pill-sized prenatal vitamins, we were off and running toward a fine new adventure. Shame be damned, this was about the joy of new life.

In Unification tradition, like most faiths, one would typically marry prior to conceiving. I had not been orthodox since my matching days, yet I still felt twinges when social propriety harassed my self-confidence. My custody battle had made me acutely aware of how fragile relationships could turn upside down in an instant. Besides, my residual religious convictions made me feel like a class A hypocrite. I had preached chastity before marriage in the past, yet I was not living that ideal. Little did I know how much the scarlet A would come into play.

Before my pregnancy, Michael and I had been public companions, but living together unmarried had an uncertain quality. Alex and I had moved in with Michael at his behest. While Michael and I spent a good deal of time together publicly, we nonetheless remained distinct creatures. We were classified as perpetually dating rather than joined in matrimony. Shifting from a life of public promiscuity to Pamela had entailed a 180-degree turnaround for Michael's reputation as a man about town. I had to earn my spot in his society to prove that I was something more than his latest conquest from the *New York Review of Books* classifieds.

The pregnancy added more heft to our public unity as my weight accrued. Instead of carousing with the singletons at department parties on Halloween, we took Alex trick-or-treating. We joined the choir at the Dutch Reformed Church, where we rehearsed weekly and sang for Sunday service. We took the dog to training classes *en famille*. George, Michael's academic birding friend, recognized me as Michael's "new love" in a short story from his latest book. Our married friends invited both of us to their gatherings.

But despite these subtle local changes in status in New Jersey, we had not yet told anyone in our respective extended families. As far as they knew, Michael and I had an uncomplicated boyfriend-girlfriend status. Alex and I had yet to meet Michael's extended family. Michael had never met my parents.

The summer came and went; we embarked on a new semester of classes. As Thanksgiving approached, Kay, Michael's mom, invited all of us, including Sadie the dog, to Glastonbury. It would be a major kinship fest. I still felt like a newcomer even though I'd already met his parents. I wondered whether his extended family would accept me. I wanted to win their hearts but felt clumsy and awkward compared to Yulia or the countless other women that had preceded me.

Naturally, acute morning sickness took hold just as Thanksgiving arrived. I was still barely showing and wore seasonal, loose-fitting sweaters. I looked nonchalant yet felt anything but. Pretending not to be pregnant was a challenge.

Roiling hormones, morning sickness, and preoccupation with regular doctor appointments meant hiding my condition took more effort.

As Michael drove us around the outskirts of New York City on the Merritt Mill Parkway, morning sickness exacted only a couple of emergency stops for vomit breaks. When we arrived in Glastonbury, I tried to be chipper, but claimed to have some sort of flu in order to wrest time away from the hubbub and take a lie-down upstairs. Thanksgiving and Christmas were big holidays with Michael's parents. Plenty of food, banter, and the mandatory game of charades kept everyone busy downstairs in the kitchen and living room.

I met Michael's sister Gertie, her husband Leon, and daughter Maya; Cousin Donna, husband Callum, and their three children; the cousins Eugenia and Sylvia, Aunt Betty, and Aunt Peg from Montauk. Everyone was talking and milling about. I managed to get through supper without incident. Afterwards in the kitchen, Aunt Betty chatted me up. She had short white hair, a slight frame, and clear blue eyes—like my maternal grandmother. Soft-spoken and slight of build, she had a tough, no-nonsense character I appreciated. Her kid sister, Aunt Peg, was built square and strong. She had a loud voice that suited her colorful language. She enjoyed hitting the liquor hard and often; but with or without it, she was a hoot. All the little cousins and Alex scrambled around on the floor talking and making vehicular noises with toys. As hoped, Michael took Alex and the cousins hiking in the woods together with Sadie while I slipped away again with "the flu."

On the way home, Alex nodded off in the back seat and Sadie rode with her head out the window. Michael said he wanted to marry me. "Okay then," I said, half-joking, "I want a ring!" ending the discussion before Alex awoke.

I knew Michael felt committed to me for years to come, through raising not only Alex but this second child together. Intellectually, I wondered if all the family festivities had made marriage seem more natural than the deconstruction and analysis of kinship traditions in academic discourse. Without me saying so, Michael knew I felt embarrassed in front of his parents being pregnant with his child and unmarried. His mother's definition of sex as a good form of exercise made shacking up together seem more like an extended trip to the gym than an indication of an enduring relationship. We spoke no further of marriage, nor did we tell Kay and Stan about the pregnancy.

It was sort of fun keeping the news to ourselves. A year had passed since we'd gathered for Christmas at Yulia's. This year, we would have Christmas at home with Alex. We invited Kay and Stan to join us in Highland Park. We put up a tree, a crèche, and sang Christmas songs around the piano. I was fatigued and glowing, though still hardly showing. To teach at Rutgers, I wore baggy clothes to disguise my thickening middle. Even by late January, I could disguise my growing belly by wearing Michael's sweaters, graduate-student style. However, by March there was no disguising it—I needed maternity clothes.

Michael was never concerned about clothes, so it was unusual when he told me one morning to dress up for an evening outing. Puzzled, I looked over my misshapen Michael hand-me-downs and decided I would have to do better than that. So, I went shopping and found a tunic and pants with Indic patterns on thin, flowing cotton fabric with little sparkly mirrors and strings that tied at the neck, wrists, and waist. I felt positively folkloric. We left Alex with a sitter. Michael tenderly latched the seatbelt over my growing tummy before driving the Isuzu off into the dark. Like our first date, I did not really know where we were going, but unlike that first voyage, I trusted that wherever we ended up would be just fine. As we passed the Grover Cleveland service area on the Turnpike, I knew this was no ordinary outing.

We rarely went past Hightstown unless it was daylight and we were headed for the beach. Michael seemed set to burst with cheer but remained staunch in his refusal to say where we were going. We soon crossed the George Washington Bridge into New York, where we met up with my college friend Jeanne and her beau on the Upper East Side. From there, we walked to a French restaurant. Jeanne and Michael looked smug. We were seated in a private alcove toward the back, out of range of the swinging kitchen doors and the hubbub of the front dining area. For the main course, I had something sublime with truffles. The presentation, as artful as it was succulent, had squiggles of sauce swooped in John Hancock swirls around the plate. Our conversation effervesced with good cheer, though I stuck to water, not champagne.

Michael rose from his chair and bent toward the floor, looking for a dropped napkin, I thought. I looked down to help him find it whereupon I met his eyes looking with bold concern into mine as he knelt by my side. Taking my hand, he said, "Pamela Ann Claxton, I'm lost without you; make me the happiest man in the world and marry me."

Dumbstruck, I paused and a bubble of silence embraced the two of us for a moment. "Yes, I will marry you Michael Moffatt." He fumbled a small box out of his pocket and put a ring on my finger. It was way too big, but that didn't matter. At the moment, I'd not noticed the restaurant had gone quiet, but then applause exploded around us. Not only our table and wait staff, but also it seemed New York City herself blessed Michael's Big Apple proposal.

The excitement of our evening expedition quieted as we drove home. Like the encounter with Michael's nude portraits when meeting his parents for the first time, I discovered that Michael had another little surprise up his sleeve. I delicately inquired as to when we might get married. My belly was not getting any smaller and I wondered if we might manage to wed before I was completely enormous. He informed me that we might encounter a delay in our nuptials. I mentally ran through forthcoming conferences and other professional duties scheduled, but I could come up with nothing.

"Why is that?" I asked.

"Um, technically I'm still married."

This little afterthought gave me pause. I took a deep breath. I fancied myself the sort of person who lived some semblance of an ethical, principled life. Dating a married man did not fit that paradigm. Had I known, I would not have dated him, never mind move in with him and have his child. Michael explained how his ex had left more than fifteen years prior and that, furthermore, she had left him for a woman. It was a definitive break between the two of them. In hippie fashion, Michael had simply neglected the legal paperwork.

This bit of unexpected news demanded an ethical response. I revealed that I wanted Father Moon to bless our marriage. I was no longer in the church, but given the spiritual experiences I'd had with Michael, I wanted to have our marriage blessed with the interdenominational and divine clout Father had.

"I thought you said Rev. Moon was not God," replied Michael.

He was referring back to our very first date, when he had asked me if I thought Rev. Moon was God. If I had thought so, that would have been a deal-breaker for further courtship on his part. However, given that he was still legally married—a very clear deal-breaker for courtship on my end—I thought it only fair to drop my own ethical bombshell.

"True. He's not God, but he is the Messiah," I said

"What?"

"The Messiah is not the same thing as God," I said. "The word means 'anointed one'—anointed or chosen by God. Consider Jesus. Jesus prayed to God the Father. He did not pray to himself. He prayed to a spiritual being of infinite love. Jesus and God were intimates, that is, Jesus understood and responded to the heart of God such that he would never do anything to hurt God's heart. That is why they were one. They were one in heart."

It was similar, I explained, with Rev. Moon. I believed he had a workable teaching that could help bring peace on earth, that he was not only intimate with but also chosen by God—the way Jesus was. My courtroom declaration about my belief in Father's teaching had not been long before I had first met Michael. However, since my divorce, I had for the most part cut my ties with the church. While I still prayed on my own, there was no place for a divorced person in the movement, nor support for single parenting. I had lost friends and certainly any fragile standing I may have had in the movement by divorcing. Furthermore, I didn't agree with the far-right political positions many church members assumed. Yet I still had a spiritual relationship with Father. I felt it. It didn't have anything to do with the church organization; I wanted Father's blessing because I loved him.

"Well," Michael said, "from what I've seen, most religions, if you examine their theology in terms of devotional practices, look equally nutty. I suppose the Moonies aren't really much different from any other faith in that regard."

Coming from a man who had devoted years of study to the venerable practices of Hinduism, this sounded oddly reassuring.

"Unificationists," I corrected him. "The term 'Moonies' is considered pejorative."

Despite this gale of unexpected news, we shared the rudder and scudded along. A determined Michael told me emphatically to plan a wedding. "Just make it for late April," he said.

So I did. We still had Alex to care for, Sadie's obedience classes, prenatal doctor appointments, classes to teach, research to perform, and now, a divorce to negotiate—in addition to planning a wedding. Leaving divorce negotiations to Michael, I took on the bulk of event coordinating for the wedding, though we discussed everything. Michael worked with our lawyer, who could have moonlighted as a stand-up comedienne. They succeeded in extracting the needed signatures with amicable generosity as Michael's ex had moved on well over a decade prior. We wanted everyone to be happy—we were, and love seemed as irrepressible as my ballooning belly.

I reserved a church, arranged for catering, invited fewer than one hundred guests, and found a wedding gown. I chose a rather large size to accommodate a second person beneath the lace. I had a substantial bustle on the rear to balance out the package—a Victortian conceit that my black-belt Taekwondo friend and confident, would rib me for on the day of the wedding.

Evenings remained cozy. After reading Alex to sleep from the likes of *The Wind in the Willows, Charlotte's Web,* or *The Lord of the Rings,* Michael would join me in bed for more read-alouds. We went through all of Dave Barry and Miss Manners, who I found hysterically funny—maybe it was the hormones. We mutually guffawed over Margo Kaufman's *This Damn House—* the title spoofing the TV program *This Old House,* where tens of thousands of dollars in repairs magically rendered shacks into palatial mansions in a single episode.

Other night reads included chapters from various books on anthropology or sociology as well as Father Moon's words. Of the latter, we'd mull over interpretations of texts translated into English from Korean. We discussed everything. Michael's insights grounded faith traditions in cultural perspectives, while mine emerged from spiritual experiences and diverse theological studies. We united on the gist of the Divine Principle—true love.

Late one night after reading and talking in bed as usual, Michael expressed his reservations about the reality of the spiritual world. Propping himself up above his pillow on one elbow, he turned toward me and said, "You know, if I'm right we'll both be dead. But if you're right, you'll be telling me, 'I told you so!' for eternity!"

We laughed, hugged, and—well, I have fond memories of that night. I believe this is how we surmounted most spiritual disagreements.

Easter arrived and Alex went to Oregon. Michael made the cross-continental flight to pick him up as my pregnancy was too advanced for me to fly. Vincent had already met Michael on several exchanges. He was generally less irate talking to Michael than to me. Contact at the exchanges was minimal and always in a public place. Michael stayed with the Baggins in Washington and took Alex hiking up Mount Hood. Having attended Reed College, Michael knew the Portland area well. I stayed home with Sadie to teach and write.

True to his word, Michael's divorce papers were finalized as hoped, and we did not have to postpone our wedding. Since we were regulars with the Reformed Church choir, we asked the minister there, Rev. Richard Blake, to marry us. He met with us several times, both together and apart, to confirm that we had the same expectations of marriage.

Blake and I had hashed over theology in numerous discussions. He had a doctorate in English, besides being ordained. Michael and I had regularly hosted Bible studies that Blake facilitated and other academics attended. Regarding marriage, Blake was quite stern with Michael. Blake understood my theological commitments in ways Michael did not yet fully understand. And as an academic and a child of the sixties, Michael had lived a lifestyle very different from what mine had been prior to meeting him.

Blake also knew that being married with me could be a challenge. I could be stubborn and it would take someone stout of heart to be my life partner. If Michael hadn't been so crazy about me, this would have been a rather sobering perspective. His dad, Stan, was stoic, but Michael took after his poetic mother. His agile mind could find clever reasons for just about anything. Fidelity was an issue that contemporary society and academia in particular defined as situational rather than absolute. Although comfortable with monogamy, Michael hadn't considered the topic the way I had. Philosophically, he came from an anthropological perspective, which held as much credence for the behavior of Bonobo monkeys as it did the Bible to determine sexual mores. Yet our marriage was not solely for the children; it was a commitment of fidelity to one another.

For children of the sixties like Michael, it was perhaps not so much their upbringing as the general ethos of the time that made them somewhat heedless of fidelity. Certainly, Kay and Stan were faithful to each other, and so were most of their friends. For many of the WWII generation, marriage meant sticking together through good times and bad with love and determination. Flower children, though, seemed less inclined to lend credence to such moral issues. The "have your cake and eat it too" opt-out clause emotionally reduced marriage to something short of a Boy Scout oath by way of commitment and rendered divorce something more than a speeding ticket in terms of inconvenience. There were several on-going faculty scandals we personally knew of at the time that attested to this attitude.

Since imbuing myself in Unificationism, studying comparative theology, and investing endless hours in my own spiritual life in prayer, I had concluded that marriage was a public declaration of the spiritual and physical bond between spouses centered on the divine. The ceremony was an invitation to the community to support a couple's union and for the couple to unite their efforts to support their community. Given my previous marriages, this was a new paradigm for me, to some extent. That is, my attitude toward marriage continued to evolve.

In the arranged match and marriage with Boris, I felt the marriage ceremony was a strict commitment I was making to God alone. In a sense, the human being assigned to me was incidental. My actual commitment had been to follow my own spiritual path and seek to love the stranger standing next to me as a child of God. When he spurned the most primal and universal ethical taboo by being unable and unwilling to control his lust for children, I felt justified in divorcing him. Knowing I wanted someone with drive and accountability I felt my ex-blessing partner lacked, I made an intellectual choice with Vincent. In that marriage, I had a piece of paper from Washington State that a justice of the peace and a bailiff signed as witnesses. Given his later run-in with the law, that last detail now appears to have foreshadowed our future life together.

However, with Michael it was altogether different. I experienced our spiritual union and relished our intellectual compatibility. We both loved nature, honesty, and adventure. By talking over everything, we unpacked the baggage of our respective philosophical matrices and life experiences. We discussed and debated Unification Thought and consulted each other on how to help our children or our friends. We made an effort to understand each other, accepting and even embracing each other's flaws and insecurities.

All that talk enabled us to heal ourselves, recreate ourselves, and honor in one another our individual wholeness. Thus, we found a shared path that was not a reaction to or a rehashing of old pain and suffering, but a fresh journey together. Finally, we engaged in spiritual practices together that were our own shared offering and prayers. Praying together, we became two children before our beloved Heavenly Parent, joined in heart and in absolute love. Our shared spiritual practices invited the presence of the divine to join us, to be in the midst of our marriage, not on the outside as ritual, but on the inside as a spiritual bond that resulted in nothing less than a feeling of love.

Invitations went out for the wedding and, with three full months to spare, we told both sets of parents about the pregnancy. Kay was thrilled, Stan pleased, and my parents polite. Our local friends and colleagues, who were well aware of the pregnancy, were festive and supportive as the day approached. Our family friends, Lisa and Marc (Marc was Michael's best man), agreed to take Alex, our ring bearer, overnight for the duration of our brief honeymoon. Briana, my old friend from seminary, would come down to help. And Jeanne, my buddy in Manhattan and maid of honor, would provide music. Michael's extended family would come, and they said they would put themselves up at a local hotel.

My parents were interested but distant, both geographically and emotionally. One of the deepest acts of love Michael would make for me was to take on my parents about rejecting me for my faith. He became, as people would say in Unification-speak, the Messiah to my family. My involvement with Unificationism had made my father want to disown me while my mother enveloped herself in Catholicism and was utterly ashamed of me. Because of Michael, they were able to see a different side to my religious journey. He was able to explain it to them in terms they could understand and that did not belittle or patronize me; he also took them to task for not loving me, for not trusting my judgment, for not being more open-minded about something that had obviously brought me a great deal of support, love, and positive feeling. And Michael did all this without preaching or evangelizing.

My parents had refused to respect anything I had to say about the movement. They trusted the misunderstandings in the popular press of the time. They distrusted me because they remembered changing my diapers. Somehow, if Michael praised anyone or any activity within the movement, they could receive what good he had to say because they trusted him as a Unificationist outsider. Still, however much they may have preferred Michael to any of the other men I had brought into their lives, they did not attend our wedding.

Nevertheless, I did get my wish for a blessing of our union by Father Moon. Briana, my seminary friend, was one of the two Unificationists who had first met me years ago. After reconnecting at seminary, we'd stayed in touch over the years. She drove down from upstate New York to bless us. The night before our wedding, she traced a cross with holy water on Michael's hand and mine. I felt heat from the cross that endured with supernatural warmth. The moment Michael and I held hands as she blessed us, I felt a powerful current flow between us, circulating through us like one body. Once again, I felt our spirits were completely united, as I had back in my Mommy apartment when we were first ping-ponging email to each other.

From our Christmas Eve date after our Jersey City dinner and Russian Orthodox service with Yulia and Michael's parents, through countless choir rehearsals and Sunday services, Michael and I seemed bound for a church wedding. At the Dutch Reformed Church of Highland Park on an early Sunday afternoon, Stan led me down the aisle, walking on my right. Alex walked on my left, holding my hand, wearing a little boy tux. Michael and I said our "I do's," celebrated with our guests, then kissed Alex, and skedaddled for the beach.

We stopped at home to change, where Michael insisted on carrying an enormous me over the threshold. We paused to admire how huge my belly was when not hidden beneath my wedding dress. After an overnight honeymoon where we repeatedly failed to read to one another, we arose the next day, ate an enormous breakfast, and returned to the bustling routine of classes and home life in somewhat bleary bliss.

— CHAPTER SEVENTEEN —
FAITH AND PRACTICE

Michael, the Darwinist, would lovingly tease me about my faith, saying that I singlehandedly incarnated "the Church of the Living Pamela." I seized moments to pray whenever possible: before driving, before eating, before bed, before any difficult conversation or public event. Sometimes my prayers rolled right along, gaining momentum with supplications for divine intervention to bring peace in the Middle East; for harmony between people of different races, religions, and ideologies; for America to help brother and sister nations worldwide; to comfort the heart of those who had lost loved ones and for other concerns of our neighbors; to express gratitude for our family that we could connect with God's heart; and so forth. My zeal had the unsavory tendency to delay eating until dinner was cold. Michael was particularly fussy about fish, which in the best of circumstances required eating straightaway. "Fish prayer!" became our code for when an abbreviated prayer needed to suffice. Thus, we accommodated one another's faith expressions—with freedom to express and to express a little less.

Most days and nights we taught classes, did research, and wrote, but one night per week we "Hee-hee-hoo'd," sitting on the gray-carpeted floor in our birthing class at the hospital. We learned methods to distract attention from pain and what to expect in an emergency C-section. It had been some six years since my last delivery. Though much of the information was the same as before, it was reassuring to hear it again. With Michael by my side, I felt ready to handle anything. It was the kind of confidence that made me want to play John Philip Sousa marches for birthing music.

Birthing classes required a babysitter—a big expense for our budget at the time. Taking advantage of the luxury, we played hooky from birthing class one night. Instead, we ducked into a B-rated Eddie Murphy movie. Both of us were inveterate nerds. Skipping class to go necking in the dark recesses of the movie theater was high drama in our little world—a fugitive delectation of such proportions I expected to see our mug shots on the "Most Wanted" line up on the post office wall.

Winter days lengthened, and soon came the spring thaw, which scarcely softened the clay soil of our postage-stamp-sized yard. I dug into every inch of it. Inspired by English, Zen, and French gardening styles, I planted in shade and sun with a palette of plants to create winter structure, fragrance, successive blooms, and a pleasing view from upstairs. Michael painted the inside of our hundred-year-old row house—the whole of the downstairs and the entire stairwell too. Revamping our nest made it ours. Michael had shared it years ago with his first wife. Nothing of hers remained in the space, but the melancholy of Michael's depression after she had left, the gray walls, the neglected garden, each spoke of a different era. After I put in my flowerbeds, he happily mowed the pipsqueak lawn that remained with a motorless reel mower that whirred with a productive metallic chinking as it left a trail of cut grass in its wake.

The summer days hummed along like that earnest mower, both mundane and magical. My mother once again sent me the wicker bassinet that my sister, brother, and I had each slept in as babies. Having since survived Alex and his cousins, its graying and fraying presence was oddly comforting. At the Englishtown flea market, we idly browsed for a crib. A large, round-faced African woman beckoned us to her stand of woodcarvings. She chanted "Baboo" over and over as I admired the round-bellied doe nursing her fawn among the objects on her table. We left with the statue and postponed the crib, her incantation hovering in the air with her Cheshire grin.

Crossing the railroad tracks into Jamesburg, to breakfast at a country flapjack house, Michael pointed out the dimorphism of the male and female cowbirds to Alex as we watched them congregate on the grass near the rails. In dimorphic species the female and males can look very different—in the case of the cowbirds, the males were flashy with their sleek iridescent bodies and striking brown head, whereas the females looked like another species altogether, appearing a wispy gray. At Colonial Park in Franklin, Michael and Alex skipped stones, threw sticks in the stream for Sadie to fetch, flew kites, or played ball while I dawdled in the rose garden or took prayer walks in the woods. Midsummer approached. Alex had to fly to Oregon for his annual visitation. At the airport, we handed him over to Vincent, who remained blessedly civil.

One bright and sunny Saturday afternoon, Michael rented a power washer to clean the white vinyl siding of the house as I pored over my research. For supper, we strolled along Main Street to the Pad Thai, a restaurant between the video parlor and Jerusalem Pizza. I savored each morsel of satay and lusted for Michael's lips as he slurped up his eel. We walked home at the new pace we had adopted since our growing "Peanut," as we called him, had slowed me down. Indeed, Michael now called our evening strolls "constitutionals." They had decelerated from vigorous, to steady-paced, to stately. I flowed down the sidewalk, as Michael would say, "like a ship in full sail." We both enjoyed my enormous pregnancy.

That evening, my contractions started. Michael telephoned the hospital. The nurse on call instructed us to time the contractions and call back when they got closer together. An hour later, Michael was so nervous when he phoned, he told the nurse the contractions were coming "every six months." The nurse said it was time to come to the hospital. Immediately, Michael called Marc, an old friend, to ask him to please return the power washer so we would not get charged an extra day's rental. Despite dining out on occasion, we counted our pennies. Michael had inherited a penchant for Scottish frugality from his ancestors that even a mad dash to the delivery room would not curtail.

Unlike my last birthing experience, I welcomed intervention for pain this time. "Leave Stoicism to the masochists!" was my shameless motto, defying at once the homeopathic righteous and those of greater will. I paced the room to encourage the contractions; they remained strong but irregular. Hours ticked by as I walked nonstop through the night. With dawn arrived exhaustion. I had to lie down.

Strapped up and wired to monitors, I observed that each contraction caused our little Peanut's heart rate to plunge like a diving submarine. I reported this to the nurses. Whenever they checked in, I was between contractions, so the machines would blip and beep their optimistic lights to spell, "No problem." However, following another strong contraction that caused the baby's pulse to plummet, a nurse rushed in with a gurney.

"I'm sorry, but we must prepare for an emergency C-section," she said.

It was late Sunday afternoon, July 21, 1996. After fourteen hours of labor, an anesthesiologist put in an epidural. Michael donned a hospital gown. White-coated orderlies slipped me from the bed onto the gurney and whisked me into the OR. There, they strapped my arms to boards and put a tent from my chest over my knees. The epidural did what it was supposed to do, while Michael and I, fearful for the baby, started singing.

We began with holy songs and hymns. The anesthesiologist was Korean and recognized some of the songs. The tent hid from view what was going on below my waist. In his cheery way, Dr. Graybell called out from down yonder, "Do you mind if I keep the placenta?" (He was doing some sort of research).

"You can have it," I retorted, "but not until the baby's done with it!"

Having run out of songs, Michael and I were down to "I've Been Workin' on the Railroad" when I saw in Dr. Graybell's hands a pair of chubby legs with afterbirth clinging to them. Michael moved close to the baby but declined the offer to cut the umbilical cord. Within moments, he brought a swaddled-up Jacob close to my face, where I could nuzzle his cheek. My arms were still tied out to the sides on boards like a crucifix, so I could not hold him. Michael nestled Jacob under my chin. Recovering from the epidural, massive chills wracked my body. When they ended, I could finally hold Jacob and keep him by my side through the night.

Michael went home for some rest. When I awoke the next morning, Jacob was missing. I fumbled out of bed, dragging my IV pole, crumpled in pain like a century-old woman with osteoporosis. I padded down the hospital floor in bare feet and a bare you-know-what. A kindly nurse put slippers on my feet and a gown on backwards to cover my rear. All I could say was, "I want my baby! Where's my baby?" as maternal panic washed over me, momentarily drowning out the searing pain travelling across my middle.

The nurses had taken him away to the nursery for routine measurements and weighing. I told them I wanted him by my side always. One of the nurses said, "You know, this may be a chance for you to get some rest."

"I want him with me," I said in a low growl.

I didn't recognize my own voice. Some beast within prepared to lunge and take down whatever came between my child and me. Soothing smiles evaporated. A nurse slipped down the hall and Jacob's bassinet appeared at my side. He was warm, sleeping. My inner beast said, "My baby, not yours!" as I hobbled back to the room with him. Michael soon returned to the hospital.

The next day, I prepared for discharge—I'd been given the forty-eight-hour C-section stay. Although I had been quite civil once Jacob was returned to me, I suspect the nurses were not sorry to see me go.

Michael drove us home in the Jeep, the new baby seat secured in the back. The smallest bump sent a shot of searing pain deep into the gash across my belly, penetrating each muscle strand of my abdomen ripped through by the C-section. After an especially large jolt, I wondered wryly if Dr. Graybell had been more concerned about preserving the placenta than how I would feel afterwards. Nevertheless, Jacob was well and that was the priority.

I was not supposed to go up and down stairs for at least a week, but our bedroom and the only bathroom were upstairs. I inched up each step. Once upstairs, I camped out for the next couple of weeks. Neighbors brought us full-blown comfort-food meals, which sleep-deprived Michael and I both deeply welcomed. He regularly jumped in to help with baby tending. I would nurse Jacob during the day and we took shifts through the night. Michael loved feeding and diapering Jacob—he was thrilled to be a dad.

As we settled in, it became routine to have Jacob in bed with us. Sadie slept nearby on the floor and, upon his return from Oregon, Alex slept on the floor beside us or in the bed too. A whole house up for grabs and the five of us, with Sadie, slept packed like sardines in the smallest bedroom. We were cozy, and we loved it.

Michael and I continued to sing in the Reformed Church choir. Hence, we attended Sunday services, choir rehearsals, and, as Michael dubbed them, "wild choir parties" that were in fact fairly buttoned-down affairs. We became good friends with Susan and Keith, whose two boys were about the same ages as our two. Susan was a veteran choir director, musician, music teacher, and homeschooler. She helped me get started homeschooling Alex and networking with others to share curriculum and field trips.

Though Michael and I had received a Unificationist marriage blessing from Briana—my old friend from seminary and CARP—Father Moon had not yet prayed over our marriage. A little over a year later, we heard there would be a blessing ceremony in D.C. with Father and Mother Moon. We decided to attend and rededicate our marriage.

A few days before the blessing, Father came to Michael in a dream. The next morning, Michael spoke of Father with a new seriousness, as though he'd encountered Father personally, in the flesh. His recollection of the dream was that Father conveyed some important information behind the scenes—quite literally, behind a curtain before going on stage. Although neither of us were what Eric Hoffer would call a "true believer," it seemed that God and the spirit world had their own way of guiding us.

It was bitter cold on the 333rd day of 1997—a Saturday in November. We only had time for a day trip to D.C. and back. Afraid Jacob would catch a cold, we left him with a sitter, but brought Alex with us. We piled into the Jeep, prayed, and Michael drove us over two hundred miles to the Robert F. Kennedy Memorial Stadium. The event would be broadcast live to some thirty-six million people. We arrived in time to find seats in the nosebleed section, alongside about forty thousand others. The rest attended via satellite at fifty-four other locations worldwide.

From the stage below, cameras relayed a live feed onto large screens. Religious leaders of different faiths and cultures conferred their blessing upon us to establish and rededicate our marriages and families for peace. Clergy, in addition to Mother and Father Moon, included Sri Swami Satchidananda of India, a Hindu; Sul Jung Jeon of Korea, a Buddhist; the Rev. Francis Xavier D'Sa of India, a Jesuit priest; Archbishop Ioan of Russia, head of the Orthodox Church of Mother Mary; the High Bhai Kirpal Singh of Malaysia, a Sikh; and the Honorable Minister Louis Farrakhan, leader of the Nation of Islam. Kenneth Kaunda, a former president of Zambia, also spoke.

The array of speakers extolled with tenderness ideals of love and peace. They prayed with a variety of accents and faith perspectives and wore festive, traditional ceremonial clothing. Mercifully, none of them spoke for too long. The pageantry, sincerity, and freezing temperature kept our attention, and Alex's too. Civil rights activist Al Sharpton and his wife Katherine rededicated their marriage with us that day.

We had to bundle up against the blustery chill. On top of our overcoats, Michael and I wore white sashes handed to us when we arrived. They fluttered as gusts of wind whipped through the open stadium beneath a foreboding gray sky. When Father and Mother Moon prayed, the wind relented and the sun appeared. I felt its warmth though my head remained bowed in silent prayer with them. Michael and I pledged our love and dedication to each other and to community. Having removed our wedding bands, we now slipped them back on each other's fingers.

As the ceremony concluded, it remained frigid cold despite the sun. Alex was antsy. We needed to get back to Jacob and work, so we did not stay for the entertainment. Though it seemed important to have completed the ceremony, in retrospect, what was most memorable were the small gestures of loving-kindness.

As we descended from the upper bleachers, Alex, all of seven, marched down the flights of stairs gamely. Gradually his pace slowed to a crawl. It had been a long day.

"How about a ride, kiddo?" Michael said, swinging Alex up onto his shoulders.

Alex's grin beamed between his rosy cheeks all the way to the car as he bounced along, his hands clasped below Michael's chin. Michael unlocked the car and Alex bounded inside. Giving me a hug and a smile, Michael declared, "We survived another Unification ordeal!"

I laughed before closing my eyes to pray and we started home.

— CHAPTER EIGHTEEN —
ALL HAPPY FAMILIES
ARE ALIKE

Michael and I included the boys on marches for interfaith peace as well as services in temples, mosques, and churches. On top of our academic engagements, we attended an array of religiously inflected social events. They gently encouraged peace, love, and interfaith dialog. Besides Blake's Bible study group, we hosted and attended intimate Unificationist gatherings that revolved around dinner and discussion.

We cherry-picked from the movement's various projects—participating in social or interfaith activities while eschewing political ones. I remained keen to attend interfaith conferences and Michael did too. Colloquia with diverse scholars and clergy provided an exchange of ideas—not only theologies and philosophies, but also creative problem-solving. For instance, at a United Nations conference in New York, I was impressed with a young Unificationist sister who'd founded an NGO to connect orphans and latchkey children with lonely elders in an afterschool program in Central America.

Teaching anthropology of religion, Michael arranged student field trips to various Indic faith centers in central New Jersey. These included Sikh, Hindu, and Muslim places of worship. Religious leaders opened their congregations to him and his students to encourage greater understanding of their doctrines and devotions. Thus, interfaith activities permeated our home life with me as a peace activist and Michael as a scholar.

Though we were non-traditional Unificationists, we found many of the regulars easy company. All of them had multicultural exposure and most had lived or been raised abroad. They often had first-hand experience not only studying but practicing diverse beliefs. This made them natural ambassadors of interfaith peace.

The Unification movement at that time funded conferences, rallies, suppers, and art programs to encourage dialog and an educational exchange for peace. Gathering to talk and break bread with others naturally facilitated interfaith and intercultural understanding. While most religions kept to their own kind, Unificationists prioritized outreach between faiths, cultures, and nations.

I still embraced the Divine Principle as a Dao of love, convinced we could change the world by using its teachings to bridge misunderstandings. The bright, creative, altruistic people I met at peace conferences—both Unificationists and non-Unificationists—inspired me not only with their vision but also by their dedication to others. While Michael enjoyed the emotional warmth of members as friends, I remained more passionate about the Principle because its neutral language, it seemed to me, made True Love accessible to anyone who wanted to practice it.

As an adult child of an alcoholic, I knew that not all the behavior patterns I'd grown up with were ideal. The Divine Principle offered a different paradigm. It provided me with new approaches to heal and explore my own potential as a daughter of God.

Michael, however, was less drawn to theology than he was to people who practiced it. Schmoozing appealed to him more than it did to me. At one point we both became card-carrying church members—not out of blind faith in the Unification Church, but due to our association with the broader movement. Michael enjoyed the company of brothers and sisters and regularly met with a group of brothers. He was more eager than me to attend religious services, be they Muslim, Sikh, Hindu, or Unificationist. He observed as an anthropologist, but also participated as a doting dad. Michael initiated and networked with Unificationists for various child-friendly outings, like fishing.

Father was big on fishing. He fished the way he prayed—with utter dedication, no matter where he was in the world. The ocean, he said, was the next unexplored frontier and a critical future food supply. He devised a protein fish powder to help solve malnutrition. An electrical engineer by training, he created the nimble "Good Go" motorboat—a white, sixteen-foot-long powerhouse with a deep, razor-sharp hull made to handle open ocean waves.

Michael arranged with some Unificationist brothers for our family to go fishing one Saturday afternoon on a Good Go boat. A church brother served as captain. The engine churned as we left shore for New York Bay. There, freighters dwarfed our vessel. Choppy waves rippled in their wake. Our boat went airborne from crest to crest, thwacking each time it landed. Following Father's fishing tradition, we put our lines in the water. Most of us caught nothing, but Jacob caught a sea robin—a creature constructed like a confusion of mythologies with a large, stern mouth, bulging eyes atop his head, and wing-like fins all in a nuclear-disaster mottle of orange and yellow.

Despite socializing with Unificationists and attending select conferences and ceremonial events, we rarely attended the Unification Church Sunday services. Michael, however, enjoyed watching televised sports with some of the brothers. We were chummy with several Unificationist families in New Jersey and visited with each other over dinners and picnics. So when our friend Carol—then state leader of New Jersey—could not go to a meeting in Kodiak, Alaska, she asked me to go in her stead. Michael, ever the doting dad, was all for it. He was prepared to parent solo, handling both work and the kids (now three and nine years old) the week I was gone. And so I flew from Newark to Anchorage, where a small propeller plane carried me to Kodiak.

Father had convened the meeting for leaders. At 5 a.m. each morning, as per tradition, we gathered for prayers, reports, and readings. Father spoke in Korean. I followed along with an English translation of the book he read from as he digressed and expounded on various themes. As Father read in Korean, I softly read aloud in English to a small group of us huddled to the side.

After our morning meetings, we pulled on yellow slickers, waders, and rubber boots to fish for salmon. Father would say, with a mischievous twinkle in his eye, "Jesus said to fishermen, 'I will make you fishers of men.' I say to ministers, 'I will make you fishermen!'"

The final day of the conference, each of us reached into a hat to pull out the name of a city in Japan. Leaving Kodiak, we were to go directly to our selected city and teach the Divine Principle there for over a month. I had not anticipated this turn of events. It sounded exciting, but Michael was home alone with the kids. We hadn't discussed me being gone for more than a week.

Most of the other attendees prepared to leave for Japan the following day. As leaders, they were used to a surprise directive from Father to fly to the other side of the world. I was prepared to do likewise. People chatted while waiting for the airport shuttle bus. I needed to alert Michael to the news.

I slipped out to find a pay phone and telephoned him. In one hand, I held the phone receiver, in the other, a scrap of paper. On it, written in pencil, was the name of my village in the Akita Prefecture where I was to go for forty days. When I told him of this new twist, Michael said, "I thought something like this might happen. I can handle the kids until you get back. Don't worry, we miss you, but we're doing fine."

I was grateful and amazed by his response. To entertain the boys, he took them to IKEA, at exit 13A of the Turnpike, near the airport. The warehouse-sized store had a cafeteria with picture windows where they watched planes take off and land. Besides diverting the kids, Michael went for the food—hefty Swedish meatballs and glurpy lingonberry jam.

My expedition to Akita Prefecture would outlast our last month of summer break. I was hoping to work out a compromise to return in time to teach when university resumed. At the last moment, plans from above changed. From God's lips to Father's ears, to leaders, to me. I was absolved from going without having mentioned to anyone the chaos my departure might have caused at home, not only in terms of childcare, but also in terms of my job. A Japanese sister later interpreted this turn of events to me as follows: "You and your husband, by being willing to support, made the offering in heart."

After a week away rather than a month, I flew straight home to New Jersey. We resumed our tandem childcare of nine-year-old Alex and three-year-old Jacob and prepared for the fall semester.

People who knew Michael only as a secular, hot-shot academic might have underestimated his capacity for religious devotion. Again, because of the prevailing political taboo against religion at the time, it was more shocking to be religious than to be, say, an anarchist, in the academy. While Michael had a secular upbringing, faith and practice had always intrigued him. In junior high, he'd had a crush on a girl who was a devout Baptist.

Raised loosely Unitarian and agnostic, for love at age fourteen, he became a regular at the local Baptist church. Well, at least until the object of his desire made it clear she would never have him. Yet, his interest in religion persisted. Years later, he researched Hindu funeral practices for his master's degree. After his books *An Untouchable Community in South India, Coming of Age in New Jersey,* and hefty journal reviews of ethnography and theory, he returned to his anthropological research of religion.

Living in Central Jersey, we enjoyed the international flow of immigrants in our community. With that multiculturalism came a wide variety of religious centers: synagogues, mosques, Hindu and Sikh temples, and Christian churches. A substantial South Asian diaspora had established temples, mosques, and churches with a distinctly Indic flavor. Michael knew the leaders of these establishments and regularly attended religious services at the local Hindu temple for participant observation as an anthropologist. Yet beyond his professional interest, he genuinely enjoyed the people and worship services he frequented. He often took one or both boys with him. Jacob was a regular at Hindu Sunday school, or *bal satsang sabha*. His class went from toddlers through the age of five.

An imam Michael visited once said of nine-year-old Alex, as he bowed along with the others at the service, "He should become a Muslim!"

I also visited diverse religious leaders at their places of worship and invited them to Unificationist conferences on interfaith dialog. Michael and I wove religious engagements into our daily life of teaching, writing, arranging playdates for the kids, running the dog in the woods, canoeing, gardening, and enjoying barbecues with the neighbors. Attending a devotional service with the kids at a mosque or temple was as normal for us as a trip to the playground. I made a Unificationist-style altar at home—a low table with a picture of Mother and Father Moon along with songbooks, holy books, and a flower arrangement. We gathered near the altar for family prayers and brief ceremonies on holy days. But when we ventured outside our home, we honored God at the altars of all faiths.

The backyard garden planted before he was born grew lush as Jacob mastered walking and running; Alex learned to ride a two-wheeler without training wheels. Michael and I passed the childcare baton back and forth when we didn't do things en famille. Alex still flew back to Oregon in the summer for visitation. One summer, I taught in Paris for Rutgers. Michael again single-handedly managed childcare. He said that whenever an airplane flew overhead, toddler Jacob would point at it and squeal, "Mama!" or "Aya!" (his name for Alex).

Michael's theory was that young Jacob thought that whoever was gone spent their entire absence flying back and forth inside a large gray bird. Michael and Jacob's trips to IKEA probably helped reinforce this concept. Other summers, Michael taught at Rutgers. While he earned summer-school salary, I could write.

In the winter of 2000, Michael and a friend in sociology, Ben Zablocki, attended Father Moon's eightieth birthday celebration. Ben had researched the Bruderhof, a communal group practicing Christianity in upstate New York. He attended the birthday celebration as an opportunity for sociological research as well as an outing with Michael. I did not go due to my teaching schedule at Rutgers and in order to tend the kids. A friend in the movement, Betty, went in my stead. She was a Reiki practitioner, mom, and wife of a Japanese brother.

It was a long day trip to D.C., but Michael, Ben, and Betty returned well-fed and each toting a couple of heavy volumes of Father's speeches. Although I disagreed with Ben over the concept of brainwashing within the movement—an idea he professed albeit with his own sociologically nuanced definition—I appreciated that he considered Marxism an ideology that required a leap of faith. At the time, a romantic interpretation of Marxism endured among literary scholars who often presumed the validity of atheistic materialism as the foundation of many critical approaches to literature.

Literary criticism, though immersed in the search for meaning—or lack thereof—in texts seemed to gloss over the dehumanizing aspects of Marxism. Ben could see that the philosophy itself in practice was vulnerable to critique in a way many literary scholars of the time ignored. It was refreshing to have a scholar recognize this discrepancy for sociological rather than pure ideological reasons. He had similar reservations about Unificationism, but my confidence in that philosophy was based on my own experience. Besides endorsing free will and disavowing violence, Unificationism had opened the door for me to explore my own relationship with God. The fruit of its philosophy resided in my friends who consciously applied its principles and lived their lives as genuinely loving people.

Our lives were full and busy, but I felt restless despite our kind neighbors, academic community, and family activities. My restlessness increased due to a recurrent dream. In it, I found myself rocking gently from side to side sitting in the rear of Michael's heavy, green Old Town canoe; Michael sat in the front, the boys in the middle. We were bobbing just west of the Verrazano-Narrows Bridge in Upper New York Bay.

The rough sea was peaked with white caps and the bay water churned with violence around our canoe in my dream. I should have been terrified. Seeing us in my dream, I thought, "Why aren't we wearing life jackets?" Michael never would have allowed us to embark without them in real life. Oddly, instead of bouncing airborne over the whitecaps, the canoe—in real life highly unstable in rough water—rocked in peaceful cadence. I felt divine protection cradling us amid fury.

In the dream, we were in the middle of the bay with a view familiar from the Staten Island Ferry as it approached Battery Park. But from the rocking canoe, I saw flames lapping the skyline—Manhattan glowing red. Though in my dream we seemed to have escaped harm, when I awoke, a disquieting urgency pressed upon me. I had to get my family to safety. I didn't know why. I didn't take the dream literally, but my instinct told me it was a warning. Even if we had to leave everything behind, we needed to go.

Viewed as a practical matter, this meant that, with the family growing, Michael and I would have to move. We visited houses as far north as Easton, Pennsylvania, and as far south as Little Egg Harbor, north of Atlantic City, in New Jersey. Still unsure where we would end up, we prepared our house to put it on the market. Our home inspector lived in Manahawkin, a town in South Jersey. His son, it turned out, had studied homeopathic medicine at the University of Bridgeport, the college Rev. Moon salvaged from financial disaster while he was in prison in Danbury.[10] Our inspector's praise of Manahawkin so inspired Michael that we house hunted there. We found one inland, near the causeway, in a neighborhood we could afford.

Meanwhile, the same dream and sequence of emotions about Manhattan in flames repeated every few weeks. I would note the danger of the rough water, feel surprised by how gently our little canoe rocked in the bay, and observe the unperturbed peace within our family. The conflagration I felt helpless to stop would blaze over Manhattan in the distance. Each time the dream ended, I felt stunned gratitude that we had escaped. Fear, peace, flames, helplessness, the need to escape. I would have the exact same dream several more times. August approached. The pressure to move increased.

On September 11, 2001, we were scheduled to close on our house in Highland Park. We went to the real estate attorney's office and waited. He did not show up. No one at his office seemed to know where he was, so we returned home. The telephone rang from the kitchen. Michael strode across the living room and lifted the receiver with one hand while detangling the cord with his other. It was the elder secretary from the Department of Anthropology, said Michael. All she would say was "Turn on the TV."

Replays of the South Tower collapsing were already being shown, but we saw the North Tower collapse in real time. We gasped as the sides of the tower began to fall away and smoke billowed upwards, engulfing it as it disintegrated into rubble. Every station continuously replayed the tragedy. Jacob, now five years old, thought the towers were continually being hit and destroyed so we turned off the news. The telephone rang again. It was the lawyer. He and his daughter, a paralegal, had been on their way to the office from Jersey City. Stuck in a traffic jam, they had seen the whole thing from the highway but they had made it to the office and he told us to come on over.

Still in shock, we drove Jacob to a neighbor's daycare. Michael waited at the wheel. I got Jacob out of his car seat and carried his bag of belongings as we walked to his locker inside. I kissed him and left him surrounded by kids playing, drawing, and counting neon tetras that flitted in bursts of color in the fish tank. Back in the Jeep, Michael and I resumed our somber drive. Prayer seemed superfluous. We were in a living prayer. Every breath felt like an act of hope to defy this tragedy.

We spoke little, but held the grief there with us, held the space of the sacred,

---

[10] Some background on this episode in Father Moon's life is available at Carlton Sherwood, *Inquisition: The Persecution and Prosecution of the Reverend Sun Myung Moon*, (Washington, D.C.: Regnery Publishing, 1991).

of all those whose lives and loves were lost. We were overwhelmed. When we arrived at the lawyer's office, I moved like an automaton, the falling towers sinking in slow motion in my head, our hearts sinking, smoldering, going cold with them.

The law office felt like our church that day. We came for fellowship, to gather with others who had witnessed this tragedy. The shock was too large to contain as grief. I felt bewildered, lost, unable to fathom what to do next. How could we resume "normal" life? How could I do mundane things like take out the trash, run the kids in the park, teach the importance of some obscure exception in French grammar the way I had yesterday? What was the point if the world was this insane?

The lawyer pointed out that if we responded with fear, the bad guys would win. As the towers still smoldered, we laid pen to paper to declare that life would go on, that we would extract order from chaos, that fear would not bind us, that there was grace in the midst of hell. The power of ritual, of gathering with others, of committing to a contract, felt like we were making a covenant with hope. Hope not just for our lives, but for all those around us, that civilization would endure not by violence, but by the authority of words that articulated the law as guarantor of peaceable exchange.

Later that night, after Jacob was asleep, we turned on the news for updates. The tragedy had blocked communications and roadways—only rescue officials could pass. The George Washington Bridge connecting Manhattan and New Jersey was closed. Phone lines were down and cell phones disabled. I was unable to reach my friend Jeanne in the city for days. When we did make contact, it was a grim relief. She was not directly harmed but was engulfed in the tragedy—not only metaphorically, but literally: acrid smoke and particulate-laden air clung to the city and filled everyone's lungs.

As soon as the George Washington Bridge reopened, Father Moon initiated a peace rally at the Manhattan Center, near Madison Square Garden. Michael and I invited Imam Chebli, a big bear of a man who was the head of the Islamic Society of Central Jersey. Accustomed to outreach, he knew the governor and often spoke on the radio. With his leadership, his large congregation gathered regularly at the mosque not only for worship services but for daily projects and afterschool programs. He was eager to attend the peace rally. When Michael called to offer him a ride with us, he said, "Wait—I will call you back about that."

We figured he was debating the risk of controversy in attending a Unification-sponsored event, or that a cultural taboo could prevent him, as a religious leader, from riding with us. But when he called back, he said to Michael, "I wanted to check with the police first. I wanted to be sure there would be a police car in the parking lot when you came to pick me up."

"Why?" I prodded Michael to ask.

"For your protection. I don't want anything to happen to you," said the Imam.

Michael shrugged his shoulders and looked at me as my eyes filled with tears, moved that this man was so concerned about us.

At dawn, as planned, we drove to meet him at the rendezvous spot. In the parking lot by the mosque, a police car sat. The Imam, in his turban and flowing robes approached our homey, red Jeep with regal stature and stride. He towered even over Michael, who was himself six foot four. I quickly got into the back seat so the Imam could stretch his long legs out in the front. I figured he and Michael would want to talk; they'd known each other for years. But Imam Chebli said firmly, "No. You must sit in front. You are married. It is only fitting. Husband and wife should be together," as he squeezed himself into the rear seat behind me.

I scooted the seat forward as far as I could, humbled by his humility. As we drove, he said, "I am sorry to say, but I will have to leave the conference early."

Knowing how busy he was, we started to assure him that it was fine; we would drive him back whenever he was ready, but he cut short our polite assurances saying, "I must tell you why." Michael was watching the road, but as I glanced over at him, I knew we were both thinking the same thing: *You don't have to justify your schedule, particularly at this time...*

"I must tell you, I have to return to meet a member of my congregation at the airport who is returning home."

We started to say, "We completely understand—" The Imam added, "He is coming home in a coffin."

We silently sighed. I bent my head down and closed my eyes for a moment. Imam Chebli continued: "He is coming home in a coffin—" His voice cracked, and then he continued: "He was pumping gas into his car at a service station in Texas. Someone saw that he was wearing a turban, so they shot and killed him in retaliation for the bombing of the towers."

The Imam's shoulders shuddered as he swallowed a sob. Then, he swept a large hand over the crows' feet on either side of his eyes. His hand paused for a moment, holding his face beneath his bushy brows and above the wiry ruff of his salt-and-pepper beard.

We drove in silence, save the growl of the Jeep engine. The suspension's usual cheeky squeak and bounce sounded more like a dirge now. Pointing his nose toward the sunrise coming in through the side window, his mouth drawn and resolute, the Imam added, "This is why it is important for me to attend this conference. We must stop the madness and educate people about peace. I am meeting with the governor later today to discuss this, how Islam is a religion of peace. These terrorists are bandits."

Imam Chebli had known the young man returning home in the coffin since he had been a small boy and started attending the mosque. His airport rendezvous weighed upon him with the urgency and sorrow of a father meeting his own son. At the same time, the Imam was called upon to bring dignity, grace, and comfort to the immediate family of the young man. He needed to give the family members space to mourn and to halt, before it arose in their throats, the turbulence of hatred. Sorrow in that moment overwhelmed the vehement cry of injustice.

When 9/11 occurred, Father Moon said that it was like Jesus going the way of the cross; America was on the cross. The injustice of the attack had turned the world's heart toward America in sympathy. Citizens spontaneously gathered in nation after nation, lighting candles, offering prayers, and sending condolences. And here within the microcosm of our own state and community, Imam Chebli was partaking of that global prayer by attending a peace rally in New York the very day he was to meet a member of his own congregation murdered by an American. The crown of thorns was firmly upon the Imam's great head, I thought, as we bounced and squeaked our way into the gray cloud of dust and debris that still hovered over New York City.

Rev. Joseph Lowery, a civil rights activist who had marched with Dr. King, was among the eclectic group of speakers at the conference. During breaks, hundreds of people milled about in the lobby. Over the din of burbling voices, service projects and other announcements came through the loudspeakers. I looked up and saw a young man bounding back upstairs from the lobby. It was a young pastor from the Reformed Church of Highland Park, whom I had invited to the conference. He held a deep interest in civil rights and, like Imam Chebli, needed to pastor people grieving in his congregation. I was glad he was able to attend.

As arranged, we left the conference early to chauffeur the grieving Imam back to his duties. When we arrived at the mosque, he thanked us and slowly unfurled his long legs to exit the Jeep. He not only had to bring divine compassion to his congregation and the murdered young man's grieving family; he also had to make televised public statements together with the governor of New Jersey to dispel ignorance about his faith. I hoped the New York conference had helped support him, that he had found comfort in interfaith solidarity, in sharing prayer and the accord of other religious leaders committed to building peace.

— CHAPTER NINETEEN —

GLASTONBURY

Within days of the conference, as search dogs continued to probe the wreckage for casualties at Ground Zero, we prepared to move from Highland Park to Manahawkin. Though we would be further away from them, Michael's parents, Kay and Stan cheered our move. They knew Michael loved the ocean. We had received a good price for our old house and found a new one within our budget.

The mosquito-infested Pine Barrens surrounded our new neighborhood, yet our tiny dead-end road had the auspicious name of Pennsylvania Avenue. I now had a half-acre to garden; the boys and their friends could enjoy the in-ground pool and Michael was mere minutes from the ocean. But within days of our move, something went amiss with Kay. Her family doctor couldn't resolve her enduring backache. She thought it was a sprain that had started around Christmas.

She rallied us on for the move by telephone, yet Kay seemed to suffer more than usual with this dogged sprain. Her aged doctor was reluctant to test for anything else and she balked at getting a second opinion. She didn't want to be disloyal to the doctor she'd seen for decades. When the pain became unbearable, she finally went for a second opinion. This time, she received a new diagnosis: cancer. It had spread from her lungs to other organs and was now too advanced for treatment other than palliative care to keep her more comfortable. The news anchored our hearts in Connecticut just as we were launching a new life down the shore.

Kay opted for home hospice. We and the extended family in New England alternated stays in Glastonbury to help Stan care for her. With the kids and the dog in tow, the bump and wiggle of the Jeep defined our familial line dance to Kay and Stan's. We would wend our way north on the Garden State Parkway to the New Jersey Turnpike, across the George Washington Bridge, and up the Merritt Mill Highway. Crossing the bridge over the Connecticut River, whoever was awake would call out, "There's Glastonbury's steeple!"—words as reassuringly familiar as the trip was grueling.

In the music room where she used to play piano, Kay rested on a rented hospital bed. We responded to the tinkle of her little bell requesting food or meds. During night vigils, we adopted a routine of watching movies in the alcove near her bed. Holding hands, Michael and I would doze upright, ready to respond if Kay needed tending.

In the wee hours one night, shuffling feet and a muffled grunt startled me from a doze. I saw Stan in the shadows. He was carrying Kay from the bed to the potty chair. It squatted like a chrome-legged beetle in the middle of the room. Its strange modernity invaded the house's early eighteenth-century calm. Every surface in Kay and Stan's house had a comfortable, dusty patina of age. But the new medical devices—the hospital bed, the potty chair, the sheen on the disposable bed pads—refracted light with a sharp, sterile glare that shattered the soft, round, organic flow and fade of time. Stan's silhouette stretched tall in the golden beam cast by a streetlight—its bright glare softened by the bubbly glass of olden-day windowpanes. His every step seemed so precarious, as if a puff of an updraft from beneath the door could have sent them both crashing to the floor. Kay was not a small woman. I was sure Stan would break a hip. I roused Michael. He said, "Dad, let me help!" and dashed into the room to wrap his arms around the other side of Kay.

Stan protested, with a gravelly "No! I've got it!"

Michael backed away and stood by me, ready to catch the two of them. Together we strained to will Stan strength, as if by watching we could steady his balance as he struggled with his precious bundle of Kay. As he half-hoisted, half-dragged her from the bed to the potty chair, he wheezed and slid his feet. Each lurch caused Kay's body to sway in front of the antique upright saloon piano. When he plopped her onto the seat, her torso flopped forward, threatening to keel her onto the floor. He relented then, allowing Michael to help him reposition Kay upright.

Stan had sustained faithful attentiveness to Kay over the course of their more than fifty years of marriage. She had been the frail one emotionally. She had tried to kill herself at one point and received shock treatment when Michael was but a boy of eight or nine. Michael said that she was never quite the same afterwards. Stan had soldiered on, tending to Michael and his sister while working fulltime for Pratt and Whitney. There, he garnered some five patents for, among other things, a device that cooled airplane engines. The company took credit and proceeds from the patents but awarded Stan commemorative plaques. There were no plaques for his heroic care of Kay, however.

Only months prior, Kay had been laughing and eager to take outings with the grandchildren and friends. It was hard to believe how quickly our lives had turned around. A good sport, she joked about Stan's passion for restoring their house. She said that the historic sign outside their front door should have read, "One Fucking Olde House!" instead of "The Thomas Hale House."

Stan tended the homestead as if raising a child—seeking to do what was right, but improvising as life demanded. Built in 1714, the house had so many layers of memories, it felt like a family member. In Colonial days, it had been a pub or "publick house." Stan had restored it with steadfast devotion. To maintain authenticity, he refurbished the chimney—hauling mud he dug by hand from the Connecticut River. He mixed paint with natural dyes for the walls in historically accurate hues.

To assure early Colonial inexactitude, Stan hired teenage Michael and his high school classmate to work on the house one summer. They were to extend the beam-and-plaster kitchen ceiling. When they completed their work, they proudly showed Stan the new ceiling, fully square and plumb. Stan had them rip out the fresh plaster and redo it without using modern tools: he wanted authentic Colonial imperfection, not perfect right angles. Outside the house, Stan built a brick courtyard and fountain. Around it each year he planted a garden of heirloom flowers from seeds. History carried on, lived, and grew there.

We couldn't believe Kay was dying. Kay and Stan were as much a part of our lives and their community as the house was a monument in the historic district. We loved them to pieces and so did the kids. Going to Glastonbury was like returning to some fairytale world.

From the smell of Kay's pies to Stan's artistry in the woodwork and creative electrical wiring, the Glastonbury house was both homey and magical. Stan's artistic conviction and engineering inventiveness made the house come alive like the Beast's enchanted castle in Cocteau's rendition of *La Belle et la Bête*.

Stan imbued everyday hardware with creative candor as well as Colonial-era authenticity. Each object that he crafted contained a tangible, fulsome history—the way a hammer that has been used for countless hours rests differently in your hand than a new one: decades of oil and sweat add heft, deepen the color and sheen of the handle—age makes it smooth, soft even. The weight of memory resides in the wood as if it remembered everything it had ever repaired. Those memories become yours as you take hold of the hammer, even if you've never held it before. New hardware and tools don't have that vibration.

The towel rack in the bathroom was no mere dowel but by Stan's inventive hand it became the long back of a dachshund—the head at one end, the tail at the other. He carved a dainty Victortian hand to clasp a stained-glass light shade; a heron whose neck curved in folds like ribbon candy beneath his graceful head, the top of which served as a shelf.

Woodcarvings adorned the house in an exotic pastiche of Indic vines and curlicues with Colonial sunflowers and pineapples, for Stan had been raised in India. The son of a missionary, he and his sisters had attended school from childhood through high school graduation in the Himalayas at Woodstock School. There, he counted among his pets a mischievous monkey and, always, a beloved dog. Endless stories of India were in the walls of the Glastonbury house, along with family tales from holidays past.

The house and Kay and Stan formed a single entity: Kay-n'-Stan's. Adding to the confusion of Kay's illness was how she could no longer fuss over Stan and all of us. He always seemed the more vulnerable one of the two. He would break a collar bone here, injure himself there with his tools or ambitious tree trimming. Before she was dying, we thought Kay was the strong one keeping him alive. I think we assumed she would outlive all of us.

Kay continued to decline. Michael and I were concluding yet another extended three- or four-day weekend when we discovered that neither we nor Michael's sister would be able to assist Stan with care the forthcoming weekend. That would leave Stan to care for Kay alone. When she had been more self-reliant and able to walk, Stan could handle things solo. Not wanting to hurt his feelings, I recalled his wizened silhouette when he tried to lift Kay to the potty chair. In our absence, they could both be hurt.

For the weekend we would all be away, I advocated for respite care to help Stan. Kay could stay in a nursing home for a few days. The all-nighters were taking their toll. In between her naps, Kay would be awake at all hours, ringing her little bell. As we were discussing this, Kay rang her tinkling bell and requested breakfast. I brought her two small pancakes with butter and syrup and the kids brought her a cup of tea. She polished her plate of food and smiled. The morphine patch was doing its job and keeping her out of pain for the moment. In the next room, Michael and I continued talking with Stan about nursing home respite for the weekend he would be alone. Stan was staunch: "I can handle it," he growled, his voice sounding as if it flowed through tumbling river rocks.

The conversation paused. I went into the music room to check on Kay and found her immobile, her head tilted to one side, her mouth open. Her spirit had quietly slipped out. I knew instantly—she had no intention of going to a nursing home, not even for a weekend. She had escaped for freedom.

We called the nurse and the mortuary. They would arrive later in the evening. Michael's sister was on a camping vacation with her husband and daughter, far from a telephone. Cell phones were not prevalent. Margie, the church nurse, arrived, took Kay's pulse, and confirmed she had died. Still holding Kay's wrist, she asked, "Would you like me to clean her up?"

Grateful for help, I quickly said yes. Phones rang and the doorbell sounded. The hospice nurse arrived and reconfirmed Kay's death. Family poured in by early evening. Cousin Eugenia brought a banquet of Chinese food. Multiple pairs of hands spread the dishes in a colorful row down the kitchen counter, just the way Kay used to for buffet-style meals. I returned to be near her. People chattered and clinked dishes in the kitchen two rooms away as I lit a holy candle on Kay's bedside table. She looked peaceful, but not asleep. Spanish guitar music—her favorite of late—strummed from the CD player by the candle.

While there had been so much frenzied dispatch when Kay died, I now embraced this lull in catastrophe. It was mid-July, but felt like Christmas with the familiar sounds of family bustling, talking, and laughing in the next room. I served myself a plate of Chinese food and returned to sit with Kay. Alone with her, I pulled up an old wooden chair with a cane woven seat. Its oak legs wobbled a little on the uneven floor as I sat down at her shoulder. It felt both homey and sacred to sit with her. As the candlelight flickered and the Spanish guitars softly strummed, kids played in the next room. The wide-planked floors creaked as they had over two hundred years ago. I felt peace.

After dinner, everyone left but Stan, Michael, the boys, and me. The undertakers arrived well after dark. Bypassing the front picket fence, their black van's heavy tires crushed the grass as they backed up to the front door and parked askew. Through the pitch of night, they rattled forth a gurney and brought it through the Colonial front door, thwacking the wood-paneled frame of the foyer as they entered. I felt accosted by modernity, by clinical sterility, by a loveless world.

The undertakers knocked and jangled the gurney through the door into the music room, where Kay reposed by the still flickering candle and the guitar strumming from the CD player. Their practical world of metal objects on wheels and plastic zipped bags seemed alien to her tender home: the earthiness of the cotton linen sheet and blanket pulled up under her chin; the fine wisps of gray hair she kept cut short; the little cards from friends lovingly taped on the windowpane—just hours ago, she had gazed at them and smiled.

Before sliding her onto the stretcher, they pulled back the covers that had hidden Kay's curled toes.

"Wait!" I said.

I ran to the armoire, grabbed a pair of socks and pulled them over her cold feet before they took her away. Kay could not go out the door with bare feet. The world was a harsh, cruel place. I could not let her go out there without socks. Although she wished her body cremated, I did not want her to leave half-clothed.

Sliding her onto the gurney, the morticians quickly zipped the black bag over her face.

They bumped their way back through the door frame into the foyer. Exiting the front door, they lifted the gurney over the two front steps then rolled it to the rear of the van. They slid Kay into the cavernous dark. Then, they collapsed the gurney and loaded it beside her to share her final car ride.

I stood alone looking out the door, watching as the two shadowy figures loaded their cargo. I felt connected with Kay and prayed for her safe journey. I was pulling for her the way I would every morning for Michael when he left to commute to Rutgers. I would will for him safe travels through the deer-filled woodlands and the hazardous highways cherishing him with all my heart, filled with intensity, as if any moment could be our last.

Upright Stan. Vertical time. We, too, had reached upward to reorient our lives during hospice. Commuting to Kay's bedside in Glastonbury had become part of our weekly rhythm, like going to work, or running the kids and Sadie in the woods to blow off steam. Now that routine was over.

CHAPTER TWENTY

UNIMAGINED VENTURES

During the months caring for Kay in Glastonbury, stolid Michael became shaky and anxious. His doctor had prescribed Xanax "to take the edge off." Problem was, the Xanax took the edge off his coordination and driving skills too. He had always loved to drive. I had a robust fear of heights and fast highways. Our route to Glastonbury over the George Washington Bridge, skittering through and around New York City traffic overwhelmed me. Rather than drive myself, which would have required confronting my own phobias, I preferred to pray. As in the days of Vincent's mad rages, I silently focused, willing the wheels to remain between the yellow lines.

On Pennsylvania Avenue, we settled into new routines. I'd taken time off from teaching at Rutgers due to Kay's hospice, prepping our old house to sell, and moving. Frugality and our move from an expensive cosmopolitan area to a rural one provided us with a different lifestyle. We ate out less often and enjoyed nature more. I homeschooled both boys, doubling my class prep. Michael had a long commute—some seventy miles. Manahawkin was affordable but farther from our old friends, like the Howells, and former activities like choir.

Michael would head for campus before dawn. I arose with him to see him off and pray. I consciously sent energy to will him safe travels as he navigated the narrow, two-lane road through the Pine Barrens' shadows, dodging the occasional deer. During the day, I alternated working one-on-one with the boys. At nightfall, until I heard Michael's car wheels crunch on the gravel driveway, my every cell remained on alert as I prayed for his safe return home.

Though we lived in a wooded area on the mainland, it was close to the beach. On sunny days, even in winter, Michael enjoyed taking the boys and Sadie to ramble along the shore of Long Beach Island, just across the causeway. He'd take the whole family birding on the Jersey Shore, a critical habitat for migrants and local shore birds to feed and nest. It seemed like an ideal habitat for us too—we had a fish shack around the corner from our new home and a public library in the village a scant mile away. We seemed to be in a great location for all that we needed—nature, books, food, and access to work.

Putting down roots, I befriended some local ministers and homeschoolers. Michael planned field work for a potential ethnography of the Pine Barrens. He also continued to pursue his interest in the anthropology of religion. Swaminarayan friends back in Edison, in Central Jersey, connected him with some Hindu families near Atlantic City, closer to our new home. It was exciting to start anew.

Yet, Michael grew broody as we entered the bleak days of late February. When he took long walks on the beach, he no longer returned happy and refreshed, but distant. He insisted that it was not the loss of his mother, that he had internally said his goodbyes to her years prior in college when she had tried to kill herself. At Rutgers, the Anthropology Department was undergoing an internal review to establish its academic rank. Michael had office politics and job performance on his mind in addition to his regular teaching load and research. I figured the stress of work was getting to him, but worried about his broodiness nonetheless.

Homeschooling was taking off. The internet made it easier to find interesting educational activities and to compare curricula. Studying Renaissance art, the boys and I painted a mural on the living roomwall with gold leaf we got from a craft shop. We took study breaks at the beach and attended events at the local library—talks on opera and Impressionism. After one such talk, I met a professor from Stockton University, about a half hour south of us. We corresponded and it looked promising for me to teach French there eventually.

After fleeing Central Jersey due to my dream before 9/11, my sense of devotion in prayer continued in Manahawkin. I felt profound gratitude and responsibility to God, not only for the personal blessings of our life—our children, food, shelter—but also for public concerns like the direction in which America was moving as a nation.

I was attuned to look beyond the ordinary. I experienced two more spiritual encounters in Manahawkin. One was a dream of Father Moon telling me, "First, I spoke French." Korean was the lingua franca of the movement. I had been praying and studying the Divine Principle quite apart from the leadership or any church organization for years. Of late, I'd been studying the Principle in French, a language I loved. At the time, this dream solidified my connection with Father. It assured me that our bond in spirit was personal and that it went beyond organizational hierarchy or definitions of leadership. This helped me to envision myself as a spiritual pioneer in Manahawkin.

To my surprise, my second other worldly encounter was a vision of Father sitting on our living room couch. He had to brace himself to hold his torso upright, the palms of his hands pushed face down on either side of his hips, his elbows rigid to keep from falling over. His face sagged with fatigue, but his spirit was strong and vibrant. Like a hologram, his spiritual presence was substantial, three-dimensional, and occupied space right there in our own house. At the time, I made no speculation as to Father's health or age, but rather self-centeredly interpreted this vision as a personal message to me.

I knew then that I could count on God. Yet sometimes I felt so alone. Father—who came to me as a beloved and friendly divine emissary—understood my situation. Holding himself up by spirit, he showed me that the way to cope with adversity was to strengthen my own spirit. The surroundings didn't matter. Whether other people understood me or not didn't matter either. That was how I took the message. Intellectually, I understood the value of prayer and connecting with a higher power to endure physical and emotional duress. But Father holding himself upright on our shabby flea-market couch, using sheer will power, felt like an intervention. Beyond external circumstances, I needed to connect with divine inner strength. I had these experiences when everything seemed to be going rather well.

The kids and I were expanding our relationships in the community. Walking in the park one day, we met an elderly gentleman who had landed on the Normandy coast on D-Day. He invited Alex, Jacob, and me to his house for a first-hand history lesson. He showed us maps, his uniform, and an original WWII flyer of Eisenhower's D-Day speech. He told us how, contrary to orders, many of "the boys" had tried to bring snacks with them on the invasion. The crest of the sea, he said, held hundreds of bobbing apples that had floated out of soldiers' pants pockets as they waded ashore.

At the library in nearby Tuckerton, we met other homeschoolers. We became close family friends with Marion and Jeb. Their son, Ethan, was a couple of years older than Alex, but they got on well. Ethan was patient and solicitous with young Jacob too. Over the course of a year, we palled around, visiting the local corn maze at Halloween, relaxing at the beach, running the dogs, sharing dinner at their home or ours. Jeb took Michael and the boys boating. Marion and I traded curriculum ideas. Marion and Jeb were such easy company that they watched the entire film version of *Gone with the Wind* with us—Michael's idea. As a result, he perceived them as cut from a different cloth: they had demonstrated the ultimate measure of true friendship by enduring that southern epic.

Michael visited the local Swaminarayan congregation near Atlantic City and made plans to return. To interview locals from the Pine Barrens, he arose before dawn on several weekends to visit Dunkin' Donuts. There, at sunrise, pick-up trucks would gather like cattle at milking hour. Strong, doughy men beneath baseball caps talked through their lowered windows while they ate in their trucks before heading forth to hunt or fish. And Michael loved doughnuts. However, even this ethnographic project and connecting with Hindu friends did not seem to calm his nerves.

Anxious one afternoon, Michael placed a call to his psychiatrist, the one who had overseen his antidepressant medication for decades. This doctor had added a new drug, Xanax, which he'd readily prescribed in ever-increasing dosages as Kay was dying. After she died, Michael's MAO inhibitor, Parnate, which had been effective on its own for years, seemed to stop controlling his symptoms of depression. Consulting his doctors, he agreed to switch to a newer antidepressant, an SSRI. But first, he had to stop taking the old antidepressant for two weeks. He'd taken Parnate for decades and felt the loss.

To bridge the gap while he was Parnate-free, Michael's psychiatrist prescribed Xanax alone. Since he had been Michael's doctor for over twenty years—and was paid seventy dollars per fifteen-minute monthly visit where he checked Michael's blood pressure and refilled his prescription—Michael trusted him to oversee the switch. But when asked for help with Michael's increased anxiety, the psychiatrist said, "I wash my hands of this. He'll need to check himself into a hospital"—without recommending a facility or continuing as Michael's doctor.

The psychiatrist saw no contradiction between having been Michael's doctor for over a quarter of a century and his current disinterest in Michael's well-being. His job description, apparently, had been to assure that Michael's blood pressure did not exceed recommended norms when on a particular med, but that was as far as it went. I called Klaus, Michael's psychotherapist. Of course, he was busy, but the recording, at least, said he would call back.

Michael was sitting at his desk in the bedroom we had converted into our joint office at home. I leaned over his shoulder to see his computer screen. We had dial-up internet and he had performed a search using an internet search tool called "Google" to find a psychiatric hospital. Across the screen splashed the homepage of Belleview Haven.

"I want to check myself in," he said.

I took a deep breath and looked over the description of the place and their treatment plans. "They specialize in ECT—electro convulsive therapy. That's shock treatment, Michael!" I said.

The website promoted the procedure with excessive enthusiasm—the way a yoga retreat might feature vegetarian cuisine or deep breathing seminars. The center's normalization of an extreme procedure shot a chill through me.

"Why don't you wait and talk to Klaus first?" I said.

At last, Klaus returned my by now frantic calls. He spoke to Michael, who was not very cooperative. Whether in too much anguish, or out of New England stubbornness, Michael had made his decision. He did not want to consider other alternatives. Having a clear plan brought him relief. It was as though he could not afford to relinquish having made a decision, even if the decision made was not the best choice.

Having decided that he would go to Belleview Haven, Michael called Jeb, who offered to drive him there. I had schooling duties with the children that day and had to get through their lessons. Marion and Jeb were like family by then; I trusted them completely. Yet as I watched Michael climb into Jeb's blue truck, I felt my heart sink.

It didn't seem right for Michael to enter Belleview Haven as a patient. Those medical strangers didn't care about him. I hoped Jeb might help Michael reverse his decision. It was a long drive through the Pine Barrens up to Princeton—they'd have time to talk. But Jeb could be passive sometimes and Michael looked determined. I did not know that it would be the last time I would ever see Michael truly in control of his own mind.

My thoughts flashed back to our previous Manahawkin Christmas. That day, I'd found a deep-wood dwelling bird, a woodcock. The poor thing was frozen to death on our back stoop. Any bird in such a state would have saddened me, but the woodcock is so shy, it was a rare sighting. Usually an event to celebrate, my "life bird" was frozen into rigor mortis. (A life bird is one that you see for the first time in your life.) He must have been desperate for warmth to come to our door.

I had absorbed every detail of the woodcock's bearing and plumage: his lifeless, closed eyes; soft, cryptic, brown scalloped plumes; the gentle curve of his long bill. Remorse and foreboding had clutched my heart with cold, steel jaws even though it had been Christmastide, when I usually felt a warm glow. As I watched Jeb drive Michael to Belleview Haven, the woodcock's little round head, arched bill, and partridge-like body flashed before my eyes. I felt again that ominous warning chill. I felt it was a sign from the spirit world, a warning I didn't want to accept it because it seemed too awful to contemplate.

Klaus called again and asserted that ECT was not what Michael needed therapeutically. His certainty combined with the spiritual warning threw me into action. There was no time to make plans. I called a neighbor to please feed the dog. Without packing, I trundled the kids into the car. Now desperate to see Michael, I made sure Alex and Jacob were buckled, said a prayer, and set off for Princeton. I could not drive the Turnpike, as it was beastly fast and stressful.

Instead, I took Michael's route through the Pine Barrens. Halfway to Hightstown on Route 571 I stopped at a Wawa, a familiar convenience store, to make a telephone call from the pay phone.

I called the only people I knew near Princeton, our old friends from choir, Susan and Keith Howells. Grandma Jeannie, Susan's somewhat deaf mom, answered.

"Hello?" she said.

"Jeannie! Jeannie, this is Pam," I said.

"Who?"

"Pam Moffatt."

"Oh, Pam. Hello! Susan's not home!" her voice boomed through the receiver.

I asked her if I could drop the kids for a couple of hours while I visited Michael in hospital. She thought it would be all right but said to call back when Susan was home. Onward I drove, wondering how I would juggle the kids and the hospital. A half hour later, spotting another Wawa payphone booth, I swung the car left from the road into the gravel parking lot. I asked the boys to stay put while I called again. Pulling out a quarter, I pushed it through the slot and gripped the cold, black receiver on the end of its metal cord. I waited for the dial tone to connect and again mashing Susan's number into the metal buttons.

This time, Jeannie put Susan directly on the phone. "Michael's in hospital?" she asked.

"Yes, Belleview Haven," I said and spilled the whole saga.

Susan, without hesitation, said, "Bring the kids over. You can stay with us."

The black neck of the telephone receiver had warmed up in my hand as I held it. Hearing her invitation, the relief of peace flowed from the phone through my body, transforming the receiver into a homey talisman. I leaned into the grimy booth as though standing in my own living room. Cars spewed dust and gravel as they exited the parking lot.

Oblivious, strangers paid for their gas and snacks inside the convenience store a few feet away. I huddled in the booth against the cold and wanted to stay there, an unwilling skydiver facing the open bay door. I wanted to curl up in that booth in fetal position, safe in the womb, connected to another human being.

"I'll go with you over to the hospital," Susan added.

I thanked her again, clunked the receiver into the cradle hook, and thanked God. Ready to plunge into action, I took a deep breath, mustered a smile for the boys, and climbed into the Jeep to continue our journey. Somehow, the universe was supporting me, dispelling the agony of isolation. When I had begun the drive, I had no idea what I was goingto do. I had not seen Susan since we had moved to Manahawkin.

Two years had sped by, yet we picked up conversation as though we had seen each other the day before. A true friend, she was. But even beyond that, I felt it was really The Big Cheese, Heavenly Father, who had reached for my hand. As Susan and her family embraced us, I felt the whoosh of God's love. Not only in their offering to receive us in their home, but also in the heart and warmth behind their offering.

I felt safe, as if God was protecting us. At a crucial moment, when Jeannie could have dismissed taking in a couple of noisy kids out of hand for so many reasons, she welcomed us in. And so, despite Michael entering a facility that seemed dangerous for him, I felt secure in gratitude and hope that God's love would prevail.

CHAPTER TWENTY-ONE

THE BASE OF THE LIGHTHOUSE

"Pam, be prepared. Michael may never be the same again," an old friend had warned me when Michael first entered the psychiatric ward. Leaving the boys with her mother, Susan and I went to the hospital. I was grateful for her company. We cleared security and found Michael in the jammed reception area. Patients, their families, and hospital personnel bustled nonstop. Without a quiet corner to talk, Susan, Michael, and I settled ourselves at a dingy, gray metal table on a noisy hallway.

Michael's eyes were glazed over and he seemed distant. On hospital medications, he spoke in a flat voice, shied from holding my hand, and seemed lost. He sounded and behaved like a different person—docile to hospital personnel and suspicious of others, including me. The drug regime they administered sedated and nauseated him. His roommates turned over quickly. They were prepped for ECT and left while he stayed. He longed to be put out of his misery.

His monotone voice and dull responses were not the depression talking but the drugs distorting his capacity to reason. Mental health laws created a vicious circle. In the name of patients' rights, doctors had free rein to drug and control the people they were treating. The HIPAA (Health Insurance Portability and Accountability Act) law of 1996 kept family away in order to guarantee the patient's privacy. A severely sedated patient, however, couldn't make choices that were in his own best interest.

The next day, I returned alone. Hightstown drifted behind me as I steered along the two-lane road to Princeton. Normal moments of our life crossed my mind—Michael painting the house before Jacob was born, his competent hands holding the paintbrush and roller with ease. His hands—*The ones that should be on the steering wheel now*, I thought to myself as I drove to the hospital. *He was the driver, not me.*

His capable hands were strong yet gentle. When we lay together for the first time, I took his hands to my cheek. Nestled in them, I found a peace there I didn't know I had yearned for—I knew he would never strike me. Safe in those hands was nine-year-old Alex dangling upside down as Michael held his ankles. Swinging him back and forth like a bell clapper, Michael would chime, "Dong! Dong! Dong!" while Alex giggled and shouted, "Do it again! Gong me like a bell!"

Michael's hands secured infant Jacob's swaddled caterpillar body against his chest. With a single hand, he would wrap his fingers around the back of Jacob's noggin with tender strength. I could see Michael's silhouette in the woods at dusk, his left hand raised aloft holding a stick dripping river water as one soggy Irish Water Spaniel eagerly poised to launch herself off the riverbank for another f e t c h , h e r almond eyes blazing in anticipation.

Overnight, the man who once sketched lifelike drawings of his colleagues during long, boring faculty meetings; the man who made still lifes leap from the page with his expert shading in colored pencil; the man who wrote vivid, scathing, and satiric responses to advanced anthropological theories in the margins of his books, could scarcely hold a pen to sign his own name due to the drug cocktails given to him at Belleview Haven.

What had they done to him? What were his hands doing in the asylum? His mind? Why would he stay there instead of working out his issues with his counselor Klaus? How could he trust hospital personnel more than me? I could not puzzle it out.

The abrupt decline of Michael's motor skills frightened me. Food—a perk that distracted Michael from the severity of his overly medicated state—left me forlorn, unable to compete. Unlike the medical staff, the cooks and servers were easygoing African-American brothers and sisters with hearty laughs, which they bestowed as generously as they did their hefty portions of heavily caloric comfort food—fried chicken, mashed potatoes and gravy, beans with bacon, apple pie swimming in ice cream. Michael, ever the food hound, could eat like a teenager. His robust food servings left his trim one hundred and seventy pounds or so unchanged on his six-foot-four frame. I used to joke that when he ate, he was just "feeding his tapeworm." Sometimes I wondered if it was true, that perhaps he'd caught something when he lived in India.

Day after day, I visited Michael on my own, hoping for a heart-to-heart talk away from the other patients, the blare of soap operas or sports on the television, and the ongoing chatter and clatter of phone conversations, beeps, and droning in the lobby. Once, we snuck into his shared bedroom to talk in private. The walls were Pepto-Bismol pink. The temporarily vacant bed next to his, he explained, belonged to a roommate who had undergone ECT. "That is the only way people seem to leave," Michael said with childlike wonder.

"They arrive and take Seroquel," he said, familiar with medical terms that all the patients had mastered—they knew the names of meds the way kids know the brand names of cereal.

"Until they feel so sick they would do anything the doctor ordered," I said.

Michael paused a moment, then nodded. Sick and docile on Seroquel, his unquestioning roommates would be whisked away on a stretcher for ECT. After convalescing from the "procedure" they would be discharged, often the same day. Michael's room resembled an ER triage more than a healing sanatorium for switching medications. The bed next to his was earmarked as "high turnover." Most of his roommates received ECT regularly. They repeatedly submitted to the procedure because it failed to cure their depression.

Forgetting why he had admitted himself in the first place, Michael started to see ECT as standard operating procedure to leave Belleview Haven. Alarmed, I tried not to react. He said that the nurses thought ECT was good and that the doctor was going to talk to him about it.

At the nurses' station, I asked to attend the ECT meeting with Michael, who clearly wasn't in his right mind. The nurses and doctor said I was not permitted. Only later, should he alone decide to take ECT, would I be permitted to meet with Michael and the doctor. At that point, it would be mainly to sign off on the risks.

The HIPAA law to protect patients' privacy did not prevent random nurses from accessing every detail of my husband's treatment. But they did create barriers that denied us family members access to our own loved one's treatment. Regulations designed to protect patients from abusive and dysfunctional families also isolated patients from their involved and caring families. Rather than including a patient's family as an integral piece of a healing modality, the institutional policies enforced estrangement, as if no one outside Belleview Haven had the patient's best interest in mind.

However, ECT remains controversial. It was developed in Mussolini's Italy in 1938 by Ugo Cerletti, who published in fascist journals. Electrodes applied to the patient's head would send electrical current through the brain to produce a grand mal seizure with violent convulsions, unconsciousness, and brain damage. Subsequently, the patient would experience memory loss and cognitive impairment—the equivalent of an electrical lobotomy. The FDA today classifies electroshock devices as Class III, the category for equipment considered the most high-risk and dangerous.

But ECT continues to be profitable, not well regulated, and the concussive euphoria from the resulting brain damage can appear to be a quick, temporary fix for depression. When Hemingway experienced the procedure, he noted, "What these shock doctors don't know is about writers and such things as remorse and contrition and what they do to them...What is the sense of ruining my head and erasing my memory, which is my capital, and putting me out of business? It was a brilliant cure but we lost the patient."[11]

Despite other available beds, Belleview Haven cycled ECT patients to bunk with Michael instead of patients undergoing standard therapy for depression. The rapid succession of ECT roommates normalized the procedure to him—a procedure that could leave him permanently damaged. He was as vulnerable as a child, his brilliant mind compromised with mind-altering drugs. Given his fragile state, I couldn't speak with him as a competent adult—the person he was before he'd entered the hospital.

Distraught by his withered condition, I doubted he could comprehend the rational risks of ECT. Mentally, I reviewed what I could say to reach him: *Michael! Don't you want to remember our lives together? What about when Jacob was born? When we went to the airport to pick up Sadie and you fell in love with her as soon as you saw her almond eyes peering up at you? Or the time we went canoeing with the Manganaros? Remember when the canoe with Paul Salem capsized and Alex was mad as a wet hen? What about making love on our wedding night?* The list of sweet nothings seemed endless: funny things the kids had said, our little family adventures, countless recent events: Jacob's birthday, singing "Silver Threads among the Gold," the scarlet tanager in High Point State Park, laughing with friends.

Returning to Keith and Susan's in Hightstown, I adjusted the rearview mirror and enjoyed the warmth of the sun at my back as I drove. Yet I resented that the stressful familiarity of daily asylum visits was now associated with a road that used to bring familial delight. It was the route Michael used when he drove us out of town to run the dog and kids in what we fondly called "the Princetitute woods" (the forest behind the Institute for Advanced Study at Princeton). There, years ago, in a fluffy, down jacket Michael had wrapped around me, I'd playfully posed for Alex with my new engagement ring, extending my arm and hand

---

[11] From A.E. Hotchner, *Papa Hemingway: A Personal Memoir* (Cambridge, MA: Da Capo Press, 2009), 279–80.

to show him the delicate ring's main diamond nested between two smaller ones—like our little family back then, already in the making.

I fretted for Alex. What would he say about his dad being willing to fry his brains to smithereens, perhaps forgetting us all forever? My eldest was clever, brooding, and already taking his dad's hospitalization quite hard. Alex adored Michael, his true father. His trips to Oregon had ceased by court order not long before we'd moved to Manahawkin. Michael had provided Alex with loving nuts-and-bolts parenting for over half of his young life. At twelve, Alex needed Michael and his guidance in a way six-year-old Jacob did not yet. Jacob was still so young that he lived primarily in the immediate present.

Remembering that Michael's psychologist Klaus had advised Michael not to go to Belleview Haven in the first place, I telephoned to tell him Michael's latest plan. Klaus had known Michael for over a decade. When I told him Michael was set to meet with a doctor about electroshock, Klaus wailed into the receiver, "What? We're talking about a professor here who needs to be able to, say, find India on a globe after he gets out!"

His outrage reassured me that I was not crazy for considering the procedure untenable. Similarly, when I brought up ECT with Susan and Keith, Keith had plenty to say. His grandmother had received electroshock at a nursing home. "Which came first, depression or being in the nursing home?" I asked.

"Hmmmm, let's have a think about that one," said Keith. "She was a bright, perky woman who could be a little morose from time to time. Aren't we all? But after they gave her electroshock, there was nothing there! She would have the same conversation over and over again. Her short-term memory was shot. So, you would go to see her, have a conversation, and two minutes later, she would ask the exact same questions all over again. It was maddening! And impossible to communicate anything of real importance."

I continued to read up on the procedure. Although I was sensitive to Michael's mental anguish, I knew that ECT's irreversibility could obliterate his brilliant mind and career. A single ECT blast to the brain sent enough electricity to stop the human heart. Hemingway had killed himself after electroshock. Despite propaganda endorsing ECT, it did not guarantee an end to depression, just an end to certain parts of your memory. Permanent short-term memory loss was common.

One Flew over the Cuckoo's Nest echoed with sinister realism at Belleview Haven. Michael's psychiatrist there, Dr. Foster, had trained in Zimbabwe—a country with sixteen official languages, a problematic human rights record, an average life expectancy of a little over fifty-five, and rudimentary psychiatric care. Although a fan of multicultural understanding, I did not have confidence in Foster's expertise given Michael's treatment plan. Adding to my concern was the "Grim Reaper," as I nicknamed Nurse Creighton, an eager advocate for ECT. She repeatedly encouraged Michael to go for it.

Dr. Foster added and removed prescriptions to and from Michael's daily regimen faster than titration could occur. At first, Michael could and did write down the drugs they gave him. I was aghast.They were hugely powerful, literally mind-blowing drugs, dispensed like Pez candies from one hour to the next. Michael was carefully documenting all this, a guinea pig who could think. And let's face it, a researcher. You have to be a little bit compulsive to make it through a PhD or little things like plagiarism and negligence of fact arise.

As Michael initially documented what Foster prescribed for him, Keith and I would go over the drugs. British by birth, it was not only Keith's accent that was clear and sharp. He had worked with a data company that analyzed pharmaceuticals for FDA approval. He knew how to access data to find out what the hell these drugs were. Both he and Susan loved Michael. Keith and I were livid as we discovered the stats on these chemicals and the quantity flooding Michael's lean frame.

Michael recounted daily, from his notes, all the little pills he took in docile communion every few hours at the altar of the nurses' station. Foster, it seemed, did not like this information making i t s w a y t o the outside world. Michael had admitted himself to hospital for support while he switched antidepressants. He was compliant with his own treatment to manage withdrawal symptoms from his MAO inhibitor, which was incompatible with newer SSRI medications. He needed counseling support and his blood pressure monitored for the temporary "dry out" between medications. However, Foster put Michael on a drug used to put raving lunatics like t h e Son o f S a m on their ass in a chair so they would stare at the wall instead of attacking people with knives.

Michael was in no way psychotic or violent, but Foster saw Michael's information leaks via the telephone as problematic, so he put a stop to it. Keith and I were horrified to find Michael a zombie the next day—complete with a Thorazine shuffle, something he did not have before entering the hospital. The doctor said that Michael writing down the medications and doses given to him was "obsessive-compulsive." Naturally athletic and accustomed to taking his exercise outside—biking to campus, canoeing, hiking in the woods—inside Belleview Haven, his only exercise was pacing up and down the hallways. There was no gym or jogging track. The nurses said his attempt to exercise proved he was "agitated," and so they gave him medication that made him sit in a chair and drool. The only access to natural light and air to be had was when the security guards unlocked a small, enclosed balcony for smokers to drag on their fags. Michael would dodge outdoors, surrounded by second-hand smoke, just to feel a little sunshine on his face. He began to smell of cigarette smoke although he had quit smoking a decade prior.

Driving back to Susan and Keith's one evening, having prayed, breathed, and willed myself to relax after visiting Michael, I peered through the dark for the mom-and-pop gas station. It marked a right turn that was easy to miss. Night driving was hazardous for me. There were few streetlights and the Jeep's headlights seemed feeble. Once around that curve, I followed a long straightaway past fields and farms to the edge of East Windsor and Hightstown. As the sun settled behind me, I focused on the road's shoulder so oncoming headlights on the narrow two-lane highway did not blind me. Worried despite my desire to trust that God had everything under control, I prayed.

"Dear God, may this be an offering to you, that somehow you can use this for your Will."

I could not fathom how the ignorance and cruelty of the psychiatric ward could possibly serve a loving God. I thought of *The Seventh Seal*, Bergman's classic film where a medieval knight plays chess with death. Only my chess game had consequences in the real world and it was between me and the devil. I only hoped the good angels were rooting for me. Then, a waltz came on the radio. As the Vienna Philharmonic played, I had an out-of-body experience.

I was no longer in the Jeep bouncing along the Princeton-Hightstown highway, but in a ball gown dancing a waltz with Michael. We glided in step, whirled gracefully around the dance floor. Many eyes were upon us, recognized us. No longer insignificant pawns, we were the principal couple of a presidential inaugural ball in some timeless place, where everyone understood everything with a clarity that surpassed mortal limitations. A parallel history was unfolding in the unseen world, another story beyond the story we were living on the mortal plane. In this parallel world of spirit, all that mattered was love, not money, drugs, or degrees.

The vision lasted only an instant, and then I was back to my white-knuckled grip on the steering wheel as I sped along, keepingto the right of the oncoming lights as I headed toward the Howells', the kids, and the dog.

My vision of waltzing with Michael somehow put me at peace. In real life, he hated to dance and I was a klutz. We were nothing like this vision of our spirits, except for the love I felt binding us. But the vision to me meant that no matter what we endured, if our love was true, it would draw forth the divine. And divine love, I knew, was more magnificent and wonder-filled than any drug, psychiatrist, or clumsy dance step could destroy.

After this vision, I planned for Michael's release, even though it seemed impossible. My mind, with renewed determination, anticipated his return to work. I knew the commute from Manahawkin to Rutgers would be too great for his now fragile condition. A move to Hightstown made sense for its proximity to friends and Rutgers. I added house-hunting stops on top of my hospital visits and put the Manahawkin house on the market. I had to make ends meet and we needed a home.

Returning from visiting Michael in the hospital, I would drive up Hightstown's Main Street, bypass the road to the Howells', and take the next left past a cute, renovated Colonial with a "For Sale" sign out front. It was actually a neo-Colonial—new, stick-built, and way out of our price range. But the word "colonial" for me had become imbued with a sense of history due to Kay and Stan's place. No mere real estate term, it corresponded to a culture of the past. Past lives, our past life, Michael's competence, the love we'd shared; I missed all that and missed Kay.

Modernity seemed a sham. I resisted this heartless world we called "modern," the instant gratification American culture venerated, where popping pills or zapping someone's brain would "fix" them to fit in. Fit into what? Some doctor's concept of sanity? I missed Kay and Stan's warmth. Living together with them through hospice had given me a sense of rootedness, not only as a family but with history. That historical perspective gave me strength because it looked beyond the petty to what endured—love.

Love excels in the presence of imperfection. The pristine neo-Colonial did not have the lumpy and lopsided, worn and weary authenticity of the old Victorians and Arts and Crafts houses in Hightstown. It had all the working parts on the surface but lacked soul. It had drywall instead of plaster; a shiny, fake fireplace where a real chimney should have been; fancy walk-in closets instead of a practical third bedroom; squidgy, steep, slick, un-pockmarked stairs; perfect, square corners in every room; and the chintzy creak of new flooring unsupported by the sturdy joists of yore.

I felt the earth around it still reeling from its construction. The trees bulldozed down screamed murder. The earth's surface, torn asunder too close to the road, heaved in silence. The foundation had been scarcely poured before the framing had begun—quick and flimsy as a balsa-wood model airplane. It reminded me of the way Foster added new drugs before the old ones had time to titrate. This could never be our house, even if we had the money to buy it. It would never feel like home. I wondered if Michael's mind would ever return home.

Susan had graciously taken our boys under her wing with her own two. She saw to Jacob's and Alex's schooling at The Studio, a community alternative school. I was in an emotional time warp, loving Michael for how he was, how we were, unable to understand the person he seemed to have become on the drugs in hospital. House hunting for the family helped me envision future possibilities even as I knew the life we'd known and planned had ended. It forced me not only to imagine, but to improvise in real terms ways we could reconfigure ourselves and create happiness even as everything that mattered was being destroyed.

Once parked, I grabbed my knapsack out of the car and pulled up my coat collar against the night air. In the distance, I could hear cars churning along on the New Jersey Turnpike. Walking to the Howells', I felt connected to every shrub, leaf, and tree as if they were a direct extension of my own nervous system. Their energy and life resuscitated me after visiting the emotional wasteland of Belleview Haven. So, too, did the Howells themselves.

Susan and Keith were quite the duo. Susan was so organized that she boxed her children's outgrown clothing by size. Each August, she would drive to Pennsylvania and shop at the warehouse sales to purchase designer clothes for the kids at bargain prices. Our kids were the lucky recipients of multiple gifts of nearly new clothes from her. I was always amazed, not by the quality of clothing—it was like everything Susan bought, nothing but the best—but by the fact that Susan's two boys did not seem to tear and stain their clothes as our boys did. I secretly wondered if Susan's kids had ever worn any of the hand-me-downs before we got them.

Once our boys wore a pair of jeans or a shirt, it was just a matter of days, not weeks, before it became personalized in some distinctive way. Colors bled in the dryer, holes appeared out of nowhere. Cloth would unravel in one place, tear in another, and acquire ink stains as pens traveled like astronauts in training round and round in our washer and dryer. Furthermore, finding a clean pair of pants on the closet floor in the kids' room was a challenge that required a good deal of mental fortitude. Susan had things boxed by size and year worn? This level of organizational effort for personal items mystified me.

Rounding past the trash bins to the Howells' back door, I climbed the porch steps to enter. Inside, I stepped on the heels of my boots to pull them off my feet before ascending the steps to the d e n a n d kitchen to greet whoever was in the room. Susan's mom, Jeannie, was listening to the news seated on the plaid couch to the right of the door, across from the open kitchen. Slightly deaf even with her hearing aid, she rarely noticed my arrival until I shouted in greeting. As usual, the boys were nowhere in sight. Keith or Susan would reappear closer to dinnertime, so I decided to take Sadie for a stroll. Throwing down my pack,

I opened the gate of Sadie's crate to release my furry brown companion as her tail thwacked against the sides of the crate.

Susan was a fastidious housekeeper and I was grateful she allowed Sadie in the house at all. The miracle of the Howells' generosity and unerring kindness was to me divine intervention of the sort only true friends would attempt. Their schedules were loaded with worthy activities. We added plenty of chaos and confusion, yet they took us in as family. When I protested that I couldn't receive all that they offered, Susan said, "Pam, listen, we talk all the time about 'What would Jesus do?' I don't get a chance to do this very often. Let me do this, okay?"

Walking Sadie to take in the evening air, she and I followed the periphery of downtown, crossing the green bridge over the lake, past the house with the carved-wood goose flying low beneath the front porch eave. As night settled, warm, golden light beamed from windows nestled in their turn-of-the century frames. By day, Hightstown bustled as a satellite metropolis of New York, but once rush hour passed, it quieted into a rural village. Retro gas lamp streetlights glowed. Church steeples punctuated the nineteenth-century roofline. The lake extended five acres of serenity beneath the night sky, reflecting a shimmer of lights from houses on the opposite shore. A pair of canoes moored in the moonlight gently bobbed by the house with the flying goose. To the west, the library faced a dashed line of park benches that hugged the shore where at dusk purple martins swooped and swallowed mosquitoes.

I recalled walking past the library up Main Street when, between visits to Michael, I had visited Reverend Sheila. She was Susan's long-time friend and a kind soul. Her specialty was funeral sermons. In Rev. Sheila's kitchen, I met a woman whose husband had walked into the Hightstown Lake and drowned. The woman was elderly but vigorous—in her early seventies or so. She had pale skin and dark circles under her eyes, like someone who had seen too much grief. Her husband had been gregarious, a solid breadwinner—the kind of guy people enjoyed having a beer or a talk with on a regular basis. He voted, tithed at church, paid his taxes, kept his car in good order, and raised his boys to love baseball. Then, he got Parkinson's. Slowly the disease ate away his body and mind. As it did so, he became an increasingly depressed alcoholic. One day, he just up and walked into the lake and never came out.

I always wondered, given how small Hightstown was and how much smaller the lake was, how could it be that no one noticed this guy in his Sears khaki pants and L.L. Bean floppy hat as he wandered into the lake? This was the kind of town where the firemen still rescued cats out of trees; where Santa rode in the Thanksgiving Day parade and tossed candy to eager children. It was the kind of place where people paused to greet each other at the grocery store. Looking over the lake, I couldn't avoid thinking of Harry walking into it. I wondered where his soul had gone.

Sadie, water hound that she was, broke my reveries as she looked into my eyes, longing to swim regardless of weather or time of day, her webbed feet eager to test the waters. Even as a puppy, before we had properly introduced her to major bodies of water, she had a built-in affinity for any puddle encountered. When she was under six months old, still covered in soft puppy fur before her adult curls had grown in, I once heard an odd splashing sound from the bathroom. I thought Sadie was drinking an awful lot of water from the toilet. In typical, lackadaisical style, we used the commode as her water dish once she was tall enough to drink from it. But the splashes seemed far more significant than a single Irish Water Spaniel tongue would make. Concerned that one of the kids was getting into mischief, I charged into the bathroom: there was Sadie, up to her elbows in toilet water, happily splashing away with both front feet.

Soon thereafter, we took regular forays into every possible woodland that offered her a chance to swim. The joy was as much ours as hers. To see her leap into the water for a thrown stick was like watching an athlete swan dive from the highest board at the Olympics. Her focused intensity, the way she knew how to live completely and fully in the moment, was contagious.

But tonight, it was late and dark and cold. Even though her instincts were tuned to the ready, I asked eager Sadie to hold herself back and keep to dry land. Reality was, I was preparing internally for a conversation with the kids I'd never imagined having. Tonight, I glumly determined, would be the night to broach Michael's treatment plan of ECT and the potential consequences.

After putting Sadie in her kennel, I only wanted to snuggle with my boys. But I had to tell them about their daddy's awful plan. This discussion was not in my repertoire, nor was it covered in childrearing manuals. I felt so alone with this knowledge, abandoned by my Michael who, in his own world of pain, couldn't help me explain. As I stood on this parenting precipice, overlooking the valley of the shadow of death into which I would have to lead our kids, I wasn't ready to invite my well-meaning friends. It wasn't their journey.

I had to take time to center myself and pray for the right attitude before talking with the boys. We three would need to unite to consolidate our inner energy and love so we could cope with whatever outcome arose.

I wasn't thinking only about this night, but about the endless nights afterward, how things could be, how we would need to hold ourselves together, and how my attitude would set the tone for the boys.

I grabbed the kids' washed and folded clothes from atop the dryer. Their fresh-baked warmth steadied my resolve as I navigated the slippery, waxed oak stairs to their bedroom. The air was cold. Susan liked to sleep with the thermostat set low. It kept everyone moving in the morning, although poor Ian would crouch in the hot shower for a good half hour to soak off the chill before dressing. As I entered the bedroom, the boys were making vehicular sound effects, pushing Matchbox cars around Lego creations on the floor. I asked Ian if he could come back later so I could talk with Alex and Jacob *en famille*.

Ian, ever affable, said "Sure! I'll just be downstairs," and bolted for the computer to play some games.

I set down the clothes, took a deep breath and said, "Come here you bugs, give me a hug!" taking them both in my arms. Our cuddle felt like the old us, the normal we used to know. I asked them about their day. They squared away what they'd each done and how they were feeling about things.

"Boys, you know your dad has had depression. He can't see a way out of it just now. Doctors have a procedure called electroshock. If your dad decides to do this, he may or may not get rid of his depression. He might lose parts of his memory. Including his memory of us or what we've done together. If he does, it doesn't mean he doesn't love you. We just have to be patient and love him, okay?"

I wondered how they would react. The concept of clinical depression was rather abstract to fit within their range of emotional empathy; it was baffling more than anything else. But they could see that their mom was sad and serious. They hugged me up, and then made some boy fart jokes. It was a vintage family moment. Something I'd worried over for days, rolled right off their backs: they, like Sadie, lived in the moment.

Nestled under the covers, their little heads and bright eyes peered out from the shadows like a couple of elfin children. Snapping back to practical issues, I indicated the clean clothes for the morrow, gave them each another squeeze, and exited to tell Ian he could rejoin his buddies, though it was bedtime for all by this point. The three boys slept in the same room. I went downstairs to give a goodnight pat to lovely Sadie, whom I wished I could take into my room with me. She looked up with her knowing eyes and thumped her tail against the bars of her kennel.

— CHAPTER TWENTY-TWO —
THE POINT OF NO RETURN

The hospital summoned me by telephone to a meeting with Michael and his doctor. They wanted to talk about what they called his ECT "treatment plan." I agreed to meet, arranging my words in a rational, grammatical order. Since Michael had entered Belleview Haven, I'd regularly felt stupefied, as if confronting a tidal wave of unreason. Now the murky wave had risen and crashed over me. Keith and Susan pulled me up for air, but even with their help, I felt stunned. How could I be expected to discuss the possibility of my husband's intentional mental demise as if it were a rational option? Keith offered to go with me to Belleview Haven. He drove. I got out of the car with every nerve a live wire—and this was without coffee.

Keith rang the bell outside the locked entrance. As usual, we identified ourselves to the faceless intercom and waited for the buzzer to sound. After it did, the heavy, gray metal door reluctantly yielded to a hefty push. The next stop was the security window. We checked all our belongings and signed in.

"We're here to see Dr. Foster," said Keith, in his clipped British accent.

I was relieved that Keith was there. He knew the "real" Michael—the loving father and sharp-witted academic. Since Michael was not sounding at all like himself, I needed another adult at my side who understood him in ways no one at Belleview Haven could.

Before they'd put Michael on Seroquel, he had phoned me from the hallway pay phone across from the nurses' station.

"I overheard the intern and Doctor Foster talking," Michael told me. "The intern said, 'We need to do this quickly before the insurance runs out. We can schedule him for ECT eight times next week.'"

A scant two days prior, when he could still think and write, Michael had sounded apprehensive about that much electroshock in one week. Furthermore, since they only did ECT on weekdays, that meant fitting in eight sessions would require them to do more than one session per day. Unbelievable! *How could they possibly think they could get away with this?* I shouted to myself inwardly. Outwardly, I had to maintain my composure because Michael was now in such a fragile state.

An administrator at a different New Jersey facility would later tell me that Doctor Foster made a thirty-five-hundred-dollar kickback each time he administered ECT.[12] How, I don't know. But that would have meant he stood to gain a tidy sum of twenty-eight grand for the eight sessions on Michael alone— eight sessions the insurance would pay without question because a psychiatrist ordered them.

Mentally impaired, with dementia from the drugs he obediently took in the hospital, my husband was being coerced to make a decision that would endanger his quality of life for the rest of his days. I researched ECT, something Michael was neither capable nor at liberty to do. Such a procedure would affect not only the patient's life, but also his or her spouse and family, who would be forever dealing with the aftermath.

I felt trapped in some absurd science fiction novel. Due to limited visiting hours, the medication schedule and his restricted access to the one shared public pay phone, we'd scarcely had a chance to talk. I considered how to broach the downside of ECT with Michael while remaining empathetic to the real pain of his depression. Besides having to reach the real "him" beneath the depression, I also faced a person disoriented by the side effects of mind-altering drugs in an institution full of distracting noises and people with their own problems. Legally, Michael was deemed capable of making his own healthcare choices through the mental haze his prescription drug cocktail produced.

"Are you a family member?" the guard asked Keith.

"No, a friend of the family who has been asked to join the meeting," said Keith.

"Only family," said the guard.

"What?" I said. "My husband and I both want Keith with us as a family friend." By now, I could see Michael through the small windows set high in the next set of locked doors. I waved and smiled at him, trying to hide my own frustration with the guard's unanticipated rebuff, but he was adamant.

Keith said, "You go ahead, Pam. I'll wait here in the lobby."

The emptiness of the hallway swallowed me up as I walked to the second set of doors. There, I stopped and waited to be buzzed through. On the other side, I met Michael who, reassuringly, was still wearing street clothes and not a hospital

---

[12] I've withheld this person's identity to protect their privacy. Our conversation took place in March of 2003.

gown. I hugged him. Just beyond, the doctor stood with a large entourage of nurses and an intern in training. This gaggle of strangers was all set to join us for our "family only" meeting.

I protested against the intern and extra nurses joining us. Foster relented but insisted that Nurse Creighton stay. She was a tall, thin woman with steel-gray eyes and hair to match that was tightly curled in place at the nape of her neck. We entered a glass-enclosed meeting room. A desk squatted to the left of the door. Kitty-corner from the desk, a TV sat on a stand with several plush, stackable chairs in front of it. Nurse Creighton ushered Michael to a chair in back while I sat across from the doctor, who'd settled behind the desk.

"So, Dr. Foster, you want me to sign off on your liability should Michael suffer permanent memory loss from this procedure?"

"Yes, it's a standard form," he said.

"And you can't be sure which memories could be permanently erased?"

"No, we're not sure how ECT works. But it is very safe."

"And you admit that some two-thirds of the people who receive ECT have permanent memory problems subsequently?" I asked.

The square-shouldered doctor sat stiff and upright. His smooth forehead and chubby cheeks seemed so innocent that I could hardly reconcile his manipulations of Michael with his professional appearance. But, Foster's eyes were out of character with his face. They had a hard sheen with "non-negotiable" written all over them.

Michael, who, days ago, was vigorous and athletic, now needed help to sit down. He clasped the arms of the uncommonly plush waiting-room chair to watch a video playing on the small TV. It was a film of a young woman receiving ECT. Nurse Creighton sat near Michael, watching both him and the video with keen determination. When the images became excessively chilling, she rearranged the little cups of pills on her tray. I thought she was doing this to distract and assure Michael that they were professionals who knew which end of the electrode went up.

The screen flickered with the violent shuddering of the young woman's feet despite her anesthesia and the thick straps that bound her ankles to the operating table. Her bare feet twitched wildly as electricity went zinging through the stainless-steel electrodes attached at her temples with a rubber head strap. An announcer's voice calmly rattled off disclaimers about the procedure as her body writhed and contorted against the restraint straps around her torso, arms, legs, and head. The camera soon panned to her feet to de-emphasize the disturbing images of her facial expressions, partially blocked from view by the large rubber biteplate in her mouth. As it panned, it blurred the view of her body gnarling and twisting in seizures.

challenge authority figures on behalf of a loved one?

"No medical procedure is without risk. We don't know how ECT works," said Foster with the assurance of someone who had repeated his explanation many times before. "It's like hitting the side of a television set when it doesn't work "."

Except my husband is not a television set! I wanted to scream. Instead, I said with deliberate calm, "Right, so you don't really know what memories might get erased. You can't tell if you are erasing, say, just the memory of being depressed, or the memory of his child's first steps."

"The procedure is very safe," Foster repeated. "But we can't guarantee that the memory loss will not be permanent. Usually, the memory returns after a couple of days. We can't guarantee that, no, but it is very safe."

"Let me put it this way, Dr. Foster: Is it so safe that you would do ECT on yourself?"

"I am not a patient," said Dr. Foster.

Nurse Creighton, overhearing our conversation, chimed in from across the room: "We administer ECT to the elderly all the time because it is less risky."

"You mean, it is less risky for you because they have no one to advocate for them once their memory is gone," I said.

Doctor Foster's cheeks took on a ruddy hue. He drew a deep breath, puffing out his chest, and then slammed both his wide palms against the desk. Leaning his weight into them to stand, he said, "I have never had a meeting like this!" He was so furious I thought he was going to hit me—I checked to see if Michael would be a witness, but he sat frozen, watching the video. Foster stormed out the door.

The doctor was evidently unaccustomed to having his diagnoses questioned. Nurses truckled to him with efficient discretion and patients behaved in docile, if not fawning, fashion. From what I'd observed, few patients had family that visited except on the weekend. Those family members who did visit were not in the habit of questioning a doctor's white-coat education and authority. He was supposed to know what he was doing. And it was accepted that what he did was somewhat mysterious. Sort of the way I see my car mechanic—somewhere on the spectrum between a shaman and a minor deity.

Nurse Creighton pursed her thin lips, gathered up the slick brochures on how to recover from having your brain wiped clean,[13] and left the room clicking her tongue in reprimand. I thought, *Right, it's a grave mistake to resist erasing your*

---

[13] Many testify to having not only permanent memory loss, but ongoing issues with retaining information and persistent short-term memory loss. ECT remains controversial as it works by damaging the brain. Letters to the Editor, *The Atlantic* (May 2001) regarding the article "Shock and Disbelief" https://www.theatlantic.com/magazine/archive/2001/05/letters-to-the-editor/302208/

life, as my own body, taut with tension, repulsed the sweat that surfaced and met chilled air as it ricochetedoff the waxed floors, metallic fixtures, shiny counter surfaces, and reinforced soundproofed glass of the meeting room.

The decision remained in Michael's hands. Drugged—as was the new normal—he stared into space, his hand limp and unresponsive as I held it. Visiting hours were over and I had to leave. I helped him up from the chair and held his arm as we made our way back to the patient lobby, where a handful of residents sat around the TV waiting for the loudspeaker that would call them to line up for medication.

If Michael decided to take ECT, he would have to stop eating by midnight. In the background, the TV squealed with commercials. I hugged him tight, pressing my head against his heart, which I could feel thumping through his wool sweater. The buzzer sounded, releasing the double doors. He watched me leave through the tiny windows of the doors until I arrived at the guard booth. Then, he slowly turned and disappeared from view.

Keith, bless him, was waiting in the outer lobby.

Numb from the meeting, I remembered that Kay, Michael's mother, had undergone electroshock. Perhaps that explained Michael's fascination with it. His mom had tried to commit suicide when Michael was in college. It had devastated him, he said, because, "I realized my mother didn't love me enough not to kill herself." There it was—he had not been enough to keep his mother going. And neither were the boys and I enough for him. It seemed like cosmic karma, or a test for the boys and me to go beyond the torment he had experienced.

Michael did not really believe in God or the afterlife. I was sure that the stress of our commutes to provide hospice care for Kay, along with the pressures of work, had contributed to his depression. He wanted to give up. I was convinced he had not dealt with his mom's death. Now his explanation echoed in my mind, "I didn't grieve her death because I had already gone through all that when she tried to commit suicide. I said goodbye to her then."

I knew Michael—in his right mind, before the Seroquel—would not endanger himself with ECT. I told Keith and Susan about the meeting with Dr. Foster and Nurse Creighton.

"Boy, I bet Foster wanted nothing more than to get you into that electroshock machine and turn it all the way up on high!" said Keith. Laughing, he mimed turning a knob and attempted to look sinister, knitting his brows and grimacing. I threw back my head, closed my eyes, and laughed great guffaws right from the belly, grateful to have a perspective that differed from my own somber reflections.

Susan played the straight cop: "I don't think you want to rub them the wrong way; they can make things difficult for you."

Keith, having visited Michael many times with me, stood up for my position: "But you don't know how these people are, Susan," he said. "They'll do whatever they can. It's all about the money. Just follow the money—it's a business. What we have to do is get Michael out of there. He checked himself in; he can walk right out."

"Really?" I asked, incredulous.

"Of course, Pam, he went in of his own free will; he wasn't committed, so he can walk out whenever he wants to."

"Thing is, he's so weak and dependent, he trusts the nurses more than he trusts me at this point. Plus, they're still putting pressure on him for the electroshock."

"Why don't you call him?" said Keith.

Each call to Michael was an ordeal. First off, I had to get through to the pay phone in the hallway by the nurse's station—it was often busy or turned off. If the phone rang, I had to cajole the random, drugged-up patient who felt inclined to pick up the receiver to a) find Michael (a person perhaps unknown to the patient) and b) convince Michael (who might be napping) to come to the phone. Sometimes this worked. When it failed, I would have to call the nurse's station and beg them to help the inmate find Michael as I called the hall phone again. Getting him on the line could easily take a half hour or more.

At Belleview Haven, the phone receiver would be left to dangle from its cord in the hallway while people shuffled around looking for Michael. Sometimes an overly efficient passerby would simply hang up the phone, breaking the connection. Meanwhile, the person tasked with finding Michael could quite easily forget what they were asked to do in their drug-induced haze; perhaps they forgot they had even answered the phone in the first place. In limbo myself, I could hear the TV playing in the background and the clanking of medical trays, people talking, moaning, and the squeak of shoes across the linoleum.

This night, Michael could not be found. He was, apparently, meeting with the doctor. Uncharacteristically helpful, the nurse said, "I'll have him call you when he gets out."

"Thank you!" I said, thinking that maybe they could be human in this place after all.

I took Sadie for a quick walk and then waited for Michael's call. The phone rang about twenty minutes later. He sounded strangely calm, firm.

"I'm going to go for the electroshock," he said.

"Why?" I said as calmly as I could; by this point, an icy chill had swept over my body.

"I see other people come here and the only way they get out is if they do ECT," Michael said, repeating what he could grasp through the haze of drugs.

"But Michael, you checked yourself in; you can check yourself out whenever you want. You don't have to have ECT to leave that place."

We talked for a while. Michael again told me how his successive roommates had gone through the same process. Foster would put them on Seroquel, which seemed to make anyone who took it nauseated. I surmised that they, like Michael, would do anything to get off the Seroquel. They'd be prepped for ECT as for surgery, have ECT (and make Foster his thirty-five hundred dollars), and then away they'd go. Talking with his roommates, I learned that they regularly returned to repeat the process. Patients could permanently lose parts of their memory and still not lose the depression.

I talked to Michael as I would a child: slowly and patiently. I said matter-of-factly how I'd already prepared the children in the event he chose ECT that he might not remember key events in their lives, or perhaps not even remember them. I reminded Michael of what Klaus had said about "needing to be able to find India on a map" so he could resume teaching.

By design, the psych ward was fully insular and alienated from the rest of society. Unlike a regular hospital, nurses and the doctor treated non-patients on the "outside" as irrelevant to the patient's constellation of care. Neither family, nor co-workers, nor friends mattered for the patient's "treatment." Nevertheless, these irrelevant entities would be the people upon whom the patient would be cast upon to live out his or her life after treatment.

"Well?" said Keith, after I settled the phone in its cradle.

"He said he had to go. They're only allowed to use the hall pay phone for ten minutes so as not to monopolize it."

Ten minutes, I thought, ten minutes to discuss a situation that would have repercussions for the rest of our lives.

"Well, what did he say?"

"He's going for ECT," I said with that calm that comes over a person in extreme emergencies. I had to make myself disassociate from my own situation to steady myself. "I've got to go for a walk," I said.

"I'll come with you," said Keith.

We drove over to Etra Park with Sadie; as we walked, Keith and I talked about the situation. Having gone around the better part of the park, Keith said he'd wait while I ran Sadie in the meadow past the farm fields and nature area. Striding out past the rows of peppers and corn, I remembered the walks with Michael and how he had taken a photo of me, my belly protruding under blue-jean overalls with the basketball that was our Jacob. All I had been missing was a piece of straw in my mouth to complete the image of a farm girl. My life with Michael passed before my eyes as though I were about to die. I prayed.

Immediately, I received the message that this was how God felt when His son was crucified. Of course, I thought. This was God's position: helpless to help his son. Satan had had a field day with God's own son, and God had been powerless to stop the forces of evil. And that was how I felt—powerless.

I said to God, "Not my will but thy will," and I let go of Michael. Michael did not belong to me—this was now clear. He belonged to God. I could not help Michael keep his life if he was willing to lose it. At that moment, divine peace settled over me in a cocoon of love.

As God's heart embraced me, I felt protected, an eternal spirit walking through a world centered on temporal dreams. I returned to Keith transformed by this love. I said, "It's okay, I understand now: It's like when Jesus was on the cross and God had to allow his beloved son to be killed. It's like that."

I accepted the path before me. I did not know what would come of it, but I was ready to accept it and just trust God.

Keith and I drove back to the house. We had scarcely entered the backdoor when the phone rang.

It was Michael. I took the phone from Grandma. "Hello," I said.

"I've decided not to do ECT," said Michael. "I couldn't do that to you and the kids."

I was stunned, and silently gripped the receiver as I took this in. "You said I could walk out of here anytime?" said Michael.

"That's right," I said.

"Well, I'll have to think about that. Gotta go. They're serving dinner. Chili tonight. Love you! Bye!"

"Love you, too, Michael! Bye!"

I started shaking, tears rolling down my face as I crumpled in a heap on the floor.

"He's not going to do it! He asked about being able to walk out of there," I gasped, looking up at Keith and Susan.

They began to work up a plan to spring Michael from a place he never should have checked into. Keith said, "He needs to know that there's support for him on the outside, that we're here for him."

"Right," I said.

"Why don't we all go over to visit him this evening?" said Keith.

"Yes, I can do that tonight," said Susan, who usually had innumerable choir, chimes, and pageant rehearsals at church.

We went during evening visiting hours. Susan spent a good hour talking with Michael about her own battles with depression. He seemed much more chipper after their chat. Keith and I each had our turn alone with Michael, or as alone as one can be in a reception area full of dazed, ambling patients, nurses summoning patients over the loudspeaker to queue up for medication hand-outs, TVs blaring, and other visiting families milling and talking nearby.

Most children were not allowed to visit—the environment was too unpredictable—but it seemed that toddlers and babies could pass security. So there was the raucous, ambient noise of little children fussing on top of everything else. Keith and I had been putting together one of the numerous puzzles strewn about on tables—one of the few recreational activities available besides smoking breaks outside, or sitting and watching TV. We had been there so often we'd nearly finished several puzzles. Of course, all of them were missing a few pieces; it seemed an apt metaphor for the place itself.

As the three of us returned to Hightstown, I felt profound gratitude for such loyal friends as well as the divine help that had manifested in Michael's turnaround. The ordeal was far from over, however. Susan reported how shaky Michael felt about reentering society. Keith, Susan, and I immediately began conspiring how to help Michael bolster his confidence to leave. As Keith had rightly pointed out, "He has no reason to leave unless we can help him have confidence that where he's going will be better than where he is."

The following week, we carefully orchestrated each day to ensure that as many of Michael's friends as possible would visit him. A couple of pastors from the Unification Church came one day; our dear friend Rev. Dr. Sydney Sadio, a minister from the Methodist church another day; our old friends from Cuba, the Marquez family—the dad, Luciano, was a Baptist minister; Hindu and Jewish friends; Keith and I, of course; even Klaus, Michael's long-time psychologist, visited. I rounded up friends from throughout the region to come calling. Michael became a veritable celebrity in a place where people hid their presence and where clandestine operations were the status quo.

Furthermore, Keith and I had been working on the legal end of things. I visited a couple of lawyers with whom Michael and I had worked in the past. With Keith's help, and that of the lawyer husband of a minister I got a crash course in care-planning law. And, with the more specific help of a power of attorney that Michael had signed so I would be able to purchase a house while he was in the hospital, I determined to make a legal case with the authorities of Belleview Haven regarding their detaining my husband. Their approach to ECT—by convincing the patient that it was not only necessary but also the only recourse available if the patient hoped to exit the institution—was not only dissimulating and unfair but surely a violation of fiduciary responsibilities vis-à-vis the family as well as the patient.

We had come up with quite a document, Keith and I. We added to it a critical legal document that a lawyer friend from Highland Park had hand delivered to us at Belleview Haven: a health-care power of attorney. After negotiating with staff, she was able to get Michael's wobbly signature and notarize it on the spot. Belleview Haven was decidedly uncooperative with this last bit. Health care power of attorney made it possible for me to make decisions on my spouse's behalf that aligned with his wishes when not drugged, and to protect him from being able to sign away his life.

Still, despite the numerous visits of friends and family, and the legal oomph on my side (we had submitted the legal documents not to Foster, but to his superior, the director of Belleview Haven), it remained touch-and-go with Michael because of all the damn drugs they prescribed, and which they guaranteed he took. These drugs made him slur his speech, shuffle his feet, and numbed his mind. This could have continued indefinitely as insurance generously and unquestioningly paid for extreme psychiatric treatment. Belleview Haven, and Foster in particular, were not done milking this cow for cash.

But finally, after more visits and repeated phone conversations under the duress of the payphone process, I had Michael's confirmation that he wanted out. We arranged with the hospital for me to pick him up the following morning. But when I called to confirm our appointment to extract Michael, the nurse at Belleview Haven said, "You can't pick him up today: it's snowing."

"Oh yes I can; my Jeep has four-wheel drive and I'm on my way," I said.

Keith and I would drive separately. His Toyota had front-wheel drive and snow tires.

We entered Belleview Haven together, and again, were met with delays. Foster could not be found; he had to sign the papers to release Michael. While we waited, the snow piled up. At last, the doctor appeared, but refused to sign for Michael's release. He preferred to keep Michael confined for ECT treatment. Instead, Michael and I signed off on papers that indicated we were leaving without the doctor's consent.

Michael was now firm in his desire to leave. He had the rest of his belongings in a plastic bag and his winter coat over his arm. I helped him put it on. As we slowly approached the first set of locked double doors, a guard stopped us. We explained we were checking out. There was a long delay as the officer had to consult his superiors. He returned and confirmed we could continue. The doors buzzed open, but we were not free yet.

The next threshold was the front desk. From there, I could see that the snow flurries had accrued into great drifts. I signed us out in the binder and asked the receptionist to cut off Michael's ID bracelet. She fumbled to find scissors, but at last cut off the white plastic band around Michael's wrist and unlocked the next set of steel doors. We pushed our way through to the foyer, where Keith gave Michael a hug.

Outside, we trudged through drifts to the Jeep as the snow continued to fall thick and heavy. I helped Michael put on his seatbelt and we turned on the radio. Soon the blaring of three distorted C major bleeps warned of a National Weather Service announcement about what would be a category 4 blizzard. Not only would we have snow but strong wind, poor visibility, whiteouts, and dangerous travel: all of central New Jersey remained under emergency conditions.

I followed Keith's black Toyota. It shimmered through the falling snow, a vague black ghost. We crept at five miles per hour as we headed to the extended-stay suite Keith had reserved for us for the week. It was some twenty miles away, north of New Brunswick. To get to the Sierra Suites from Princeton was usually a ten to twenty-minute drive; with the blizzard, it took a full two and half hours. We inched through the snowstorm, surrounded in white, as if driving inside a cloud.

Halfway, we stopped at a Walgreens to fill Michael's prescription—a formidable cocktail of eight different meds he was to swallow six times per day. No wonder the poor dear was so ill, I thought. It was enough drugs to knock out a horse. I'd already contacted doctors at the psych unit at Rutgers for help. I couldn't yank him off the drugs cold turkey, they said. They thought they could take him as a day patient and were onboard to help me to support him through the transfer and process of weaning off the excessive medication.

Keith was truly a saint. He stood chipper as a schoolboy with rosy cheeks from the cold as Michael and I approached the front desk at the Sierra. He paid for it all. I was broke, but protested anyway. Keith said "Nope! Won't hear of it! Now you have a great night, you two." And off he went.

We went to our room. Despite the storm, we were able to have a pizza delivered for supper. It was New Jersey; nothing stops Italian food from finding its way to an empty belly. I sorted out Michael's meds, wrote down each drug, dosage, and frequency to keep track. That night after eating, we lay down together in that huge bed, the snow still softly falling outside, and made love for what would be the very last time in our married life on earth.

— CHAPTER TWENTY-THREE —
THE SHADOW OF DEATH

Michael became an in-house resident of the Rutgers psych ward for several more weeks before graduating to day-patient status. At Rutgers, doctors oversaw his switch from an MAO inhibitor to an SSRI form of medication by reducing the Belleview Haven cocktail and providing supportive counseling. We both looked forward to his recovery and Michael's return to lecturing at Rutgers. After all, for over twenty years until only recently, one tiny pill of Parnate had kept his depression at bay.

Yet despite counseling and careful doctoring, Michael struggled. By the time he graduated from the Rutgers facility, he still took a complex cocktail of drugs, albeit one that was less onerous than the concoction from Belleview Haven. The Howells continued to extend their generous hospitality to us as Michael and I house hunted in Hightstown. We wanted to stay close to our friends and Rutgers, anticipating Michael's commute to the Department of Anthropology.

Meanwhile, my father was diagnosed with throat cancer. I began regular treks to Florida to visit my parents. Dad's tracheotomy, which was supposed to be a temporary measure, endured. To talk, he covered his trachea hole with his hand. To eat, he poured liquid down a feeding tube that connected to his intestines and bypassed his stomach. After a meal, he tucked the tube away beneath his button-down shirt.

Each morning, he rose, showered, and dressed as if for work, with an undershirt beneath his white Oxford shirt, which was in turn tucked into his slacks and belt. His moccasins were the only compromise to his career attire—formerly slippers, he now wore them both indoors and about town. He and Mom still slept in their four-poster bed but switched the queen mattress for two singles so Dad's restlessness wouldn't keep Mom awake all night. Medical paraphernalia for the feeding tube, trache, and diabetes monitoring dominated their bathroom sink counter. Various medicinal implements made regular appearances in the kitchen dish-drainer.

Normally optimistic, my parents struggled with the severity of Dad's condition. I knew they did not approve of my faith. I visited them out of love and to support Mom—not to peddle religion. My faith resided within me. I relied upon divine succor for strength to cope with my own challenges at home in New Jersey, which I monitored from Florida when visiting. Michael remained ill, the children were young, and we hadn't yet found a home of our own. By habit, I prayed upon waking, on walks during the day, and before sleeping. While I was away, the Howells and other friends watched over Michael and the boys.

I empathized with my parents' emotional suffering. I also sensed their conflicted feelings toward me, the black sheep. To ground myself and stay connected with God, my own center, and my spiritual life, I slept on the floor. This simple shift, closer to the earth's energy, felt peaceful. Each night, I placed bedding on the floor and curled up to rest after prayer. Each morning, I arose early, prayed, and arranged the sheets and covers back on the bed.

One evening, having unrolled my bedding on the floor, I was preparing to pray and rest. It was late and I was tired. I breathed in peace looking at my traveling altar, which I hid in my luggage during the day. It included a small two-by-three-inch photo of Mother and Father Moon along with photos of Michael and the boys. The small black and white photo of Mother and Father Moon made me smile because it was from RFK Stadium, taken the day Michael and I were blessed, the year after Jacob was born.

The blessing photo showed Father and Mother wearing holy white robes and festive crowns. Behind them stood some dozen brothers and sisters loosely lined up, also in holy robes. One brother's head and shoulders tilted to the side in a comical way. His candid, casual pose reflected the joy of the moment. It was a blessing to join with people who loved God and each other to celebrate eternal true love.

The brother peeking out to the side personified the way I experienced God, in a kind of unconventional wink. I loved the informality, the down-home feeling, the "It's okay if your shirt is wrinkled, we still love you" message of the photo. On prayer walks, I would collect a seashell or a dried blossom and add it to the little altar, my mini-sanctuary.

This particular evening, long past midnight, my weary head sunk heavy into my shoulders as I prayed. Already in my jammies, I sat on the floor ready to lie down and sleep when the door flew open. My father blasted into the room without knocking. He saw my mobile sanctuary and screamed, which, with the trache, sounded more like a loud whisper, "I will not have a photo of that man in my house!"

Dad was fully clothed. Despite his illness, he loomed far larger and stronger than me. He planted his legs wide below his shoulders. He held one arm close to cover his trache. His free arm ripped through the air. His eyes snapped like brown firecrackers in his flushed, scowling face. My little girl fears of his anger, the force he once used to hit me with his wooden fraternity paddle and his rejection, left me. Instead, I felt only compassion for this dying man, who yet protested the inevitable together with my mom. He was waging his own battle with God.

The people in the photo he despised had given me courage to face impossible odds—from selling roses in the dark of night in a snowstorm on a backwoods Vermont road, to going up against two lawyers and their three clients on the witness stand thousands of miles from home to battle for custody of my son, to Michael's miraculous turnaround after I prayed and marched him out of Belleview Haven in a blizzard, and indeed to this very moment. I had not relied upon generic, formulaic prayers from a book to live my life. Rather, I had relied on God incarnate, on principles and love that I had experienced because of the teachings of Father Moon, because I had experienced spiritual guidance and love not only with Jesus and God, but also with Mother and Father Moon, and Michael.

That little photo reminded me of happy days when Michael still enjoyed good health; of the quirky ways that God seemed to work in my life; that somehow, there was a bigger macrocosm out there that knew me, knew my heart, knew Michael and I loved each other. The things we had been through, only God really understood. The day we were blessed, Michael had driven the Jeep to D.C. He was competent and strong back then, able to direct his mind and body—not the person he was now who needed help getting in and out of a chair.

Our blessing was before 9/11, before Kay died. When Michael could easily swing a tired, squiggling Alex up onto his shoulders and carry him. The God I related to was one beyond pretense, who knew the sacrifices big and small that we had made as a family. That little photo represented the absolute love that Michael and I had in a way Father Moon had taught me, and my dad had not. The photo was not an object of desire for me in and of itself, but it represented years of living with faith in the Unification tradition, years of devotion that had borne the fruit of love in my life. It was not some superstitious token.

In his own way, I think my dad acknowledged the power of love that photo represented by the degree to which he found it reprehensible. Like Vincent, it seemed as if he wanted me to adore him instead of God. He wanted me to be the compliant little girl he used to visit at night when Mom slept. He wanted to own my heart. But Father Moon had taught me about a greater love, and I was not about to give that up.

As Dad ranted, he moved toward me from the threshold, towering over me. I gathered my bedding and scuttled backward, placing the little altar behind me. I crouched to dodge Dad's swinging fist. My back reached the wall beneath a window opposite the door—the only exit. The double bed occupied most of the room. Dad approached, blocking the door. As he fumed, I held my breath, calculating how to evade him. Scrambling over the bed, I thought, I could bolt for the door.

Fury had puffed him up like an angry grizzly bear. Suddenly, his outrage exhausted itself as quickly as it had flared. Deflated, he weakened. His eyes left me and focused on the closet by the open doorway behind him. Lowering his arms, he turned away as though I no longer existed. He slid open the closet door, removed some clothes, and left. I closed the bedroom door behind him and locked it this time.

I figured my mom's disapproval and dad's hostility arose from misinformation in newspaper and magazine articles that dated back to the seventies. By sharing my activities in the movement with my folks, I hoped to dispel their fear. I'd had fun, made friends, and had seen positive results from conferences. I wanted to bring them up to date on the reality of my experience, rather than let their superstitious fear continue to create a barrier between us.

On my next visit to Florida a few months later, I brought a videocassette with a film of a typical Middle East Peace Initiative trip to Jerusalem. It had footage of a peace march through the ancient city, candid conference shots, and excerpts of talks by various international religious leaders. Though it was not a film of my own trip, it captured a peace demonstration and conference like those I had attended in Jerusalem after Michael was safely graduated from the Rutgers psychological rehabilitation program.

One evening, Dad, Mom, her brother Leo, and I sat talking in the living room. Leo mentioned a trip he'd taken to hear jazz music in New York City. He'd stayed at the New Yorker Hotel, which Father Moon had bought and renovated. I told him how sisters and brothers had fundraised to help pay for it and how I'd stayed there on several occasions. This segued into me mentioning the video that I'd brought. Leo and Mom wanted to watch it. Dad, to be polite in front of Leo, said nothing. I popped the videocassette into the player.

"See, that's where we marched in Jerusalem, singing 'Peace, Shalom, Salam Alaikum.' We followed the Via Dolorosa, the path on which Christ carried the cross, to there," I said, pointing to the steps of the Dome of the Rock.

I was excited to show them where I'd heard impassioned speeches for peace and seen rabbis, imams, and Christian ministers hug one another. As the video played, we watched demonstrators singing as they walked through the old town to Independence Square. Religious leaders led the march, chanting as they held a banner calling for peace in English, Hebrew, and Arabic. The international parade of demonstrators behind them chanted, too, as they marched.

Watching the film, it was easy to see the multiple ethnicities and religions of the marchers. Buddhist monks wore orange robes; Hindus had saris and saffron robes; Sikhs wore turbans; an Amerindian elder marched in a full traditional headdress. There were Asians, Caucasians, African Americans, and Africans; rabbis and others wearing yarmulkes, ministers in a variety of holy robes, imams, and others in prayer caps or keffiyehs.

I did not mention to Mom and Leo that I had initiated and organized an all-night prayer vigil for a group of clergy who went to Gaza to meet with Yasser Arafat, the head of the PLO. It was a dangerous time and the US State Department did not protect civilians who went into Gaza. President Bush had started the Iraq War in March, 2003—the year I went for the peace rally. A day or two after our December arrival in Jerusalem, we heard Saddam Hussein had surrendered.

In Jerusalem, I'd prayed at the Wailing Wall and shed tears with other brothers and sisters at the Holocaust Museum. I'd visited Nazareth and seen Jesus' birthplace outside Bethlehem in Palestine. We'd traveled by bus to the Sea of Galilee and eaten fish there. I'd brought back some water from the Jordan River and prayed where Jesus had given the Sermon on the Mount. We'd visited the church where Gabriel had appeared to Mary about the forthcoming birth of Jesus. And I'd prayed in the Garden of Gethsemane. It was an extraordinary journey— one that had been made possible by friends both in and outside the church who'd visited Michael and the kids and brought them meals while I was gone.

After watching the video, Mom and Leo looked inspired. Their faces had lit up when they saw people of different faiths come together to march for peace in Jerusalem. The video captured a second event—footage of ministers releasing doves for peace in North Korea. Rev. Dr. Sydney Sadio, a minister friend from New Jersey, had attended that expedition. I hoped Dad would appreciate this part. He'd served on the ground with the Air Force at the end of the Korean War. I did not want to proselytize, but I wanted to show the people I loved the most, my parents, some of what I'd been doing with a movement they misunderstood. I wanted to share my life as an adult, as a world citizen, not the sickly child who'd always been bedridden.

But my father, a man who had raised me to think for myself, was livid that I'd dared to present anything associated with Father Moon. He fulminated in silence, but his anger created a palpable tension in the air. Mom and Uncle Leo arose with the soothing determination of their dinner routine. They invited me to eat with them at the table.

Dad, because of the feeding tube, did not join us. I felt uncomfortable eating when he could not, but Mom and Leo continued to set the table with plates of food and silverware. Dad, still fuming, settled into his chair to watch something on TV while we ate. As I turned to walk toward the dining area, feeling remorse that he still "didn't get it" and embarrassed to eat in front of him, I heard a spiritual voice.

This voice from beyond was male. I heard it say, "Thou preparest a table before me in the presence of mine enemies."

It sounded familiar, but I couldn't place the quote. Although I'd attended seminary and read the Bible quite a bit, I was juggling enough real-world emotions that precise citations eluded me. Later, I tracked down the verse. I'd forgotten the full context. When I looked it up, I felt stupid. Of course, it was from the well-known *Psalm 23, The Lord is my Shepherd:*

The Lord is my shepherd; I shall not want.
He maketh me to lie down in green pastures;
He leadeth me beside the still waters.
He restoreth my soul;
He leadeth me in the paths of righteousness
for His name's sake.
Yea, though I walk through the valley of the shadow of death,
I will fear no evil; For thou art with me;
Thy rod and thy staff, they comfort me.

Thou preparest a table before me
in the presence of mine enemies;
Thou anointest my head with oil;
My cup runneth over.

Surely goodness and mercy shall follow me
All the days of my life;
And I will dwell in the house of the Lord Forever.

Although I did not recognize the voice, whoever it was, he seemed fond of the King James Version of scripture. Furthermore, the verse resonated with me in a couple of ways, the immediate one being that I was being served food and my dad was not. I felt sad about that. His anger still scared me. His hatred of the movement and Father Moon dismayed me. Someone in the spirit world saw his persecution of me as him opposing one who belonged to God. This verse gave me courage.

The verse spoken at exactly that moment seemed to indicate that God "had my back." But the words in their judgment call also made me feel more compassion for my father's miserable state of prejudice. I longed for his liberation from ignorance, that he could come to understand the truth about God's love for him. However many flaws they may possess, the mission of all parents is to be

True Parents, parents that embody True Love. It is in our DNA but gets lost in all the jumbling about of the world.

I felt we all needed to serve as the messiah to one another, to transmit divine love, truth, beauty, and compassion to each other. Although I had visited many places of worship and studied how other faiths taught these ideas, Father Moon had delivered them in a form that made sense to me. I knew my dad had a good heart and mind. I was sure that it was his idealism that had prepared me to meet the movement. I wanted nothing less than the happiness of God's love for the man who had been my first love as a little girl.

I was relieved when the visit ended so I could resume caring for my kids and ailing spouse while finding a place for us to live.

Some months passed. Dad was hospitalized for more tests. Leaving Michael and the boys with the Howells again, I flew down to support Mom. My previous visit, Dad had still been able to dress, walk around and feed himself by pouring liquid down the feeding tube. Mom was now taking care of him much more, he was not improving and he'd been hospitalized for a while.

It was a tough moment. There was no longer hope that Dad would get rid of his trache or the feeding tube and recover. Test results indicated it was time for hospice. While Mom went out of Dad's hospital room to talk with one nurse, another nurse approached me with the release papers to sign so Dad could leave the hospital. I knew he loathed hospitals almost as much as he did my involvement with Father Moon. Following Dad's orders as he commanded from his hospital bed, propped up on pillows, I signed his release papers. The next order of business was to find a wheelchair to roll him out of there.

Mom, typically calm or slightly lost with loved ones hospitalized, strode into the room. Tears of rage framed her eyes: "Oh Pam, how could you! He's my husband! Why didn't you call me?" she sobbed.

Her reaction shocked me. She and Dad had already decided he was to go home; I was simply a warm body in the room trying to facilitate what they wanted to do. In retrospect, I imagine she was desperate to do everything possible for her husband. But jealousy was there, as well. From my childhood, Dad and I had had a rapport that rightly belonged to her—I was his emotional confidant when he'd visit my bedroom at night. Despite my childhood fear of his explosive anger, we also shared a sort of camaraderie. He could be a loving father.

At this pivotal moment, I'd arrived simply as a daughter to help with the hospice situation. But years of what my mother considered estrangement made me a different creature to her. Mom, with sincere devotion and dedication, had endured much travail caring for my dad. The same way in which she'd found comfort in the rituals and rules of Catholicism, she trusted the expertise of doctors—a leap of faith my Dad and I did not take. She had a script in her mind of protocols to follow. The day I arrived from the airport, she was under duress coming to terms with dad entering hospice. Her anger toward me for signing Dad's release papers was so acute that she did not quite get over it until after he died.

In the moment, I was grateful to be able to free Dad from an institutional existence I well understood—not only from my own time spent in hospital but also from the kindred Protestant-based faith I shared with my dad. He and I knew that doctors, lawyers, and administrators, no matter how well intentioned, could not live our lives for us. The real freedom to live was not contingent upon experts, but upon being cogent and able to define our own terms, to claim our lives as our own by taking responsibility for our choices.

Susan and Keith had again stepped in to help with Michael and the boys during my absence. Upon returning to Hightstown, besides tending family, I had to oversee the sale of the house in Manahawkin and search for a new home suitable for Michael and the boys. They say that moving and selling a house creates stress equal to that of a death in the family. I was handling both at once. Prayer was indispensable for me—not the flowery kind of prayer you read in books; no, the kind where you spill your guts then float outside of your body while the spirit of God takes you up and holds you when no one on earth fully understands what you're going through.

As when Michael was in Belleview Haven, I felt that every act—be it grocery shopping, putting gas in the car, folding laundry—was an offering. I could only offer my heart to my parents and then trust God to work out the details. My trust came not only from my experience, however, but also from the inspiration of the Principle.

The Divine Principle framed my life in a bigger context. It taught me that as a blessed family, Michael, the boys, and I had a responsibility that extended beyond the family level to the community, nation, and world. In the post-lapsarian scenario, the disorientation from true love due to the separation of humankind from God had to be restored step by step—from the individual, to the couple, to the family and extended family, to the community and beyond, to the nation and the world. So, sorting out misunderstandings was worth our while—not only for the immediate benefit of more harmonious relationships, but so that harmony could expand.

The historic loss of true love needed to be recreated within people's hearts to reverse the history of fear, violence, and despair. This concept of being in a deliberate process of re-creation from within gave me strength. As emotional difficulties arose, I searched to consider the broader context of spiritual history and my place in it. This vantage point helped me to contextualize my situation differently. I could perceive what might have been devastating personal confrontations as problem-solving challenges. This took effort—it meant constantly inviting God into the situation through prayer rather than relying only on my own feelings and perspective.

CHAPTER TWENTY-FOUR

DIM EARTHLY DISCERNING

My brother, sister, and I alternated trips to Florida to help Mom with Dad's hospice. As his final weeks approached, all three of us, along with Jenny's husband, Corky, convened in Florida at Mom's to take turns keeping vigil. When I was away, the Howells, again, took care of my family back in New Jersey.

In death, according to the Principle, one's spirit parts from the mortal sphere of the physical body yet remains intact to reunite with our original spiritual parent in our eternal spiritual home. I felt that my duty to my family was to serve as a spiritual midwife for Dad's departure. My mom desperately wanted him to stay on earth as long as possible. But I knew that in his heart, my dad's spirit was ready to go home. His body, which was already causing him great suffering, was shutting down.

I lobbied for permission for Aunt Mary Lou to see him before he died. Mary Lou's husband, Bill, was a Methodist minister. Besides a particular jazz piece he wanted played at his funeral, Dad had specifically asked that Uncle Bill conduct the funeral service. Though he had always liked Bill, Dad did not get along with Mary Lou, his somewhat prim, older sister.

Bill and Mary Lou knew the family secret of my dad's decades of alcoholism, but they were unaware of how it affected me. While Mom and my siblings had lived through Dad's years of alcoholism, they, too, were unaware of Dad's nocturnal visits to me as a child and teenager. My younger siblings had lived a somewhat different childhood than mine. They united with Dad's version of family history—one that, as far as I was concerned, was seeped in historical revisionism.

Though generally kind toward others, Dad wanted us to inherit his resentment toward his sister. He had trained us to detest Mary Lou as a matter of course. To fail to despise her was to be disloyal to my father. My younger siblings, consequently, maintained that she was not to be trusted and that she would be a source of discord and trauma for my dad.

When I suggested that Mary Lou be allowed to come see her nearly expired brother (at this point, Dad was mostly in a coma), my siblings were furious. Jenny furrowed her handsome brunette brows together and shook her head in protest. My brother Rick, a strong fellow, stood facing me in the hallway by the kitchen. Stunned, I watched him pull back his right arm and cock his fist, which appeared aimed at my face. Frozen in place, I prepared for the blow and prayed. At that moment, Mom walked between us. Rick lowered his arm. As a loving dad himself, he would never do this to one of his own.

Yet such is the tension that arises around unresolved family history. I wished Michael could have been there—I wanted to feel safe and loved. Instead, I felt that my siblings misunderstood my motives and took me for some sort of monster. As Dad's death became imminent, Mom and I bonded wordlessly, sharing the nearness of the unseen world. Empowered from beyond, Mom said, "I will make the decision. And I say that Mary Lou should come."

That was the end of it. I had not advocated for much of anything with my siblings except to suggest this one thing. I was outnumbered, the black sheep of the family in their eyes. This was so not only due to my faith, but because I rejected a revisionist perspective that made our family history with Dad adorable. I loved my dad, but our life had been far from perfect. Although Mary Lou had problems of her own, including unresolved grief for the death of her son, my cousin Craig, I felt that for the sake of history and restoration that a sister be able to say goodbye to her brother.

As evening settled and the tree frogs burped, Bill and Mary Lou invited me to sit inside their airconditioned car to talk in private. They asked how I was doing and encouraged me to be frank about how I felt about Dad. I shared some of the challenges I had experienced in our relationship, his night visits when I was a child, his stormy outbursts when I was a teen, his fury when I joined the movement, but I also told them how I had forgiven him. It was a relief to be able to talk to elders about some of the difficulties without being taken for a traitor.

Over supper that night, we gathered around the circular table off the kitchen. Bill invited us all to hold hands in prayer. Mary Lou helped cook and made the sweetest sweet potatoes I'd ever eaten. They were full of butter, brown sugar, and pineapples—just smelling them practically made your teeth ache. Bill had each of us share memories that we cherished. We told stories of kind and funny things we'd loved about Dad—omitting the bad memories. We were sure he listened in, though he remained deep in a coma—a state like sleep but with the singular omission of his melodious snore. With his hospital bed set up in the den near the dining area, he was easily included in the conversation.

We kept vigil around the clock. I took the 3 to 6 a.m. shift; when I was done Jenny and Corky took over. Corky made Alaskan gold rush coffee that kept us alert. Rick remained suspicious of me. He was reluctant to leave me alone with Dad, as though I would do something to upset the man I had known longer than he had. Rick was beside himself with grief already. He had taken after dear old dad in many ways and was no shrinking violet. They were both Leos. Rick also had Dad's soft heart for the downtrodden, quick wit, ready laugh, and a clever knack for fixing things. You could count on him to do what was honest and true.

Day and night, I felt "on call"—not only for my dying father and my suffering mother, but also for my siblings who did not see death like the spiritual transition I did. Already grieving their anticipated loss, they concentrated on Dad's physical well-being over the momentous spiritual change I saw him approaching. I was more concerned with Dad's journey than my loss. Witnessing the intensely spiritual nature of death's transformation was like being in the passenger side of a vehicle looking at the road through the windshield: I was not driving, but I could read the map and see the road ahead. And I knew that I would have to get out of the car before he reached his destination.

I was also in the middle of major financial negotiations. On the phone and by email after hours, I handled back-and-forths with lawyers over multiple contract details—not only on the sale of our old house, but also on the purchase of our new one. Michael could not manage these affairs. To ignore or postpone them was to risk losing both our buyer in Manahawkin and our home-to-be in Hightstown. Given Michael's vulnerability, I could not delay establishing a place for his security. On top of this, handling resentful siblings, a distraught mother, a dying father, various well-meaning but superficial busybodies from mother's church, doctors, hospice nurses, medications, and Dad's biological and spiritual needs on very little sleep was a challenge.

Prior to going into a permanent coma, Dad one day sat up and swung his feet over the edge of his bed. His head slumped down and we were ready to catch him. Suddenly he jolted his head up and announced, "God is my co-pilot."

As we took turns tending Dad, we swabbed his lips to keep them moist and gave him morphine if he groaned in pain. He would slip in and out of a coma—a place beyond deep sleep. I sensed that he was visiting the other side, the spiritual realm. On my watch, to ease Dad's transition, I invited Heung Jin Nim, one of the children of Father and Mother Moon, whom I'd met just before his fatal car accident, to come and help Dad find his way. I spoke to him as if he were there in the flesh, "Dear Heung Jin Nim, please watch over my father and help him find his path on the other side." The next day, awakening from slumber, Dad said, "I found my guide."

He had a sudden burst of energy, unseen for days. He insisted on sitting up in a chair. We obliged him, helping him into an armchair where he was secure. Soon after settling in place, his head slumped until his chin met his chest.

Moments later, he jerked up his chin, full alert; "Oh," he said, and after a long pause: "You are mortals."

It was clear to me that he was communing with the next realm and staving off death to tell us about it.

"What's it like in Spirit World, Dad?" I asked.

"LOVE, LOVE, LOVE!" he answered.

My sister, angry with me for using the term "Spirit World," thought I was imposing my religion. She interjected: "What do YOU call it, Dad? Do you call it 'Spirit World'?"

"I call it 'Spirit,'" he said.

Jenny remained upset despite this answer. She was a devout agnostic back then. Years later, after adopting children, she became a Sunday school teacher. I imagined that the challenges of parenthood were sufficient to drive even the sturdiest of souls to seek divine intervention.

Sitting up another time, Dad expressed happiness at having Mom, Jenny, and me—three women—around him. He said he wanted to give me a kiss. I bent down to kiss his cheek. To my amazement, he swung his arm up in a surprisingly powerful grip, grabbed my neck, and thrust his tongue down my throat. I abruptly left and washed up in the bathroom. I was sure he knew who I was at that moment. It was so devilishly like him, imposing himself, wanting to physically dominate me.

The incident disturbed me all the more thinking of Mom's already heightened sense of jealousy and her need to be uniquely responsible for Dad's care. She wanted to be first in his heart. And I felt horrible that Dad had expressed this desire to dominate me on his deathbed. I wanted to hope that he had mistaken me for Mom. But I knew he had not. The depths of my repulsion from this were not only due to how it violated me, but how it violated Mom, her trust in and devotion to him.

Dad owed Mom a major apology. He had been a very demanding patient. Mom had waited on him hand and foot for ages and subdued her own opinions for years in deference to him. Her submission to his tantrums and denial of his drinking was not an image of marital partnership that sat well with me. She did the best she could, but it was not the kind of life I wanted. Furthermore, his illicit desire for me, his emotional plundering of me as a child and a teen, made his resentment of people who taught me about unconditional love, true parental love, even more understandable. It was a love he himself needed, but from someone other than childhood me. No one saw Dad grab me and go for my lips on his deathbed. Evening had fallen; we were in the shadows and the others were chatting on the far side of the room.

Later, Dad settled into a final coma. At Mom's request, I shaved his head—that had been his habit when he stopped covering up his bald patch long before the cancer had set in. I had also, for Mom's sake, taken that moment to cut a lock of his hair. Jenny proposed that the next day we should all go for a walk on the beach at sunrise. We should go, she said, no matter what. Dad had been in a coma over a week, without food or water except for the swabs we passed over his motionless lips so they wouldn't get chapped.

Mom still didn't want to let him go. But Jenny's proposal of a sunrise walk—the new day proof of life's continuity with the next day and the day after—was its own message of hope. We went and something shifted inside Mom. More at peace, she was able to let go. I felt sure that Dad sensed her change. His spirit was not free to leave until she could let go. Mom had to release him. Jenny's suggestion of a beach stroll had helped Mom to let go.

Mom, Rick, and Jenny gathered around Dad's bedside after our walk. I paused with them, and then went outside to work on the garden. As I was arranging mulch around the butterfly bush, Corky called: "Come quickly!"

Mom, Rick, and Jenny had their heads next to Dad's as they cried and held onto him. He had died—or rather, his spirit had been set free.

"I'd like to offer a prayer," I said.

"NO! You must let us all grieve our own way!" Jenny said.

Her response stunned me, but I could see she was in pain. I walked quietly out the front door. I felt Dad's spirit exit with me. I was walking in a spiritual cloud. The sandy soil beneath the hair-like straggles of grass gave way under my feet as I cut across the lawn to the neighbors' front door. They were kind Christians, but their family's woes irritated Mom's sense of propriety. I always thought this was incongruous, but then, I had never told her about Dad's nocturnal visits with me or my abortion. Our family was not exactly proper, either.

Still in a cloud, I knocked on their door. When their son answered, I blurted out like a zombie, "My dad's died and I'd like to say a prayer. My sister won't allow me to pray with them."

The young man gathered his parents and sister in a heartbeat. Wordlessly, they hurried through the door to join me outside. The five of us gathered holding hands in a circle under the tree in their front yard. Such energy and power transmitted from our little circle that I felt we must have beamed a spotlight to the outer reaches of the universe. I offered a prayer for my father's ascension and prayed in the name of the Father, Son, and Holy Spirit, True Parents' name and my own name. They humbly honored my prayer with amens and each said one of their own prayers in support of my loss at that moment.

Love rather than grief enveloped me. I felt sorry my own biological family could not understand. As usual, I was closer to God with strangers than with my birth family. I felt Dad there with us too, celebrating his ascension in the sunshine, a substantial energy force. I also sensed the presence of the spiritual realm; and the ancestors gathered to collect my father. They, too, radiated energy, like the force of chi. I don't know if the neighbors perceived that side of things. But I hoped they could feel the lingering sense of benevolence and divine love that surrounded us. I felt this cloud of love accompany me as I walked back and rejoined the others at Mom's.

Within days, I had to return to Hightstown to my own family, whom the Howells tended in my absence. Michael could offer no emotional support for what I'd experienced in Florida. He was unable to see beyond his own needs at that point. Not only had he protested me leaving to help with dad's hospice, he'd been adamant that I stay at his side rather than attend the funeral. Keith talked with him at length to convince him that it was important for me to go. Michael was not in any shape to travel or I would have brought him along.

Cogent agency, something my dad kept intact in the face of death, was something Michael seemed to have lost. His will to self-manage had suffered severe damage through his stint at Belleview Haven. To bring him back to life, I took him house hunting with me. I hoped it would stir his imagination for resuming life in a new way. We imagined our way from house to house in our price range until we visited a slightly dotty Arts and Crafts two story on Hightstown's Main Street. It had recently dropped in price and felt like home, right down to the mouse droppings in the kitchen drawers. We closed quickly and sent for our belongings in storage.

The moving van arrived in a downpour. We didn't yet have a key to the house, so we loaded everything into the garage. After the movers left, Michael and I sat on the front porch in plastic armchairs. We watched the clouds rattle with thunder and pour buckets of rain on the ivy-covered hillside below. Even locked out of the house, it felt like home. Within a few days we had the house key and moved everything inside from the garage.

Upon graduating from day-patient status at the Rutgers hospital, Michael resumed teaching. Emotionally, he remained fragile and his motor skills were not up to par. Yet his brilliant mind could still churn out ideas and facts. But I noticed that he'd lost something profound and permanent: his own executive management. He could no longer self-initiate, self-direct, or process the array of variables needed to manage a class. Although I could help him to write his class lectures at home, at the podium reading his notes, he would lose his train of thought. He was falling apart. Together, we finished out the semester, but the prospects for him continuing his professorship looked bleak.

Although losing his ability to teach was tantamount to losing his livelihood, far more debilitating was the emotional fallout of him losing his mind. He did not suffer the loss alone, we all did—our family, his colleagues, and friends. I'd lost my emotional champion and confidant. Diminished by the confusion of drugs and disease, he was incapable of empathy when my dad died. It seemed like Michael had bailed on adulthood. Emotionally, it felt like he'd bailed on our marriage. Yet, despite his frailty, Michael and I framed his disabilities as temporary. In the past, he'd coped with depression through counseling and support with minimal medication. With that goal, we searched for the right doctor to oversee his meds so he could resume teaching the following term.

Meanwhile, I'd applied for and was hired to teach ESL to post-doctoral foreign students at Rutgers. I enjoyed my colleagues and international students. My supervisor liked my work and encouraged me to apply for a forthcoming permanent full-time position. Susan picked up Jacob on school days to take him along to the alternative school where she taught. Alex had a scholarship to attend a local private school of science and math within easy walking distance, but he preferred to homeschool with me, which I arranged around my college teaching.

Michael didn't rally the way we anticipated. We soldiered on from Hightstown, visiting doctor after doctor throughout the region. Each of them prescribed a different cocktail of medications. But nothing brought back the "old" Michael. Researching depression in the town library, I found the name of a local psychiatrist who'd handled complex cases, Dr. Schroder . He provided actual counseling that went beyond the typical fifteen-minute meeting to rubber stamp medication prescriptions.

Dr. Schroder spent hours talking with Michael and reduced the size of Michael's antidepressant combination. Yet Michael remained wobbly. As a resident, Dr. Schroder had interned with a neurologist, Dr. Jacob Sage, at the Robert Wood Johnson University Hospital at Rutgers. Dr. Schroder encouraged Michael to see Dr. Sage for testing. We'd already seen other neurologists at Princeton. Unlike the previous doctors, who attributed the quivering of Michael's hand to "familial tremor," Dr. Sage diagnosed it as Parkinsonism. This revolutionized and expanded Michael's treatment.

There was a drug Belleview Haven had insisted on giving Michael. I'd read articles that said it was known to produce signs of Parkinsonism in those who took it. These side effects were supposed to disappear once the patient ceased taking the drug. In Michael's case, this drug had opened floodgates for Parkinson's disease (PD) that refused to reclose. Though this news was a tough blow to receive, Michael was relieved to have a name for a different beast to fight. I was numb but determined to fight it with him.

To deal with the diagnosis, I rallied family and friends for emotional support. When we told Michael's cousin, Eugenia, the matriarch of Michael's family now that Kay was gone, she said, "Well, have a nice life."

Her remark felt like a slap in the face, a rebuke to assure that we'd keep our distance. She was establishing her own boundaries having done hospice for her own parents and working a high-pressure job as a university department chair. Still, it left me feeling abandoned by Michael's family. I would pursue my own research to cull best coping practices in an attempt to follow Eugenia's advice without her help and to live as fully as possible for the sake of our kids and community.

Besides consulting doctors and friends with medical experience, I directed my years of training in literary criticism and teaching to research traditional allopathic treatments and complementary holistic approaches. Rather than pursue a lawsuit over who was to blame for Michael's condition, I wanted to do everything in my power to assure his quality of life according to his priorities, not the priorities of some institution or pharmaceutical company.

Determined that disease would not define our family, I put God first in our lives. We were beings of spirit and love before all else. From that love came inspiration to think creatively about what we could do instead of moaning about everything we couldn't. Daily, I had to remind myself and the family of our primary purpose: to live with true love. In that context, Michael's disease became a series of problems to solve, choices to make, inconveniences to navigate—not a taskmaster to rule over us. Our lives belonged to the origin of love, not to the fear of death, poverty, or social rectitude.

At Family Camp (an annual retreat founded by Unification brothers and sisters at Hickory Run State Park, in Pennsylvania), I learned that a brother who was a musician and an old friend from CARP days, Bard, also coped with PD. He and Michael encouraged each other when we would gather for our annual camping trip in the Poconos to meet with other Unificationist families. In later years, they would share a room at the infirmary at night for ready access to electricity and an adjacent bathroom, while the rest of us campers slept in cabins without such amenities. At times, they goaded each other like the Odd Couple, but they also looked after one another in little ways the rest of us couldn't imagine, sharing a story of encouragement, or saving each other a seat at the dining hall.

Back in Hightstown, we investigated every form of technological support available. Keith found Michael the most up-to-date computer possible. We stuffed it with the latest software called Dragonspeak. It was designed to take dictation and transcribe as a person spoke into the microphone. However, the program did not work for Michael. His voice was too shaky, his pauses too long, and he'd lose his train of thought.

Conceding that the old Michael would not be back, we reluctantly applied for Social Security Disability. At first, filling out the questionnaire made me turn cold. Then, as I enumerated all the functions that Michael could no longer do, which included filling out the application himself, hot tears poured down my cheeks. Prior to filling out the six-page form, I'd refused to admit to myself the extent of his disability.

Answering the questions forced me to review all the details of Michael's personal life: how he needed help to get dressed; how he ate with difficulty; how he couldn't drive or handle money; how he couldn't write. Written in black and white, it all added up to a radically changed life. The picture of Michael that emerged was of a hopelessly dependent person with serious mental debilitation from depression. We visited a doctor who confirmed by examination what I had described on the form. It was official: Michael was not just taking early retirement; he was "disabled."

To this day, I maintain that the insidious drugs administered to him at Belleview Haven, along with the facility's mismanagement of his psychiatric treatment and the resulting stress, induced his condition.

I yearned to help him snap out of the spiral of depression and to see him fire up his will power and defy the rigid mask of Parkinson's, which immobilized his face around a bland stare, regardless of what he was feeling. But I had to resign myself to the "new" Michael. And so together, we decided to change our environment. He didn't want to be around his old haunts at Rutgers now that he was unable to do the things he loved. No longer tied by work to New Jersey, we put our house on the market and furniture in storage. Although we'd happily settled into the wonky Arts and Crafts house in Hightstown—and I loved it there—we needed to reinvent ourselves yet again. We would make a fresh start by the ocean—this time in Florida.

Stan, Michael's dad, was onboard for our move. He and I had bonded over the fact that we both had been drafted to care for spouses who suffered with depression. Though Stan's mind remained sharp and his hair thick, at eighty-four, his physical health took a sudden downturn. Just months before our move, he became frailer. Before Kay died, he'd led an ambitious life, and faced the busy routines he set for himself with resilience; if he lost a finger to a table saw or a bit of bone to a fall now and again he carried on. His habit was to bounce back from near death. We'd come to expect this of him.

But his recent episode was different. Something had twisted in Stan's gut. Doctors saw fit to remove several feet of his intestines and put him on a feeding tube. He was to pour thick, murky-looking liquid down the tube that was permanently attached to his intestines. I hesitated to move so far away, leaving him in New England.

However, Stan's spirit remained strong. Like Michael, he remained enormously fond of sturdy comestibles. The gray shake doctors prescribed resembled—and must have tasted like—worm droppings. Stan persisted to eat solid food which resulted in his frequent visits to the ICU. We thus said our "final" goodbyes more than once, complete with I-love-yous and tears. By nature, subtle in a British sort of way, he had to ratchet it up to speak such words. But then, in classic Stan style, he miraculously recovered just prior to our proposed moving day. This made for a much gayer departure.

With the pod loaded atop the Jeep, everyone seat belted in place and Sadie wagging her tail, we backed out the driveway for the last time. We turned south for Fernandina Beach, where Mom lived. Without Dad fulminating about my faith, I hoped to solidify the bond that had grown between her and me since his death. Weather in the Sunshine State boded well for Michael's mental health and I'd investigated Florida's homeschooling regulations and found them feasible for the boys. Things looked promising.

As we backed out of our Hightstown driveway for the last time, like the day we first moved in, it began to rain.

— CHAPTER TWENTY-FIVE —
TO THE BEACH AND BEYOND

Bridges frightened me. To cross even small ones, I'd follow close behind another car, focusing on their bumper in lieu of the dizzying, wide-open expanse that produced terror within me. Tall bridges catapulted my entrails into the sky like an airplane on lift off. I had planned our Florida route to avoid such panic triggers. After wending through South Carolina's side roads, we slept at an inn near a swamp, serenaded by tree frogs, far from the bustle of Myrtle Beach.

The next day, an unfortunate digression somewhere in Georgia shunted us onto a busy highway. As we sped along, a bridge with colossal girders rose on the horizon and our roadway disappeared into the stratosphere. Chills shot up my spine as my breathing halted. Braking, I pulled into the emergency lane, stopped, and turned the key to cut the engine.

"Michael, if you don't drive us over this, I'll have to turn around and who knows how far out of our way we'll need to go," I said.

"Well . . ."

His eyes lit up at the prospect of driving. His Parkinsonian face freeze held his countenance fixed, unable to register the nuances of emotion we humans anticipate—a smile, a frown, a wince. Instead, hands on his lap, he turned his torso to look me in the eyes. Michael was still inside that body, willing to help. Hope welled within me; not only would we be able to cross the bridge, but Michael would challenge the inertia of his comfortable dependent status—this was a victory.

It was Christmas Eve, and desire to keep the trip as short as possible was unanimous. Mom's house on Amelia Island was within a few hours' reach. Michael looked down at his hands, shrunk back into the seat, then mumbled, "Okay." I moved the seat back to accommodate his long legs, slipped out my door, sped to the passenger side, opened his door, and unlatched his seatbelt. He slowly inched out of his seat clutching the car roof. Sliding his hand down alongside the windshield, he leaned heavily against the hood progressing to the driver's door. I opened it for him from the inside. He lurched into the seat behind the wheel and closed his door. From the passenger side, I pulled his seat belt and shoulder strap across his chest and buckled him in.

"I pray for a safe journey in the name of Pamela and Michael Moffatt of a Blessed Central Family," I said quickly; we both were going to need God's help to cross the bridge. Reaching around Michael's right arm, I turned the key in the ignition. His hands searched for a grip on the steering wheel as if it were a strange, foreign object instead of a familiar form. I waited for his grip to hold steady, then took a deep breath and said, "Okay, Baby, you can do this. I'll help you pull out."

I scanned the lanes. Behind us, traffic zoomed toward the bridge like machine gun fire. Spotting a solid break, I said, "Okay Michael, GO!"

He stepped on the gas and the Jeep crawled onto the highway. Cars whizzed around us. At last, our V-6 engine chugged up to speed. Inwardly, I prayed with a familiar desperation—one from the days when Michael drove us to Connecticut on Xanax to do hospice for his mom. Back then, he insisted he had full control of the wheel despite taking prescription meds. His psychiatrist, who wrote the scripts, was never in the car when Michael drove.

Straddling the lines as if they were mere suggestions, Michael meandered as we ascended the bridge. I grabbed the wheel to help him choose a lane. Cars whipped past. We seemed airborne. My heart zoomed from my chest to my throat seeking a safe place to land. Praying, weaving, and arguing, we made it down the other side. The five-minute trip felt like it took a half an hour. Michael and I were spent from the exertion. On solid ground, we wobbled down the highway. I took another deep breath to steady my voice and conjure peace, patience, and hope for success. "Okay, let's pull over!"

Michael jerked the wheel to the right. Brushing by his chest, I flipped up the right turn signal. The car eased to a stop. Michael burst out, "I don't ever want to do that again!"

"Me neither!" I said.

But I was grateful for two things. First, we made it over the bridge. Second, Michael could see for himself that his performance behind the wheel was not what it used to be. If he no longer coveted the role of driver, it was one less issue between us.

We resumed travel. The kids nodded off as usual in the back as Sadie wagged her tail. All seemed well with the world. We sped through monotonous miles of Georgia flatlands on a six-lane freeway. Traffic buzzed past us on all sides at warp speed. Savannah's old town approached. Its peaceful dock, Gothic charm, and trees dripping with Spanish moss beckoned. I remembered them from my CARP fundraising days. When I suggested we take a pit stop there, I could almost hear the water lap against boat moorings. But Michael and the kids protested the slightest detour. "So much for spontaneity and culture," I lamented as we crowded into a hot highway rest stop.

At last, Exit 1 released us from the roaring highway into quiet Florida backroads. Turning east toward the Atlantic, the day yawned into dusk, blurring the horizon that separated land from sky. We passed unmanned, ramshackle stands advertising oranges for sale, an oddment shop, a vacuum repair, a Home Depot, a church. Michael mocked the puny steeples of small Southern Baptist Churches; "In New England,' he said, "steeples have proper heft and lift!"

I joked back with him about phallic competition, then caught my breath. Another bridge loomed ahead. It spanned the Intracoastal Waterway separating Amelia Island from the mainland. I'd crossed the bridge many times by taxi or with others at the wheel but I'd never driven over it myself.

I pulled over to contemplate this insurmountable obstacle. My options? Risk slamming head-on into oncoming traffic with Michael driving or facing my own panic to drive over the bridge myself. Not a simple choice, despite our recent experience trading places. Both options felt death defying. Arguing with myself, I silently weighed the options as Michael could not.

"Perhaps, if I did it just this once, I'd never have to do it again," I told myself.

"Impossible!" I answered. "Amelia Island is too small and the town of Fernandina, limited. Once 'on island' we'll still have to venture back to the mainland."

"No! Once across, I'll stay there!" I protested.

"What about hurricane season, huh?" I said, projecting the Jeep swirling midair in a hurricane to the theme of Miss Gulch from *The Wizard of Oz*. Even if I switched the scene from black and white to Technicolor, it seemed less scary than traversing the bridge. But the immediate potential for a head-on collision with Michael at the wheel stacked the odds in favor of me confronting my fear. There was a strange hush in the car. Even Sadie waited without whining to leap out and swim.

I pulled out of the emergency lane and back onto the road. Internally I chanted as I used to do in fearful or painful situations, "Glory to Heaven, Peace on Earth, I pray for the success of True Parents' mission. Glory to Heaven, Peace on Earth, I pray for the success of True Parents' mission. Glory to Heaven . . ."

Everyone was awake and talking now. They looked out the car windows at what was to be our new home on the other side of the bridge. I slid onto the two-lane road behind a logging truck laden with pine trunks still fully sheathed in bark. Reaching the apex of the arch, the point of lift off, my stomach grew light, but not with the abject terror I'd anticipated. The bridge gently eased earthward as the land rose up to meet us. My hands were not shaky, white-knuckled, or sweaty. We regained solid ground as the sun set which turned the brick buildings into inky silhouettes. A smiling pig outlined in festive red neon smiled atop a barbecue joint. Maybe there was something in the air since it was Christmas Eve, but I felt peace surround us and carry us over the causeway and onto Amelia Island. The kids and Michael, to my surprise, all shouted, "Yay! You did it, Mom!" It was a moment of triumph. Not only crossing the bridge, but the family rallying to support me.

We followed the directions into Fernandina, where Mom and Dad had moved half a dozen years ago. Left on Citrona, and then, about a mile down the road, another left onto Orca Court. The white and blue trimmed "C-Van" that they'd bought to travel around North America stood parked, unused since Dad died. The garage door was sealed shut. No outside lights were on. The L-shaped ranch looked asleep. A dim beam from a streetlight gestured toward the front door.

Above the roofline, the arms of live oaks jerked skyward. Bent at odd angles, their branches looked like an angry mob shaking fists in protest. Following the shaft of streetlight, we made our way to the dark front stoop and rang the bell. After a long few minutes, the lock clicked. The inner door eased open, revealing a thin line of light. Mom said, "Hello," without unlocking the screen door that darkened her face.

"Hi Mom, we're here!" I said. "You wanna unlock the door?"

She sighed, fumbled with the lock, and slowly the screen door eased open. The kids piled into the house: "Hi Grandma!" they shouted.

I held Michael's arm to steady him should he trip on the threshold and guided him into the foyer.

"Well, hello there," she replied, somewhat gravely. Turning to me, she said, "Pam, I'm not sure about this. I don't think it's a good idea for you to stay here."

"Whoa! Where did that come from?" I wondered. Mom sounded enthusiastic the last time we spoke a night or so ago on the phone; her current reaction was nothing like that. Having driven some nine hundred miles after packing and moving our belongings into storage, we all needed a break. I'd have to negotiate with Mom before the family disintegrated in exhaustion. I needed a way to stall to conjure options from my tired brain.

"I need to walk Sadie, Mom. Could the kids use the bathroom? I'll be back."

I left Michael and the boys inside, relieved to find Sadie's smiling eyes and wagging tail; I snapped on her leash and strolled with her into brighter light along the street. As Sadie snuffled the ground, wagging her tail, I looked up to the sky and prayed. "No room at the inn," was the answer I received.

In an instant, I understood. I remembered Jesus' course, how he was rejected before he was born. Mary and Joseph found no room at the inn. Strangers in a foreign land, Mary and Joseph had traveled a great distance. They were weary and people didn't know their story or care about them and their unborn child.

Although mom was rejecting us, I knew that God was with us, that love was with us. What we'd been through together as a family, our faith and offering, was known in the realm of spirit. I felt our family was connected to the original lineage of God, that we had a divine spiritual lineage through the blessing. This birthright belongs to all people but easily goes unrecognized. It's a bond of love with the divine. Michael and I had tapped into that spiritual energy and had created space to honor and cherish it. We shared a spiritual bond of true love whether we were accepted or rejected even by my own family.

Although the warm Florida weather would help Michael, I knew that our move to Fernandina was not for our convenience alone. We had a family responsibility to restore relationships and make amends for misunderstandings of the past. That meant serving others without any expectation that we would be served in turn. But before we could do that, I needed to ask Mom for a huge favor now that it was getting late on Christmas Eve.

"Would it be possible, just for tonight, to sleep here in sleeping bags?" I asked. "We can find another place tomorrow. I'm not sure where we could get a hotel right now."

Mom conceded. She looked at Sadie with dismay. I imagined her calculating the thousands of dirt molecules that would enter her white-carpeted home on those four doggie paws and the four pairs of human feet already in her foyer. Having reversed her position, true to form, she insisted the boys sleep not in sleeping bags on the floor but on a blow-up mattress in the living room. Likewise, Michael and I were to take the master bedroom. She would sleep in the guest room.

Her complete turnaround in attitude astonished me. She let me borrow her computer to deal with real estate transactions ongoing back in Hightstown. She soon insisted we stay until we found a new place. I tried to piece together what had caused her initial hesitancy when we arrived.

It was Mom's first Christmas without her husband of over fifty years. His office remained intact. Reluctant to displace his things, Mom squeezed her affairs into a small corner of a guest bedroom instead of colonizing Dad's desk and file cabinet. She'd kept his old diabetes paraphernalia and the feeding tube like icons in the master bathroom. When I asked her about them she confided, "I'm not ready to let them go."

These objects weren't reminders of my dad, but of his illness and what she'd done for him. These now useless medical devices had transformed into sacred totems of her last connection with his body, of their shared suffering, the farewell tears for their dreams that were left unrealized—the golden years they would not experience together on earth.

A few weeks later, I brought up Dad's attitude about death and the body. "Remember, Mom, the cicadas back in New Jersey? How they molted and left behind hollow shells of their bodies? I remember Dad telling me that when we die, our body is left empty as those cicada shells. That our spirit lives on, while the body left behind is but an empty shell. Remember how he said everything in spirit world was 'Love, Love, Love!'?"

She did remember. Her face grew brighter. With fresh determination, she gathered all the old medical remnants—tubes, needles, and pills—and threw them into the trash. Rearranging her toiletries, she restored the bathroom to its original, non-hospital condition. I felt hopeful that she seemed to be finding a way from grief to renewal.

We soon found a place to live on the north side of the island, some two miles from Mom's so as not to intrude. We bought it with a bridge loan so we could move out of her house more quickly. Nevertheless, by then, we'd created a routine with her. She invited the kids to identify birds with her from the back porch and took them on little outings about town. She and I walked together almost daily and she enjoyed talking with Michael, too. He found her easy company.

Sadie ended up charming Mom, who took to calling her a "fine old girl" and praising her "dignity." Dignity was not the adjective that came to my mind to describe Sadie—in fact, quite the opposite, with her crazy coif, rat tail, laughing eyes, counter-surfing habits, fear of thunderstorms, and fondness for the trash bin. Mom was not what I would call a dog person, but she was kind to our hound and didn't seem to mind wiping Sadie's paws clean each time they crossed the threshold from the sandy outdoors.

We moved from Mom's into a ranch house with a huge sunroom—ample space for gatherings and homeschooling. School was not about being in a building, I told the kids, it was about learning something you could take into the world with you. Michael and I worked with them in the sunroom surrounded by tropical plants that grew outside. In the late afternoon, at community soccer practice, slapping mosquitoes while the kids played, we met other parents and their offspring. Networking with colleagues at the university in Jacksonville, I looked forward to a potential job teaching there.

As hoped, the mild climate and proximity to the ocean lifted Michael's spirits. Wandering uptown one day while the Jeep was being repaired, I found a bike shop with adult tricycles. This was a revelation to me. Soon, we were the new owners of an adult trike—a "Miami Sun" complete with horn, bright-orange safety flag atop a pole, and a roomy basket on the rear.

Instead of stewing at home, Michael pedaled to the beach downhill from our house with a book and towel in his rear basket. His Parkinsonian tilt didn't faze the trike. He could swim, read, and bask in the sun. The return uphill was steep, but the draw of home and food was strong. Michael could walk leaning on the trike for balance. He said the Miami Sun made him "the envy of the six-year-old set"—and even, it turned out, of some grownups. One irreverent and slightly sloshed older gent said to Michael, "Sure wish I had me one o' them thar things. Then I wouldn't get arrested for drunk drivin'! Why, I could put my six-pack right on in that basket thar behindja and just bike my way 'round the island! Thanks for the idea, Buddy!"

As his biking and reading forays on the beach brought the luster back into his eyes, Michael tried to help with homeschooling. Despite the improvements in his condition, this proved too much for him. The sparks of his intellect did not kindle flames of sufficient duration to manage lesson outlines and tutoring. My career plans teetered as I focused on the kids' schooling. The university job opening in Jacksonville, the nearest large town, was a good hundred-mile round-trip commute. The time away from home, given Michael's condition, was too great.

As the summer heat settled in, I didn't. Palm trees growing in the forest continued to feel wrong somehow—like cream cheese in a salmon sushi roll. Deciduous trees and pines called to me. The "live" oaks seemed more dead than alive. They shed brown leaves year-round, sprinkling morbidity like fairy dust. Brittle leaf litter crunched underfoot, smothering all but small patches of green lawn. The persistent decay stifled me.

I'd found a dried-up gecko in the sunroom before we moved in. It haunted me like the dead woodcock in Manahawkin—an omen. Michael was fighting death. I worried about him dying in obscurity. Besides Mom, we had no real ties. And although she was a cookie-baking grandma, she was still coping with Dad's death and not prepared to offer real emotional support. I bore the brunt of coping with Michael's incapacities alone. I found a homeschool academy in town that helped me arrange for the kids to receive public school credit. The curriculum offered flexibility and assured that they'd be able to earn a high school diploma. It wasn't too expensive and I was grateful that Alex, now a budding teen, could have someone besides me to whom he could be accountable.

Shooting uptown on his bicycle, Alex received private tutoring and a personalized curriculum. By now, he was in middle school. Jacob was doing fine with Singapore Math and the Calvert School curriculum. Both boys played with neighborhood children after hours. The local high school was not stellar, but there was a certain charm to kids playing hooky on days when the surfing was good. It reminded me of repairmen at the Jersey shore who wouldn't show up when the bass were running.

We connected with the Unification movement in Jacksonville. The pastor there, Francis, was an old salt. Together with his wife, Darya, he'd helped to pioneer the church's shrimping business in Gloucester, Massachusetts, where their kids were born. They'd weathered tough situations with their humor intact. Richard did various odd jobs for money, but lived for his service work, which included a food bank network. He negotiated with food shops and restaurants to collect surplus food they'd usually discard. Boxing it up, he delivered care packages of food to needy families and congregations.

With his ruddy cheeks, stout helping hand, and ready smile, he charmed both the donors and the recipients of food that otherwise would have rotted. Darya, like her husband, sported a smile broader than her ample figure. A former geologist and academic, she sold bras in the lingerie department at Nordstrom's. Commenting on her career shift, she said, "I never miss the old days. What I do now is low-stress. I enjoy the people and I don't bring my work home with me."

One of their children was blessed by Father Moon and raising a family with his Canadian wife north of Vancouver. Their younger son lived at home. He was often on the computer, when not away at college. Francis and Darya offered housing whenever church members from Asia or South America visited, so their home remained lively with guests and projects.

Church services rotated between the living rooms of various members near Jacksonville. Afterwards, we'd all tuck into a broad selection of potluck dishes that hailed from around the globe, as did the small gathering of motley church members. Michael enjoyed the food and good company. I appreciated that Richard's and everyone else's theology was grounded in praxis.

The North Florida church family had a casual, earthy tone—the congregation was more interested in going fishing than dressing up for long sermons. We hosted services at our home followed by fishing expeditions, which all the kids enjoyed. I helped with fundraising by working at a church member's flower shop on rush holidays like Valentine's or Mother's Day.

In this way we gathered bouquets of happy moments. But as the year progressed, "off island" seemed worlds away. From Fernandina, Jacksonville was a long expedition over bridges, past desolate wetlands and roadside shops that hung on by a shoestring—an air conditioner repair joint, flea market, fruit stand, pawn shop, bail bondsman, muffler shops, and the occasional Jamaican, Mexican, or Chinese restaurant. Most of the folks spoke "Southern" and their pastimes were church, football, and fishing—much like in Alabama.

Amelia Island was historically segregated with a proud tradition of free Blacks pre-dating the Civil War. We lived on the north side, closer to the historically Black area. However, Florida also boasted being the third state, after South Carolina and Mississippi, to sign the Secession Acts of the Confederacy.

Although Union troops occupied Fernandina early on in the war, they hadn't modified the culture and North Florida still felt like the Deep South to me. I struggled with this, as I felt more at home in places—like France—without a history of slavery.

Despite Michael doing better, the down-to-earth church members, and the kids having reasonable access to academic resources through the internet, the retiree culture that predominated suffocated me, too. Up to my neck in so many withered leaves, I wanted to break free—free the way Sadie made her "run for the roses" charging for the woodlands as we walked the perimeter of the soccer fields where Jacob played.

I needed to move away from death, decay, and sticky Southern history. Apart from the beach, with its day-trippers that included families, the middle aged, and young folk, when I ventured to places the "natives" frequented—the grocery store, video parlor, post office, or hardware store—I saw mostly tanned and wrinkled seniors, ebulliently fending off death. Some called Florida "God's waiting room."

Michael's marked improvement gave me hope that we could move back north. I took an exploratory trip to upstate New York. Briana, my old friend from the movement who'd blessed Michael and me, met me at the Albany airport. She put me up while I searched for employment. Briana and her then husband, Charles, lived in a ranch house near the old Christian Brother's building that housed UTS, the seminary we'd both attended, in Barrytown, New York.

Sitting at her dining room table, I pored over the classifieds in the Kingston newspaper. Spotting a small posting for an upper school French and Latin teacher at Woodstock Day School (WDS), I called. The French teacher had recently resigned and I landed an interview.

The next day, I drove a dinged-up Rent-a-Wreck van that chugged its way up switchbacks into the Catskills. The campus had wooden buildings painted in rainbow colors. Inside a forest-green cabin that served as an office, I waited to interview with the Head of School, Dr. Steve Coleman. While waiting, I took in a poster on the wall.

With the authority granted the Ten Commandments, it defined WDS's philosophy, which prioritized creative, artistic, intuitive, holistic, problem-solving right brain activities over left brain activities. Students practiced yoga for gym class and I could hear African drum rhythms playing from a tent in the center of campus. Children and adults were all on a first-name basis. The librarian, wearing Birkenstocks and a long patchwork skirt, smiled warmly as she shook my hand through a cloud of patchouli.

The interview seemed to go well. Dr. Coleman gave me a tour. As we passed students studying or playing, they cheerily called out, "Hi Steve!"

I returned to Briana's, and within a few hours, learned that the job of upper school French and Latin teacher was mine. I flew back to Florida the next day. Finding work seemed a mandate from beyond, a divine rescue from life in Fernandina.

On the plane ride back, I sat next to an artist, an elderly woman with perfectly coiffed platinum hair wearing a navy-blue suit, matching pumps and shiny hose. She handed me her crisp, colorful business card. I confided in her about my job hunt. She said, "Well, don't tell a soul you have a PhD. Men won't like it and it will work against you." I thanked her for the advice and wished her well. Inwardly, I couldn't wait to leave Florida and its retro roles for women.

Within a couple more weeks, Michael and I flew to New York while the kids stayed with Mom. Once again, I rented a vehicle from Rent-a-Wreck—this time to find a home. Briana put us both up and we slept on her living room floor. Within three days, we found a funky Victorian at a bargain price. It sat just around the corner from an elementary school and only a few blocks from the High School in Saugerties. It was a short commute to Woodstock for me and a short walk to the bustling village center for Michael.

It seemed like we'd found a good home. Saugerties sat on the Hudson south of Kingston—roughly across the river from UTS. I still had friends there and enjoyed walking the labyrinth on campus. Furthermore, Saugerties had both a decent town library and school system. I could work at Woodstock Day School and rely on the public schools for the boys and the walkable village for Michael.

The library was a short block and a half from our house, as was a small beach park on the Hudson. Our new backyard stretched deep, offering gardening possibilities and room for Sadie to frolic. Kids of various ages lived on our street. Besides the public school, there was a private Catholic school two doors down in the cul-de-sac. Lilacs bloomed and apple orchards blossomed. The place teemed with life. Our street name was Cedar—the name matched where we'd lived back in Highland Park, New Jersey, before Michael fell ill. Again, I felt our move north had divine sanction.

We returned and put our Florida house on the market. Within days, we had a solid full-price offer that more than paid for our move as well as the fresh paint and gardening I'd done at the old house. During the past year, Michael had regained his autonomy, managed his own medications and had a fresh outlook from triking about the landscape. The final good news was that Mom and I had become closer on our walks even as it became clear we were leaving.

At last, I'd been able to confide in her about some of the marital difficulties I'd had to overcome with Michael's illness and medication side effects. She said she never had liked the house she lived in now. She and Dad had bought it in haste when they'd moved from Pennsylvania. She hated living on the corner of a busy street. It was not 8th Avenue in New York, but Citrona was a major thoroughfare from the bridge to the north side of the island. People littered. Kids threw grapefruit from the trees into her yard. It was noisy despite the fence she and Dad had extended along the roadway.

Although Mom knew we'd be leaving, we talked about getting a place together. She wanted a room of her own, a bit apart from the family. She said that even a room above a garage would have suited her. I pictured her moving up north with us. The Victorian Michael and I were moving into had just such a garage. She wanted autonomy but could handle a shared kitchen. Being part of our family appealed to her as she took down barriers of faith that she used to harbor against me. Back at her house, she showed me her prayer bowl. Its little snippets of paper held names and concerns she prayed over each day. She prayed for the whole extended family.

With this spirit of love, that we were really going to be a family, I felt relieved and happy. For a moment I felt that, with Mom's camaraderie, I'd be able to handle Michael's inevitable decline. A warm fuzzy cloud of love embraced the two of us as we conspired about our future adjoining living arrangements. I felt we'd realized a new, higher level of trust in our relationship even though it was all fantasy. When we were getting along like this, my new job and our forthcoming move seemed far away. Despite our looming departure, she arranged for the two of us to look at condos in Fernandina. She wasn't trying to convince me to stay, but looking at houses for her was a sort of hobby—she'd once been a realtor. Mom knew we were buying the Saugerties Victorian closer to my new job, but looking at real estate together was a way to bond the way some folks do playing cards or ice skating or having a brew at the pub.

Some of her realtor enthusiasm rubbed off on me. Each time we'd moved, I'd considered how the house we were buying might someday generate income. Although I improved the interiors with paint, windows, lighting, and wood floors, and the exterior with landscaping for my own aesthetic pleasure, I always planned for changes that might add to the resale value of a house we'd scarcely lived in. I fixed things up not for my own amusement, but with an eye to investing for the future.

Mom and I discussed her coming to live with us in upstate New York. Elated at the thought, I imagined our cockeyed garage in Saugerties transformed into a cute cottage with Swiss chalet flower boxes. If she decided to be a snowbird, spending part of the year with us and part in Florida, perhaps we could rent it out when she was gone. With the thought that Mom might join us, I felt even happier about our forthcoming move. The only damper on my enthusiasm had been leaving her. With that problem eliminated, I could enjoy anticipating our departure for a new life in the Catskills, a scant month ahead on the calendar.

The move imminent, Mom and I met daily at dawn to walk on the beach. One such morning, we enjoyed the crazy gulls and the Royal Terns that reminded me of Bozo the Clown with their reverse black crests. They also reminded me of dad's ducktail and baldpate. Mom mentioned that she had a pain in her side. She rarely complained. When she said she was going to have a doctor check it, I was concerned but she clucked that it was probably nothing.

CHAPTER TWENTY-SIX

MOM

I drove with Mom to Jacksonville and met her solicitous doctor. She gushed as she spoke with him. *A paid friend*, I thought. He wanted to do an MRI so I went with her for the scan. I held her free hand as she took the radioactive serum into her vein. Then, we sat in the dark, windowless room for what felt like hours. She was still, quiet like a sparrow, uncertain of whether to fidget or preen as she looked about the room. I was glad to be there for her. I'd always wondered how she could have attempted nursing school given her tendency to faint at the sight of blood.

"Remember being in hospital in Aix, Pam?" she asked.

Hard to forget. It was another one of those six-week stays along with surgery. But there was more. I had to miss class at *lycée* where I was in *sixième*, or sixth form. Luckily, classmates brought me homework as the hospital was just up the hill from my school. My brother and sister's elementary school was not far from the hospital in the opposite direction. Mom happened to be visiting me when we heard an ambulance siren below my window. In France, the tone of an ambulance was a minor fifth *nee-ner, nee-ner*, not like the slurring octave *arrrrrrrrr* of an ambulance in the US. Dad used to whistle in the same tones as the French ambulance to call the dog or us kids home for dinner.

From my hospital bed in France, I'd written to the National Wildlife Federation in the US regarding my ecological concerns. They responded, and Mom brought me the stamped manila envelope stuffed with illustrated articles regarding nuclear power, effects of pollution, and endangered species. Thrilled with my booty, I spread the brochures and reports across the smooth linens of my hospital bed as I recovered from surgery, an IV needle in my arm. A nurse appeared at the door, "Madame Claxton?"

Mom stepped into the hall but soon returned looking confused and pale, the nurse at her side. I had to translate. On the road in front of the hospital, a car had hit my little sister Jenny. She was walking from school to meet Mom at my bedside. Jenny was already in surgery and would need a cast on her arm and leg, but other than that, she was fine. Mom, of course, was not fine, but didn't let on at the time.

Back in Jacksonville, as we waited for her MRI, Mom told me how much she'd appreciated my nattering on that day about the impending pollution crisis, the benefits and risks of nuclear power, and the need to balance ecological priorities with development while Jenny had her surgery. At thirteen, I was a hospital veteran and pleased to have Mom's full attention about what I thought was the most important thing happening on the planet.

After awakening in the recovery room, Jenny joined me as my hospital roommate. The casts on her arm and leg would need to be on for six weeks, a good match for my stay. We became known as *Les Américaines*. To minimize our notoriety, we tried to synchronize our bedpan requests. Jenny was younger, so I suggested we recite nursery rimes together to pass the time. This served the same function as talking about ecology with Mom.

Hospital memories. Waiting for mom's procedure in the dark. Our bodies make us frail and fragile creatures, but our minds may provide us with succor or terror. I stayed at Mom's side until a nurse wheeled her away. Afterwards, we left with no news except to wait for a doctor's phone call. The call came. Mom's gynecologist had found a cyst on one of her ovaries. Mom granted him permission to perform a routine hysterectomy.

My brother Rick flew out to join us for the day of surgery. We took Mom to the hospital. A nurse told me to put her street clothes in a large, clear plastic bag as Mom put on the surgical gown. We stayed with her while she waited for surgery. I had an ominous feeling putting Mom's clothes into the plastic bag. She was smiling and chattering about how much she liked her doctor—like a little kid going to summer camp. "I'll just get this done and be good as new," she said.

It was a routine procedure. But her clothes in the bag seemed so definitive. I wondered if she would really be putting those clothes on again after surgery. We saw her off and went to the waiting room. The operation went longer than expected. Rick and I were just returning from our visit to a machine that spewed brown water labeled "coffee" when a nurse summoned me to take a phone call at the waiting room desk. The doctor had paused surgery to talk to me. He said, "I'm sorry, but we got in there and there's cancer everywhere. It's all over her bowels. I need permission to go ahead and take out what I can see."

I felt numb. Time was of the essence. I asked a few questions, mumbled an affirmative reply, and clicked the phone back into its cradle. I pictured the doctor's hands, his surgical gloves bloody. Mom out cold, her entrails on view to the world. I turned to my brother and told him. He agreed with me that granting the doctor permission to carry on was the right choice. Mom was anesthetized already. Why open her up twice?

What were the ethics of us knowing more about Mom's condition than she did herself? I wondered. Rick and I strategized how things would play out after surgery. Who was going to tell Mom about her condition? Going under anesthesia, she thought she was completing an anodyne procedure. She was to awaken to a death sentence. The clear plastic bag with her street clothes flashed in my mind.

We waited to see her outside the door of her hospital room. Her pain would have been tremendous, but an IV dripped major quantities of dope into her system, keeping her somewhat drunken and disconnected from her body. In this state, she was to learn that she had cancer. Rick and I watched the doctor enter and go to Mom's bedside. He clearly had affection for her. He held her hand, "I'm sorry to tell you, Connie, but you have cancer. I'm going to pull in an oncologist to work with you."

She gazed up at him with total love and trust, her adoration fueled with the drugs cursing through her veins. Oblivious to the reality of her body, she crooned, "Thank you, doctor, yes, that will be fine."

She seemed unfazed by the diagnosis. Under the influence of the dope and shock, she retreated into her best Southern Belle composure: "Doctor," she said, "I want you to know how wonderful you have been."

I thought she was going kiss him through the tangle of tubes and devices plugged into her short body. Rick and I stayed in the room as the oncologist entered. He was a calm, thin, dark-haired man with commanding, dark-rimmed glasses. He said in a matter-of-fact tone what Mom's doctor had known but had not said. The cancer was stage four; it was throughout her intestines; they would do all they could; they would use chemotherapy. He checked the surgical site. Instead of a small incision, she had a huge swashbuckling slice across her entire abdomen. Recovering, I knew from my C-section—a far smaller incision—would be no cakewalk. On top of that, Mom's immune system was surely compromised by the cancer.

Half-listening to the doctor, I mentally composed a resignation letter for the job intended to liberate us from impending death in Florida. Rick postponed his return home to Arizona. I researched on the web about stage four colon cancer. To be succinct, there was no such thing as stage five.

However upbeat and diplomatic everyone tried to sound, this was not a simple uphill battle, but a futile one. In the cancer community, though, one does not admit to such fatal ideation. Death-defying optimism is required to participate in cancer remediation. The "treatment" could be lethal.

As more test results confirmed Mom's grim prognosis, I increasingly questioned the value of treatment. Would it not render her last days on earth even more unbearable? Coping with her recent surgery was challenging enough. Convinced that cancer treatment was a cash cow for the medical establishment, I wanted to protect Mom from torture for the sake of profit. Doctors presented chemotherapy as inevitable, disregarding the patient's quality of life under treatment. Death was inevitable—not chemotherapy, but I didn't dare say so.

After a few days, Rick had to return to work in Arizona. Jenny stayed in touch by phone. I listened as Mom chose to take chemo with her full decorum intact. Why, it was simply the thing to do. However, I suspected that deep down Mom wanted to leave this world to go be with Dad. Once he died, something within her had died too, something neither her grandchildren nor her children could satisfy.

She recovered from surgery and was scheduled for chemo. We took regular walks together at dawn. One morning, standing in her kitchen, I saw another side of Mom. Holding open the freezer door, she pulled out some frozen blueberries and burst into high dudgeon: "When I think of how I ate enough roughage to feed a horse, yet I got this darn cancer, I could just spit!"

I prepared to resign from my job in Woodstock and back out of purchasing the house in Saugerties. Since we were already under contract to sell our house in Fernandina, I consulted my realtor about relocating on the island.

One afternoon, standing under the live oak in what was still our front yard, Mom said, "I want you to go, Pam, you hear me? You must go to Saugerties. I'll be all right. I have Jackie and Leo close by. I'll be fine. I want you to go!"

Mom's sister and brother—they lived in South Carolina and Georgia, respectively—would take turns traveling down to support her through chemo. So I prepared to deploy our little family. I researched doctors in New York for Michael, schooling for the boys, and movers for our belongings. Yet, once it was certain we were leaving, Mom became nostalgic.

Our dawn beach walks became a farewell regimen. As though neither of us had a care in the world, she'd talk about us moving into a new house together, a place where she'd have her own separate apartment. My heart soared: we'd happily lived with Kay and Stan in Glastonbury; I longed for that familial coziness with Mom. Sharing the fantasy was her way of coping.

Given the severity of her condition, I was prepared for hospice. Meanwhile, Mom prepared for recovery through the magic of chemotherapy. I felt God's grace had given Mom and me time to reconnect on a deeper level. The core of our bond was not mere theology, but the spiritual presence of love, what I felt was God himself. This vertical relationship transcended mere biological, rational definitions—it was heartfelt. That spirit ran through Mom's unsolicited blessing of our move to Saugerties and my simultaneous plan to stay in Fernandina without her asking. Swimming in a divine stream, we each wanted to support the other.

Mom insisted that we go, however. So, we packed and drove to Saugerties, hoping she'd join us there in the cottage I'd prepare for her. I loved our new home and my new job. In addition to the town library, the village shops and Michael's doctor were all within easy walking distance, as were the kids' schools. There was even a small beach on Esopus Creek, a tributary of the Hudson River, within triking distance. Mom and I phoned each other regularly and she coped with chemo, as promised, with the help of her siblings.

With the trike exercise and the air of the Catskills, Michael stayed alert and active. Yet we knew his mobility and mind would fade. At this point, Michael was forgetful, but didn't have full-blown dementia. Bit by bit, day by day, and hour by hour, his dependence upon me increased at a slow creep. Stubbornly, I denied that our relationship was unusual. Out of love, I naturally took over the extra gestures to help him get through the day. I refused to accept that people in the world beyond doctors could detect his frailty, despite the painfully detailed description I'd had to provide of his daily limitations when I first filled out his social security forms.

Perhaps it was my years of practice living in denial of Dad's alcoholism that made this possible. Or perhaps it was just love. Other than calculating my students' grading—I was a stickler for numerical objectivity—I became much fuzzier about math. That is, measuring. Measuring time when I never knew how long it might take Michael to ladle a spoonful of food to his lips. Measuring effort when I knew that pulling on his own socks required supreme dedication and concentration. You don't measure love, you just live it. And you measure moments in eye sparkles, or wobbly smiles. I would travel to the ends of the earth for an eye sparkle from Michael or his effort to make a wobbly smile.

I refused to allow disease and doctors to define our lives. American doctors had a way of telling you everything you could *not* do. Their fingers twitched with eagerness to write prescriptions for drugs that clouded your thinking so you wouldn't notice all the things you weren't doing anymore. The more drugs, the more side effects—and for these, of course, they simply prescribed more drugs.

You could fill your days seeing nothing but the inside of doctors' offices and waiting rooms. You could measure time by clocking when and how many medications you took. You could let disease run your life. In your spare time, you could go to support groups and talk about the disease some more until you eliminated anything extraneous to the disease from your life. That way you could live with the clear conscience that you'd done nothing less than make the most mathematically verifiable, acutely precise, scientifically safe choices to honor the disease in your life.

Instead, Michael and I both wanted to create the best memories we could while we had the chance. This meant that travel became a high priority. We planned a trip so Michael and the boys could see where I grew up in France. On another trip, we'd visit Oxford so the boys could see not only where Harry Potter was filmed, but also where their dad had gone to school.

Scraping together our savings, we flew to Paris. After spending the night in Montparnasse, I rented a car and drove the family to Mont Saint Michel. Traveling west out of the city, rain fell steadily. As the tidal island rose into view, the sun was setting over the low-lying fields. I stopped the car and Alex eagerly tromped through a muddy pasture taking photos of sheep in the marsh. We followed him, taking in Mont Saint Michel hovering in the mist beyond like a mystical vision, as bleating lambs and their woolly mothers milled around us. According to legend, the archangel Michael himself requested a church be built upon the island's summit in the eighth century. At low tide, pilgrims could access the abbey by walking over the causeway from the mainland, but high tide surrounded it in water, rendering it a moated fortress.

When we visited, the car parks, dam, and bridge from the mainland did not exist. I had to find a high sandbank above the incoming tides to leave our rental car. We crossed the sandy causeway in the rain. The island rose beneath our feet as we hiked uphill and over slick gray cobblestones, following switchback alleyways lined with walls over five hundred years old. Like salmon swimming upstream against the current, we met day-trippers descending en masse via the switchbacks to leave before the tides rose, isolating the island.

About a third of the way toward the summit, we arrived at our lodging—a medieval stone building that melded with the granite mountainside. Drenched, we checked into our room. Its windows were portals. Safe within, we watched the tidal bay rise around us. Alex, tired of being soggy, sensibly chose to stay in the room and watch soccer on TV, allowing us to bring him leftovers for dinner.

My food hounds, Michael and Jacob, ventured forth with me into the drizzle to find sustenance. Streetlights glittered on glistening stones as we explored the now empty rain-slicked streets. Michael, in good humor, commented on the lethal combination of slippery stones, steep ravines, and his inelegant gait. "Just what a person with mobility impairment needs," he joked. "Wandering around at night on cobblestones and thousand-year-old stairs in the rain!"

I walked on one side of him to body-block a fall onto the cliffs below. Jacob walked on the opposite side, taking his other hand to help him navigate. We found shelter from the rain in a seafood restaurant. With most of the tourists gone, we had the place to ourselves.

Jacob boldly ordered *fruits de mer*. A platter larger than him arrived with exotic marine life quieted into cooked repose. Curious geometric forms awaited cracking, slurping, and sucking—sea urchin, eel, mussels, and crab. Jacob, scarcely up to my waist, was game for it all. He helped Michael dig in, happily breaking open carapaces and poking meats from shells to feed his dad. Barely eight, Jacob had a wisdom about him that enabled him to look after his father without asking anything in return. As I watched the moonlight play over the water outside the window, and Jacob's little hands become expert at eating creatures he'd only ever seen in books, I felt that by coming home to France we'd in fact discovered our real life. We'd safely, I let myself think, left behind in America the bad dream of doctors and disease.

The next day, the skies cleared. After breakfast, all of us—even Michael—hiked to the top of the Mont to see its namesake, the Archangel Michael, slaying the dragon, and other medieval accoutrements in the abbey museum. Descending the fortress, we fetched our belongings from the hotel and headed back to the car, where I'd parked beyond the tides. The sun returned and warmed us to the bone. The boys whooped and charged into the water, splashing as they scampered across the windy shore. Michael wiggled his toes in the gray sand before we left for Caen and the train to Aix-en-Provence.

Aix was the birthplace and hometown of Cézanne. I led my little brood on foot to his atelier, a distance of under two miles. As we walked, we left behind the town's soothing, burbling fountains and shady squares. We emerged into the parched, rugged countryside of Provence and could see Mont Saint Victoire shimmer in the dry, sunny heat. My joy was tempered as my once happy crew complained that I was leading them on a death march in my enthusiasm for art. Luckily, Cézanne thought to have an ice cream stand outside his atelier in addition to some leafy plane trees. Once they had resuscitated in the garden, I herded my charges into Cézanne's studio to take in his sacred space and the northern light coming through his windows.

The following day, I took them to my childhood haunt—the Club Hippique just outside of Aix. This time, I took the precaution of driving, although when we were kids, my brother and I sometimes walked there after school—it was only about three kilometers from town. To celebrate old times, one of the main instructors and owners of the stable, Marie Christine, put each of the four of us on horses for a gentle ride around the grounds. We walked our mounts down past the *rivière*, where, legend had it, Cézanne had painted "The Bathers." Marie Christine had assigned us mild-mannered steeds so no one had to manage any equestrian excess. Afterwards, we watered our horses at the old fountain, removed their tack, brushed them down, cleaned out their feet, and put them back in their boxes, just like the old days—not just mine, but as it had been done for hundreds of years. The Club Hippique was one of the oldest riding schools in France, a national tradition.

After our ride, rounding the corner to the tack room, Marie Christine said to me, "*Pam, il est vraiment perdu sans toi, hein?*" (He's really lost without you, eh?)

It hit me hard to hear Marie Christine—my teacher, my sensei—say this. I wanted to imagine that nobody but us could see Michael's disabilities, as if that would mean he could carry on indefinitely. I was happy to help him bebop over cobblestones or ride a horse—activities that subverted the protective, traditional American approach to caregiving for those with neurological disorders. I saw his body's resistance to mobility as a challenge rather than a limitation. Working together, him trusting me as I ushered him, enabled us all to share experiences that typical medical practice would have restricted.

While many Americans think of France as a place with fancy food and mannerisms, I felt the essence of my adopted mother country to be her understanding of human frailty. People were kind not out of pity, but empathy. Michael was too large for me to lift or carry. Taking public transportation, strangers would lend a gentle, loving hand to help me get him situated. In French restaurants, renowned in America for their snobbery, waiters never complained or looked askance at his awkward table manners or crumbs that missed the plate. We were not judged for being unfashionable and clumsy, but rather treated like family.

I felt grateful to be included in regular society instead of delegated to the sickly sector, sequestered in clinical settings. Americans liked to categorize and house people by ailment and age. Not so in France, where multiple generations rubbed shoulders and elders, more often than not, aged in place. Physical disability was just part of the human condition, not something to pity, fear, or hide from the city's bustle. It exacted compassion, acceptance, and adaptability. The profound kindness and acceptance we experienced in France made me feel like God was with us.

After we returned to the States, I reconnected with UTS. There, I regularly walked the labyrinth, either with my old friend Briana or on my own. Its sacred geometry allowed for prayer grounded in the body through movement. Beyond words, it provided a moving meditation.

UTS sat across the Hudson River from Saugerties—far enough to make going there a trek. This meant that our family had a great deal of independence and felt no immediate geographical pressure to jump when the church sneezed. However, when Michael's dad sneezed, it was another issue. During our stay in Florida, Stan had managed his affairs on his own. Gertie, Michael's sister, though she did not get on with her dad all that well, would visit Stan periodically. Once back up north in Saugerties, our trips to Glastonbury resumed. Stan was slipping. He could no longer handle his own checkbook to pay routine bills and his driving days were over. He had a full-time live-in Congolese caregiver named Charles. The upstairs boarder, Abigail, helped him too. She'd literally saved Stan's life at least once by calling an ambulance when he'd fallen and couldn't reach the phone.

Asked whether he wanted a "Do not resuscitate" order (needed for hospice), he said, "It's natural to want to live, right?"

In that spirit, he ignored doctors' orders and ate what he wanted despite the feeding tube. This resulted in regular near-death experiences that would land him in the ICU. There, once revived, the doctor would send him home. Once, when Michael, the boys, and I visited him in the glass-encased room, he said to me in a raspy whisper, "Come closer!"

I leaned over past his shoulder to put my ear near his mouth to listen as he said, "We can break out of here. Use this piece of wood." He gestured to the plank that braced his arm with its embedded IV tube. Another time, having entered the ICU during the night, he was found the following morning sitting upright in a chair fully clothed. "I want to go home!" he growled.

While other elderly folks might ponder their own mortality, Stan refused to let death enter his thoughts at all. He had far too much he wanted to do. Yet, despite his attitude, Stan became more dependent and homebound. Hence, our trips to Glastonbury from Saugerties became more frequent. My new job required attention too. Beyond classes, there were meetings with parents, colleagues, and weekend fundraising events on campus. Commitment to family and work stretched me thin as I lost sleep and, increasingly, my temper with the regular commutes across the Berkshires to Glastonbury.

To regain composure, I'd take slower paced back roads lined with trees and plan a prayer-walk pit stop in a state park. This had the added bonus of giving Sadie and the boys a chance to run through a forest. Michael would throw sticks for Sadie to fetch from the river that burbled over boulders into waterfalls. After our jaunt, refreshed, I could resume driving.

Come Thanksgiving, it was clear that Stan's health was failing. His death looked imminent. I gave notice at work so we could move to Glastonbury. The commutes were too much for me to manage on top of Stan's hospice, Michael's illness, and raising the boys. But within days of the Thanksgiving festivities, Stan died in the middle of the night. The night nurse awoke me alone as the family member on duty. I prayed and talked to Stan as he lay that final night illuminated from the streetlight shining golden yellow through the antique glass. As day broke, I notified the others.

When the undertakers arrived to carry Stan out the door, I alone saw him leave. After putting him on the gurney and zipping up the black bag, they pushed his body through the kitchen and the ell where he used to spend so much time at his workshop, past the greenhouse he'd built himself, where he'd used an old screwdriver as a door handle, and out the back door into a black minivan that served as a hearse. It was bitter cold in Glastonbury that November. I recalled how the funeral parlor had taken Kay boldly out the front door into the night, yet Stan out the back, like a secret, as if death might upset the neighbors.

Days later, we had his memorial service at the church next door. Stan's Brittany spaniel, Annie, broke loose from the house, burst through the church door, and scampered into the reception hall. I felt Stan had a good laugh at that from beyond. I had a stone for him made to match Kay's. We held a more intimate memorial service where, with all the extended family standing around, Jacob lowered the box of Stan's ashes into the ground. Now Stan, Kay, and her parents all reposed in the old cemetery plot by the village green. A large Victorian stone stands guard over their plot. The epitaph reads:

> Remember me as you pass by,
> As you are now, so once was I,
> As I am now, so you must be,
> Prepare for death and follow me.

Kay had erected that stone to honor her mother long before Alex, Jacob, and I had entered the scene. Michael took ghoulish delight in the Gothic theatricality of the verses. I enjoyed the humor of the dead speaking to the living. In some ways, it made Stan's passing easier imagining that he wasn't really gone. Though neither of us had planned for death to enter our lives so soon, the Victorian familiarity with mortality offered a sort of morbid comfort. Acknowledging the reality of death helped relieve the idolatry of youth that dominated American culture.

The acceptance of mortality as historical fact pervaded the cemetery, which dated back to the Revolutionary War. In those days, death was not antiseptic and clinical; it was more a part of daily life. Its allegory arose with the sun's illumination while the extinction of each day in darkness made death's shadow a regular guest. There were fewer heroic measures to deter its power. The preciousness of life was perhaps more apparent.

Michael, who now had dementia more severely, could find his way around Glastonbury, his childhood home. We talked things over with Gertie and offered to buy her out of her share of Stan's house. She agreed. We were set to make Glastonbury home for good. Michael, Jacob, and I stayed on at Kay and Stan's.

Jacob was thriving at school nearby while Alex opted to homeschool with church friends in Northern California.

Having tried high school in "Soggy Cheese," as Alex called Saugerties, he wanted to homeschool instead, yet needed mentoring. Between work, Stan, and caring for Michael and Jacob, I was unable to tutor Alex. I turned to the Blessed Teens Academy (BTA)—a school founded by a couple of church members. It gave Alex a chance to homeschool, but alongside other kids and with adults supervising in an embracing, kid-friendly, homey environment. The academy was located in Berkeley, near the university campus.

The separation would be difficult, but BTA gave Alex the support he needed for his education. It had been years since he had visitation in Oregon. His biological father and grandparents there had preferred to keep their rifle collection and privacy to themselves rather than permit social workers to visit in order to approve Alex staying with them.

I wanted to provide Alex with an environment where he could enjoy being a kid, without constantly dealing with illness and death. He was at that vulnerable stage of teenagerdom: "Go away! Love me! You don't understand me! Where are you? Stay out of my face! You never help me! Leave me alone! You don't care!"

I couldn't do anything right for him. When he arrived at BTA, there was a brief honeymoon period, during which he was happy to be away and make new friends. Then, the reality of schoolwork sank in. I began to receive regular phone calls from Alex about how miserable he was. While visiting Mom who was having chemo in Florida, I flew Alex out to see her too. He'd matured and seemed quite competent flying on his own. I felt proud of him—his long blond hair made me smile. "Prince Valiant," as Michael called him when his hair grew out. He resembled a pre-Raphaelite knight straight off the canvas lacking only a horse and armor.

Alex returned to Glastonbury for holidays too. One Thanksgiving, snow turned us back from the ordeal of driving to Rhode Island to join the extended family. We hunkered down at home at Kay and Stan's and enjoyed the best Thanksgiving ever. Michael cooked. Each bite filled us with all the cozy family warmth that the Main Street house could bestow. I felt that both Kay and Stan were there in spirit. The snow hushed the landscape into a sacred white tableau. Jacob made his famous Redwall trifle and Sadie pillaged the trash afterwards—it was wonderful: a bit of bliss shared by all.

While I wanted to spare Alex the challenge that constant caregiving for Michael imposed, Jacob seemed to handle it better. He was younger and had a different relationship with his dad. Alex was grieving the "old" Michael who used to be so competent. Homeschooling in Berkeley appeared to be a great opportunity for him. He did have fun, despite his complaints.

BTA made a number of road trips with the students. They helped to fundraise—working in pairs mostly at supermarkets to chip in on travel expenses—for expeditions to places like Lake Tahoe.

Interacting with the public was a good experience for Alex, though challenging for his then shy nature. He learned how to relate with strangers, this boy who had been afraid to so much as ask a clerk at a department store where to find socks. He gained confidence and composure learning how to interact with a wide variety of people. He also learned that dirty dishes did not magically wash themselves—all good things for Alex's personal growth and life skills as far as I was concerned. And perhaps most important of all, he had several sets of adults without illness with whom he could converse, learn from, and who genuinely cared about his spiritual and emotional well-being. I wanted him to have the freedom of youth instead of acting as my "right hand man" for a while.

Michael, Jacob, and I visited Alex in Berkeley in February, which coincided with a regional and international Unification blessing ceremony in San Francisco. We stayed at the BTA house. It had formerly belonged to Randolph Hearst and subsequently had become a dormitory before BTA rented it out. It was a rambling mansion among townhomes and apartments on a hilltop, two blocks from the University of California's Berkeley campus. Sitting between Tilden Regional Park and Golden Gate Fields, the house was smack dab between nature, funky Telegraph Avenue downtown, and campus. *What a great opportunity to live here!* I thought.

At the time, Alex seemed mostly oblivious to his good fortune, though somewhere in the deepest regions of his subconscious he must have recognized there were good things happening. He was learning how to get along in community and take responsibility for his own actions. Furthermore, as Michael had deteriorated in his parenting ability, I found myself having to be both the "good cop," providing nurturing compassion, and the "bad cop," handing out discipline and setting boundaries. It was exhausting.

For the year he was at BTA, Alex was free to challenge the two sets of adults that ran the school. They could take turns playing the dual roles that I had to singlehandedly take on while tending all the other familial causes. I was especially grateful that another adult could address Alex's teen challenges for a while. This way, he could see that it was not only me, the ogress, who set boundaries for behavior at home. He was not a bad kid, but like many teens, he regularly tested one's entire parental skill set.

One day, I received word that Mom was fading. I had to take the next plane to Florida with an open-ended return. En route, storms kept me grounded in Baltimore where, waiting for my connecting flight, I'd befriended a pair of African American ladies, one of whom was in a wheelchair. The three of us ate lunch together. I offered to push the wheelchair and its occupant back to the gate. Speeding down a ramp, we were sharing a hearty laugh when my cell phone rang.

Mom had died before I could get to her. Stunned, I turned to my new friends and told them. They embraced me to their big motherly bosoms and the three of us prayed. Afterwards, I thought how it must have been God's grace to be there with them. Sharing with these two women felt natural, as did calling upon God together at that moment. God's love embraced all three of us.

Nevertheless, that rainy moment in the Baltimore airport was challenging. I wanted to be at my mother's side as I had been for Dad, Stan, and Kay. I called an old seminary roommate, Robin, in Washington, D.C. Listening to her voice soothed me as she inquired after my state of mind and heart. Robin stayed on the phone with me, her voice holding my heart, until I boarded the airplane again for Florida. Though we hadn't spoken in years, we could pick up right there, at a moment of life and death, with a feeling of natural rapport. The sense of continuity, commitment, and love everlasting was solid and sure. That was an experience I had with multiple sisters and brothers in the movement, even though our politics or geography may have been vastly far apart.

After landing at Jacksonville that night, I went straight to the funeral parlor. My sister and brother had directed the morticians to leave Mom unadorned. I entered the dark chapel and saw her pale face in the dim light that beamed from above the open casket. The morticians left and I stayed and talked with her for about an hour. It was a relief to visit Mom outside of the hospice ward, detached from IVs, the colostomy bag, away from nurses, buzzers, beeping machines, blinking lights, white sheets, stethoscopes, and sanitizing sprays.

The funeral would be another performance of processions, incense, and Latin incantations. From atop the closed casket, a nun would give me a golden cross with a dead man in a loincloth hanging on it as though that could replace Mom. But that night in the chapel was a blessed moment. I could talk with Mom's spirit without her gussied up into a caricature with big hair and gaudy makeup that would be the mortician's Southern fantasy of beauty the next day.

When I left the funeral parlor, the night air was foggy, starless, and pitch-black. A bat wibble-wobbled through the shadows of live oaks and palm trees as autumn toads sang chorus. Their silly voices held me in their unpretentious embrace, the kind Mom and I had shared walking barefoot along the beach at dawn. She'd not minded the wind mussing her hair. On the beach, there'd been no incense but the salty spray of sea air, no holy robes, no holy rollers, just the rhythm of the tide, playful gusts of wind and sticky sand between our toes.

— CHAPTER TWENTY-SEVEN —
RISING UP FROM SORROW

Leaving funereal Florida behind me, I flew back to Hartford and took a taxi home. The cabbie knew the route well—past Old London Turnpike to Main Street. I was eager to hug my little family and excited at the thought of settling into our new forever home. Leaving the cab, I walked up to our front door just as a couple was arriving to view the house with their realtor.

"The house is already under contract," I said, knowing we had taken it off the market.

"But that's not what the listing says," replied the couple's realtor.

"There must be some mistake," I said, pushing open the door. They left as I pulled my suitcase inside and closed the door. I hugged Michael. Laughing, I said how this crazy thing happened, people were looking to buy our house. Before climbing out of my traveling clothes, though, I called our real estate agent to make sure the listing was removed. She told me the house was back on the market.

"What? How can that be? We are due to close on the third of January. We've already locked in our loan with the mortgage company."

"Gertie and Michael put it back on the market," she said.

"Gertie and MICHAEL? He has dementia. I have power of attorney for him. He can't sign without me!"

The realtor, however, insisted that Gertie and Michael had put the house back on the market.

It was illegal to obtain a mortgage for a house still on the market to be sold. When the sales contract is signed, the house must, by law, be taken off the market. Putting it up for sale again voided our contract and meant we had to forfeit a couple of thousand dollars in closing costs. Not to mention that I had already invested in bringing the furnace, heating ducts, and circuit breakers up to code. These were long-term fixes; I anticipated that we would live there until our kids brought grandchildren home. I felt happy to be part of Stan and Kay's legacy and lineage. The history of Stan's and Michael's Indic experiences resided in the woodwork. I relished how Michael knew and could navigate the old homestead.

Hanging up the phone in disbelief, I said to Michael, "Do you remember putting the house back on the market?"

"I don't know," he replied.

"Do you remember signing any papers?" I asked.

"Oh yes, Gertie and the realtor had me sign some papers," he replied.

Do you know what they were?" I asked.

"No," said Michael.

"Could it have been something to do with the house?"

"Maybe."

He looked dazed and disinterested, with that faraway look from drugs and dementia.

Spotting a pile of papers on a shelf in the music room, I rummaged through them. Beneath junk mail advertisements for lube jobs and dentures, there were yellow carbon copies of papers to put the house on the market again. They'd been signed just the day before.

A chill went through me as I recalled talking to Gertie by phone two nights prior. She'd asked me three times if I would be at my mother's funeral all day the following day.

"Yes," I said, "but if you need me to confirm anything about us buying the house, just send me an email and I will get back to you as soon as I can." It seemed odd, her repeating the question, I thought at the time. But I was busy with the funeral, helping select a modest casket liner, responding to the Brylcreem-slicked mortician with understated reserve when he asked, "Doesn't she look lovely?" Revolted by the beehive hairdo he'd given Mom, I wished James Cagney would appear dressed as a gangster and say, "I'm gonna punch your lights out!"

Leaving Florida this time felt like an escape from the Twilight Zone. Returning to Glastonbury was a homecoming—home where we belonged, where ancestors who'd nurtured and embraced us reposed, where familiar memories kept Michael safe amidst his childhood haunts. We'd quickly moved from Saugerties when Stan needed hospice. Though it was a financial stretch for us to buy out Gertie, our house in Saugerties had sold in less than a week. It seemed like we were moving with the blessing of Providence.

I'd planned to keep upstairs rented, as Kay and Stan always had, to cover taxes. Though the place was old, the bones were good. We could limp along, doing repairs now and again as time allowed. I had a repair schedule strategized and we'd paid to upgrade the heat and fix some electrical issues while interviewing contractors.

Gertie needed the money from the house sale. I'd assured her I could communicate by email should questions arise while I was away at my mother's funeral. The loan was locked, loaded, and ready to go—she was to have her money within a few weeks. But Gertie decided she could get more for the house from someone else. Gertie, as Michael would say, "was very good at looking after Gertie."

Losing Kay and Stan's house was like another death in the family to me. Now we were, in essence, homeless. I negotiated with Gertie for us to stay on temporarily at Kay and Stan's. There was no time to be angry. I now had to launch plans for yet another move.

After moving to Glastonbury to help with Stan's care, we'd sporadically attended Unification Church Sunday services in Bridgeport. It was a long trip, but I enjoyed the services there because they were intelligent, theologically coherent, and embraced individual difference. A couple of old friends were pastors there—Ash and Ashly Wren. They'd both been in my seminary class at UTS and I knew others in the congregation from those days.

At the Bridgeport service, I met Ash's spiritual father. Like Ash, he was Polish and had a deep heart. A simple exchange of words with him felt like entering an ancient temple on a mountaintop—full of wisdom yet with a broad view. He beamed such love to Michael that I felt our marital couple was fondly supported and accepted just as we were—a feeling I didn't sense often from extended family.

After church service one day, there was a drawing for our tribes. Each tribe was associated with an area of the world for which we would take responsibility, like a missionary or social worker. Each of the twelve tribes, reminiscent of the Twelve Tribes of Israel, was to be led by one of Father's children. Our tribal assignment was like a home team—one you loved, win or lose—only it was chosen for you, random selection giving free rein to the hand of God.

I settled Michael in a chair in the balcony, prayed God's will be done, and nipped down the steps to the stage. There, Ashly held a box containing slips of paper with numbers. I didn't know if we'd wind up with Argentina or Zimbabwe. Holding the box above her head, Ashly blindly rustled through its contents. The colliding folded papers made a soft crunchy sound, like boot leather compacting fresh powdered snow. At last, she pulled out a single prophetic slip of paper. Unfolding it, she read, "Ten."

Hallelujah! I thought. Perfect! We'd be part of tribe 10, Europe 1, a territory which included Albania, Andorra, Belgium, Bosnia and Herzegovina, Bulgaria, Croatia, the Czech Republic, Cyprus, Denmark, Finland, France, Germany, Greece, Greenland, Hungary, Iceland, Ireland, Luxembourg, Macedonia, Malta, Monaco, Netherlands, Norway, Poland, Portugal, Romania, Serbia, Montenegro, Slovakia, Slovenia, Spain, Sweden, and the United Kingdom. Funny, although right next to France and Monaco, Italy was part of Europe 2, as was Switzerland. Nevertheless, I was ecstatic to have essentially been given the blessing by God to migrate back to France and nearby European areas that seemed familiar.

Drawing tribe 10 offered consolation for the loss of the Main Street house. I understood now that my ultimate mission was not to make a central foundation for outreach in Glastonbury, however at home Michael may have been there, but to move to Europe and make a foundation there. Hence, feeling "uncomfortable" in the US was fine and dandy—it was not to be our real home anyway. We, as a blessed family, had a mission in Europe, to restore something and to unite with our tribe there. In that sense, Gertie's rejection of us merely helped move us along in the right direction.

So Jacob could finish his schooling, Michael and I began looking in earnest for a new place to live in Connecticut while maintaining the upkeep on Kay and Stan's aged house until it resold. Going to Europe was a fine plan, but we had to wrap up loose ends in the States first. Alex would continue homeschooling at BTA while Jacob continued elementary school in Glastonbury. Michael's health pursued its wobbly and precarious course. While house hunting, I was still coming to terms with the loss of my mom and Stan. Even Sadie missed Stan.

For ages, a little green and overpriced Cape Cod had been for sale on Douglas Road—the same street where Aunt Betty used to live. It was nearly visible from Stan's front door. Next to the Cape Cod was a pizza parlor with which Stan had enjoyed a longstanding dispute. Like many of the upscale neighbors in surrounding historic homes, he thought the humble pizza parlor brought down the neighborhood. Like leaves falling in autumn and daffodils rising in spring, there was an annual hearing about this commercial enterprise. Upstanding Glastonbury citizens opposed the crass modernity of pizza, which marred what they considered a showcase residential neighborhood in their prized historic district. But Michael had fond memories of when the pizza parlor was a shop where he could buy candy and look at the owner's coin collections.

Secretly, I thought it great fun that an authentic family-run enterprise should be in this otherwise snooty, old-moneyed neighborhood. In keeping with my cheeky attitude, I wanted to set in roots with Stan and Kay's house to make it more of a community center, Unification-style. Its possibilities tantalized me: a school out back in the barn, meeting rooms downstairs, and rental income from upstairs that could easily be two apartments. Those hopes dashed, the Douglas Road house was serviceable. Jacob could ride the same school bus and continue his friendships with neighbors. Because it was so close to his childhood home, it had a comfortable familiarity for Michael too. It was close to the library and an easy walk to town.

So, we purchased the green Cape Cod instead of Kay and Stan's. Like a prophecy, Sadie, who was rarely ill, vomited when she went to the green cottage for the first time. One morning the week we bought it, I had what seemed another omen about the house. Waiting for a break in traffic, I saw a doe prone on the roadside, hit by a car. She held her head up like a dog looking straight at a police officer who drew a handgun. Extending his arm, he held his pistol in one hand, but he was shaking as if he feared the doe would rise up and charge him. He managed to miss a lethal shot even though he stood scarcely three feet from her—she was obviously too injured to move. The deer writhed in agony so he had to shoot twice more. This drama at close range left me shaking. It happened at the foot of Douglas Road, in front of the funeral parlor.

Before moving in, we painted, primped, replaced the roof, and gardened at the new place. Yet however much we fixed it up, it lacked the hominess of Kay and Stan's and our shared memories there. The day we moved from the old homestead, Sadie uncharacteristically bolted through the front door and ran. I tracked her down at the dog pound by the police station two blocks away. They agreed to keep her in a dog run for the day while the commotion of moving continued. When I picked her up, Sadie was glad to see me, but she was not herself, distracted.

Later that evening—our last night sleeping at Kay and Stan's—I let Sadie out, and she again took off. When I called her, she ignored me and made a beeline for the dumpster across the street. She was moving fast, so I jumped in the Jeep to catch her. When I hopped out from behind the wheel and called her, she did not even turn her head at the sound of her name. When I grabbed her by the collar, she turned on me growling and biting—completely unlike her. I gave her a shake, spoke sternly, and put her in the car to drive home. She returned to normal, responding with her usual doggie smile. That night, she slept, as was her custom, on the floor at our feet.

Upon waking the next morning, I went straight to Sadie, for her first routine outing of the day. Without rising from the floor, she looked up at me through her curly topknot. I patted her, ruffled her ears, and then clicked my tongue for her to go outside. She strained to raise her head but could not get her feet under her. This was her best effort. After that, she could not even get her head off the ground. My heart pounding, I found Michael to help me carry her to the car to take her to the vet. I backed the Jeep over the lawn to the front door, just as the hearse had come for Kay. As I watched Michael, tottering with PD, I had a flashback of Stan tottering with Kay to the potty chair.

Sadie weighed a good sixty pounds. With my back out, I couldn't lift her. I coached Michael down the front steps. As he lurched in disequilibrium with Sadie in his arms, I had another flashback of him driving over the bridge in Georgia. I felt so alone. Together we got her settled on a large towel in the back of the Jeep. I helped Michael into the passenger side, sped to the vet, talking to Sadie the whole while, wishing I could have been in the back holding her.

I burst through the door and told the receptionist what had happened. She sent a pair of young techs to the Jeep with a doggie stretcher. They carried Sadie into an examination room and the vet took x-rays. When Sadie returned from the x-rays, she still could not lift her head. The vet said that she was riddled with cancer. Surgery, even if successful, would not give her more than six months, and the operation would cost thousands of dollars. I knew the time had come.

My only panic was that with every passing moment, I knew she was in pain. I wanted only for Sadie not to hurt anymore. Michael stood by me as I caressed her head and the vet injected her with serum to put her to sleep. Sadie's eyes closed in death and it was the saddest moment of my life before or since. Sacrilegious as it sounds, her death hurt more than any of the human funerals I'd attended. I grieved her more because she'd been an extension of me, so intimately involved in my life. All my happy memories of Michael not being sick had been with Sadie at my side. She was the one being in my life I could trust who was not in perpetual crisis. I looked to her to connect with earth, health, healing, and unconditional love. I prayed to an invisible God, but in Sadie's joy for life, I saw the divine incarnate.

Each day I continued to go for prayer walks the way I used to with Sadie. I traipsed through the woods, along the river, up trails, and through town. And I sobbed uncontrollably on every outing. I missed my best friend and repented to have let human concerns consume me the past few months. I felt Sadie had somehow soaked up all the pain and grief of Stan, Kay, my dad, my mom's cancer, losing the house, Michael's depression and PD. It felt like she sacrificed herself, absorbing our family's torment, to save her wretched people, especially me. She, more than any person on the planet for the previous eleven years, had shared my sacred space and had been one in heart with me through every challenge.

When I retrieved her ashes from the vet, I paid the sizeable bill. The receptionist handed me a little gift bag. I cringed; it seemed like a party favor. In the bag, besides her ashes, there was a plaster paw imprint from her foot—a canine equivalent of a death mask—complete with a red ribbon to hang it upon a Christmas tree—a grisly souvenir.

Instead of Sadie bounding through the woods, I had this paisley-print bag and tidy little gift box of her ashes. I wondered what to do with them. I called my sister, Jenny, in Alaska. She said, "I keep Chloe and Jack's ashes out in the garage," referring to her long-ago dogs. She continued, "I know exactly where they are among the stacks of furniture we don't use, piles of magazines and other stuff. I can't bear to get rid of them." This from the girl who used to live in a cabin and have an outhouse. Married life had rooted her in ways that had not occurred to me. I didn't want to keep a garage full of stuff. Besides, I had a strong feeling about dust-to-dust and following nature's course, despite our "civilized" lifestyle.

The paisley bag with its little red ribbon seemed trite and foreign to the gusto for life that Sadie always expressed. Her death merited a natural memorial, one that joined her with the earth and stars, for she embodied the natural world in a fuzzy brown package of pure joy. I was not going to carry around her ashes in a designer box. That was not where she belonged. I couldn't bury the ashes in the garden of our new home. Its impermanence was already certain. Yet, I couldn't leave her at Kay and Stan's because we'd sold the property—it would be in the hands of strangers. I needed a place of permanence in the natural world.

Although it was against the rules of the cemetery to bury pets with the people there, I mixed Sadie's ashes with soil and planted daffodils and hyacinths around Kay and Stan's tombstones. The circle of flowers united them as a married couple. Stan was a dog lover and Sadie knew it. I figured he would be glad to have her around, as would Kay. The subversiveness of Sadie joining them in the prim Colonial cemetery would have pleased both of them.

To top off the garden, I added a small statue of a cherub reading—rather Catholic for a New England cemetery, but the only time Stan was without a book under his nose was when he was walking his dog, cooking, or fixing something. I fancied saving up for a bench one day. The cemetery was the closest thing I had to home. I guess that is why, although it was inconvenient, Gertie kicking us out of Kay and Stan's did not deter me from seeking to order my life around love. The temporal, physical world would not endure like the spiritual realm where my allegiance remained.

At dusk, my habit was to take a prayer walk around the cemetery, where I often saw a red fox trotting along the woodland's edge. After Sadie died, the fox would stop and sit like a dog looking at me. Tending the gravesite, I would commune with the dead buried there. I prayed for them all, walking around the cemetery. The spiritual realm understood more about our little family and the challenges I faced than the physical creatures who formed our extended nominal family yet remained distant strangers in terms of heart.

As Michael continued to lose control of his mind and body, I knew it would only be a matter of time before he would join his parents in the dirt.

On a lark, years before Michael was ill, we'd purchased gravesites in a Unification plot in Washington, D.C. At the time, neither of us imagined using the damn things; they were being sold as a fundraising effort and we didn't mind helping the movement. Since our mission country at the time was the US, it seemed fitting that our graves would one day be there. Death in those days seemed theoretical.

Having lost the family homestead and drawn tribe 10, I was no longer certain that the US would be our final home and I'd thought about selling those grave plots. But rather than stew over such things, I instead looked forward to taking the family back to France. To that end, I enrolled in an ESL certification program there, in Mauzac—a tiny village east of Bergerac, a couple of hours east of Bordeaux. I hadn't yet visited this region and hoped to make the best of the trip with my three "boys." I lobbed Michael into the category of "child needing love and assistance" rather than "adult patient losing his mind." The former made me feel maternal and loving toward him. The latter made me feel woefully inadequate for I was not much of a nurse. From our last trip, I knew that the food, climate, and people in France would do Michael and me a world of good. It felt homey there and offered respite from the pain of recent losses.

Through the ESL program, I found reasonable housing for the whole family for a little over three hundred dollars. That made our month-long stay in Mauzac feasible. I added a prior week of family travel to overcome jet lag and prepare myself for study. Michael lobbied to see Normandy. I secured travel and lodging arrangements for our trip while job hunting stateside.

Dismayed by the lack of support in Glastonbury, I applied for work wherever the environment and school system looked attractive for Michael, the kids, and me to live. My applications included an ESL position in Hillsborough and a French high school position in Durham—both in North Carolina. One of my main objectives was more sunshine. Although it had beautiful late-afternoon light, Connecticut's frequent overcast days felt depressing.

I was looking forward to leaving for France: I loved how road trips ensured family time. Traveling gave us a chance to see the front of the boys' faces rather than the backs of their heads as they stared at computer screens. And since Alex had been homeschooling in Berkeley, traveling together would give us all a chance to reconnect. I was convinced that our relationships needed quantity as well as quality time.

Though our trips provided ad hoc learning about history, art, and culture, most of all, I wanted to encourage every possible chance for the kids to connect with Michael. Mauzac would give us that opportunity. Being together in a foreign country was a retreat from our usual chores and gave us time to work on our relationships. On the practical side, the ESL program would advance my professional credentials, which meant I could better support the family. We left at the end of the school year, soon after Alex flew home from Berkeley.

Once in Mauzac, while I studied, Michael read or strolled along the Dordogne River. Jacob and Alex joined him. The boys went biking and reverted to their naturalist days from Manahawkin. They spent hours in the surrounding riverside meadows observing bugs and ducks—often taking astoundingly good photos. Although I'd hoped they'd speak French by talking with friends their own ages, they wound up to be the only kids in the village that summer. We made daytrips to caves with prehistoric drawings, *châteaux*, forests, gardens, and medieval villages when I was not in class. The Dordogne, though a hotspot during the Hundred Years War, had avoided much of the bombing during World War II. Thus, its hillside villages remained more or less as they'd been for centuries.

After completing my coursework and final exams, I felt joyful for having gained new skills and friendships from my studies and deepening the rapport within the family living abroad but sorrowful to leave France. The day of our departure, as I exited the garden of our rental overlooking the river, my eyes met with two enormous rainbows. Their brilliant arcs looked as if they'd been painted across the sky. Only someone relentlessly focused on their shoes could have missed seeing them. They soared into the sky-blue vault of heaven over the entire village, and then cascaded in shimmering ribbons of brilliant color on the far bank of the river. One alone would have been magnificent, but the pair made me want to dance in the street and sing. This was no ordinary rain refraction, but a gift from God, an omen, like the rainbow for Noah.

We said goodbye to Mauzac and drove west toward Bordeaux. We stopped en route at the Château-de-Montaigne, the birthplace and home of Michel de Montaigne, the Renaissance philosopher who had penned what some say are the first true essays in the Western world. Next, we paused in Saint-Émilion, a

UNESCO World Heritage Site. The children didn't exactly revel in the international regard long garnered by its vineyards, architecture, and civilization, but it was a glorious day nonetheless—a moment of whimsy that resulted in an enjoyable romp around the town for Alex and I. Jacob stayed close to Michael, near a church in the center of town. Alex hopped upon walls and took photos through ruins as we explored medieval alleyways; I caught a photo of the *tricolore* waving in the breeze above a government building that had housed a monastery in the twelfth century. Ice cream convinced the rest of the gang that the visit was tolerable, if not as magical as it was for me.

Indeed, a sense of spiritual bliss carried me. I felt I belonged in this land, among its people, living and dead. We spent a night in Bordeaux before taking the train back to Paris. This French-inflected pause provided space to breathe; drink in the sun, the stones, and the beauty of the vineyards, the happy clinking of wine glasses, quiet conversation, and appreciative laughter from cafés before resuming life in the States.

Though I'd been happy in France and had savored the moments the boys and I had shared with Michael, upon our return, even my new books could not compensate for the loss of our beloved Sadie. Our house felt vacant without her. With Kay and Stan gone, and their house of happy memories sold out from under our feet, there was nothing comforting in town but the cemetery. Glastonbury's Yankee coldness had become as stifling as Florida's sultry heat.

Maintaining our summer tradition, I shelved my paraphernalia on Montaigne, Sarlat, the *châteaux* and medieval villages we'd visited, as well as my ESL notebooks, and pulled out sleeping bags. We began preparations for our annual trip to the Poconos for Family Camp.

From our touchdown from Paris to our departure for camp, we had one week. To keep pace, I visited my chiropractor. On the way home, I stopped by the Magic Pet Shop in Wethersfield, where there were puppies from local breeders to visit. Playing with a litter of pups, I found a roly-poly one that behaved like a total people person. Ignoring food and toys, she came right to me. I knew she'd be perfect for our family, and so I put down a deposit for Polly without telling the kids or Michael about her.

On schedule, the Jeep loaded with gear, we headed for camp driving west through the Berkshire Mountains, down the Hudson along the Catskills and into the Poconos. Just past White Haven, we met in a restaurant with Unificationist friends with whom we'd camped every summer for years. Parents ran the camp and over the years so did their older children—teenagers and young adults. The elders taught Unification Principles to the younger ones and held adult discussions in the morning. In the afternoon, there was free time for hikes, volleyball games, swimming, climbing trees or just hanging out. Throughout the day and evening, there was time to commune with nature in prayer or participate in service projects. There was always plenty of singing and talented musicians to accompany on guitar. The purpose of our camping retreat, though, was to rekindle our relationship with God.

One day at camp, I had to break away from a group discussion around a picnic table to take a call on my cell phone. I walked into a woodland meadow. The call was coming from North Carolina, and the person at the other end was interviewing me for the second time. Within an hour, I received a follow-up phone call from an administrator who broke the good news of my employment: "We'll need you here in Hillsborough next week for orientation. School starts the following Tuesday."

I took a deep breath of mountain air. I had less than two weeks to move us down there. Managing life felt like I was both playing and inside a pinball machine. Bells pinged as I maneuvered flippers that launched me from one activity to the next: pack, move, sell the Douglas Road house, drive the family seven hundred miles, find us a new place to live, situate Michael, get the kids enrolled into school.

"Sure, I'll be there," I said.

I cut short our week at camp and trundled the family back across the Berkshires to Glastonbury to pack and leave—Hallelujah! For good! Hillsborough was not France, but it was a chance for a fresh start. I interviewed realtors and put the green cottage on the market within days. I touched up the landscape while a contractor helped me spiff up the house. I arranged for movers, prepped our aging Jeep for the trip and assured each person had essentials to last for the next few months. The Jeep soon sat in the driveway loaded with suitcases so we could leave as soon as the movers emptied the house. I moved at warp speed; a pace, I had learned, that tended to keep chaos at bay.

The movers arrived on schedule and packed their van. I swept the floors clean, released the holy salt house blessing, and loaded the family into the car. Bouncing southwest in the Jeep toward North Carolina, there was just one more item on my to-do list. I made a surprise stop at the Magic Pet Shop, where, unbeknownst to Michael and the boys, I'd arranged to pick up our new four-footed family member.

The white-and-brown spotted little girl was smaller than Michael's shoe. She happily rode in the back with the kids. As night fell, we stopped at the nearest EconoLodge, which, conveniently, allowed dogs. The next morning, we arose and were off to North Carolina without saying goodbye to anyone but Jacob's friends.

I was grateful for the sense of freedom that fluttered in my breast and that we had Polly. Hope flew with us toward new adventures.

CHAPTER TWENTY-EIGHT

CIRCLING TO CENTER

"Put your kids in the Chapel Hill-Carrboro schools," said Clara, the principal of the Hillsborough middle school. I figured she should know. So, I found a house in Carrboro, rather than near the school in Orange County. The commute was familiar from one of my many temp jobs when in grad school at UNC. The drive past cow pastures and woodlands had scarcely changed. Following the asphalt ribbon of road between the fields, I reflected on events and people in my life, how they overlapped and twisted back on one another like ribbon candy. I felt something more than modest weather and work had drawn me to bring the family back to Carrboro and Chapel Hill.

I recalled how Chapel Hill had enchanted me before meeting the movement there. When I later left to travel the lower forty-eight, selling flowers and trinkets, I did not imagine returning. Yet a few years later, I was back in Carrboro, enrolled in graduate school and married. After divorcing Boris, I parted from the movement while completing my master's degree, traveled to the USSR, and returned to Carrboro and to Vincent, whom I married. After birthing Alex, I'd left the area again, for Alabama, New Jersey, Oregon—where Vincent and I divorced—again New Jersey—where Michael and I married—and then Florida, New York, and Connecticut. Here I was again in Carrboro. This time, I thought it was my final incarnation—blessed for real with Michael, two children, and our second family dog in tow. I needed the strength familiarity seemed to provide, and this part of the world felt homey and apt for raising kids.

Yet part of me still felt lost, invisible, a servant to my family and job. Like sedimentary stone, my identity compressed into a thin layer beneath the weight of Michael's increasing disabilities. Now, teaching full-time, like attending to Michael's and the children's needs, also demanded full-time attention. At school, I enjoyed my colleagues and students, but I had a steep administrative workload. An initiative called "No Child Left Behind" required me to produce and maintain intricate additional documentation for each student. I often stayed after school until evening and came in on Saturdays to complete paperwork.

Our district's team of ESL instructors gathered weekly to prepare curriculum together outside class hours. When the high school's ESL teacher resigned, the rest of us wondered when the district would hire her replacement. We each had a full schedule of students, faculty, and parents to tend at our respective schools. Right before winter break, the department supervisor informed me that I was selected to replace the high school teacher. I was to add her workload—students, parents, faculty, and a commute across town— to my full-time middle school schedule. I was to do this with neither an increase in salary nor an increase in the number of hours in a day. I resigned.

It was just as well. I needed more time to help Michael with daily tasks at home, transportation, advocacy with his doctors, and support to maintain his social life. Since we lived in a suburb, I was the on-call chauffeur. I needed more than prayers, I needed hands-on help. We had limited contact with the Unification movement in North Carolina despite our annual summertime pilgrimages to meet old friends at Family Camp. The Unification Church in North Carolina seemed to prioritize service as a form of PR and evangelism over pastoral care. Although we participated in a few blessing rituals, I preferred to avoid the local church's dogmatic approach and right-wing politics.

I spent hours in prayer on my own seeking answers. To keep within earshot of Michael, I prayed in a closet or while walking in the yard, an activity that reminded me of the labyrinth at UTS. I soon planned a seven circuit Petite Chartres Labyrinth as a meditative garden. Using field-marking paint, I drew the pattern I'd been pacing in prayer. Over the course of the year, I wore a path in the grass of our front yard and covered it with weed cloth. With the help of a hired hand, Juan and his friend, I laid bricks and gravel to mark the path. Around the labyrinth, I planted a peace garden and found used benches to place on the perimeter. A friend blessed the labyrinth.

On September 21, 2008, International Day of Peace, Michael and I officially opened the labyrinth to the public. I'd posted signs around the neighborhood and visited various religious centers to invite folks to come. We named it the Crossroads Peace Labyrinth, as it was on the corner of our property, at the intersection of two roads. I held public new moon walks that sometimes attracted a half-dozen people. Regardless of the numbers—and often it was zero—I would light candles, pray, and walk.

Walking the labyrinth, I'd receive answers to questions or at least a sense of peace to deal with the daily chaos. The sacred geometry of the labyrinth opened a portal between this world and the spiritual realm. My walking meditations there made accessing divine inspiration easier somehow—the way practicing scales on the piano allows your fingers to feel more at home on the keyboard, less focused on mechanics, and more reliant on sound. In the same way, walking the labyrinth freed my spirit to commune with the beyond even as my body remained earthbound—turning first one way, then another, balancing left and right, but focused on the breath of spirit rather than the constraints of my body.

These experiences reminded me that I needed to find my own spiritual support independent of any church. Brothers and sisters in the movement had their own agendas. It seemed that as Father Moon aged, the Unification movement concerned itself more with its own preservation rather than living in alignment with the principles he'd taught us. I still honored the Divine Principle and the divine in our daily life. We had individual friends within the movement (most of them up north), but I felt divorced from the local church. God, I felt sure, was bigger than any organization.

The spiritual essence of Father's original message of love as a continuum of the love of Christ embracing all faith traditions was what I held dear. The labyrinth was the fruit of an experience in prayer I'd had the prior year when we still lived in Saugerties. Marion and Jeb, our old friends from homeschooling days in Manahawkin, were visiting us in upstate New York. Together we crossed the Hudson River from Saugerties to visit the seminary. The kids played on a swing by Massena House while we adults chatted and walked the UTS labyrinth. At one point, I wandered off solo to a rock outcropping on the seminary grounds where Father had once prayed.

Peace enveloped me like a warm hug; my feet seemed to grow roots into the earth. That moment punctuated my long-time connection with God with a firm message: That rock, that moment, the inspiration I felt, I could summon wherever I went. Father's rock of prayers and God's history of love could be found anywhere through understanding the Principle. I could recreate that rock, the solid sense of home in its wordless testament to God's love, anywhere in the world. It was not the literal rock, but the essence of God that set the stone to join heaven and earth.

Re-creation was within my grasp. The Divine Principle had taught me that we mortals have the spiritual authority to reclaim and express our common divine origin upon this earth, our true love heritage. The labyrinth seemed to facilitate that process and I held on to that feeling of finding one's core spiritual center and then transcending it. Perhaps the sacred geometry didn't hurt. The memory of that day at seminary is what motivated me over a year later to make the labyrinth in Carrboro.

Curiously, the license plate on our Jeep at that time began "XRD"— "crossroad." Literally and figuratively, we were at a crossroads. I felt this keenly as Michael's abilities declined. We were at an intersection in our lives between this world and the next. Aware of this reality, Michael and I prioritized creating the best memories we could with the boys.

Michael wanted to visit the Grand Canyon with them. I arranged for us to go when the boys had spring break. The canyon's chasm was so vast that early explorers ran out of mythological names for its countless rock formations. They borrowed from all the world religions to describe its inner landscape of buttes and plateaus. Like God, it was bigger than any one religion. Names explorers gave to the canyon's natural sculptures included the Vishnu Schist, Brahma Schist, Rama Schist, Buddha Cloister, Shiva Temple, Solomon Temple, Jupiter Temple, Tower of Ra, and the Shinumo—the word for peace in Hopi—Altar.

My memories folded back and forth at the Canyon too. I'd hiked the Tanner Trails there as an undergraduate at the University of Colorado at Boulder, long before I ever met the movement or Michael. On that trip, during the steep descent into the canyon, my knee was still somewhat fragile from surgery from one of my regular bouts with osteo. I was struggling where the trail had washed out. There was no rail along the path to prevent a stumble from there to eternity in the canyon below.

My walking stick wobbled as I braced to traverse the washed-out crevice. I almost went down and began to doubt my ability to endure a week-long journey of hiking for miles with a heavy backpack. As I started to crumple into a heap before this obstacle, a hand appeared before me. I took hold, navigated the rough patch, and because of the confidence gained in that moment, I was able to make the rest of the journey.

The history that had unfolded for me that day concerned not underestimating others or myself. The outstretched hand belonged to a young man who, unlike the rest of us, was not from Boulder. The Tanner Trail hike had limited access and required permits years in advance; he'd traveled across the country to join our expedition, I discovered as we walked together for a pace. It turned out that he and I had not only lived in Westfield, New Jersey, at the same time—we'd shared the same fourth grade class with Mrs. Kovacs. Despite the years that had passed, I recognized him.

He used to be one of the "bad boys" who sat on the opposite side of the classroom from me when I wasn't home with rheumatic fever. Someone, whom

I, as a child, had judged to be naughty and perhaps feared as wicked, had helped me with sensitivity in an embarrassing and dangerous situation. I did not recall seeing the young man who had helped me for the rest of the trip. Perhaps he was among the more competent hikers ahead of me. But his assistance had done more than help me catch up to the other hikers.

In that moment, the Grand Canyon had brought us together and taught me that my childhood presumptions of his character were wrong. Anyone could change—including me. It also taught me to have confidence in the face of my own frailty. Once he'd helped me over the crevice, though I kept my walking stick, I no longer doubted that I had the fortitude and the courage to complete the trek. His compassion had given me confidence. It felt as if the hand of God himself had reached out to guide me.

Michael, the boys, and I watched the sun set across the canyon. I sat a little to the side, near a scrub pine above the edge of a cliff. Red, gold, and blue light glowed jewel-like as shadows chased over the canyon walls. My memories of the Tanner Trails compressed into a past transcended by the present, as we absorbed the enormity of geological history from the rim. I remembered how God had reached out to me before when I hadn't expected it, when I was afraid. At peace taking in the sunset, I felt that somehow Michael, the boys, and I would be able to handle Michael's fatal disease.

After returning from this trip, we travelled more, pressed to seize the moment. Within the context of history and the cosmos, the world seemed small. Living within this bigger framework was more important than whether we ate reheated frozen pizza or shopped at Walmart for shoes.

We went back to France, this time to Nice, and stayed near the port. Michael indulged in his love of the sea and French food. Jacob earned his diving license. I befriended Marie Uliana. In her nineties, she still played a coquette of the 1930s pretending to be a mere eighty. She was half-blind and lived in the apartment beneath ours. She encouraged me to move to Nice. The weather would be good for Michael, she said. I took her advice to heart.

Just as we had not needed to stay in New Jersey once Michael went on disability, we did not need to stay in North Carolina once I no longer taught full-time. We were free to go. I hoped the kids' lives would be enriched attending French public school as mine had been. We put our Carrboro house on the market, our stuff in storage, and moved to France.

Nineteen-year-old Alex opted out, preferring to stay stateside with friends. Michael, Jacob, Polly, and I arrived in Nice. I enrolled Jacob in a school near the port, one Marie knew well. I found Jacob a guitar teacher to continue his music and doctors for Michael to manage his medication. The local Unificationist community was international, supportive, and deep hearted. Polly was as welcome at Unification services as she was at the local cafés. Michael continued to decline, but I felt a sense of community in France I hadn't experienced as a caregiver in the States.

Socially, I felt a sense of acceptance and belonging despite Michael's Parkinson's whereas in the US, the cult of youth made infirmity or growing old a flaw. In French culture, there was no shame or embarrassment about aging. The quirkiness of our family felt acceptable in ways it had not in the States. There, it was routine to sequester elders by grouping them together in housing compounds restricted by age—as if growing old itself were a disease. French culture seemed more tolerant of eccentrics, whether artists or those who behaved in peculiar ways from disease or disability. The wonkiness of humanity was a fact of life.

Soon, I learned that there was a different philosophy about medication in France. The French approach, to my relief, helped us to simplify Michael's prescribed drug cocktail. All this boded well for our continued stay. However, financially, I'd relied upon the sale of our house to afford renting abroad. When four different buyers failed to close at the last minute, it left us with both a mortgage and rent to pay. Having exhausted our money, we had to return.

Sorry to leave Marie, who'd adopted us as much as we'd adopted her, we departed Nice to live in our empty, unsold house in Carrboro. I extracted our sleeping bags and cooking gear from storage. Staying until it sold, we would find a different place to accommodate Michael's needs. Once the Carrboro house sold, we moved to Hoot Owl Lane in Chapel Hill. Alex moved back in with us and worked at a restaurant owned by church members. Jacob continued with school. Polly was happy to be on Michael's lap wherever we were.

Perusing the internet from home one summer evening in 2011, I stumbled upon the website of Earthtones, the photography studio owned by my spiritual father, Paul, the person who first introduced me to the Unification movement in Chapel Hill. After the matching and blessing of 1982, his Catholic parents had subjected him to deprogramming. He eventually married his childhood sweetheart in his home state of Wisconsin. We'd not spoken in some thirty years. From the online galleries, I saw that he'd turned his artistic eye and passion for photography into a full-time business. I contacted him by email and he responded warmly.

On the phone, Paul spoke as he did when we had first met. He had the same Midwestern drawl and goofy laugh. It was easy to respond to his gentle observations and inquiries into my life. I made it clear that though unorthodox, I was still associated with the movement and that, together with my family, I'd maintained a rapport with the Principle. Enthusiastic to reconnect, he still spoke to me as though I was his spiritual child and he my spiritual "pop," talking about agape love—the kind that wows you in a sunset, or a cloudscape, or makes you laugh at goats in trees. He had a poet's eye for nature, through which he found his deep connection to the divine. He and his beloved, Althea, did not have children together. He soon broke the news to me that he was dying of cancer.

"Paul," I asked. "Do you want to be blessed with Althea? I can do it, you know. Anyone who is part of a blessed couple can."

"Yes, it would mean a great deal to me to be blessed with Althea," he said.

This was a rather significant turnaround for him. Paul had left the movement in a flurry of publicity, which included interviews with *People* magazine and an appearance on the *Today Show*. Furthermore, when he'd become a deprogrammer, he called my parents and offered to deprogram me. Since then, he'd retreated to the western countryside with Althea and focused on his nature photography. His photos were poems of his love for God.

Paul and I had always enjoyed an easy camaraderie—purely brother and sister without a trace of romantic attachment. He and I had shared a different sort of intimacy, that of praying together, sharing our most tender longings for a world of true peace and love to be made manifest on earth. His love of God as the Original Artist was as apparent in his prayers as in his photographs. It was that aspect of our divine parent—God—that endeared him to me. For all his willowy height and inner fortitude, he was a gentle man and we were able to be forthright with one another. I didn't bring up the deprogramming incident with him. I knew his desire to receive the holy wine spoke for itself. His earthly energy was already waning.

The holy wine of the blessing ceremony was blessed by Father Moon. Sharing it, along with their prayers of commitment, would eternally join the couple in spirit. This was believed to be the substantiation of God's love, the eternal unity of yin and yang, joined in spirit and flesh. Because the blessing was to be eternal, some took the holy wine with a partner already in spirit world, holding the cup into the air for the spirit person to drink after sipping half themselves.

Of the many theological ramifications of the blessing, the essential one was that of including God, and thus eternal love, within a couple's love relationship. Although he'd left the movement, worked actively to oppose it as a deprogrammer, and remained estranged from it for some three decades, Paul not only remembered the blessing, but wanted it for himself and Althea. Some might have seen this as the return of the prodigal son. I just saw it as another chance to share God's love.

I had the spiritual wherewithal to bless him (although unorthodox, I was blessed with Michael), but I needed to find holy wine. I contacted a brother in

California, Roy Frieden, who had a vineyard. He and his wife Phoebe bottled and sold holy wine. Their idea to produce holy wine had evolved from their initial experimentation growing grapes in their suburban backyard and fermenting homemade wine. Over the years, their crop yield increased, and with it, their bottling. Ultimately, they purchased a vineyard and expanded to full-scale grape cultivation and wine production, blessing the earth and grapes as well as the wine.

As a blessed couple, the Friedens pioneered this venture themselves, not because the church directed them to do it. Their enterprise came to Father's notice and he visited their ranch. Roy most affably sent a bottle forthwith to Paul.

Paul confirmed by phone that he received the wine, adding, "Guess what day it arrived? On my birthday!," which was a Friday, August 26. This date would prove to be significant.

Together with my family, I arranged to bless Paul and Althea the following day, Saturday, at 5 p.m. his time. I would hold the ceremony at our home in North Carolina while they received the gift of spirit at theirs across the United States, in Wisconsin. Uniting in prayer transcended mere miles.

To prepare for the ceremony, I cleaned and holy-salted the living room and prepared an altar by putting a white cloth over a low table with a picture of Father and Mother Moon, a vase of flowers and a holy candle. I set up the room as for Pledge, putting a throw rug in front of the altar so we could all sit and kneel comfortably on the floor. On the rug, I placed four Family Camp songbooks, one for each of us to consult for the words to Pledge and to various songs. For the blessing, I helped Michael into his holy robe and put on mine, the same ones we had worn at our three-day ceremony after we were blessed at RFK Stadium in 1997. I gathered the boys and the four of us stood in front of the altar, Michael and I side by side, the boys behind us.

First, I led us in three full bows to our Heavenly Parent, True Parents, and brothers and sisters throughout the world. We recited Pledge in unison and then I prayed, "Heavenly Father we are gathered here to bless Paul and Althea as children of True Parents in the eternal marriage blessing of love."

I continued praying, explicating the significance of the blessing, the four-position foundation, the purpose of God's Providence and the pivotal role of the blessing in re-establishing God's eternal Kingdom of True Love on earth. When I got rolling, I had to measure my discourse by how much the kids and Michael fidgeted. I paid close attention to Michael especially, as I did not want him to topple over. I concluded the service with a holy song, then we all joined hands in a circle for three cheers of *Mansei*.

Mansei is a Korean word for "Hooray!"—but more of a declaration than a cheerful exclamation. The church's cheer of *Mansei* originated with the March 1, 1919 Samil Independence Movement. *Mansei* was the rallying cry for Korea's liberation from Japanese occupation. It meant, "Long Live Korea," or "May Korea live for 10,000 years." The church added *Aboji* (Father) to *Mansei*—in other words, calling for the liberation of Heavenly Father. So, the cheer of *Mansei* resonated with a vigor that defied spiritual and political barriers—divisions between heaven and earth that had endured for millennia.

The Korean-style cheers included raising our hands high above our heads so the cheers were both loud and vigorous. After the three cheers, we clapped loudly to congratulate Paul and Althea. I was grateful to stand together with Michael at my side as he encouraged the kids to unite with me. They were not enthusiastic about ceremonies. Michael, ever the anthropologist, had spent many hours in various temples and led by example. I cut a strawberry cream cake into slices for the family. The boys and Michael happily tucked in, enjoying their reward for having again indulged Mom in religious ritual. I felt the palpable spirit of God embraced us together with Paul and Althea.

Paul and I stayed in touch less after the blessing. He needed all his strength to commune with his family and friends in Wisconsin prior to ascending. Until nearly his final days, he wrote entries on his blog, *My Journey Home*. He wanted to leave an account of his experience as he died. I prayed for him and his family, appreciating the example he set of living fully with love even as he was dying.

Meanwhile, our life bustled along. Both boys lived at home: Jacob was attending high school and, having completed one marathon, he was training for the next; Alex worked at a sushi restaurant and was saving up to buy his first car. I tutored from home and tended to Michael. I did not think of him as old, but his medications and neurological decline increased his forgetfulness and decreased his mobility. A social worker advised me to sign him up for Charles House, an eldercare day facility, so I could have some respite.

I decided to meet the director and register Michael, but as I drove to Charles House the road dimmed to a blur through my tears. I didn't want to admit to myself the severity of Michael's decline, or that the constant care he needed was more than I could handle alone—it was as if doing so would be disloyal. I lived for flashes of insight, the moments when Michael and I were still "us," although we'd not made love since the night when Keith and I had busted him free from Belleview Haven nearly a decade prior.

Cozy, and with a friendly and competent staff, Charles House operated in a suburban home in Chapel Hill. There, Michael befriended another participant, John Jenkins. John's wife, Susan Linn, turned out to be the daughter of Chuck Linn, one of Michael's beloved former teachers from his middle school days in Connecticut. Michael had kept in touch with the Linn family through high school then college, visiting them in Connecticut and, later, after they settled in New

York. Susan remembered Michael from those early years and we became instant family.

To encourage his independence, I sought new ways to keep Michael active and engaged at home. Our little Polly was part of that plan, serving as a comfort dog. When Michael was home, she would perch on his lap and tidy up his whiskers like a mother cat after meals. That made him smile. But she could hardly hold him up if he faltered. To this end, I decided to find a dog large enough to help steady Michael when he walked and smart enough to learn a command like "home" to guide Michael back to the house should he become bewildered.

I'd read up on Parkinson's dogs and was eager to train one for Michael. When someone with the disorder "freezes," meaning they're unable to advance, the dog puts a paw on the person's foot. That contact prompts neurons to fire, jumpstarting the person from inertia. I met with a dog trainer who had MS. She'd taught her Dalmatian to serve as a counter-weight and balance assistant. The dog was large enough to steady her as she walked and would stand at her side so she could lean on him to get in and out of a chair. Combing pounds and adoption centers, I found a gentle creature for the job, part shepherd, part golden retriever, whom we named Riley. We soon began puppy classes with him.

My life orbited around Michael's needs day in and day out. In the middle of the night, if he arose to use the bathroom, I was on the alert to spot him. I accustomed myself to a night's rest consisting of several naps—the way a parent tends a newborn. I lived in a world beyond time, where my every waking moment was given to caring for someone else, not unlike hospice.

Michael's weekday routine included catching an EZ Rider, a shuttle for those with mobility impairment. It picked him up at the end of our little road and took him to the senior center or Charles House as needed. The neighbors at the end of our street let us put a folding lawn chair in their front yard. In the morning, once dressed, fed, and washed, Michael would walk the length of our little road, all of two houses long, and wait for the bus comfortably sitting in the neighbors' yard by the stop sign.

One day, after helping him dress and get out the door, as per our last visit to the doctor, I encouraged him to use his walker. His inability to balance had advanced from sporadic to routine. We had the speedy walker with wheels we'd picked up in France. There, encouraged by Marie, Michael had strolled briskly and safely around Nice with his snazzy racing walker. But back in the States, he could not abide using it.

"Michael," I hated to remind him, "the doctor said you should use your walker. I put it by the front door for you."

Dressed and shod, Michael pretended not to hear me and skedaddled out the front door. He wobbled down the steps and took off on the straightaway of the gravel driveway to the street, tilting precariously to his left, almost enough to fall over. I grabbed the walker and ran after him, pushing it in front of me as I jogged to catch up with his lengthening stride; he might hit the ground any minute. But the closer I came, the faster he went—a speeding, human leaning tower of Pisa. His sprints made it impossible for me to catch him. I ran all the way down Hoot Owl Lane calling out after him as he power walked at a tilt to the crossroad.

Catching up to him when he stopped at his chair for the bus, though my wifely duty might have been to scold him, all I could do was laugh. He looked proud of himself too. I was grateful that he was so determined and independent— I loved his resilience. Capable of being hardheaded myself, I admired stubbornness in others.

Later that day, though, I received a phone call.

"Mrs. Moffatt? This is Carol at the Seymour Center, Chapel Hill's senior center. We've had to call an ambulance for your husband, but he refuses treatment."

"What happened?"

"He fell down."

"I'll be right there."

Grabbing the car keys, I hopped into the Jeep, rumbled to the senior center, and parked behind an ambulance with its rear doors agape. A bevy of elderly folks milled about, tottering with uneven steps, leaning on a variety of walkers and canes beneath the portico. Walking toward them, I prepared myself for blood. In the center of the hubbub sat Michael on the ground, cheerful to be the object of so much attention and happily chatting to his entourage.

An elderly woman with a walker had jostled him as he went out the door, provoking his fall. Prioritizing litigious concerns, the Seymour Center personnel had called an ambulance, rather than helping Michael up off his tush. They feared liability for injuries, though Michael seemed fine. Another absurdity of American culture, I thought.

Michael smiled at me in triumph and said with pleased determination, "I told them I would not go to hospital unless my wife approved."

"I'm so glad someone had their wits about them!" I chirped. Wrapping my arms around him, I gave him a kiss on the cheek and helped him up from the ground.

Several days later, on a Tuesday, after long bathroom visits struggling with constipation, Michael complained of pain in his side. I took him to the doctor. Our trusty physician, Dr. Withrow, poked around Michael's abdomen and gave him an x-ray. He said with a compassionate tone that Michael would probably be better served in hospital, that he had some "blockage."

Within a day, as anticipated, Michael was unblocked. But the hospital wanted to keep him for more tests. The nurse speculated that it was some small thing amiss. No big deal.

I returned to the hospital on Sunday afternoon. The weekend doctor on duty said he had some news for me. Perky to have the test results, I was prepared to fend off extraneous medications that would only make Michael worse. The doctor stopped me in the hallway. He said that he needed to talk to me, in private first. "Based on our tests, your husband needs to be in hospice."

My mind froze as my mouth snapped, "What do you mean? Why?"

"It's his swallow test. Everything he swallows passes into his lungs."

Flashes of Stan, Kay, my dad, my mom, several others whose deathbed we had attended flashed and fizzled. My inner voice screamed: *Not Michael! Not yet! He's still lucid between bouts of incoherence; we have another five years! You're wrong! This isn't the plan!*

"This changes everything," I said, stunned, then numb as my circuits overloaded.

I grilled the doctor on specifics, got my answers, and accepted the diagnosis. Then the doctor and I went to tell Michael. He was lying in his hospital bed. He looked a little drowsy from all the tests, but otherwise, comfortable. He took in the diagnosis. The doctor gave us a moment alone together.

Michael looked into my eyes. "You need me," he said.

We talked, holding hands. I knew he was afraid of the precipice, that he dreaded a catastrophic depression. In dying, he had to go to a place his antidepressants could not reach. The PD was a perfectly designed hell. It removed all the things Michael loved most: reading, walking in the woods to bird watch, eating, even breathing. But what frustrated him most of all was the loss of his mind. He would careen off road, lost and confused in the land of dementia and know he'd been away.

We locked in on each other's eyes. I told him how David S.C. Kim—the president of UTS when I was there and one of Father's first missionaries to America—had just died. I reminded Michael of what David Kim would always say: "When I die, it will just be a change of address!" and how he would laugh in that deep, guttural Korean style.

Michael took this in and liked it. He calmly looked into my eyes and said, "Tell them . . . aqpqoiajpoijfjafdkj, apoiqeffj."

I couldn't understand as his voice faded for lack of breath. I put my ear right to his lips and said, "Tell me again, Sweetie!"

He said, "Tell them I am not afraid."

The doctor, ever solicitous, returned. I reported to him and the nurse what Michael had said.

Looking at Michael, the doctor asked, "Is there anything else you'd like to tell us?"

Michael replied, "Travel! Go to France! Eat French food!"

Facing death, this was Michael's advice to his white-coated caretakers.

The news and efforts had exhausted him. He settled to sleep. I had to go home and tell the boys. Night had fallen. It was a long walk across the pedestrian bridge, through the deck to find the parked Jeep in the dark. When I settled behind the wheel, the enormity of the loss we were about to experience hit me. Tears blinded me. I punched a button on the radio repeatedly until I hit music. Hearing a pleasing note, I turned the volume way up to drown out my own thoughts.

Some random station was playing a song I'd never heard before, "Baba Yetu," from Christopher Tin's album, *Calling All Dawns*.

I exited the parking lot blasting the song without understanding the words. All I knew was that the music, the voices raised on high, held me up. They imbued my limp arms with strength to drive, cleared my eyes of tears to peer into the yawning black of night, gave me the wherewithal to look beyond the headlights and find my way home. I later learned the lyrics were the Lord's Prayer in Swahili.

— CHAPTER TWENTY-NINE —
TRY TO ENJOY THE EXPERIENCE

The next day, I called ahead so the nurses could lift Michael from the hospital bed into a wheelchair. Upright would be better for him and the boys to greet each other. The kids and I conspired to bring Polly by tucking her into an ample handbag. Its woven straw and worn leather handles were redolent of France—picked up used from a flea market where we had visited Marie Christine's brother-in-law. As the elevator rose, Polly's nose poked up, sniffing over the edge of the basket. The kids shushed her and covered her up with a blanket.

As we arrived, nurses wheeled Michael into a private family visiting room. He had rallied and sat erect in the wheelchair, one arm attached to an IV bottle on a pole. As Polly curled up on his lap, it all seemed so normal, the five of us together, despite the medical paraphernalia. Michael asked after the kids' day at school. We made small talk. The usual kind. The kids knew the drill of hospice from their grandparents. They were tender with Michael, aware yet accepting of the situation. No momentous pronouncements. Just together, hugging. Sitting. Standing. Talking. Tucking a blanket.

Within days, an ambulance moved Michael to a rehab facility to receive palliative care. I chose a place close to home so it would be easy to spend plenty of time there. His decline seemed rapid. He could move little on his own. Well over six feet of him had to be turned in the bed every few hours to prevent bedsores. The round-the-clock care he needed was more than the boys and I could provide at home. Hospice could last six months or more. When I told my brother the news, he asked, "What if he improves?"

"Hospice isn't going to hit him over the head with a frying pan to keep him there!" I said. "If he gets better, he leaves hospice. But the prognosis is not in that direction."

I could not waste what could be, what were likely to be, what were in fact his final hours.

What was sinking fast was his mind. His brilliant, beautiful mind went walkabout much more often. I knew that it was important to connect with everyone who would want to say goodbye.

Michael was a public figure to many people and beloved by others. Moreover, for his soul to feel at peace to take leave, he needed to say his own goodbyes. I began a blog and launched a quest to invite those who loved him to speak with him. How much better to say goodbye, rather than to eulogize after he was gone. I wanted to share the precious gift of time that remained. And connecting with people gave me something to do besides watch helplessly as Michael prepared for his ultimate spiritual journey.

Emails and phone calls came in, and people visited. Mostly locals, a few from out of town, some childhood friends. I prioritized Michael's emotional well-being, tried to protect him, to keep him comfortable and spiritually at ease. Once I let a therapist in to visit him. Michael scolded me for having done so. It was a waste of his internal preparation time. He needed space to process his own life. Gifts of live plants and flowers arrived, greening up the room. Out the window was a bird feeder. I filled it with seed. I set a blue bowl with pebbles, water, and some Paperwhite Narcissus bulbs on the windowsill to remind me that from death we resurrect in spirit. Out of the bulbs, little green shoots slowly began to appear.

I saw this painful interlude in our marriage and Michael's suffering as stemming from a cause greater than the ravages of a disease on a man's body. It was, rather, providential. Although he was the grandson of missionaries, Michael had been a devout Darwinist; he was not seeking spiritual adventures. Yet, one week before Father and Mother Moon blessed us in RFK stadium on November 29, 1997, he had had a dream of Father. And one week before entering hospice, he had had another dream of Father, though he had been unable to articulate its details.

I felt Michael was shouldering a burden for all of us with the way he accepted and braved his Parkinsonism. Others in his position would express anger, resentment, and bitterness at their lot in life. But he never did. People loved that about him. He remained positive, gracious, and with his sense of humor intact. He never cursed God for his disease.

Michael was from Connecticut, born in Hartford. As such, I always felt we had a responsibility for Father's wrongful imprisonment in Danbury. Father's cell number in prison was 13. When Michael went to Belleview Haven in 2004, his room number was 13. It was at Belleview Haven that the drugs triggered Parkinsonism. Furthermore, his room number at the hospital, when the doctors told us Michael was not going home but to hospice, was also 13. To an outsider, these things might seem trivial. But from the inside, every gesture, each molecule of air that surrounded us, seemed weighted, momentous, and significant, not random.

Searching for meaning, I imitated Father's application of the Divine Principle in his life choices. I wanted to put our lives into a similar historical context. In terms of the Unificationist theology, what counted were the offerings we made to God. Topping that list was the blessing offering of our marriage to God. Michael and I had been blessed on November 29, 1997, fourteen years prior. Going back in time, I had been celibate for the past eight years due to Michael's meds and his physical condition. My time with Vincent had been its own unique course. Before that, I had been blessed with Boris from 1982 to 1989. Overall, I had completed my twenty-one-year blessing course—much of it celibate. Michael and I had worked together in France, our tribe being Europe 1, and we had blessed my spiritual father, Paul, who would die ten days before Michael.

When we met, Michael had served as a foster father to Ivan, whose father had been a dissident Russian artist. In the former Soviet Union, this man had been forced to take pharmaceuticals to destroy him as "treatment" for being an enemy of the state. Michael's mental demise originated with pharmaceuticals in a US institution most people would consider prestigious. As his life ebbed, I searched for cause and effect, how to stop it, how to accept it, how to understand what was emotionally incomprehensible.

I believed that our union served not just each other, our children and community, but that we lived for a greater purpose, that we served America herself. And I still looked to Father Moon's example, how he dealt with adversity in order to cope with what was unbearable to me. I craved some sense of order, of purpose, of higher meaning.

The good that America embraced included the ideals of multiculturalism, religious plurality, and freedom. The mortal enemies of these ideals reside in corporate greed, religious intolerance, and unethical behavior. Father's imprisonment in Danbury proved that unethical bigotry still reigned. Yet Father's reaction was to found a university in Bridgeport, Connecticut. He did this from prison. His reaction to hate was love—in this case, loving unconditionally the very state that had imprisoned him. Father remained steadfast in his objectives to serve God. I felt that all these afflictions of America against Father were being borne in Michael's disease.

Even as monks chanting can benefit and bless people on the other side of the world, or perhaps even future generations, I felt that somehow the afflictions Michael bore without resentment were a foundation for God to reclaim America— a land of high ideals and abysmal ethical distortions, from slavery to the KKK and hate crimes—a place where heaven and hell resided side by side.

The conscious sense of offering had been our life for over seven years. Heaven and hell side by side? You betcha. Michael loved to read; he became legally blind. He loved to hike, canoe, and birdwatch; his mobility was removed. He loved intellectual discourse and a fine turn of phrase; his intellect disconnected. He loved food and had been a gourmet cook; he got to the point where lifting food from the plate to his mouth took supreme effort—ultimately losing the ability to swallow. Instead of a vehicle of joy, his body closed down into a living tomb.

The marriage blessing Michael and I received from Mother and Father Moon united us in ways I imagined we did not understand. Our own very personal miracle had been when God had blessed us with Jacob even though Michael had been told he had such a low sperm count that it would be impossible for him to father a child. Supporting interfaith endeavors together—marches, lectures, roundtables, home meetings—Michael and I had worked to build a world of peace.

He loved the down-home earthiness of our Unificationist friends and had actively participated in key public events and family outreach before becoming ill. We had fought his demons of depression together and as a family. We were so entwined with each other's lives; I could not imagine being disengaged from his energy, insight, and love. I had to find a higher purpose in everything that happened. I needed meaning and logic to bolster me to face the sorrow of his dying.

While Michael was ailing, he continued to inspire others. A then homeless man—named, coincidentally, Mike—had befriended him at the senior center. He wrote a piece on Michael for *Talking Sidewalks*, a journal the men's homeless shelter published. Michael's steady striving, his commitment to doing his best despite his illness, had inspired this man with gratitude for his life and opportunities. Mike ultimately found work and a home. Years later, he told me how Michael had inspired him as someone who had kept a positive attitude despite losing even more than he had lost in his challenging life.

After Michael moved from the hospital to the rehab facility, visiting him became easier. Visiting hours were relaxed and Polly was welcome—it felt less clinical than the hospital and more family friendly. Few people were in hospice there. Some were long-term patients; others came for therapy only and would soon leave to resume their lives.

Michael's room was private and the boys could visit on their own. One afternoon they gaily rode Michael's old Miami Sun tricycle and another bike a couple of miles to the Harris Teeter grocery for food with Polly in Michael's basket. Then, they biked up to the rehab center for a visit—a miniature parade. Jacob took some days off from school to sit and read at Michael's side. He cancelled his scheduled second marathon run, although he had been training for it. I could not spare the travel time away from Michael to drive him to Charlotte for the race.

I tried to get to know all the nurses on duty. They provided hands-on care and could report to me how Michael was really doing when I went home to rest. When they assigned him a liquid diet, the nurses insisted he use a wretched gel thickener. Instead, I took him mango smoothies, which he loved. One afternoon, as I helped him navigate from the wheelchair to the toilet and back, his hand took a viselike grip on a metal hold bar. Pausing, he forced words through his unresponsive jaw, ejecting each syllable with a little explosion of air: "I . . . know . . . I . . . mean . . . ev'ry . . . thing . . . to . . . you . . . and . . . you. . . mean . . . ev'ry . . . thing . . . to . . . me."

Soon thereafter, he settled into heavy somnolence punctuated by a rare word, coughs, and wheezes. Nights, I curled up next to him in bed, holding him; he snored and increasingly made a rattling sound in his throat. I was grateful for the prayers that surrounded us from friends near and far. I felt their lives intertwine with ours, their stories mingling with our stories, with Michael's life and his passing. I envisioned spiral swirlings of others on their life journeys, like the labyrinth, how they would continue their lives after Michael was gone. How the pause that they made to think of him was a beautiful, eternal thing, a shared point in the cosmos. And in that shared pause was love. As my seminary sister, Robin, texted me, "This may sound funny, but try to enjoy the experience." Vintage Robin.

Thanksgiving arrived. What would have been a rather somber event for the boys and me was brightened when our old friends from Hightstown, Keith and son Ian, arrived for a visit planned before hospice had ever been on the menu. Through all our moves up and down the East Coast, our families had remained close. They were as eager to see Michael as the rest of us. The kitchen grew lively with cheery talk and Ian's ebullient piano playing filled the house. I was still on vigil, though, and Michael was fading. The day Keith and Ian were to leave, they took a cab to the airport. I could not spare an hour away from Michael's bedside.

I talked, read, and sang to him, for his spirit could hear me even though his body could not respond. His eyes remained closed and he no longer spoke. His breathing became irregular. I snuggled alongside him and held his limp hand as his body shut down. A few days before, as I had exercised alone at the gym, Stan had appeared to me. I knew Michael's ancestors awaited him in the spiritual realm. That night, I told him, "Michael, I love you and you know the kids do too. But you are free to go. People are waiting for you in spirit world. We'll be okay."

I had to let him go. As for us being okay, it was not a complete lie. I hoped saying the words would make me believe it too. I knew he couldn't escape the tomb of his body as long as he worried about us.

Every few hours, I would stand up and pass my hands over him to check the aura over his body. Exhausted emotionally and physically, I captured little in the way of extrasensory information. Soon, physical evidence arrived, with coldness that settled first in his feet, and then crept up his calves. Several more hours in I said, "I need a smoothie myself to keep up with you! I'm going to Whole Foods and I'll be right back."

I wanted to remain upbeat and encouraging for Michael's sake. His spirit was taking the equivalent of an ocean cruise and I from shore was there to see him off and wish him safe passage. But of course, on another level, I felt at wits end. I called Sofia, a dear friend from Family Camp who was, like Robin, a nurse. She asked about symptoms. Clutching my cell phone, sitting in the Jeep, I was able to have a bit of a cry and a "buck up" from her to keep going. With Sofia's coaching, I could try to monitor Michael's fading as "progress" toward spiritual lift-off.

When I entered the Whole Foods to purchase a smoothie, people beamed at me. I felt engulfed in a glow of love. As I returned to the rehab facility, a magnificent sunset blazed across the sky. I took photos with my little flip-phone camera, saying aloud, "Michael would love this!"

I felt him with me looking at the sunset, unconfined by tubes or a bed that beeps if the occupant arises. My heart filled, exhilarated with joy. Glowing from this interlude, I walked down the corridor and turned into his room. Two nurses were standing at the foot of his bed. One of them approached me and said, "He's gone. Just now."

I said, "I know. He was outside with me looking at the sunset."

They left. I prayed then called the boys to come for a final goodbye. I phoned the cemetery, Fort Lincoln in D.C. A secretary said they would arrange for a local funeral parlor to come collect what would henceforth be referred to as "the body."

My big boys arrived. We hugged, held hands in a close circle, and prayed. I sent phone messages to those who had reached out to Michael in his final moments, attaching a photo of the sunset we shared. The boys went home. I waited for the funeral parlor to collect him but couldn't watch as they put him in the black bag and zipped it up. Standing around a corner in the hallway, I left after I saw them push the gurney out the front door from a distance.

Besides Robin, Sofia, and the Howells, I called my Unification brothers: a Unificationist pastor in Baltimore, Larry Moffitt, a longtime writing chum and international peace advocate in D.C., and two brothers from Family Camp who loved Michael. I confided in Teresa, a sister in D.C. who helped nurture those going through the grieving process. People rallied to support me as I planned the ascension ceremony, or *Seung Hwa*. I was grateful they were there. Father had taught us that death, from a spiritual perspective, was really a cause for celebration—that it was meant to be as joyful as a marriage because at that moment the soul returns to God. Of course, joy was a tough thing to recognize while missing the person whose soul had departed.

Nevertheless, planning a *Seung Hwa* resembled planning a wedding in that there was a service, a setting, particular clothing, and a reception to host and orchestrate. Internally, I was praying and processing not only recent events but also our marriage, the kids, and my life course. Michael's departure required a huge recalibration of my every waking moment.

A Japanese friend from Family Camp offered to drive us up to D.C. in our Jeep from Chapel Hill. Robin and her family took in the boys and me to stay at their home while we prepared for the *Seung Hwa*. One evening, Robin and I stole a walk along the banks of the Severn River. She said, "True Love never hurts."

"Nothing hurts more," I replied.

Each night, on a conference call, I spoke with Bruce, Larry, Randy, and Teresa for hours to process Michael's passing. Together, we planned his *Seung Hwa* ceremony. For guests unacquainted with Father's teachings on *Seung Hwa*, I found relevant quotes for the bulletin to be distributed:

Sunghwa (Peaceful Ascension)

A Sunghwa Ceremony is actually comparable to a wedding, when men and women get married. It's not a sorrowful occasion at all. It's like an insect coming out of its cocoon, getting rid of a shackle, and becoming a new body and a new existence, a new entity. That's exactly the same kind of process.

—Sun Myung Moon, April 13, 2010

In our way of life and tradition, spirit world and physical world are one, and by our living up to that kind of idea, we bring the two worlds together into one. In the secular world, death signifies the end of the life. However in our world, death is like a rebirth or a new birth into another world. For this reason, we should not make those occasions gloomy or sad or feel discouraged.

If we here on earth become very mournful or gloomy, it is like pulling the person who is going up to the heavens down to the earth.

—Sun Myung Moon, January 7, 1984

Therefore we are always confident and know that as long as we are at home in the body, we are away from the Lord. We live by faith, not by sight. We are confident. I say, and would prefer to be away from the body and at home with the Lord. So we make it our goal to please him, whether we are at home in the body or away from it.
—II Corinthian 5:6–9

Often Father would compare our life on earth to life in the womb. Within the womb—the world of water—the fetus prepares to live in an unknown world—one of air—by growing lungs, fingers, and toes. So foreign is the world of air, the baby cries upon leaving the watery world. Yet, prepared from the womb, the baby can breathe and inhabit this world. Similarly, on earth we live in the world of air. Yet, during our lifetime in this earthly womb, we must prepare for the eternal life hereafter. In that world of spirit, we no longer breathe air but love. Just as a baby in the womb grows lungs, fingernails, and eyelashes preparing to live in a world unseen, so we must grow our hearts of love to live and breathe the air of love in the spiritual realm after physical death.

The Seung Hwa, then, celebrates the soul's journey into this realm of absolute love. And in keeping with that purpose, it was to be a joyful event. I'd felt Michael's spirit with me when he had transitioned; I knew he had rejoiced in that sunset with me. And I continued to feel him with me, his living spiritual presence.

Halfway in spirit world myself, I would say, "I'm not sad that he's dead, but joyful that he is alive."

For secular folks, that would seem to be an odd statement. But the disciples saw Jesus after he died. Spiritualists, too, can sense people on the "other side." Combined, my spiritual experiences, theology, and the loving support of friends made it possible for me to frame the Seung Hwa not as a dour funeral, but rather as a celebration of Michael's life. I wanted, as Father had taught us, to give Michael a joyful send-off for his new life. People all over the world were praying for him—hundreds of Swaminarayan (our Hindu friends), also our Baptist, Catholic, Presbyterian, Buddhist, Muslim, Sikh, Jewish, and Unificationist friends.

The day before the ceremony, four brothers came to the funeral parlor and gently lifted Michael into his Korean holy robes. They did this prayerfully, as was the Unificationist custom. Bruce Bonini from Family Camp prepared songs for the service and made a little songbook especially for us. He had included the song Michael and I had been singing when Jacob was born, "I've been Workin' on the Railroad."

The following day, we would have the service. Two anthropologist colleagues of Michael's would drive from Rutgers to attend; another dear family friend from Rutgers days, Lisa—who happened to be visiting D.C. from Beirut—would attend as well. Susan Howells would drive with Ian from New Jersey and other church friends would drive up from North Carolina. Our Hindu friends would send two emissaries from the local Swaminarayan temple in Washington, D.C., Michael's cousin Eugenia would fly in from Rhode Island, and my sister was to arrive early from Fairbanks, Alaska. She would help set up the Indian food for the reception afterwards at the home of our friends Kate and Cory. Kate was another seminary sister and our families had crossed paths regularly at Family Camp over the years.

The day arrived. The boys did not have clothes for the occasion, so Robin's husband took them shopping at Goodwill for suits to wear. People showed up to help fill the gaps with whatever was needed—suits for the boys had not crossed my mind. About all I could handle was to provide Michael's holy robe for the viewing, plan the service, and deal with him being dead.

Larry arrived early to drive us to the chapel. I was in a daze but felt such affection as I watched him with Alex and Jacob as they lined up in front of Robin's bathroom mirror side by side. Uncle Larry showed them how to tie their neckties. It was a tender moment, something Michael would have passed on to his sons. Although in truth, he was not much for wearing ties. Still, I felt his presence watching with me—loving the boys with me.

At the chapel, somewhat corny music was playing—not what I had planned—but there was a slideshow of photos from Michael's life that was very touching. All this had been arranged through hours of effort by people I hardly knew, but who helped out of love for God. They honored Michael as their own precious brother. When it was time to close the casket, the pastor quietly asked me if I wanted to kiss Michael one last time. That was a shocker. I felt that Michael's body was a shell, that his spirit was standing outside the coffin with me, so why would I kiss a corpse? Putting the morbidity of the well-meaning offer aside, I helped lower the casket lid, patted the top of it, bowed, and sat down with the boys beside me.

Playing guitar, Bruce led with some songs from Family Camp, which made sitting in the funeral chapel a little less strange. Larry emceed, inviting family and friends to the podium to share their memories of Michael. When my turn came, I glanced down at my pages of typed notes, then up at the audience. I decided to wing it instead. "When I look out and see all these precious faces here today," I started, "I see Michael living on in each of you."

And I meant it. One of the Swaminaryans gave a beautiful testimony from their faith tradition, and the other presented me with a plaque.

Michael had died on November 26 and his Seung Hwa was December 5, 2011—a bitterly cold, overcast day in Washington. But the sun came out as we left the chapel for the Won Jun (burial) ceremony at the graveside. We sang an upbeat hymn, "I Want to Sing Halleluja Christ Is Here," as the pallbearers carried the casket. Jacob led the procession, carrying a photo of Michael. Bruce played the guitar. As we stood by the open gravesite, more people shared tender testimonies of their love for Michael. One of the Swaminarayan offered a singsong prayer in Gujarati. Larry spoke with insight that included, I thought, comforting words for the boys—they had been so brave and caring with Michael over the years. As the casket lowered into the earth, a pair of Japanese sisters handed out long-stem roses to each person. Single file, we circled the lowered casket; some knelt or let their roses fall down upon the top of the casket.

A mound of loose, unfrozen soil and a shovel had been prepared. The pastor offered the shovel to me, but I scooped up the cold dirt with both hands, held it tight, then released it with a thud on the lowered the casket, saying "Goodbye, my Love," so only Michael could hear.

The boys were next. Alex grabbed the shovel with vigor and hoisted a large shovelful of dirt into the hole. He later said he wished he could have stayed to bury Michael singlehandedly. Jacob took the shovel and added his load into the hole with careful precision. He remained serious and reflective. One by one, the others picked up the shovel and followed suit.

We reconvened in a circle and held hands for a final send-off prayer. Greg led three cheers of Mansei, for Michael's life, for his ascension, and to bless our family. I stood between Jacob and Alex. On my left, Jacob squeezed my hand. He did not want to raise his arms for Mansei, which I understood. So for each cheer, I had one arm up and one down. A flock of geese flew overhead. After some chatting at the gravesite, all those gathered headed to Karen's for the Indian food my sister had arranged. The anthropologists from Rutgers had brought a bottle of Spanish red that was nectar from the gods.

My awareness of each moment and interaction was keen; it seemed that data flooded my system not only from my eyes and ears, but from the hair on my arms and head, as if they were antennae. Exhaustion was a welcome relief.

The next day, the boys and I drove back to North Carolina. It was my first solo drive from D.C. without Michael by my side. I felt raw, weak, and unsteady, even with the boys. A bridge rose on the horizon: we were headed right for it. I braced for the inevitable panic. Yet as we approached the base of it, I felt Michael carrying us up into the clouds with him, freed from his body of death, his living prison. He was so happy, I laughed as we reached the apex.

We took a rest break in Virginia by a shop with used items for sale. In a far corner was a picture of Jesus standing on clouds embracing a man whose back faced toward the viewer. The man looked just like Michael, right down to the wisp of hair at the nape of his neck, the little ducktail that Jacob had too. The shop owners insisted on giving us the picture.

I felt grateful for the true love I'd experienced with Michael. Of course, I lamented his physical departure. But the Seung Hwa service recognized Michael's spirit as part of our ongoing lives. This reality reassured me and made me feel a little less crazy for having so many spiritual experiences with him. For well over a year after he died, I would sign his name along with the rest of us on letters, unable not to include him.

His physical disability was temporal; his love transcended time. He loved the world's peoples and cultures as well as its natural wonders—loved trekking through the woods with kids, paddling a canoe, peering into treetops in search of warblers. After he died, I felt his presence all around me as I pondered some of his final statements to me from his deathbed: from "I've always loved you;" to "I'm sorry you have to go through this;" to classic Michael when he noticed me talking to a visitor, "I'm dying here and you're upstaging me!"

I was glad for him, glad that he was free. I felt connected with him on the other side more than I felt a part of this world with him gone.

— CHAPTER THIRTY —
A PROMISE IS A PROMISE

Returning to earth, I grappled with countless appointments and phone calls regarding the likes of death certificates, social security paperwork, and insurance. One recording announced, "Push 5 to report the death of a loved one," followed by a second recorded message, "We're sorry for your loss. For Alternative Benefits Program, press 3. For Cobra, press 2."

Frank, my insurance representative added, "For more sincere condolences, press 7."

There's nothing quite like resuming life after your spouse dies. The increasingly complex caregiving at the end of Michael's life had connected me more with him than ever. The least thump in the night sent me scurrying to his bedside. I was used to living in his universe, with brief forays into a world where people chose how to use their time as though it belonged to them.

Reentering the non-dying world was a journey. During the first phase of my bereavement, I could have imagined throwing myself on the funeral pyre. Despite my beliefs and worldly experiences, I felt like my life was over and had no meaning. Next, I wanted to swim around in the ether of the unseen world looking for my disembodied partner. That was due to my understanding of the Principle and my own spiritual experiences. Then, there was functioning with the lack of him apparent everywhere I went. His empty shoes, his vacant chair at the dinner table, the stop sign where he used to wait for the bus—abandoned.

Hoot Owl Lane had been our sanctuary, the place where I imagined our children would bring grandkids home to visit. Without Michael, it felt like an empty tomb. I longed to sell the place: every square inch reminded me of his absence. Moreover, as mom and wife, I felt my duty was to honor his memory and comfort everyone else missing him—our kids, the dog, extended family, his colleagues and friends, old and new. This kept me in a public role, representing him when instead I needed to retreat and recover.

The boys resumed their routines of school and work after Michael died. They had friends in the community. Caregiving full-time, my community had narrowed to Michael's doctors, pharmacists, physical therapists, and other caregivers. Despite tutoring, taking classes, and writing from home, I'd lost my professional identity. For years, the goal of nearly every foray beyond the front door had been to serve the family or Michael's needs.

Prepared to catch him if he faltered, to help him dress, to find or remember something—being "on call" had become my life. At home, the boys and I had learned to cooperate like a NASCAR pit crew to keep Michael up and functioning. Both of them were good sports when I needed to pass the baton on Michael tending to fetch groceries, walk the dog, or taxi the other sibling somewhere.

So, when old family friends and neighbors from Rutgers—Mike and Evelind—invited me to stay with them in Phrao, Thailand for a change of air after Michael's death, I trusted that Jacob (sixteen) and Alex (twenty-two) could manage at home without me for a spell. I could leave them with a full larder and a list of contacts. Besides our kindly neighbors, both boys had a strong network of friends with parents willing to help out if needed. Northern Thailand differed little from North Dakota in terms of communicating with the boys. Though I'd be out-of-state, we could use the internet and talk with Skype or by phone.

I relished having a project unrelated to disease, doctoring, and death. Both Mike and Evelind had taken early retirement—he from a professorship in political science at Rutgers, she from a high-powered business career in New York—to found an NGO, Warm Heart, in the agrarian valley near Chiang Mai. Honoring the local hill tribes' efforts to maintain their culture, educate their children, and improve village revenue, Mike and Evelind began by serving the kids there. They built dormitories and provided meals and tutoring for the children so they could live in the valley during the academic year to attend public school.

Life in the isolated hill tribes was hard on youngsters as their parents relied on subsistence farming. Few mountain schools went beyond fourth grade, the average education level of the parents. During monsoon season, their switchback roads washed away—floods and mud rendered them inaccessible. I would be visiting in the winter—the dry season. School would be in session so I could help tutor the kids in ESL. I was happy to postpone the discovery of other details until after I arrived. I planned to stay through Michael's birthday, February 8, my first without him.

Waiting for my plane at the RDU airport, I prayed at dawn as usual, taking in whatever was going on around me and talking to God about it. "Has my best already left me? You seem capable—are capable—of infinite creativity and sorrow; surely the horrors of this world must surpass the goodness you see. I hope that slowly, uniting with others, we can change that."

Watching sea creatures play across the airport television screen, I marveled at their intricate beauty, rippling life and radiating color as they gamboled in all directions yet moved together in the swell and rhythm of the vast murky waters. The spirit realm resembled the deep sea—mysterious yet present, animated with countless beings both beautiful and nefarious. I felt God's tears, too, were vast, that they surpassed oceans as He saw his children brutally mutilate each other not only physically but in spirit. I constantly spoke with God, and now I included Michael in that conversation.

Despite my individual prayers, I thought Michael's *Seung Hwa* would conclude our church activities. Though I'd led my family to bless my spiritual father following church rituals, I felt reluctant to engage with the movement. Not only had it grown large, impersonal, and doctrinaire, it was imploding from within as Father's leadership waned. The original heart of love that had first attracted me was lost.

Father Moon was elderly, over ninety-two years old. His poor body had been beaten, bloodied, and every bone broken through multiple torturous prison sentences dating back to the Japanese occupation of Korea and his later internment in a North Korean concentration camp during the Korean War. Now, infighting among his children vying to lead the movement squandered and misdirected energy and resources freely donated by members who had sacrificed their all. Father, having spoken for years of how he could die any time, had appointed Hyung Jin, one of his younger sons, to succeed him.

This followed the principle of restoration whereby the younger brother (Abel, Perez, Jacob, Jesus) would lead rather than the elder brother (Cain, Zerah, Esau, John the Baptist). The Moon's elder son, Hyun Jin, whose Romanized Korean name was nearly identical to his younger brother's, had taken umbrage at this turn of events. Followers who had dedicated their lives and their earnings to the movement for years were confused by this brouhaha from the inner sanctum. I was not involved with church politics. My own family's needs had claimed all my devotion and effort. My rapport was with God and the Principle as a form of holy writ.

Nevertheless, I did have a dream of Father not long before Michael died. Michael had dreamt of him the same week—just before he entered hospice. While he had forgotten the details of his dream, I remembered mine.

I was walking down a long corridor ablaze with white light. It was pristine. In my dream, I noticed how the light reflected off all the surfaces, like the hall of mirrors at Versailles, brilliant refractions illuminated the passage as I walked. As

I kept walking, gradually, I became aware that it was not an ordinary hallway, but a long passageway on a boat.

The vessel was huge—a great ark, solid and sure, and it was bathed in this white light. I emerged from the passageway onto a deck as big as a football field. At the prow on the horizon, I could clearly see two figures with their backs to me: Father, seated and holding the end of a fishing rod, his line in the water. Next to him, Hyung Jin in a hoodie and jeans, sitting on Father's left, looking up at his dad solicitously.

In the dream world, I was immediately at their side without having to walk the length of the deck. I had a pressing question for Father about ministers. In the dream, I was instantly aware of multiple issues. For one, there was no one else on the boat but us three. This seemed wrong for the ark was solid and clearly built to hold many.

Hyung Jin gazed into Father's face with filial love, a good son. However, he was missing the point, which was that Father was looking to the horizon. Hyung Jin was looking at Father instead of looking at the horizon with Father. Because it was a dream, I could see the front of Father's face as well as Hyung Jin's, even though I stood behind them. Hyung Jin's expression was full of love and concern, but he ignored the broader picture.

Father was focused, preoccupied. His scrutiny extended into the unseen realm, beyond the limit where the sky met the sea as he assessed and aligned the spiritual realm. He was preparing, anticipating. He was concerned with decades and generations hence. Hyung Jin was absorbed in the present moment and concerned about his father's well-being. Father was thinking only of God's Providence and what would have to be achieved in order to realize it. My question was, "If ministers were really serving God, how could they ever retire?"

A loud voice boomed from behind me, a voice I knew was the voice of God. He said, "Ask the son!"

I woke up.

I cite this dream as part of my spiritual journey. It reflected my desire to attend God with Father. I still felt spiritually bound to him then, yet the movement had long since abandoned the original heart for which I had joined. Looking with Father to the horizon, I wanted to sail toward world peace, even as my husband was dying. Through prayer, I sought to connect our family with our bigger providential role—one that transcended petty church politics. And by no means would I cite this dream now as an endorsement of any one of those in the current Moon dynasty. History has marched on.

Michael entered hospice the week after my dream—so the dream informed my heart but not my actions. I had no desire to engage with the movement. My hands were full at home. Meanwhile, disagreements between the Moon children produced an organizational meltdown. The implosion was caused not only due to infighting between various sons, but also due to the personal situation of one of the daughters. Spurred by her husband's drug use and infidelity, her marriage had fallen apart while she was the national leader of the US church. Since marriage and fidelity were theological cornerstones, her qualifications for leadership unraveled when it was revealed she was carrying the love child of another man who would later become her new husband. I felt confident that God and Father would have a plan no matter what other intermediaries, leaders or members of Father's own family would say. While most people in the movement relied upon the church leaders for pastoral guidance and/or employment, I did not. My faith was divorced from the organization's shenanigans.

The Principle, God, and a sense of shared mission with Father motivated me to maintain my faith practices regardless of how the church appeared to digress from its founding principles. Having been a relative outsider for years, organizational hijinks did not interest me—aligning myself to serve my family with True Love did. Was I living with True Love in my community? Was I responding to God's calling for me and my family? The church organization had lost relevance for me, though in the past it had served as a vehicle for restoration. The political dysfunction coupled with an impenetrable and rigorous hierarchy surpassed my capacity to help set things aright. Though I kept up with select friends involved with the movement, I no longer subscribed to the faith traditions the organization endorsed and mandated. However, I still felt the spirit of God.

At Warm Heart, Mike and Evelind gathered with volunteers and staff each morning at their outdoor kitchen table on a patio beneath a bamboo roof. From this spot, they not only discussed major decisions that would affect the community, but celebrated staff birthdays, and occasionally put a Band-Aid on a kid's knee. Loving all the children on the Warm Heart campus as their very own, they lived a public life day and night. Staff employees were treated like family and paid well above Thai standards. In so doing, Mike and Evelind demonstrated Father's motto of "Live for the sake of others" by loving with a parental heart. Though they had never to my knowledge studied the Divine Principle, they lived it.

They invited me to stay in their home on the Warm Heart campus nestled between mango groves and fields with floppy-eared holy cows (donated to Warm Heart, they had the same sacred status as any you might encounter in India). I volunteered to edit newsletters and the website, tutor students with English, and help paint a senior center. Warm Heart's staff included me in myriad activities, both in the valley and in the hills. Each day, I took at least forty minutes to pray, walking for miles along the red dirt paths between lychee orchards in the company of several native street dogs that Warm Heart had adopted.

At first, praying as I traipsed through the tropical paradise, tears splotched the red clay with each step. Jungle greens—banana leaves, teak, bamboo, and ferns—absorbed my outpouring as the dogs merrily yipped and raced each other, chasing rodents through the orchards before loping back to join me on the road. Oozing fruit and sap glistened under the sun like the snot and tears that ran down my face; birdsong covered my sobs. For the first time, I felt free to let go. All this yipping, singing, ruminating, riotous nature invited me to inhabit the planet and allow my body—tightly wound to be strong for everyone else—to release.

I'd been holding in my own emotions from the time I learned Michael was entering hospice. Exotic nattering of wild birds, fantastic tropical flowers, leggy roosters, and white, brown-eyed cows all spoke to me of the beauty of ongoing life on earth. Eventually, I only sobbed for twenty minutes, then ten, then just the first five minutes or so of my walk. Near the end of my stay, I had a breakthrough—a walk without sobbing in grief. My healing had begun.

Once back in the US, I invited Jacob to join me on a return trip to Warm Heart again that summer. Alex was launching his own independent life working. I felt Jacob could benefit from by volunteering in the supportive community that the staff, volunteers, and children shared. I also hoped that Mike and Evelind—having known his dad for many years—could share their memories of Michael with Jacob. Given his age, the bulk of his memories of his father were from the years when he'd been sick. Alex, being older, had known Michael when he was well. I wanted Jacob to have a sense of his dad from people who were friends, not just nurses and doctors.

I also wanted to share first-hand my love of Asian culture and communal living with Jacob. Alex had been exposed to this lifestyle when he'd homeschooled with BTA in Berkeley. Jacob hadn't had that experience. At Warm Heart, he could see how our family traditions, like not wearing shoes in the house, were common in other cultures. And since neither of us had been to Korea before, I arranged for a whirlwind pilgrimage there to visit some key places Father Moon had lived.

I hoped our itinerary would offer Jacob some first-hand cultural insight and experience so he could understand why we prayed so often while he was growing up. Whether or not he chose to accept the idea of an invisible God, I wanted to show Jacob what Father had lived through and share not only some of the deep history of Father's life but of the Korean people. So I arranged for us to fly via Atlanta to Seoul before traveling on to Chiang Mai.

My own children, in many ways, could not understand Father's life course, or my life story, without understanding our shared desire to restore some of the historical wrongs of humankind. Perhaps at the outset this sounds like a project of sheer hubris. Yet, by retracing some key moments in Father's life, I hoped that Jacob could open his heart to understand more of Father's relationship with God and what he had endured to fulfill his calling. By understanding Father's life a little better, I hoped that by extension Jacob would be able to understand my choices a little better too, how as a parent I'd made difficult decisions—not to maximize my own pleasure, but out of a hope that we, as a family loving each other and those around us unconditionally, could help make the path a little easier for others.

Father's first imprisonment had been for patriotic activities under the Japanese occupation of Korea before World War II. When the war ended, the Japanese withdrew and Korea was divided into North and South. Father defied government-enforced atheism by preaching in North Korea. Kim Il Sung, who started the Korean War by attacking South Korea, imprisoned Father in a labor camp. As the Korean War raged, a US contingent from MacArthur's landing liberated Father just before the scheduled execution of everyone in his cellblock.

Time and again, Father heeded his internal calling from God and resisted external political pressures at great risk to his life. When the political powers of the world closed in to shackle and torture him into silence, Father persevered. His internal focus, even toward those who beat him, was always to love the person with God's love.

He felt responsible for their spiritual journey and looked at his own life from an eternal point of view even when it was not convenient. He explained to us in a speech once why he could not allow himself to harbor resentment or condemn those who tortured him. If he resented them, that energy would create a barrier between his torturers and God. He did not want to inhibit their path to divine grace and the love of their divine parent. He looked beyond his own suffering to see the eternal suffering of others. In so doing, he shouldered the burdens of the weak, but he also restored the misdirection of the mighty.

And yet, much as I loved Father and admired his zeal for realizing God's love on earth, I was never very eager to go to Korea. Devout Unificationists prized going to Cheongpyeong (the location of a church retreat center in the mountains outside Seoul) the way a devout Muslim views the *hajj,* or pilgrimage to Mecca. I secretly had confided in God that Korea did not beckon to me. "France, sure!" I said. The land of Cézanne and ratatouille resonated from deep within my soul as home.

"Thailand? Why not?" I thought. I looked forward to visiting our friends and helping with the substantive work of Warm Heart.

But the idea of a pilgrimage to Korea had never appealed to me. I was particularly leery of Cheongpyeong, actually. Every church member I talked to who went there got sick. From what I gathered, the most significant characteristic of a visit to Cheongpyeong was the infamous "Cheongpyeong Cough" everyone seemed to return home with and hold on to as a souvenir for months afterwards.

The church retreat dormitories were crowded and frequently cold. The readily available food was not very healthy or nourishing. Grueling schedules in tight quarters made it difficult to sleep and easy to get run down. Typical activities at Cheongpyeong included monotonous chanting, repeated bowing, and *ansoo,* or self-tapping. These practices were initiated by a female Korean shaman related to Mother Moon—not practices that Father taught us or that the Divine Principle endorsed.

At best, Cheongpyeong seemed like a colossal waste of time to me. I'd discussed this with God in private over a decade before Michael's death, when he was robust. Yet, despite Korea's lack of appeal for me, I felt I owed it to Father to try to understand the place of his birth. After all, he had spent plenty of time in my crazy nation. So, in secret, I gave God my word that should Michael ever die, I would go to Korea. In fact, at the time, I was so sure that Michael would outlive me—I figured I'd never have to go to Korea. My plan had backfired.

So, when Michael died, and the offer to go to Thailand arose, I could hear God clearing his throat in His own subtle way, reminding me of my promise. Visiting Thailand became a catalyst for me to plan the trip to Korea I'd been reluctant to take for over three decades. Only God knew how deeply I really did not want to go to Korea.

Years of prayer conditions had nonetheless prepared me for this moment. A prayer condition was a devotional offering that required a central figure, an offering, and a time period. A central figure is a person incarnate in the physical world who reaches forth to invite divine presence, guidance, healing, and blessing upon the broader community. An offering is the object given out of devotion.

In a Buddhist temple, for instance, the offering might be fruit or flowers. In church, money might be offered. Religious people throughout history have made offerings through sacrifices such as fasting, or taking vows of poverty, chastity, and obedience. An offering can also be the devotion of reading a holy text. The heart behind the offering determines its value—prideful display of duty does not impress the unseen world, rather sincere humility and love moves God's heart.

The time period can vary, but requires a beginning, a middle, and an end. The duration of the prayer itself must be fixed—whether it is three minutes, twelve minutes, forty minutes, or two hours. The amount of time is not as significant as the focus and absolute follow-through. To fulfil your condition is to accomplish something in communion with the divine—it is a spiritual victory.

These prayers had kept me going for years. As one forty-day condition ended, I would prepare the next one. Thus, I maintained an internal focus to guide my life. Whatever happened externally, somehow, if I fulfilled my prayer condition (reading some DP or Father's words, twenty-one minutes of prayer, writing), it seemed like the day was not wasted. In some small way, I would have followed through on an internal directive and brought some positive energy into the world.

After Michael ascended, my prayers had the added dimension of seeking to connect with his living presence from the spiritual world. It had been six months since he died. I had completed one 120-day prayer condition and had resumed my 40-day prayer conditions. I thought of the 40-day conditions in groups of three. I would be two-thirds of the way through my second 120-day condition and starting a new 40-day condition as the plane landed in Seoul.

Thus, Jacob and I had two different agendas as we boarded the plane for Thailand via Korea. Though we were both en route to volunteer, Jacob was first having a cultural excursion while I was keeping my promise to God. I loved Warm Heart: the people, the culture, the work. It was the tasty worm on the hook to entice me to Korea. The plane food was surprisingly tasty too, a dinner of *bulgogi*—Korean barbecue—and a breakfast of *bibimbap*, or rice topped with vegetables, meat, egg, and chili pepper paste. I was one contented fish. As we landed, I held to the window a laminated photo of Michael I traveled with and I whispered to him, "Here we are in Korea, Michael!"

— CHAPTER THIRTY-ONE —
REBUILDING A SOUL WITH
A LITTLE KIMCHEE

As soon as we navigated from the airport bus stop to our hotel in Seoul, I called an English brother I knew living there, Julian. He was the editor of a monthly church publication, *Today's World*. We'd met in New Jersey in August 1999 when both of our families lived there and I'd returned from the Alaska leader's meeting. Julian was writing an article on the exclusive event and I had valuable photos. I wouldn't have had the gumption to take most of the snapshots if it hadn't been for Rev. Hong, then the State Leader of New Jersey.

Regular and eager paparazzi surrounded Mother and Father at formal events. I didn't want to join the shutter bugs, but Rev. Hong had taken me to the side and asked me, specifically, to take as many photos as possible. Besides feeling shy, I cringed at objectifying True Parents by taking their photo—it seemed presumptuous. I wanted to live in the moment, not record it. Yet, an awareness persisted that we were making history; we felt ourselves to be like the disciples in the early days with Jesus. Honoring Rev. Hong's request, I made a determination to take photos at every opportunity, despite my natural resistance. It was because I'd united with Rev. Hong and transcended my personal comfort zone, that I'd met Julian. Challenging my personal concepts had put me into a broader arena, connecting me with an editor who then lived in New Jersey but worked on an international level.

Julian's wife was Italian and they'd relocated with their children to Seoul from Clifton, New Jersey during the intervening years. They'd raised their brood in the local Korean Unification Church community. Typical of many Unificationist kids, their multicultural upbringing was also multilingual, so they were fluent in both Korean and English. Julian, who was fluent in Korean, had helped me plan Jacob's and my itinerary via email.

It was a relief to hear Julian's familiar voice on the phone when I called from our hotel in Seoul. Despite having traveled in Europe, the Americas, Russia, Thailand, Israel and Palestine, Korea felt challenging to me. As a Westerner who knew only a few words of Korean, navigating through the sea of Hangul (Korean lettering) felt daunting. Among the Koreans I'd met thus far on the bus and in the hotel, good will was abundant, but access to rudimentary English was not.

Julian and I hadn't seen or spoken to each other in over a decade, yet we picked up as if we'd seen each other the day before—an experience that was a regular event given the peripatetic nature of folks in the movement. To find the bus to visit the Cheongpyeong church retreat, I needed to ask the right questions of people. Julian advised me. Hotel staff who knew a little English could help me find the bus depot. Once near the depot, I could ask various store clerks to help me to find the proper city bus into the countryside.

The next morning, Jacob and I breakfasted at the hotel buffet on pastries, eggs, sausage, and fruit I had never seen before in my life. Although I recognized the brilliant red dragon fruit from my first trip to Thailand, other fruits were utterly unknown. One, a rambutan, resembled a scarlet sea urchin, with an interior fruit similar to a lychee—the size of a large grape hiding a pit the size of a small almond. Another fruit, a mangosteen, was a tough purple-brown pod about the size of a mandarin orange. It had a green acorn-like top I had no idea how to open, so I found the cook and gestured my confusion. She kindly cracked the pod all the way round and pulled up the top to reveal the pearl-white fruit inside, arranged in citrus-like wedges. It was sweeter than pears and contained no pits. I felt the mangosteen personified Korean culture: sheer toughness outside, pure love inside. Like with the rambutan, the mangosteen seemed like a perfect balance of *yang* and *yin*, strong yet tender.

Jacob and I took the metro to the bus depot and travelled through downtown Seoul, past towering apartment colonies on the city's outskirts and on into the mountainous countryside. The Unification Church retreat center had a campus behind a hospital founded by Mother Moon. The retreat center could house thousands of people and it had a chapel, a café, a cafeteria, dormitories, and lecture halls. The extensive grounds included woodlands, meadows, and ponds with walking paths, rock gardens, and pine groves for meditation. Getting off the bus at the hospital, Jacob and I paused at the chapel to take in the view from the lower courtyard before climbing a mountain path. Ascending, we paused at prayer trees and a fishing pond with valley vistas. We seemed to have the place to ourselves but for a handful of volunteer gardeners—church brothers and sisters from various nations, including Thailand.

Among the gardeners was an American sister with whom I'd worked over a decade ago in Washington, D.C. at the *World and I* magazine. Anne and her daughter, both in wide-brimmed gardening hats, were pulling weeds from one of the rock gardens. It was a typical church moment, running into someone I knew who just happened to be on the other side of the world in the same remote location as me. We exchanged greetings.

"How do we walk to the palace?" I asked and pointed to the white domed building nestled in the mountainside. Named Cheon Jeong Peace Palace, it looked a decent hike from where we stood. The sky was clear blue. Sunny hillside meadows shimmered as flowers danced in the breeze, bobbing sprays of bright orange, red, and yellow. The distant hillsides were a deep Lincoln green. The white palace leapt from the lush pine background. It resembled the US Capitol building with its tall central dome. Father said he'd built the palace so God would have a substantial place on earth where representatives of all nations could gather for the sake of peace. Church members had fundraised and provided donations to build it.

At the time of its construction some years earlier, my democratic soul bristled at the elitist concept of a "palace." Yet, I could understand wanting to create something that endured through history. Father had a long view of history (think Egyptian pyramids, Stonehenge, the Panama Canal). But I was not keen on the concept of a "palace" compared to, say, a soup kitchen. Part of my distancing from the church stemmed from the contradiction between the monumental investments and the real needs of people that went unmet within and outside the movement.

The standard explanation of this contradiction in church theology was explained by the example of Mary Magdalene, who with her tears washed Jesus' feet, then dried them with her hair and anointed them with oil (Luke 7:37-38). It was none other than Judas Iscariot who protested, saying the money would have been better spent on the poor. I came to accept the idea that the palace could endure as a monument. Unlike more sectarian monuments, like Saint Peter's in Rome, the Dome of the Rock, or King David's Tomb in Jerusalem—each dedicated to one religion—I understood that the Peace Palace was dedicated to creating and enhancing interfaith peace. Like the US Capitol its architecture resembled, I thought it would serve as a public meetinghouse: available to all, a monument to humankind's potential for cooperation on a global level.

"You can only go into the palace by special invitation," Anne informed me.

"What? Are you kidding me? Church members paid for this," I said.

Unlike the Capitol Building, available to visit because it belonged to the citizens and was the place their representatives worked, the palace was apparently more like the White House. Although it "belonged" to the world, there was controlled access to the palace for the sake of security. I had to pray about what seemed to me elitism. I wanted to give time and space to the idea that perhaps there was a Confucian or Korean interpretation of protocol that I ignored. But my emotional reaction was disappointment and irritation. I was not going to be in Korea again, much less Cheongpyeong, anytime soon.

I let go of my frustration by taking in the beautiful grounds and asking God what He thought about this whole palace thing. Then, I called upon the timeless comfort of Aesop's fable *The Fox and the Grapes*. To reduce the cognitive dissonance of wanting to visit the palace but having my desire frustrated, I adapted my preferences and convinced myself that I didn't want to see the crummy old palace anyway.

Jacob and I hiked onward. He ventured off into the woods passing a bright orange Turk's cap lily, its leopard-spotted petals refracted backwards toward the pines. I thought how his ambling suited the way we'd related to the movement as a family. We appreciated the path and its garden outposts, but we explored God's creation ourselves, feeling at ease off the trail in the wider world. I was thankful not to be a part of any organized meeting as we rambled and contemplated in our own way, taking in the pine-slope vistas that overlooked the lake glistening below. These hillsides did not have the naked, jagged peaks of the Rockies or Sierra Madres, nor were they the rolling Appalachians or Blue Ridge Mountains. Their acute, angular shapes brought to life the oriental scroll paintings I used to sell door-to-door.

The view was distinctly Asian. According to church lore, however, the view of the slopes overlooking Cheongpyeong Lake recalled the Sea of Galilee. While Galilee's shores have a gentler topography and less vegetation, they were where Jesus spent some of his happier days delivering speeches such as the Sermon on the Mount, the Lord's Prayer, and the Golden Rule. It was in the city of Jerusalem that Jesus went the way of the cross. However, on the hillside, near the Sea of Galilee, he delivered messages of love and peace. The church retreat at Cheongpyeong Lake was built to recall the halcyon days of Jesus when he spoke of the promise of peace.

Nature's beauty provides its own meditative embrace with or without theology. I recalled walking on woodland trails at seminary in peaceful solitary prayer as well as with Father, brothers, and sisters. Hiking the Cheongpyeong trails in Korea with Jacob, trails where Father had walked, felt as if the two of us were walking with Father in spirit. But I didn't dare tell Jacob that. We ambled along and took in the views, the green, the flowers, and the sky. On a practical level, it was a garden excursion outside Seoul. It provided an opportunity to spend our first day overcoming jet lag.

The second day, we took a bus to the DMZ (Demilitarized Zone) between North and South Korea because the tour company had changed our itinerary. We civilians needed to be flexible about scheduling. Visits to the DMZ required coordination through those with military affiliations, like the USO (United Service Organization). We had to sign a waiver to acknowledge that the US State Department could no longer protect us before we boarded the bus for the North Korean border.

As we traveled, we heard lectures and saw documentaries on the history of conflict at the 38th parallel and stopped to visit landmarks and museums. The hostility became tangible as we hiked into an invasion tunnel built by North Korea. It was discovered in 1978, and subsequently blocked to prevent subterranean military attack. Back above ground, we passed rolled barbed wire fences beyond which lay active land mines. A chatty US soldier recounted North Korean–instigated deaths and breaches of the border as we went into the Joint Security Area (JSA). The seriousness of the North and South Korean standoff at the JSA was as evident as the unwavering countenance on each South Korean soldier's face as they stood facing north to stare down their perpetual enemy.

Growing up in the United States, it could be easy to take freedom for granted. While American society is far from perfect, the constitutional guarantees in the Bill of Rights exist to protect ordinary citizens in their pursuit of happiness. Freedom of speech and the press, freedom of religion and the right to assemble, and freedom to petition the government to redress grievances for fair treatment under the law—these are rights we Americans expect to be enforced to protect our own individual liberty. These freedoms were not accessible—never mind readily available—for the ordinary North Korean citizen.

Though Jacob and I only visited the border, the tour highlighted the history of the Korean War and subsequent battles in the region. Visiting the DMZ was a stark introduction to North Korea—a nation militarily antagonistic to liberties we assumed rudimentary in our daily life. This cultural contrast highlighted the danger and consequences Father endured to express his love for God by defying North Korean law and preaching there in the early days of the church. The ongoing threat of North Korean antagonism also explained both the rigor and ardor in the early days of the movement and perhaps the vehemence with which more fundamentalist Unificationists clung to narrow ideological interpretations.

The division between freedom and oppression at the DMZ reminded me of George C. Scott expressing Patton's stark observation to his soldiers, "When you put your hand into a bunch of goo that a moment before was your best friend's face, you'll know what to do."

The police state of a truly communist society does not "feel" like a theory. The Marxist-Leninist utopia of ample food, housing, and access to goods and services was not realized, but the lockdown on human rights certainly was. The death toll from famine and ongoing malnutrition in North Korea was legendary.

Yet the government continued to prioritize a strong military over civilian infrastructure.

The civil-rights-crushing hand of the North Korean government was evident in the institutionalization of labor camps such as the one where Father had been imprisoned during the Korean War.

Yet, Father's attitude about this was to forgive rather than curse Kim Il Sung, the leader responsible for his imprisonment. Decades later, he and Mother Moon would return as guests of Kim Il Sung, dining with him in December of 1991. Father's attitude was one of bringing God's forgiveness and love even to someone who had tried to kill him. And risking his own life yet again, he spoke frankly about God to Kim Il Sung and expressed the need for a more open society. To this end, Father Moon founded a car company, Panda Motors. Through trade, he proposed, the Hermit Kingdom of North Korea could open up to the wider world.

I was acquainted with Father's efforts to broaden perspectives within North Korea not only through his tearful prayers, but also through the cultural outreach of the Little Angels dance troupe and peace park activities, in addition to his economic outreach with Panda Motors. Our United Methodist pastor in New Brunswick, New Jersey, Rev. Dr. Sydney Sadio, had participated in a peace expedition to North Korea and returned highly enthusiastic about his experience in general and the Little Angels in particular.

The USO's schedule change of our DMZ visit was due to a conflict at the border. The change produced some interesting ramifications. Originally slated to visit the DMZ on our third day in Korea, a Wednesday, the rescheduling moved us up a day so we visited on a Tuesday instead. Had the switch not occurred, I would have missed an amazing opportunity.

Jacob and I returned to Seoul from the DMZ by nightfall on Tuesday. Exhausted from the somberness of the day and the long journey, we exited the bus and met Julian for a much-appreciated ice cream.

Over sundaes, Julian said, that the following day, Wednesday, was a high holy day, one known in the movement as the Day of All Things. To celebrate, there would be an offering table, prayers, food, and song to express gratitude for all of creation. The dates for holy days changed each year. They were based on the lunar, rather than the solar, calendar. Since I was not regularly involved with the church, I didn't track such things anymore.

Julian had coveted tickets to the palace celebration. Furthermore, Father and Mother Moon were to be there. Had the USO not changed our schedule, we would have been at the DMZ on Wednesday. Therefore, I would have missed this rare chance to see Mother and Father Moon in the Peace Palace.

Some might say the sequence of coincidences was just happenstance, but to me, it felt like a higher power at work. As Father would be speaking, the duration of the celebration was unknown. Father could speak sometimes for as little as ninety minutes; other times, he could continue for eighteen hours nonstop. This was a gift of the spirit to some, evidence of his dedication to God for others, and to those listening for long hours without pause, either a blessing or a curse. I suspected Jacob might place an interminable sermon in the latter category. Sensibly, he decided to opt out of the celebration. Instead he would noodle around Seoul, then hang out at the hotel until I returned.

Michael, the boys, and I had attended a fair number of church events over the years besides our annual trip to Family Camp. But meetings with Father were usually an ordeal that Michael and I spared the kids. Besides their unpredictable length, Father's sermons could be grueling as they took place at dawn and entailed long hours of sitting on the floor. Formal public speeches had firm schedules, chairs for guests, and usually a printed translation of the speech. However, in-house talks, like those at East Garden, were unpredictable. The translation was consecutive and Father was subject to divine inspiration.

At home, over the years, to deliver the essence of Father's words with less tribulation, I would share excerpts with the family using video clips or extracts from speeches translated into English from Korean. I received these translations through church connections soon after Father spoke – and Father spoke nonstop. He traveled worldwide speaking. The internet made it much easier to distribute his messages as soon as devoted sisters and brothers translated them from Korean into English, Japanese, and other languages. Receiving Father's words online was the next best thing—some would argue, a far better thing—to being there. Bathroom breaks, for instance, were a real bonus with the online version of a sermon that endured for hours from dawn through the mid-afternoon.

I used to hold mini-church services at home called *Hoon Dok Hae*, which meant "gathering for reading and learning." Our family's meetings of this ilk were somewhat sporadic, but the kids received a good taste of what Father's speeches were like. His talks often explained the providential significance of a current project, such as protein fish powder, or a bridge tunnel between Japan and Korea, or the launching of the Peace Cup for soccer. But he also elucidated deeper aspects and applications of the Divine Principle. The content of his talks varied somewhat depending upon the audience sitting before him. Regular topics included God's love, internal guidance on attitude to create harmony between sisters and brothers, and in-depth analysis of historical spiritual problems and the processes needed to resolve them.

I wanted Jacob to be able to understand True Love from Father, not be mad at him for rambling on and on. So, rather than bring Jacob to the palace with me to be bored silly, I preferred to offer him a small dose of Father's words if he was interested. Perhaps, had I raised him with strict Confucian filial piety, he would have considered it an honor to endure Father's speeches live. However, I was ready to make that offering on Jacob's behalf. Father and I had been through so much together, he could not bore me. That was the power of True Love. And since Jacob had not experienced what I had with Father, or with the Principle, or with God, I did not expect him to share my interest. Julian, Jacob, and I finished our sundaes and parted ways.

The next day, I slipped out of the hotel before dawn and waited on a major artery out of town for Julian to pick me up. It felt a little like the old fundraising days, waiting for a ride on an unfamiliar road in the dark. He arrived on schedule and we drove east into the hills as the sun rose behind them. "Now Pam, you have to understand that these are just general tickets. They are good for the back of the room. If you want to go with the hard-core folks nearer the stage, sitting on the floor, you can, but know that you may be asked to go to the rear of the room because that is what the tickets say. Okay?"

I understood; there was limited space; it would be unlikely that I'd see much from the far end of the room. But simply being there was historic enough, given Father's age. We arrived, parked, and walked across the Peace Palace courtyard of white stones that overlooked the winding road and gardens below. Upon entering, as I was not a member of the media like Julian, I had to check my camera. I received a number to retrieve it at the end of the visit. We passed through security and removed our shoes, Asian-style, before entering the lecture hall. Next, with loving efficiency, sisters placed a cardboard box about the size of a shoebox in each of our hands. It contained breakfast. A security brother pointed to me and indicated I should go straight toward the area where the "hard-core" people sat on the floor. Surprised, I bowed to say thank you and glanced at Julian. He whispered, "Go for it! I'll meet you down here afterward."

Julian disappeared into a sea of people as he left to oversee the filming and simultaneous translation from an upstairs booth. I found a patch of unoccupied floor and folded my legs to squeeze in. Once seated, my head bobbled as my eyes swept over the crowd, taking in the architecture. White columns held the ceiling aloft. The room contained an enormous breadth and depth, yet it seemed that there wasn't an inch of empty floor to accommodate another precious brother or sister's bottom. Everyone was dressed in various shades of white and had arranged themselves in remarkably orderly rows. Julian's wife had loaned me a white jacket, which just fit over my T-shirt; this allowed me to appear suitably dressed— at least from the waist up—despite my khaki trousers. Packing my traveling gear, I hadn't anticipated a need for High Holy Day togs.

The stage at the front of the room had a couple of padded, ornate chairs for Mother and Father Moon. In front of the stage stood tall, colorful pyramids of stacked fruits and sweets, as was the custom for celebration days. I scanned the room again, to check if I might recognize someone.

I seemed to be the lone Westerner in a sea of unfamiliar Korean and Japanese faces. I looked to the Korean sister on my right. Hoping she knew a little English, I asked, gesturing with my hand like a bird to my mouth, "When can we eat the food?" I didn't want to be rude if we were supposed to pray or listen to a discourse before eating. She gave a little shrug and asserted, "Now or later."

Appreciating her familial practicality, I smiled, nodded, said a little prayer, and tucked into a deliciously sweet rice cake from the box we'd been given. As I munched and casually gazed around the room, I enjoyed being in the moment and felt at ease, although still amazed that I was actually sitting in the palace. I watched a middle-aged Korean man approach, stepping adroitly between the rows of people in his stocking feet. He arrived at my row, squatted next to me, and asked in English, "Where are you from?"

I pondered his question for a moment. Maybe he wanted to kick me out. "Julian?" I answered hopefully. By associating myself with someone well known in the church and with a mission-related reason to be there, perhaps I could keep my spot on the floor.

Then he asked, "Are you American?"

Was I? My brain struggled. I didn't feel American. I'd grown up in France; I was on my way to Thailand to live with people who were part Jewish and felt like family—so much so I'd toyed with moving there. I felt cozy in Thai Buddhist culture. On the other hand, when the church had assigned continents, I'd pulled tribe 10, Europe 1 out of a hat. Besides, I identified more with European than US culture. And to top it off, my spirit was feeling sort of Korean at the moment. Man, that rice cake was good!

Then my brain said, "Get real!" I traveled with a US passport and was born in a suburb of Chicago. As my Rolodex of citizenship options stopped spinning, I concluded that I was American. After what must have seemed to be a stupidly long pause, I admitted, "Yes, I am American."

I lowered my eyes and prepared for him to ask me to give up my prized hard-core seat and move to the rear of the room as Julian had forewarned. But then the older Korean brother said, "My wife is ill with a heart condition. She could not travel. Could you bow to True Parents with me representing America?"

My eyes filled with tears as I looked at him, stunned—both by his request and by a gush of overwhelming gratitude. I felt deeply honored to be entrusted with a responsibility of this magnitude and grateful to offer a bow to True Parents. It was a chance to say thank you.

I wanted to thank Father for pioneering the way of families, so we did not have to remain singleton monks and nuns of God. I wanted to say thank you, Father, for my family, for my husband, for the love and faith I'd received from our spiritual bond; thank you for the teachings I'd received, not only on an intellectual level, but in visions and dreams; thank you for the hope that had helped me endure with spiritual strength and love unbearable emotional anguish during my husband's long battle with disease. I wanted to say thank you to Father for his love of God; thank you for the vision and willpower he'd maintained to pursue his calling in the face of excruciating persecution, egregious betrayals out of ignorance or spiritual blindness, and above all for the suffering that I knew only Father really understood, what God had been through for millennia longing to reunite with His children in a world centered on true love.

The words "represent America" fluttered around my head. "Holy crap," my brain said, "I'm not worthy to represent America." Select couples from various nations would bow to represent their country to True Parents. To bow on behalf of a nation was to represent all its people. When I thought of great Americans, true patriots who had done so much more for my nation than I had, I felt profoundly unworthy. And I repented for the messy history of America, the injustice and persecution—not only of Father but also of all God's children, and the ignorance about love that prevented people from loving one another across racial and cultural divides. Yet America was so blessed as a nation. "Represent America" felt both grand and frightening.

I was a warm body in the right place at the right time, by a miracle of scheduling, a mix of shenanigans and serendipity. Less than twenty-four hours prior, I had no hope of approaching the exterior of the palace grounds. Now I found myself not only inside the palace, but called upon to bow before Father and Mother, representing America? I was not a hotshot church leader or VIP.

To this unknown Korean man I said, "Yes."

"Thank you," he said, before starting to go, as the ceremonies would soon start. "Excuse me," I ventured, "I don't know where to go!"

"Follow me."

I left everything: purse, program, radio for translation, partially eaten rice cake, and followed him, tiptoeing between row after row of sisters and brothers, my feet in thick white athletic socks that came up to my ankle. We went toward the right of the room, passing in front of the foremost of the VIPs, many of whom I knew and some of whom knew me. I did a half bow passing Dr. Yang—

broadminded, he truly loved the US, spoke English fluently and had a doctorate in theology from NYU. I saw faithful Dr. Pak and dear Rev. Hong in the audience. Archbishop Milingo, famous for marrying as a priest, was there in Catholic holy robes and, next to him, a Western brother, Joshua Carter whose sexy voice, pure heart, and expert guitar playing made him many a Unificationist sister's secret heartthrob.

The man said, "Sit here," and gestured to a patch of floor. As I folded my knees to sit, while trying to avoid putting my butt in somebody else's lap, I asked, "What is your name?"

"Douglas Joo. When it's our turn, you come up and *kyung bae* [bow] with me."

"Okay. Thank you," I said and squeezed into the front row spot he'd indicated.

Dignitaries sat behind me in chairs. All that separated me from the stage was a row of half a dozen Korean men in dark suits—security guards. From where I now sat, I could easily see the doorway where True Parents would enter the stage. In fact, I could see down the hall beyond the door. We sang some holy songs. I kept my eyes on the hallway and saw True Parents arrive. I later wrote about that moment in my journal:

I'm sorry but I hardly looked at Mother when True Parents approached. Mostly, I just sought out Father like any kid craving love. But I could see in the brief flicker through his eyes that his health is failing. He is seriously weakened and on the way to spirit world soon despite how his willpower drives through his heart to his very fingertips, coursing through his body from his mind, in a blast of determination. Mother must support him as he walks.

My eyes met Father's before True Parents entered the door, while they were still down the hallway. I could see that he was halfway into the spiritual realm, that his physical body was falling apart. Like the dream I'd had of him fishing where I'd met him on the boat, I knew not to distract Father from what he needed to do in that moment. It took all his strength to focus on the task at hand. Spiritually, I didn't want to take his energy from him—I wanted to support him. I could do that by looking away, not absorbing his strength. I knew he knew I was there because God knew I was there.

And God and Father had instant communication.

Father entered with Mother. They lit the holy candles on the offering table, bowed to the position of True Parents, and sat in the chairs on stage. The position of True Parents is God's ideal of True Man and True Woman. In a sense, no one is that ideal. Yet, we are all of us called to embody that ideal. Bowing to the position is to acknowledge God's yearning to see the embodiment of True Love manifested on earth. Mother and Father Moon represented that position to the best of their ability, but even they bowed to the position of True Parents. They bowed to God as the original Parent.

The children and grandchildren bowed to True Parents. Then the representative couples were called forward to bow in groups of three to four couples. I followed Mr. Joo to the front and bowed standing behind him. The fruit stacked in pyramids towered so high I could not even see Father and Mother seated behind it. Good thing I'd caught Father's eye back in the hallway, I thought to myself. As I offered my bow, I couldn't help but think of how many second-generation Unificationists would joke about "bowing to fruit" at holidays when we would symbolically bow to the position of True Parents. Trying not to smile too broadly, I fully embraced their perspective: at that holy moment, it appeared that I was indeed bowing to fruit.

When all the representative bows were completed, it was time to recite the Pledge, the eight-point prayer Father had established over the years and had revised on rare occasion when there was some substantial providential progress. Usually, Father stood up for Pledge, but since he was ailing, he said it sitting down. His eyes closed as he mouthed the words, words he clearly loved.

At home, I recited the Pledge in English with my family since we didn't understand Korean. Afterward, I'd run through the Korean version solo. For Unificationists, Korean—like Hebrew, Latin, Sanskrit, or Arabic—was considered a holy language, a unifying language we would share worldwide. At formal international gatherings (and by definition, all our gatherings were international), we typically recited the Pledge only in Korean. I didn't have all of it memorized, but I knew the beginning of each of the eight phrases, "Cheon il guk ju-in, u-ri ka-jeong-eun cham-sa-rang-eul joong-shim-ha-go" (Our family, the owner of *Cheon Il Guk*,[14] pledges), and the ending of each phrase, "hal-goh-sul-maeng-se-ha-na-i-da" (by centering on true love). So I started each of the eight pledge points confidently in time with everyone else, mumbled the part in between, and finished strong with "true love" at the end of each promise.

After Pledge, True Parents gave a benediction; we shouted three cheers of *Mansei*, and they distributed food from the offering table with kids coming up for candy. Dignitaries—some wearing the traditional formal dress of their nation—gave reports from around the world. In Nepal, for instance, they were broadcasting the Divine Principle on one of the major television stations. Two of the adult children, In Jin, a daughter who at the time led the US church, and Hyung Jin, the

---

[14] *Cheon Il Guk* is a term in Korean that means "Nation of Cosmic Peace and Unity." Here, "nation" is not a literal geographic area, but represents those aspiring to consciously create a world centered on relationships of True Love and True Service.

younger son Father had selected to follow in his footsteps as the overall church leader, sang "Amazing Grace." They also sang a bluesy piece together, looking at Hyung Jin's Blackberry for lyrics. Then Hyung Jin sang in Korean. An international choir performed, singing in multiple harmonies.

Father had a grandchild on his knee as he remained seated to speak. Since I didn't have my transistor radio for the simultaneous translation, I focused on his facial expressions and listened to his tone of voice. He made faces and noises at his grandson; Father seemed to babble with childlike enthusiasm. There were many smart people in that room; together, we'd all bowed in attendance, not from obedience to an abstract ideal, but out of love and loyalty to Father. The dignitaries who were there seemed encouraging, laughing, and embracing him, not as a world leader, but as their own father. This holy day was a family moment for all of us, even the political and religious leaders. They were there, like me, out of love for Father. It was not a grandstanding declaration day. I didn't believe anyone expected Father to come up with a new "direction" or make sweeping leadership decisions. I knew people had to be guiding Father as he was deteriorating, despite his strong spirit.

Reading her face, I felt In Jin was frustrated, perhaps understandably flustered by the feeling of constantly being in a fishbowl attending public engagements even as her father declined into senility, dementia, and incoherence. I understood that frustration, recalling how Michael had declined but could have irregular lucid moments when he could rally and sound like his old self. But having Father as the titular head of so vast a movement when he was in such a condition was a real stretch.

As people prepare to go to spirit world, they increasingly lose touch with the logic and priorities of this world. Father, with his heart of absolute love for God, his transparency, made me feel that his discourse could result in some "wise fool" moments. By the power of spirit, he could respond to exactly what needed to be heard. But this time, even though I didn't speak Korean, it was evident he was speaking gibberish at some points, baby talk, as he bounced his grandson on his knee.

When I had nodded to Dr. Yang, approaching the front to sit, an aura of patriotism surrounded and embraced me. I remembered how much he loved America. His love was ascendant; it was strong enough to carry a continent, move nations. This was Father's legacy. He'd brought forth this kind of heart in others. My journal notes from the day held these thoughts:

Father, beloved as he is, is preparing to leave this world and reunite with his beloved creator. Father is releasing his grip on this world and its consequences.

I looked to the next generation and could feel comfort in Hyung Jin and his wife, but also that they are so vulnerable and frail compared to Hyun Jin. And In Jin in the middle—loyal, yet needing to build reconciliation.

From the audience, as people stood and gave reports, I could feel Father's powerful spirit transmitting through those who spoke, Dr. Seuk among them. I knew him from CARP days and had seen him at the seminary but didn't expect him to know me. He was a black belt Tae Kwon Do master, besides holding a doctorate in economics. He'd served in Russia for years. In the past, I'd seen him as gaunt as any concentration camp victim. He often fasted. Today, he was quite thin, with chiseled cheekbones, but not completely emaciated. I recorded the following in my journal:

As I returned from bowing, I caught Dr. Seuk's eyes, which were completely soft with love for Father. This sacrificial, stoic man, a disciple who had fearlessly worked in the lion's den of the Soviet Union had succeeded by self-discipline. Yet, I saw a gentleness in his eyes, the tender love of Father that had united us all in that room. We had gathered out of love for Father, not because of position, rank or political connections. Just love. Only love. It did not matter if Father spoke gibberish. We were family. Father was moving to that place now, that place of spirit where his power and spirit can move into others, become incarnate within them, when he chooses.

When Father finished talking, about an hour and a half later, he and Mother left, as did the rest of us after collecting our phones and cameras from security. I managed to find Julian. Since he understood Korean, I was eager to ask him what Father had said. Julian said with a sigh, "There was no real content."

That meant nothing substantive would go out in terms of "Father's Words," as his sermons were nicknamed. A leader who was in the room might write up a report to sisters and brothers to read. But to catch the full nuance of the day, that old chestnut—"You had to be there"—now comes to mind. Those of us who were there, in terms of Unification lore, had the moral imperative of Matthew, Mark, Luke, or John to write down our experiences. Others might think us fools. But perhaps a hundred or ten thousand years from now, it would make a difference.

Unlike Jesus, whose life was cut short at thirty-three, Father kept talking and talking for decades. Many of his words have been recorded. But it is those who followed him in obscurity, aware of changes in spiritual evolution and of stasis in the human condition, who may bring forth insight for healing this world.

Father was clearly senile, but the leaders with this knowledge had failed to inform the rank-and-file members at the time. My heart went out to Father's family. And yet I felt the movement was doomed without Father's acuity combined with the depth and breadth of his heart. Mother simply didn't have his education, experience or personality. I didn't feel she was equipped to take over as head of the movement—not due to her gender, but due to her education and personality. Given the scope of the movement's projects, honoring Father and keeping him as the titular head of out of filial piety, duty, and honor, together with the unquestioning loyalty to leaders befitting Korean Confucianism, would not save the world. Father's vision went light-years beyond that, but the inner sanctum was wed to the old ways.

Julian had to stay at the palace to finish his media duties, but he found a ride for me back to the hotel in Seoul with a couple of Japanese brothers. I returned to find Jacob at the hotel, pleased with his excursions as a young man about town. Having learned to navigate the tram in Nice, he had enjoyed exploring and mastering Seoul's subway system.

The next day, Jacob and I visited Seodaemun Prison History Hall in Seoul. My hope was for Jacob to understand Father's life course, but it was also an important site in South Korean history. Built in 1907, Japanese colonial forces had used its chambers to punish Korean patriots who had opposed their rule during the forty-year occupation. In opposition, Korean patriots launched the Samil Movement and some seven thousand protesters would subsequently die fighting for freedom. Many were martyrs at Seodaemun Prison. It is today a somber museum, maintaining historical artifacts and evidence of the extensive torture and execution of Korean activists who opposed the colonization that had crushed Korean culture and enforced Japanese cultural hegemony.

Prior to Father Moon, the Korean equivalent of Joan of Arc, Yu Gwan Sun, had been imprisoned there. She had led non-violent protests for Korean independence and died in the prison from torture in 1920. She was seventeen years old at the time of her death.

Likewise, demonstrating for Korean independence, Father Moon was imprisoned there between October 1944 and February 1945. Prison guards so thoroughly beat and tortured him that they threw his spent body out of the building onto a heap of corpses, assuming he was dead. Followers came, found him, and resuscitated him. Jacob and I looked at the bricks at our feet made by prisoners, some by Father's hand. We spent a long while in the exercise yard designed for constant surveillance, reflecting on how human beings try to impose their will upon others. I imagined Father there, his will unvanquished despite his surroundings.

Inside, the museum maintained collections of torture instruments and small cage-like cells with spikes. Museum installations included mannequins reenacting various forms of brutality. Several rooms honored the dead with walls papered floor to ceiling with passport-size photos of those martyred. Jacob took photos of these walls that put faces to the numbers accounting for the dead.

This monument to one of the darker episodes in Asian history made Father Moon's vision of establishing a culture of peace and uniting historic enemies all the more poignant. Within the movement, we "restored" historic wrongs by working together with the descendants of former enemy nations—for example, Japanese and Korean, or German and American—dating back to World War II. Despite the imprisonment and torture he had experienced at the hands of Japanese colonizers, Father called Japan the "Mother Nation"—the counterpart to Korea as the "Fatherland" in his vision of a world of peace. The spiritual marriage of historic enemies was fundamental to his view of establishing peace. True Love strove for deep forgiveness to honor the eternal divine that resides within each person.

Our brief yet intense and revelatory visit gave us physical contact with Korea's history and culture. Traveling in Asia offered a different worldview, one where the US was not the central reference point on the world map. It may seem obvious: the very shape of the earth means there is no up, down, right, or left in the global community. But education, media, and cultural constructs surround and condition us with expectations and definitions. In the United States, NASA photos feature the North American continent in the center. Public schools tend to teach US history as a separate unit, distinct from world history. This fragmented perspective creates a split with "us" over here, and the "the rest of the world" over there.

I hoped to pass along to Jacob an understanding of Father's vision of one world of True Love, uniting cultures not by crushing them but by honoring their traditions and heritage. By learning more about what Father had lived through, not only as a Korean, but also as a man of vision, wisdom, and faith, I hoped Jacob could come to appreciate more deeply Father's heart. By exposing Jacob to Asian history and culture in its authentic context, I hoped he could situate Western culture within a broader framework. Where the US Pledge of Allegiance affirms "One nation under God," Father taught us to affirm "One world under God"—a place where all people are God's children to be cherished.

Our last day in Korea, Jacob chose to visit a royal burial ground, the Seonjeongneung, which dated back to the 1400s. Although within downtown Seoul, its grounds provided a large natural area of woodlands and meadows around the historic tombs. Families picnicked on the grass in little groups or strolled and exercised along the trails. We hiked along paths through leafy woodlands and past grassy fields where black and white magpies the size of ravens hopped and where the occasional flashy pheasant took long, leggy steps between beak jabs to grab a bug off the ground. Brightly painted, curved-roof pavilions and temples with open, Neo-Confucian courtyards and chapels to honor ancestors dotted cultivated fields of grass. Descendants of the kings still held elaborate Confucian rituals in the main temples on holy days.

Leading up to the buildings were two parallel paths. One, we could walk upon; the other was forbidden and roped off to pedestrians. The path we could use was the same one the king had walked upon long ago; the forbidden one was a sacred spirit path for the departed. No one could walk on the spirit path, not even the king. Those in the spirit realm had greater majesty than the king. This provided an interesting context for the average citizen. We non-royals could walk on the king's path, as we shared the common status of mortality. However, even the king could not walk upon the spirit path until he took up full-time residence in the spirit world.

I thought about the significance of this in terms of my prayers about the Peace Palace. It seemed there was an ingrained Confucian respect toward those in positions of authority. Merit was not purely determined by human measure. Even a king, who would be powerful in a worldly sense, had to bow before ancestors or those in the spirit world. The king, like us regular mortals, had to honor the ancestors. Thus, the supremacy of spirit over all had a unifying effect.

More important than the distinction between king and peasant was the distinction between mortal and immortal. This three-dimensional monument, over six hundred years old, occupied not only a physical space in the local geography, but also a conceptual space in the Korean psyche. It testified to the reality of spirit world as a substantive entity people historically recognized. I realized that this spiritual heritage infused Father's presentation and interpretation of Unificationism and perhaps his conceptualization of how history and spirit intertwine.

Korea's cultural sensitivity to spirit was evident even in the hole-in-the wall restaurant where, later in the day, we slurped five-alarm-fire kimchee soup. Jacob and I were the only Westerners there; in fact, we were the only patrons in the three-table establishment. The cook and solitary waiter were watching a traditional national sport on TV—Korean wrestling, or ssireum, which dates back to 37 BCE. The objective was for competitors to wrestle one another to the ground by pulling on a cloth band their opponent wore wrapped around the waist and thigh.

Blowing on each steaming spoonful of soup, we gingerly slurped, gulped water, and watched TV with the waiter. Exotic fanfare preceded the wrestling matches. Women dressed in gaily colored *hanboks* (traditional dress) danced in kaleidoscopic flower patterns playing traditional drums. They reminded me of a grown-up version of the Little Angels dance troupe. The women then held a container of holy salt up to one dignitary, who blessed the arena casting salt upon it. A parade of dignitaries in suits, ties, and elaborate flower corsages walked around the wrestling circle in single file. The wrestlers followed the dignitaries. What they lacked in holy salt, they more than compensated for in their regal, barefooted gait and dashing silk kimonos.

Profuse bowing ensued. I was entranced. As the pre-match pageantry continued, it struck me how much Unification Church traditions and rituals simply implemented traditional Korean customs and mannerisms. Although I'd known this in theory, it felt like a revelation at the time. What was to me an exotic, humble and earthy sport—wrestling—felt both familiar and like a high holy church event.

One dignitary in a Western-style suit and corsage gave an impressive discourse with intonation that thundered and waned. His cadence recalled many a sermon I'd heard delivered in Korean. Next, the Korean national anthem was sung. Blasts of smoke rose in two columns of dragon's breath from statues by the entry of the changing tent. The wrestlers again emerged one by one. The first two wrestlers entered the ring and faced each other. More bowing.

The tone of solemn cordiality and control was so different from the bouncy exuberance and barely controlled excess surrounding sports events in the West. As I watched, the assertive *yang* energy of traditional Korean culture struck me as stunningly familiar. It infused the event with folkloric charm and a mix of shamanism and Confucianism that characterized much of Unification culture.

Father's thinking transcended the dominant culture of the organization he founded. He appreciated the finer points of Western culture, like the ability to take initiative, put aside concepts, and value the unique individual. But general Unification Church culture was seeped with centuries-old Korean tradition.

A prior visit to the National Museum of Korea, near the Unification international headquarters in the Yongsan district of Seoul, had reinforced for me how deeply embedded shamanic belief was in Korean history and thought. While the Thai mix of Hinduism, Animism, and Buddhism was more softly observed, the Korean expression of Shamanism and Confucianism seemed to have a much more assertive quality to it. Like the powerful intonation of Korean language, Korean architecture—both old and new—reflected more of a *yang* sensibility rather than the flowing curlicue *yin* of the rooflines and the subtle assumptions of Buddhism in Thailand, where we would soon be traveling.

Both Asian countries had experienced phenomenal development in the past fifty years. Mike Shafer, the co-founder of Warm Heart, was also a professor emeritus of political science at Rutgers. He asserted that Korea—not America, as so often assumed—was the ideal to which Thailand aspired. Korea had enjoyed soaring economic success and maintained its Asian identity. The young girls at Warm Heart swooned over Korean boy pop groups and wanted to emulate Korean girl band couture when they were not wearing their school uniforms.

I tried to put Korea in perspective as Jacob and I traveled back to our hotel by metro to collect our bags before leaving. I remembered my dad describing Seoul at the time he was there (this was at the tail end of the Korean War): "There was one paved road," he said. "It went straight into downtown Seoul. The side streets? They were dirt."

Within a single generation, Korea had catapulted into the twenty-first century. I was grateful to have had the chance to visit Father's homeland. On our final day in Seoul, to visit tombs from the Joseon Dynasty of the late 1400s, Jacob and I sped through the slick metro network below Seoul's ambitious skyscrapers. Beneath the vertical cityscape on steroids, the colonized underground bustled with eateries and shops. Above ground, innovative landscaping and city planning had carved out little wilderness areas, replete with walkable parks, along the Han River. Historical artifacts juxtaposed booming commerce and bold art adorning contemporary buildings.

The metropolis we easily navigated on foot or by public transportation contrasted with the painful lack of development in North Korea. On our first day in Seoul, looking for a Korean-English dictionary in the neighborhood around our hotel, I'd asked a young Korean woman in pumps, hose, and a business suit if she knew where the nearest bookstore was. Her heels paused clicking on the pavement as she efficiently swiped her smart phone and said with impeccable English, "Yes, there is one just two blocks away. Take the first street you see there, to the right, you will see it on the corner of the next block. It is very big."

All I could stammer was "Kamsahamnida"—thank you being one of the few Korean expressions I knew other than "tongil," (unity) and some other choice Unificationist phrases. On a nearby street roaring with traffic, I'd watched a farmer bring the Joseon Dynasty to life wearing a broad, conical hat, or *satgat,* against the sun, *baji,* trousers closed at the ankle to keep out mosquitoes when working the fields, a white cotton peasant shirt, and a loose hand-sewn vest. The long pole he carried across his shoulders held woven baskets on either end, heavy to the brim with vegetables. The baskets swung with each step threatening to spill the produce he was taking to market. His graying beard stretched to a thin point mid-chest. Beneath his bushy eyebrows, his eyes were so penetrating; I seemed to be watching Confucius himself navigate the busy intersection.

Evening on the same street, I watched young Korean boys imitate their hip teen idols, their bleached blond hair gelled to perfection. They wore biker jackets and tight jeans that hissed as they jaywalked. Dodging oncoming cars, they bounced off parked vehicles making half cartwheels that set off car alarms. Laughing, they skipped into the urban landscape, balancing smart phones in their hands instead of baskets on a pole over their shoulders.

During our final evening stroll in Seoul, an elderly man in a long, dusty gray trench coat approached me rapidly. To Jacob's consternation, he grabbed my hands and looked with earnest command into my face. He blurted a volley of Korean words I could not fathom. He reeked of whiskey and sweat, had worn, yellow teeth, and crow's feet that framed his eyes. Deep lines meandered across his forehead as well. Beneath his fedora, as he spoke, his brown eyes misted then filled with tears. He continued with relentless zeal, until he punctuated at last, his monologue with "Thank you, America, thank you, America," delivered in English through a thick Korean accent.

I surmised that he'd lived through the Korean War. Bowing my head to him, through my American accent, I replied, "Kamsahamnida, kamsahamnida."

Tears spilled down his face. My throat choked and tears welled in my eyes as I made contact with God incarnate. When the man at last let go—much to Jacob's relief—we parted with mutual expressions of "God bless you."

— CHAPTER THIRTY-TWO —
NORMAL IS JUST A SETTING ON THE WASHING MACHINE

From Thailand, Jacob and I returned to America, where people contained their feet in shoes, the air inside buildings, and their privacy inside cars. Jacob was grateful for the reprieve from sweat in North Carolina. At Warm Heart, he'd worked with the landscape and building crews in the tropical sun. I missed the outdoor kitchen's jasmine vines twining over the sink, the animated conversations over meals at dusk, and the distant chants and tinkling bells from the Buddhist temple. Instead of spirit houses, mailboxes sat outside homes in Chapel Hill, jumbling the sacred and secular in piles of adverts, bills, and the rare billet-doux.

There were ways in which I felt more estranged than ever from US society—both within and outside of the Unification movement. My faith refused the constraints of the now politicized movement. Only nostalgia remained. And my new status as a widow in society left me with few friends. I appeared to be a singleton and therefore no longer fit in as "married" in social gatherings. For over a decade, I'd organized my every waking moment around caregiving for Michael; now that had ended.

We resumed our routines: Jacob walking dogs and hanging with friends until school started, me tutoring from home and continuing to edit newsletters and website articles for Warm Heart. Alex was working. Michael was still dead. I was driving to the grocery store one night and stopped at a red light. Seeing no cars in the pitch, I eased slowly into the far-right lane but was slammed by an oncoming vehicle; it sent me spinning 360 degrees into a ditch.

At the moment of impact, the aged, floppy shoulder strap had not held me to the back of my seat, nor had the airbag deployed. And yet I was safe. I'd felt a pair of spirit hands hug me back against the driver's seat. I insisted to the ambulance drivers who soon arrived that, though shaken, I was fine. The driver who'd hit me was likewise unhurt. Her hefty black SUV weighed far more than our little red Jeep—indeed, the latter was now completely totaled.

As I looked at my crumpled car, I felt like a spirit looking at the corpse of my life. A decade of moments flickered past on fast-forward—Michael latching his canoe on to the luggage rack; Alex hanging his head over the back seat as "Ralph the dog" next to Sadie; Jacob chortling in his car seat as Michael and I cleaned up the paint-can-sized load of sticky formula he'd happily dumped over his head; Michael driving as we raced Hurricane Bonnie from Ocracoke Island; field trips to meet students at mosques and Hindu temples; breaking down on a remote isthmus in Barnegat Bay, where some friendly folks who claimed they were with the Mafia gave us a lift to the park ranger's station; my Mom at the wheel backing out of our driveway in Hightstown; Imam Chebli insisting on riding in the back seat; the chug of the four-wheel-drive engine, still innocent of the future as it gleefully navigated off-road to camp in the Poconos pre-Belleview Haven; its determined churning through the snow to retrieve Michael from Belleview Haven; our joint "I don't ever want to do that again!" after crossing the bridge in Georgia; the boys and I returning to North Carolina from D.C. without Michael after his *Seung Hwa* in 2011.

The Jeep held the spiritual energy of all the people she had carried, but also the physical evidence of those happy and horrible days. In its nooks and crannies remained the faint residue of infant formula, a smudge of Sadie's dog slobber somewhere on an inside window, a whiff of a decomposing horseshoe crab the boys once kept as treasure. All that was to disappear. The Jeep was smashed beyond repair.

Assuring the ambulance drivers, again, that I was fine, I called a friend, who drove me home. After dropping me off, as she left, her car tires crunched on our gravel driveway where the Jeep would drive no more. I was grateful to her and I sank into prayer to thank God and Michael. I also felt indebted to Heung Jin.

My elder Japanese Church sisters used to tell me that from spirit world Heung Jin watched out for those driving. He was Father and Mother's second son and from a young age had devoted himself to Father, not only as a son loves his dad, but as a disciple as well. Rather than resenting his father's public duties, he united with Father's self-definition as a man with a mission from God. Heung Jin's sense of mission, it was rumored, surpassed that of many, although at the time he looked like a regular seventeen-year-old kid to me. At seminary, he used to gallop bareback on the same little barb mare I sometimes rode. She was bay with a thick, black mane and tail—feisty and fun to ride.

The seminary kept several horses back then. I was an experienced rider, not only from my time in France where I'd learned dressage, but also from high school days in Colorado, when I used to ride my neighbor's horse, Joe, in endurance rides. Heung Jin and I didn't converse or interact. Although Father's kids would hang out at the seminary sometimes, they had their own friends and didn't really mingle with the seminarians. I was busy studying and talking theology with the other graduate students, and I had chores to do.

One winter day, I was leaving the laundry room, where I enjoyed the heat from the dryers. The old stone floors of the Christian Brother's seminary held charm and cold with equal vigor. Located in the Hudson Valley, it was north of Poughkeepsie and frigid in winter. I had maneuvered my basket loaded with clean clothes out of the laundry room and was making my way up the hall toward the sisters' dorm when I met Heung Jin, followed by his friends. Upon meeting me, Heung Jin said, "Howdy."

This may not seem like a big deal, but the word "howdy" is not part of the lexicon of kids like Heung Jin raised in upstate New York and Tarrytown. However, it was not only his choice of greeting that struck me. I had a spiritual experience on several levels. The instant he addressed me, I felt empathy pierce my heart—as if he knew me to my core, everything about me, without ever having spoken—that I had ridden horses in France and Colorado, that I was struggling with my matching partner at the time, that I relished my studies, that I grieved my parents, brother, and sister not understanding what I was doing in the movement.

Complex combinations of emotion-laden data communicated at once via spirit—as if a whole lifetime of experience was relayed in a wordless heartbeat. Whether due to his love for God or how he loved Father, Heung Jin and I connected in an instant. I felt seen and accepted. But there was more. When he said, "Howdy," time slowed the way a 45 rpm vinyl record sounds when played at 33 1/3. We were face to face, a short arm's length apart, yet as he approached the small door by the laundry room to exit into the icy parking lot, he sounded miles away. A spiritual hurricane surrounded him and muffled his voice. The velocity of the turbulence that churned around him was palpable. Its force physically pushed me back. The door to the outside remained unopened—it was not a physical breeze, but a spiritual whirlwind. I thought it peculiar, but not enough to tell anyone at the time.

An hour later, Heung Jin drove along the road to Poughkeepsie. A semitrailer jackknifed on the ice and slammed into his car. He turned the wheel to take the brunt of the impact on the driver's side, thereby saving his friends' lives. This collision happened at the very moment Father was giving a significant speech in Korea at the risk of his life.

Having received the majority of the impact, Heung Jin was fatally injured. When Father and Mother took him off life support, his physical body died, but Father declared it a holy day, the Day of Victory of Love. This event and Father's response was the origin of the concept of *Seung Hwa*, or ascension—as opposed to simple funereal death—in Unification tradition.

Love's victory over death was everlasting because the eternal spirit is real. According to the Divine Principle, had the original ancestors of humankind not fallen away from God, they would have maintained the full capacity of their spiritual as well as their physical senses. Before the fall, they could see angelic beings who became invisible after the fall—not because they ceased to exist, but because human beings had lost the capacity to perceive them. Had human beings not fallen, the spiritual realm would be completely accessible, as visible and tangible as the physical world. Recognizing the Victory of Love was to reestablish the pre-lapsarian condition of absolute unity between the physical and spiritual realm. It was a return to the Edenic origin of God's ideal of creation. Therefore, Father's vision that Heung Jin lived was absolute, much like Christians believe that Jesus is alive. We all continue to live after death; it's just that most of us go unnoticed.

Father lived with a deliberation and inner vision such that whatever situation he encountered, he was determined to bring the love and clarity of God there. He interpreted his every act within the context of the historical courses of Jesus, Moses, and others who had been called by God throughout history. When his own son died, although he grieved, he maintained an awareness of God's hope for the world. Father directed his mind, focused his conscious determination as an offering to God to fulfill his mission, which he saw as recreating the lost connection between heaven and earth—the same lost connection Jesus addressed.

Therefore, his son's death became a sacrifice within the context of God's providential history. Father proclaimed the Victory of Love to solidify the unity between the spiritual realm and the physical realm and make the never-ending stream of love stronger than physical death. It was this love that would make it normal to transition from mortal life on earth to spiritual existence. This was to take another step toward establishing the original Garden of Eden where true love would guide all interactions.

When Heung Jin's physical body expired, Father asked Mother not to cry but to join him in making this offering. To some, this seemed a cruel request. Yet to live in the light of original love was to see the passage from mortal life to spiritual life as seamless. Father asked Mother, in the midst of grief, to divert her mind to this bigger context in order to claim Heung Jin's physical death as an offering—like Jesus going the way of the cross.

Mother, like any loving parent, was deeply bereft of her son's earthly life. It was so difficult for her not to cry. It demanded that she look absolutely to God and put all her energy into feeling united with the divine original spirit instead of her own pain in order to perceive her own son in the spiritual realm. Through his life course, Father had trained himself like a Buddhist monk or a Hindu ascetic to access this vertical realm on a regular basis. But it is meant to be accessible to all and Mother united with that vertical love.

The principle of indemnity in DP explains that by going through hardship for the sake of God, by making an offering of one's life, one could make the path easier for others who would follow. It was a cruel and difficult hardship to lose Heung Jin, but in making the emotional and spiritual effort to unite with God at that crucial moment, the condition for the Victory of Love was met. *Seung Hwa*, or ascension, for all humankind could be established. Mother did what Father asked her to do, but later, in private shed many tears. It was so difficult.

Heung Jin, who was therefore in the spiritual realm, was blessed in marriage to Hoon Sook, a young woman twenty-one years old in 1984 and very much alive and mortal. She was a professional ballet dancer, the daughter of one of Father's early disciples. She subsequently devoted her celibate life to her art, and later, to raising two adopted children.

Prior to totaling the Jeep, I'd last seen Hoon Sook in Kodiak in the summer of 1999, during the leaders' meeting to go salmon fishing with Father and Mother. By a fluke of good fortune, our local state leader had asked me to go in her stead, so I had been included in this elite group. I knew Hoon Sook's course had been lonely and difficult. After fishing one evening, we sat around a campfire and sang songs. To one side was a cliff over the shoreline where ocean waves crashed against huge boulders. On the other side, old-growth forest reached up to the stars in the heavens—they twinkled above the clearing where our campfire danced in the twilight. People took turns singing—most of the songs were in Korean or Japanese.

As she picked her way over some logs near the fire to sit down, Hoon Sook's eyes met mine. I sensed she knew my concern for her difficult course. I saw into her pupils, although I was a good ten or fifteen feet away from her. It felt as if the physical distance between us collapsed and I could see into her soul. I felt myself falling into an abyss of endless sorrow. Exiting her eyes, I was again sitting in my place—I had not physically moved. I felt that she had given me a glimpse of her world, the realm that only God knew. This was the broken heart of God about which Father had taught us.

The Jeep accident made me reflect upon my life—both what I believed and what I'd experienced. The spiritual protection of invisible hands holding me as the Jeep had spun 360 degrees into the ditch reminded me of how unconventional and blessed by grace my life course had been. Time and again, God had reached out to me when I was not following someone else's script of secular success or religious devotion. Even though Michael had been buried with a *Seung Hwa* ceremony, I didn't feel emotionally fulfilled by church rituals yet I felt close to Father because I related to his unconventional love for God.

Father understood God neither as an almighty superhero, nor performer of circus-trick miracles, nor foible-counting CPA seeking loopholes to keep people out of heaven with obscure religious legislation. Father's teachings had offered me the opportunity to forge my own path with God. My path—before and after studying his teachings—had led me through tears and heartbreak but also joy and love. The process of consciously applying Father's teachings made tangible for me a living God of love.

The God Father taught us about suffered with all the wisdom and knowledge of an omniscient parent who adores his children and longs for their fulfillment and healing from their every heartache. Lonely, God yearns for us to understand and relate to him as our own True Parent. It was this God of love that had bound Heung Jin and Hoon Sook—and, I had thought, over the years—would bind me with God. I focused on the transcendent quality of God—connecting in spirit. I ardently believed that living and teaching God's love would realize a world of peace. I longed for that peace.

In Thailand, at Warm Heart, I witnessed divine love in action without Unification rituals or theology. I recognized the Divine Principle being realized there as people lived for the sake of others, honored elders, and loved brothers and sisters with a pure heart. It didn't mean there weren't problems, but people worked harmoniously to solve them.

During our stay, Jacob and I had grown accustomed to sitting on the floor for meals and sharing food with unknown ingredients—exotic forms of vegetation, succulent fruit with hard carcasses almost impossible to open, and cool, golden, gooey tapiocas served inside the hollow of a piece of bamboo. Living in the moment felt as natural as kicking off your shoes before entering the house, as soothing as a Brahman calf's ear flopping against her jowl in a casual flicker to shake off a bug. Monsoon rain? No problem. Just park yourself and your motorcycle beneath the umbrella of a banana tree leaf until it passes.

After Thailand, my prayer walks continued apace in Chapel Hill, but no longer through mango groves and jungles. Instead I walked along Bolin Creek, where I'd spot the occasional blue heron or red-shouldered hawk and watch that Polly, Michael's little lapdog, wasn't picked up for a raptor's lunch. Another family had adopted the second dog I'd started to train when Michael's hospice began.

One day, I received word that Father was mortally ill. The church leadership asked us to pray for his recovery, which, given how ill he was, would be a miracle.

How much more powerful would Father be if he was unencumbered by his body?
I thought. The miracle had already been granted that he'd lived to accomplish as
much as he did. Therefore, I felt it blasphemous—or at least ignorant of Father's
course, life, and teachings—to pray for his miraculous recovery. Of all people, I
thought, Father deserved the grace of an easy, peaceful, and lovingly supported
farewell from his physical body. It was the least we could do. To pray for him to
stay on the earth plane was selfish, as well as silly on a practical level, however
raw and devout the passion behind it.

I felt the Unification leadership misguided the members by asking them to
pray for a miracle. I hadn't attended church in well over a year—before Michael's
Seung Hwa. Even when I had, I'd not gone out of religious devotion, but because
Michael had wanted to go to a Durham Bulls baseball game with the boys. A
church brother had group tickets and we met him after the service. After Michael
died, going to church at all was extraordinary for me. I was fed up with the church
in general, and the overt right-wing politics of the Durham church in particular.
Yet, I decided to attend one Sunday in September of 2012.

Several different reasons compelled me: one was to report on my trip to
Korea with Jacob and to help prepare the church members for the fact that Father
would indeed pass from this world one day. The leadership was maintaining the
position that Father "shouldn't die," and they were asking members to pray for
Father's full recovery. They were setting people up to feel guilty if Father died,
as if his death would be due to the insufficiency of their prayers or faith rather
than a natural culmination of his long life on earth. That Father was preparing to
leave the mortal sphere had been obvious to me when I'd seen him at the Day of
All Things event months prior, yet the movement's leaders, with their ongoing
requests to pray for miracles, seemed to deny this fact. Furthermore, I also wanted
to testify about my own experience with God, how the presence of the divine in
my life was not limited by my unorthodoxy. Finally, there were devout church
members who would have given anything to go to Korea and see the palace.
Supporting big families on uncertain wages, many had scrimped and saved to
make donations to help build it, yet couldn't afford to travel there and visit. I owed
it to them to share what I'd been privileged to see.

After the church band played a final song, the Durham pastor, Isaac, invited
me up to speak. "Hi Brothers and Sisters," I said. "I have a little testimony to share
about Cheongpyeong. I never really wanted to go to Cheongpyeong. Even though
I like kimchee and bulgogi, visiting Korea never really called to me like, say,
France."

They laughed.

"So, I had made a secret pact with God. If ever Michael died, I told God
once in prayer, I would go to Korea. That is the real reason I went. Michael died

and I had to keep my promise to God. Only God knew about that promise." People listened as I told my story.

Contrary to the typical glowing report, my testimony was not about how great the Peace Palace was, how wonderful True Parents were, or how fabulous the Korean people and the Holy Fatherland were. It was about how no matter how unprepared, how sinful and insignificant we might be, God does hear our prayers; and that there is a higher power at work in the world. This connection with God had nothing to do with being a Unification Church member—although more than a few rigorous old-timers might have differed with me on this. (George Orwell's *Animal Farm* came to mind, where all were deserving but some were more deserving than others.) My testimony served to assert that the power of God's love was for the everyday sinner, not the holier-than-thou ideologue.

I stood before the Durham congregation as a non-conformist. As I concluded my testimony, it was time to eat. Isaac, the young pastor, asked me to offer a prayer before lunch. As I began to pray, I had a spiritual experience and felt Father's spirit come into me. It was familiar, the sense of his presence, at once tender and supportive, completely accepting and knowing me to my core, yet at the same time, a lion of God with a roar so mighty my voice began to boom with authority, with the courage to face death for the sake of a mad, passionate love for God.

As Father's spirit gushed through me, I recognized it as a tsunami that inundated the old world, brought the water of life of a new world, a new history; it carried away the debris of temporal misgivings and misplaced priorities, ransacked all that was manmade, of rich and poor alike, and left us to scramble up the mountaintop to save only souls, not things. I felt Father's strength course through my veins as I prayed, "I report in the name of Pamela and Michael Moffatt of a Blessed Central Family."

People slowly rose to go eat. A couple of Western brothers deftly nodded or winked in thanks for my testimony so their wives could not see. Their more fundamentalist spouses turned their backs to make a beeline for the food along with the rest of the congregation as a welcome change of subject. I had become invisible. The spirit of what I said was powerful, but the content of my testimony was unwanted by those who wished desperately to believe in the leadership and keep praying for Father's miraculous recovery. They clung to the rectitude of their orthodoxy.

Folding tables stood at the back of the sanctuary, by the door. Upon them, sisters arranged dishes of potatoes, rice, chicken, salad, and cookies for dessert. People chatted amiably in English and Japanese as they took their paper plates and plastic forks and settled into little groups to eat. Restless, I walked past the buffet lunch and exited the sanctuary into the back hall that lead to the door.

Before departing, I poked my nose into a room near the main door and found the pastor sitting quietly alone in a vestibule corner. Hardly old enough to grow five-o'clock shadow, his face looked wan. Instead of eating, he stared at the cell phone in his palm.

"What's up, Isaac?" I asked.

"Father died this morning, just moments ago."

The time was 1:54 a.m. KST, September 2, 2012, 12:54 p.m. EDT, September 3, 2012—just as I had been praying before lunch. Isaac would have to make an announcement to the rest of the congregation. He was so young, I felt sorry for the heavy responsibility he bore. However, I also did not want to deal with the certain disappointment of people who had been praying for a miracle. I needed my own sacred space to digest what I'd just experienced—namely, that liberated from his body, Father's spirit was free to roam, to inhabit any of us. I told Pastor Isaac of my experience and left the center to drive home. As I drove, I prayed to support Mother in this moment and for healing, reconciliation, and peace for all their children. I knew that nothing could bring a family together like death.

The news spread rapidly over the internet. On its heels came invitations to attend the *Seung Hwa*. It was, of course, an opportunity to bring a guest. I could not begin to think of the *Seung Hwa* that way, as an outreach vehicle. Having recently been to Korea at no small expense, I weighed the cost of returning. I didn't care whether church members thought I should go or not. But I did ask myself, "What is my relationship to Father?" The reality was that I'd just communed with him in spirit. I didn't have to be in Korea to sense his presence. Nor did I need to prove something to others or myself. Father was, to me, family. Not a celebrity. Not a guru. Not only a teacher, although I'd learned things from him, and his deepest lessons had a value beyond mortal measure.

Not that I was master of what I'd learned, but my spiritual bond with him while he lived had been constant. He'd blessed Michael and me, and his teachings and spirit had seen me through some of my darkest days. I'd lived with him in heart and mind for over thirty years. Father and I had shared a sort of spiritual marriage. Without him at the heart and center of the movement, that marriage was over for me.

The movement was in an uproar. Prayer requests flew right and left as preparations for Father's *Seung Hwa* in Korea began. I wanted no part of it. Instead, I felt an urgent call to go to the ocean. Father used to joke that Jesus took fishermen and made them fishers of men, and that he took religious leaders and turned them into fishermen.

When Father died, Alex understood in ways Jacob could not just what his passing meant to me. Jacob spent the night at a friend's house and Alex and I drove to the coastal town of Carolina Beach. We arrived near dusk and stayed in the same motel where Michael and I had stayed on what would be our last trip together before he died. Alex and I were given room 119, the room just above the room where Michael and I had stayed.

Straightaway, I took a prayer walk along the shore and determined to rise at dawn for a farewell *Hoon Dok Hae* (readings from Father's teachings) and prayer. I hoped Alex would be willing to indulge me. He was. When dawn arrived, we did *Hoon Dok Hae* together and prayed sitting at a little table in our room beneath a window with a view of the shoreline.

As the sun peered over the ocean, a bright amber tangerine in a sea of rosy, pink sky, Alex said, "Look Mom!" pointing to the horizon.

Just then a tiny fishing boat slid toward us on the glittering water. As the nautical miles between us decreased, her stature rose, revealing a fine fishing vessel. I feared she would run aground as she came closer and closer, like a pet dog snuffling at the stoop of our door. Then, as mysteriously as she arrived, she departed whence she came. Churning steadily toward the sun's lengthening rays, she vanished into the horizon.

In the apparition of that fishing boat, I felt Father's spirit had visited us. I knew then that I had to return to Korea. After Alex and I took a last walk on the beach, we drove home. I arranged for lodging, travel, and whatever the kids would need at home while I was to be away.

— CHAPTER THIRTY-THREE —

THE END OF AN ERA

A few days and a long plane ride later, I had settled in Guri-Si, east of Seoul. Julian, the English brother who'd met Jacob and me on the last trip, stopped by my hotel after work. He walked me to the Unification-owned Il Hwa Ginseng-Up training center a couple of blocks away. The Il Hwa center was a complex of warehouses located behind apartments, small shops, and a couple of local churches. The surrounding neighborhood had a calm seediness. Later, I wrote in my journal:

11:20 p.m.—I need to shower and prepare for a 3:30 a.m. wake-up call. I'm here yet I don't think it makes me feel closer to Father—if anything, more distant. The church is weird. They're nice enough but clearly getting more dogmatic with his passing. In many ways, I felt my own connection with Father at the beach with Alex was profound and more sincere. However, it turns out, I learned from Gustav today that I would be facing Hoon Sook, the disembodied Heung Jin's fully embodied wife.

I felt connected to Hoon Sook, not only from my trip to Kodiak, but because of my experience with her husband, Heung Jin, in spirit world. Father would join Heung Jin on the other side. In ascending, Father, too, would be returning home to his True Parent, or God, who had loved him for nearly a hundred years during his earthly life while he'd suffered to do God's will on earth. What a great and happy day the ascension would be for God, I thought, as Father would return to his true original home with God in heaven.

I'd left the States in such haste that I'd forgotten to pack white socks. To prepare for the *Seung Hwa*, I needed to shop up some light-colored socks to go beneath my white suit. Following Unification tradition, we wore white at ascensions—the opposite of funereal black. The closest I could come was gray. As I pulled up my new knee-highs, I prayed that they would not seem "fallen" or impure. Trusty umbrella in hand, I made my way through the rain to the Il Hwa complex.

With Julian's help, I navigated through milling crowds speaking multiple languages to preregister with a smiling brother sitting cross-legged with a clipboard. At dawn the next day, I would only need to queue up in the parking lot to catch a bus to Cheongpyeong. Dawn arrived with rain. To transport everyone from Seoul to the countryside, the church had secured charter buses, which queued up along the curb bumper to bumper for blocks.

Among the thousands of brothers and sisters waiting for buses that day, I ran into an old friend from Nice—Patrick, originally from Brittany, and his wife Michiko, originally from Japan. For the first of our two trips to Cheongpyeong, we would view Father lying in state and pay our respects to the family; the funeral would follow the next day. I took my place in one of the multiple orderly lines. Everyone was dressed in formal white attire and most held umbrellas against the steady drizzle.

When my line began to board, the bus filled to capacity just before I could climb on. As I retreated to wait for another bus, a brother directing the lines told me to squeeze on in anyway. There were no more seats. I sat shotgun on a folding chair next to the driver. *The last shall be first, the first shall be last*, I thought. I took this to be God's compassionate answer about my socks not being white enough for code.

Through the windshield, I watched the downtown shops and neon signs give way to bold skyscrapers on the outskirts of Seoul. These towering monoliths sat resolute, defying gravity, poverty, middle fingers rigid against the sky, stark fuck yous to North Korea. They passed behind us as the mountains to the east rose up beneath the sun, which gently shimmered behind the haze of rain.

We wound our way through the valley on the expressway until a large green and white sign in *Hangul* and Latin letters indicated the exit for Cheongpyeong, where the ascent began. As we zigzagged through the mountain village, our steamship of a bus cornered slowly. The outer edge seemed to take days to pivot around each turn. The engine growled with relentless power—enough to easily climb hills or start from a standstill without slipping back on an incline. Our charter bus was nothing like the school buses that had transported us in CARP days—those had hemmed and hawed with each gear change, lurching forward in gasps.

In the village, banners strung above and along the streets announced the *Seung Hwa*. They had quotes from Father Moon that proclaimed the forthcoming Kingdom of Heaven, the Unity of all people, and God's Divine Love for all. The banners were white with black font and they showed Father's smiling face. Each one was over fifteen feet long and three feet wide. Some arched above the roadway hanging from streetlights; others stretched along the roadside, mounted between telephone poles, or pulled tight between fence posts in fields where peppers and potatoes grew.

We churned onward past the village and up the mountainside. Village shops gave way to the church grounds. A stadium perched facing the dorms, temple, and trails of the holy center of the church's Cheongpyeong retreat. Hundreds of buses moved tidily into place behind the white stadium. Thousands of people dressed in white mingled beneath their umbrellas in small groups. They eventually merged toward the main doors of the stadium.

Our brakes whooshed in long, slow, two-tone bellows. A guide onboard told us where to go next in Korean, Japanese, and English. I descended the bus and walked with Patrick and his wife to the stadium. I knew Father was dead, but the familiar bounce and go of gathering together made it feel like he was still alive. People chatted happily as they reunited with old friends from around the globe. It was a big family reunion.

The atmosphere changed when we entered the stadium. An usher showed us to our seats for a screening of a film on Father's life. People stopped chatting to watch. The movie depicted stories Father had often told us as parables. If we hadn't heard them directly from Father, we'd heard them from his early disciples. Or, following oral tradition, we'd heard the stories from our elder brothers and sisters. We, in turn, then passed them along to our younger spiritual siblings.

As I watched the movie, I observed the sisters and brothers in the audience shedding tears. I recognized that thousands of people, people who'd been erroneously directed to pray for a miracle they were sure God would bestow, needed to be shepherded through this process. When the movie ended, we proceeded out row by row to walk down a long hallway in lines of two or three abreast. Sisters dressed in white traditional Korean dress, or *hanboks*, and white gloves handed each one of us a single rose from a huge multicolored bouquet. As I received mine, I felt gentle deliberation from the sister, as though her prayers had been thrust into my hand along with the rose. We nodded to each other without speaking. My rose was orange: the color of the robes Thai Buddhist monks wear, and the color of the button-down sports shirt Father was wearing in the photo of him and Mother when they visited Monaco for the first time.

We had to walk briskly down the hall and up white marble stairs while preparing internally to see Father's corpse. Before the viewing, we paused to arrange ourselves in linear formation—straight rows without stragglers. Father's casket stretched lengthwise amidst a profusion of flowers, centered along the back wall of the room. Along the left wall, family members waited to greet those who had come to pay their respects. The room could only hold thirty or so people at a time. Our ceremonial lines watched each group of thirty in front of us bow row by row, place their roses, process left, bow to the family, and exit in single file.

Our group walked forward at a solemn pace. We bowed in unison. I was near the end of the row on the left. After bowing, I placed my orange rose among the others. There was little time to dwell upon the shell that was Father's body before our row processed left to greet the family. The person in front of me stopped. I did too and turned ninety degrees to see to whom I would pay my respects.

Before me stood Hoon Sook, Heung Jin Nim's wife, in a white *hanbok* and white gloves. Her eyes filled with tears as she looked into mine after we bowed to each other. She said in impeccable English, "Thank you for coming."

I was both stunned and wanted to hug her, tell her everything. We read each other's hearts without words. I felt she knew I'd been one of the last people to see her husband alive before his accident. Just as Heung Jin had seemed to know me that day at seminary, I felt Hoon Sook knew me at the *Seung Hwa*.

I had to keep pace with the procession, as did she. The next row of people awaited their turn to bow. Our eyes disengaged as we resumed our duties. Some thirty thousand sisters, brothers, and dignitaries had come to pay their respects. I said a prayer for the family members receiving the wishes pouring out from all the desperate brothers and sisters. I thought how tired the family must have been standing for hours on end in reception.

The grief of the brothers and sisters was reaching a peak. After seeing Father in the casket, people who had been happily chatting on the way into the stadium now quietly sobbed. That tenor of sorrow would remain in place throughout the ceremony the following day in the stadium. Then there were prayers and speeches, most in Korean, some translated into Japanese, English, or other European languages if you had the proper transistor radio station. Undoubtedly, there were prayers in Korean that were consistent with the *Seung Hwa* service that I'd experienced with Michael.

My mind and heart drifted. It didn't "feel" right as a service, not based on what Father had taught us. Fundraising somewhere in the southern United States, I'd learned what the attitude of *Seung Hwa* might be, or so I thought. In the course of my travels, product under my arm, I'd entered an establishment that turned out to be a funeral parlor. An African American family was conducting a service. As soon as I realized what was happening, I wanted to duck straight out the door to give them privacy to grieve. However, I noticed that no one looked sad. Young and old were beaming, beatific. Before I made it back to the door, an elder woman in the group took me by the arm, led me to the casket of her aunt and said, "Isn't she beautiful? She's gone to be with Jesus!" The other family members around us were nodding and smiling. They radiated love and joy. That family, to me, embraced the spirit of God's eternal love.

Death is the moment when we most connect with this very transcendence. It is the crossover from mortality to everlasting love. I felt sorry that Father's *Seung Hwa*, with thousands of people weeping, did not seem to capture this essence, the very thing Father had taught us. I felt like he would rather have been in that humble funeral parlor down south celebrating his love of God with that family instead of having some big, highfalutin ceremony with everyone carrying on with their hankies.

I mean no disrespect to those who mourned, of course. It's just that Father, you see, he wasn't really dead; his body had just met its "use by" date. He'd lived a life in which he had seized the opportunities to multiply God's love. He was to live on within the hearts of all those who attended his *Seung Hwa*, and many others besides. Imagine hosting a party to celebrate your spiritual birthday and everyone who showed up was crying the whole time. That's what it seemed like to me. I wished for Father's sake that more of God's joy had been manifested for his send-off.

Others might say that these earthly ceremonies are for the living rather than the departed. As such, the church ceremony for Father seemed to align with high Korean tradition—a typical funeral for a great head of state. Before my eyes was a worldwide movement of thousands of people in tears. Yet, as I observed the service and offered my prayers, I remained convinced that this was not what Father intended at his physical death.

Jesus had told the women of Jerusalem not to weep for him but for their sons and daughters when he went the way of the cross. But Father's death was not under the same circumstances. Although he had borne many crosses during his life, his determination had repeatedly won victories from the most onerous of circumstances. Furthermore, he had many faithful followers who likewise had borne crosses together with him. Father had died of old age in his nineties. This was not a defeat.

God's grief, I felt, resided in the ongoing suffering of His children around the world. Father's homecoming to the spiritual realm was an opportunity to rejoice in the victories of his mortal life. His weary body had been broken in countless places through torture in concentration camps under the Japanese occupation and in North Korea. Having lived through phenomenal physical hardship, he deserved to rest in peace. I felt his comfort would come from us carrying on his vision more than from us lamenting his departure.

Father's *Seung Hwa* was the ultimate proof of what I'd long felt—that the church was no longer a small ragtag band of misfits living for the sake of true love. It was a vast organization. The small, intimate, family-sized groups I'd enjoyed when I first joined had developed into a large, unwieldy institution. Though brothers and sisters were kind, the massiveness of the organization alienated me. Father's funeral represented the culmination of his living relationship with the church, and mine too.

My rapport with the Unification movement had unraveled as each new revisionist theory was accompanied by the political maneuverings of Father's biological children as they vied for church positions. This was not Father's way and I was fed up with pretense. True believers refused to pay attention to what was going on, or they took sides in one camp or another. These machinations ignored some of Father's most basic teachings: forgive, love, and unite. Give and forget you have given. Live for the sake of others. One (world) family under God. And above all: God is a God of True Love.

On a personal level, I was deeply disappointed that Mother had prohibited some of Father's own children from attending his *Seung Hwa*. No matter their politics, their personal situation, or whether or not they were Unificationists, I felt they should have been invited. Not because they were privileged, but because they were his kids. All people were invited to the Marriage of the Lamb. Father had blessed Jesus and Stalin in spirit world. The gates of heaven and hell were wide open. All humankind was meant to be restored. What better chance for a prodigal child to return than at a *Seung Hwa*? Besides, given the way the church leadership seemed to ignore Father's teachings, was it the leadership or the children that were prodigal?

Father's own daughter, In Jin, was "disinvited" to her dad's *Seung Hwa*. This was pure politics. It is quite probable that political leaders in the audience at her father's *Seung Hwa* had committed all manner of deviations in their lives. Yet they were there and she was not. She had made choices in her life due to her situation, for which she took responsibility. Father's way of love was such that he sought to open the path for Kim Il Sung—the man who had put him in a death camp—to come to God. Did people really think that Father would want his own children barred?

Another child of Father's, one of the elder sons, had not been permitted to visit his own dad on his deathbed. Given my own experience with losing loved ones, I had some notion of the emotional complexities that can surround death. But what enabled me to make decisions during those crucial moments was not protocol, appearances, politics, or even my own preferences: my goal was to liberate the soul of the person departing in the utter freedom of God's true unconditional love. I had sought to put Michael's eternal soul first, not my temporal convenience.

When the cage of our body releases our soul, we rejoin our source, the divine. For those who live with love, it is a moment of utter happiness and joy. As a cosmic moment, it transcends time, space, and worldliness. To have strayed from this spiritual priority, to have reduced Father's *Seung Hwa* to a petty political event, alienated me further from the church. Not that I was a "follower" of any of the children in question. They had their own issues to work out between themselves and God, without me meddling. But co-opting Father's own *Seung Hwa* for dogmatic or political ends nailed the coffin, for me, on the church.

As for family disagreements, I hoped Father's children would prioritize God's heart rather than personal gain. After all, most of the humble church members had given up everything to heed God's call in their lives. I hoped that leaders who were sincere in following Father's teachings would emphasize God's love, healing, reconciliation, and peace over Pharisaic interpretations of dogma.

As a free agent, I sought to keep an open heart to what the divine might bring into my life. Although my spiritual practice was no longer determined by Unificationist rituals, I did not regret my thirty-three years of practice nor did I regret letting it go. There was a time when I'd kept a photo of Mother and Father Moon in each room. I used to seek their blessing and participation in every aspect of my life. I stopped displaying their photo, even in the privacy of my office. Living people surrounded me, filled my heart, and challenged me to love.

I am still learning from my children who are young men now. They long ago rejected the church even as they embodied much of the Principle. I used to carry everywhere with me a photo of Michael, the one we used for his *Seung Hwa* portrait. A casual shot, I took it close up at an afternoon picnic before visiting a science museum with the kids. It captured not only Michael, but our family then, for Michael was our center.

In the photo, Michael is ruddy, with a whiskery face, the brim of his birding hat flops in casual fortitude above his ears. He appears ready to lope into the woods, gather a child into his arms, or plant a juicy one right on my kisser. Out of love, he followed and led me through a labyrinth of Unification adventures. My heart shattered as I watched him die in slow motion before my eyes. Unification teachings, friends, and Father's spirit gave me strength to endure.

My husband died having never dialed a number on a cell phone nor having swiped an electronic screen with his finger to read a text. As his senses betrayed him, he lived on the edge of life; his body became a living tomb. He would cite Paul Fussell on social class and insist he was "dead," not "passed on;" he preferred the deliberate earthiness of acknowledging death over euphemizing it.

I felt from "the other side" that he lived on with humor and a cadence that devoured the distance between earth and spirit. His will-driven walk used to eat up the miles. I had to jog to keep up with him—even a scant week before he entered hospice. That drive emanated from his spirit, his body before hospice already refusing to comply with his directives. The same way I sensed Michael's spirit, I felt Father's spirit lived on.

While he still lived on earth, I felt bound to Father Moon. However, when he died, he became more Mother's husband and less my irrepressible spiritual partner. I felt released from the movement. I used to wear my Unification ring on one hand and my marriage band on the other. I would tell brothers, "Thing of it is, as a sister, I am always married to Father first, and to my husband second."

Following Father had felt like a spiritual marriage—the way nuns and monks marry Jesus. I experienced devotion that, though not sexual, was deeply intimate, salvific, intensely personal, and absolute. Without Father at the heart and center of the movement, that spiritual marriage ended.

I began to rebuild myself from the root chakra up. Yoga practice and connecting with people helped me to call my spirit into my body. I remain curious and amused to discover what my spirit and body shall do together on earth before I die.

Several friends have noted that my stories swoop into existence at odd moments. Perhaps stories lead lives of their own and I am here simply to bear witness to them. So before I leave you, dear reader, I must relate two more stories relevant to this writing. One has to do with Michael, the other with the completion of this book.

About two years after Michael died, I asked his permission to seek an earth partner. Pacing back and forth in my office, I talked with him as I often did. I cherished him, no one would replace him, I said, yet I was lonely and needed companionship in this world. I knew he had an answer for me. But he clammed up. He would not talk to me while I was alone in my office. So I went out the door into the kitchen.

I sat down at the kitchen table, thinking Michael and I might hash things over there. Jacob, a senior in high school, was in class. Alex no longer lived with us. Besides Michael, I felt half a dozen spiritual beings sit down at the table with us.

How did I know? Imagine yourself in line at the movie theater with your eyes closed. A couple of people cut in line in front of you. Without opening your eyes or touching them, you can sense their presence, their energy, their nearness, whether they are unmerciful or benevolent. Likewise, I could sense these beings were there, that they were wise and important. I did not know their names. But I felt them lean in, serious and attentive.

Michael came and sat close to me. I made my case aloud before this unknown committee. How my earthly mission required my presence in mind and body, how I could better serve with an earth partner. They conferred, which in spirit world is an instantaneous process. There, communication is thought and emotion itself.

The committee gave Michael the floor. He gave me his blessing to have an earth partner. I felt a sense of relief in my heart, as if recognizing my own breath settling into my lungs—safe, confident I wouldn't drown or suffocate. It was not the absence of pain, but deep peace and fullness. I could feel him one with me, not reluctant, but unconditionally supportive.

At the time, this spiritual meeting seemed as normal as family gathering at the table. Once I received Michael's answer, the spirits departed. Where I had felt embodied spiritual energy, there remained nothing but air. I wept in gratitude for Michael's response, for his love, and then I went for a walk. Outside, I could collect myself in the physical world. My desire for a partner seemed clear, but I wondered how to go about finding one. When I returned to my office, I sat at my computer, unsure how to begin. Michael had always bantered easily, but casual conversation eluded me.

As if I were preparing to teach a class, I planned a theoretical encounter with a potential significant other. Dumbstruck at the thought and not knowing where to begin, I researched "conversation topics" online. I tried my hand at composing a question and typed, "What did you do in your youth that embarrassed you?"

I stared at the question I had written and thought about my own youth. I felt embarrassed. Foolishness and I were old friends. The thought of being with a man other than Michael frightened me. My body was at ease with him—comfortable, safe. Then, I felt the warmth of Michael's cheek brush against mine. "Feckless," I heard him say, loud, right in my ear.

That was his word, not mine. I laughed aloud. My shoulders shook in relief at his intervention—grateful for the word, even more grateful that this confirmed the blessing he'd already given. I added "feckless" before the word "youth."

Later, having composed a few questions for my theoretical conversation, I abandoned my questionnaire and went for another walk. I felt solemn upon my return. There was so much involved in this decision, years dedicated to theology, devotion, and praxis. I found the little box where I had kept holy candy from the first time I saw Father in 1981.

I slipped off my wedding bands and put them in the box. I hesitated to remove my Unification blessing ring. Twirling it around my finger, I watched how the ship steering wheel caught the light of the four-position foundation symbolizing our connection to God. I looked out the window. My eyes followed a sunbeam coming through the trees. It glinted against the ring. I took off my Unification ring and put it in the box too.

Late one evening a couple of years after removing my rings, I finished writing the final chapter of this book. The next morning, my alarm sounded. I looked up and saw a huge heart from the floor across the ceiling, in a dotted line of rainbows. The upper "V" and arches of the heart rose beneath the overhead light fixture, the side of it, curved down the wall by my closet door.

Whence came this apparition? I wondered. As I stretched and arose, the heart slowly dissipated; the rainbows became white light, and then vanished. It seemed like a message of divine love to me, but I wanted to figure out the cause.

I slept with the curtains closed. Somehow, the morning of this apparition, a sheath of sunlight had peered from behind them, reached the jumble of oddments upon my dresser, and ricocheted off a piece of crystal casually placed there. Next to the crystal was a heart-shaped piece of common gravel I'd picked up the day before. I often found heart-shaped stones. The humble gravel, nestled by the crystal, must have set up the perfect angle for the sun to hit it at exactly the moment I opened my eyes.

Had I, out of rude discipline, arisen far earlier, I should have missed this vision. Likewise, had I, out of indolence, refused to open my eyes to the day, this apparition would have remained unnoticed. It was the exact moment that I lifted my eyes that the sunbeam graced me with this love letter from beyond, timed to perfection.

Upon seeing this heart of rainbows, my foibles and inerrancies, my lacunae and overzealousness, the times I've spoken too much and too little, laughed too heartily and not enough, melted away. I felt the divine had given me a sign that this book was meant to be brought into the world. And so I thank you, dear reader, for being a witness to these little events of my life and wish for you and yours the joy of everlasting love.

SELECT BIBLIOGRAPHY

Rev. Moon's autobiography, written at the behest of a Buddhist Korean publisher: *As A Peace-Loving Global Citizen*. Available on Amazon and as a pdf here: https://www.tparents.org/Moon-Books/PLGC-SunMyungMoon-091101.pdf

Biographer and former follower of Rev. Moon Michael Breen's account of the first decades of the Unification movement: *Sun Myung Moon, The Early Years, 1920–53*. Available on Amazon and as a pdf here:
https://www.tparents.org/Library/Unification/Books/Sm-Early/0-Toc.htm

Early disciple and fellow North Korean labor camp inmate Won Pil Kim's words of internal guidance: *Father's Course and Our Life of Faith*. Available at:
http://www.unification.net/fcolf/.

Scholar George Chryssides' study of the origins of Unification Thought: *The Advent of Sun Myung Moon: The Origins, Beliefs and Practices of the Unification Church* (London: Palgrave Macmillan, 1991); his more recent article "The Unification Church," is available in *World Religions in America* (Louisville, KY: Westminster John Knox P, 2009).

Sociologist of Religion Eileen Barker's study of brainwashing in *The Making of a Moonie: Choice or Brainwashing?* (New York: Basil Blackwell Publisher Ltd, 1984).

Journalist Carlton Sherwood's account of Rev. Moon's US trial: *Inquisition: The Persecution and Prosecution of the Reverend Sun Myung Moon* (Washington, D.C.: Regnery Publishing, 1991).

Rev. Moon's exegesis of his original Divine Principle, developed in greater detail in his speeches: *Exposition of the Divine Principle1996 Translation*. Available at:
http://www.unification.net/dp96/.

Unification Thought as explained by his disciple Sang Hun Lee: *Essentials of Unification Thought* (New York: Unification Thought Institute, 1992), and *Explaining Unification Thought* (New York: Unification Thought Institute, 1981).

Professor of Religion, theologian and first missionary to the United States Young Oon Kim's *Unification Theology and Christian Thought* (New York: Golden Gate Publishing, 1976). Available as a pdf here:
https://www.tparents.org/Library/Unification/Books/UtaCt/utact.pdf

Philosophy professor Sebastian A. Matczak's study of Unificationism: *Unificationism: A New Philosophy and Worldview* (Jamaica, NY: Learned Publications, 1982).

ACKNOWLEDGMENTS

My gratitude for countless encounters with grace incarnate extends to people worldwide who have showed me the better side of humanity and extended irrational kindness. For friends who've leant an ear, their home, their hearts, their wisdom when I, at times with my family, was bereft of income or hope: Jeanne Ross, Susan and Keith Howells, Lisa Salem, Marc Manganero, Sarah and Dave Roberts, Susan Linn, Evelind Schecter, Michael Shafer, Larry Moffitt, Kim Brown, Robin Musiol, Frank Kaufmann, Richard LaMartina, Gillian Kampitch, Patrick Jouan, Edy Iverson, Elizabeth Wilson, JeanMarie Olivieri, Hélène Ramos Montgomery and Ricky Garni.

For those who've inspired and put up with me in my writing journey: Wayne Milstead, Nancy Peacock, Mimi Herman, John Yewell, Jaki Shelton Green, Stuart Horwitz, Amanda Steel, Stephanie Levin, Anna Dunwell, and Emma Claire Sweeney.

For Uri Eisenzweig who "saved me" from Alabama offering me a research and teaching scholarship at Rutgers and in so doing probably saved my life, and Gregory de Rocher who at the University of Alabama made me chummy with Rabelais and in so doing saved my soul. For George B. Daniel who believed in my potential when no one else did. For Rick Lockwood for being himself. For François Cornilliat who with the patience of Job and the wisdom of Solomon guided me through the labyrinth of my dissertation. And Yves de la Quérière who once told me you must shake the palm tree to see if coconuts fall.

For the man who bought laser prints while selling plasma to get money for booze in LA, for the yoga practitioner who said it was okay to fail and try again, for Dr. Thomas Boslooper who taught me how to sing in praise for unanswered prayers; for Mrs. Stoddard, my first-grade teacher who believed me when I said I read this many books after proving I understood them. For Mrs. Rainey, our babysitter, who taught me how great an adventure life could be and to find joy no matter the hardship. For the whole Famille Noël at the Club Hippique d'Aix-Marseille who taught me compassion and resilience. For Isabelle Devant and her family for taking me in.

For Aunt Myrt; great grandmothers Barnes and Bino; my twin aunts Jackie and Jeanne, uncles Leo, Doug, Bob and Bill, my grandmothers, Iona, and Mimi, who, when dating, said she could tell the difference between her husband and his identical twin, a preacher, by how they kissed; for my mom, dad, sister, and brother who remained practical when I wasn't. For Kay and Stan, Michael and our boys—Victor Alexander and Jacob Marston—in every breath and heartbeat.

I'm grateful for the blessing of life and people met in countless unforeseen circumstances. My hope is that the next generation may realize the value of the earth, one another, and their dreams.

ABOUT THE AUTHOR
PAMELA A. MOFFATT

Pamela Moffatt, a student of language and culture from childhood, raised off and on in France, has taught courses for post-docs, university undergraduates, high school and middle school students (BA, MA, University of North Carolina—Chapel Hill; PhD, Rutgers University—New Brunswick). She has edited publications and blogs in the US and Thailand, waited tables, raised two sons and several dogs, worked as a night manager at a bookstore and sold roses on street corners.

For thirty-three years she was deeply involved with the Unification movement. She lived in intentional communities, attended the Unification Theological Seminary, participated in international conferences and fundraising. This memoir is her chronicle of adventures and reflections as the movement, global politics and she encountered changes of heart.

Pamela lives in France with her dog, Louis.

- Ignores LGBT+ people in discussion
of Moon's belief — very heteronormative
- p.279 — def. of "real freedom"

Printed by Amazon Italia Logistica S.r.l.
Torrazza Piemonte (TO), Italy

60719510R00236